REPUTATION AND DEFAMATION

Reputation and Defamation

LAWRENCE McNAMARA

OXFORD
UNIVERSITY PRESS

OXFORD
UNIVERSITY PRESS

Great Clarendon Street, Oxford OX2 6DP

Oxford University Press is a department of the University of Oxford.
It furthers the University's objective of excellence in research, scholarship,
and education by publishing worldwide in

Oxford New York

Auckland Cape Town Dar es Salaam Hong Kong Karachi
Kuala Lumpur Madrid Melbourne Mexico City Nairobi
New Delhi Shanghai Taipei Toronto

With offices in

Argentina Austria Brazil Chile Czech Republic France Greece
Guatemala Hungary Italy Japan Poland Portugal Singapore
South Korea Switzerland Thailand Turkey Ukraine Vietnam

Oxford is a registered trade mark of Oxford University Press
in the UK and in certain other countries

Published in the United States
by Oxford University Press Inc., New York

First published 2007

British Library Cataloguing in Publication Data
Data available

Library of Congress Cataloging in Publication Data

McNamara, Lawrence.
Reputation and defamation / Lawrence McNamara.
p. cm.
ISBN 978-0-19-923145-4
1. Libel and slander. 2. Reputation (Law) I. Title.
K930.M36 2007
345′.0256—dc22 2007035283

Typeset by Newgen Imaging Systems (P) Ltd., Chennai, India
Printed in Great Britain
on acid-free paper by
Biddles Ltd., King's Lynn, Norfolk

ISBN 978–0–19–923145–4

1 3 5 7 9 10 8 6 4 2

Acknowledgements

This book is the culmination of a project that began in 1999 as research for an article about a very small aspect of defamation law and turned into a PhD thesis undertaken at the University of Sydney. It has become a monograph about some very large aspects of defamation law. I have accumulated debts as the years have passed. I am not sure that I can ever repay them but acknowledging them is at least a start.

I would like to thank the University of Sydney and Macquarie University, both of which provided resources and support for my research as, respectively, a postgraduate student and a member of the faculty. In particular, the encouragement of Ros Croucher, for a long time the Dean of Law at Macquarie, was always appreciated. I am also grateful for the assistance and support I received when visiting the Louis D Brandeis Law School at the University of Louisville, the Biddle Law Library at the University of Pennsylvania, and the School of Law at the City University of New York (with particular thanks to Penny Andrews). In 2003–04 I was a visitor for some months at the Centre for Media and Communications Law at the University of Melbourne. My thanks to Andrew Kenyon for kindly arranging this. Numerous people have been generous enough to read and comment on the work at different stages. Among them, Michael Chesterman and Robert Post read early drafts; Eric Barendt, John Burrows, and Des Butler examined the doctoral thesis; and Raymond Wacks read the manuscript. From time to time anonymous reviewers have provided invaluable feedback, especially those from the Media and Arts Law Review and OUP. There is, however, no reader who surpasses my doctoral supervisor, Roger Magnusson. His generosity and patience were unfailing. The move from thesis to book has benefited from the editorial help of Emily Hay and the assistance and good will of Alex Flach, Lucy Stevenson, and Cheryl Prophett at OUP.

I have been fortunate to be surrounded by a circle of colleagues and friends who have made all the difference over the years: Andrew Buck, Leo Crawford, Tanja Dreher, Ben Fenton-Smith, David Fraser, Louise Halpin, Justine McNamara, Andy Meehan, Denise Meyerson, Rachel Moss, Libby Ostinga, Peter Radan, Michelle Redford, Alex Reilly, Cameron Stewart, and Nick Weeks have all enlightened and uplifted me, and I suspect neither task was always easy. There are ties of inspiration and support that stretch back some way but without which this book would not have been completed and perhaps would never have been started: John Barry, Tracey Booth, Andrew Linklater, Richard Shapcott, and my parents all did more than they could ever know. No one has seen this project up close in quite the way that Andrew Lynch has. Even though the Mazda and the

Laser are long gone, I'm sure he would agree that it has continued to be quite a trip. Finally, I want to thank Andrée Duggan. She endured the highs, the lows, and everything in between. By way of thanks to all, I'll borrow from the very first book written about defamation law. In 1648, John March concluded *Actions for Slaunder* with a sentiment that holds true with respect to all those who have been so good to me:

And so I have quite finished my little treatise. May the Reader find as much profit and delight in the reading of it, as the Author had in composing of it, such is the ardent desire of your affectionate friend.

Lawrence McNamara
Sydney, April 2007

Contents—Summary

Contents

Table of Cases

UNITED KINGDOM

AUSTRALIA

UNITED STATES OF AMERICA

CANADA

IRELAND

ISRAEL

NEW ZEALAND

SOUTH AFRICA

Introduction

I. The Inquiry

I am not aware of any entirely satisfactory definition of the word 'defamatory'.
Lord Justice Neill, *Berkoff v Burchill*[1]

The aim of defamation law, so it is said, is to protect reputation. This view is virtually axiomatic in the cases and the literature.[2] The clarity of the rationale and the extent of agreement surrounding it is quite remarkable. Unfortunately, the same cannot be said of the law itself. The common law of defamation suffers from a fundamental deficiency: there is no principled, theoretically coherent statement of law regarding what is defamatory. It is not that the question has been neglected. The law is regularly recited but, like all aspects of defamation law, it has long been prefaced by observations that the law lacks principle and logic. The 'meaningless and grotesque anomalies' of the law were remarked upon by Veeder a century ago, many years before Prosser apologetically confessed that 'there is a great deal of the law of defamation that makes no sense'.[3]

Why has there been no satisfactory answer to the question of what is defamatory? The reason, I would suggest, is because there has not been sufficient attention paid to the nature of reputation or to the relationship between reputation and defamation. Without a satisfactory account of reputation, the law that seeks to protect it is bound to be inadequately conceived. My aim in this book is to address these shortcomings. I will do so by using reputation as the point of reference for analysing, evaluating, and proposing a revision of the law that governs determinations of what is defamatory. The relationship between reputation and the legal framework for its protection is central to the inquiry. The question I pose is asked in a very particular form, with the premise itself being a critical issue: if reputation is the interest to be protected by defamation law, then what should be the test(s) for what is defamatory?

[1] *Berkoff v Burchill* [1996] 4 All ER 1008, 1011, CA.

[2] As Barendt has explained it, 'the standard answer' to the question of 'what is the point of libel law' is that 'libel law protects the interest all individuals have in safeguarding or vindicating their reputation': E Barendt, 'What is the Point of Libel Law?' (1999) 52 CLP 110, 112.

[3] VV Veeder, 'The History and Theory of Defamation Law I' (1903) 3 Columbia Law Review 546, 546; W Prosser, *Handbook of The Law of Torts* (1941) 777 and through each edition to WP Keeton et al, *Prosser and Keeton on the Law of Torts* (5th edn, 1984) 771.

This is certainly a legal question but—particularly because it is about reputation and not just defamation—it is also much more than that. The question is, at the very least, an opportunity to explore and demonstrate the ways that disciplines other than law enrich answers to legal questions. It is, especially, a pathway to the past that traverses legal, cultural, and intellectual histories of the ways we judge those around us and the bases on which judgments are made. And it is, above all, a moral challenge. I hope to show that it compels reflection on the moral commitments that bind people together into communities in contemporary Western liberal democracies, and demands the articulation and justification of the way that moral commitments are to be mediated through the law.

II. Reputation, Defamation, and the Law

Although defamation laws differ across jurisdictions and can be very complex, the essence of the tort is fairly simple. A person may have an action for defamation where something has been said or published about them which is 'defamatory'. The plaintiff will not succeed in every circumstance—for example, if what was said was true or was an expression of opinion (rather than fact) then the plaintiff will fail—but in order to make a case in the first place it is essential that they have been defamed.[4] A brief outline of the current legal position and its flaws will help explain the legal and conceptual gaps the inquiry seeks to fill.

A. The current legal framework

The classic statement of law about what is defamatory is generally attributed to Parke B in the 1840 decision in *Parmiter v Coupland*: a publication will be defamatory if it 'is calculated to injure the reputation of another by exposing him to hatred, contempt or ridicule'.[5] Until the 1930s this was accepted as the test for defamation. During that decade the law underwent some significant change and the last 70 years has seen the emergence and stabilization of the following three tests for what is defamatory.[6]

The principal test is the 'lowering the estimation' test. Modifying the *Parmiter v Coupland* position, Lord Atkin held in *Sim v Stretch* that it was not necessary to inspire feelings as strong as hatred, ridicule, or contempt. Rather, it was enough

[4] For a detailed comparative guide to the plaintiff's case and defences to defamation, see A Kenyon, *Defamation: Comparative Law and Practice* (2006).

[5] *Parmiter v Coupland* (1840) 6 M&W 105, 108, Exch.

[6] The general acceptance of these tests is illustrated by, for example, P Milmo and WVH Rogers, *Gatley on Libel and Slander* (10th edn, 2004) [1.5]; D Butler and S Rodrick, *Australian Media Law* (2nd edn, 2004) 34–5; S Walker, *Media Law: Commentary & Materials* (2000) 132–3. To the extent that there is not complete unanimity, that is more likely a reflection of the difficulty of identifying a satisfactory definition: eg, J Burrows and U Cheer, *Media Law in New Zealand* (4th edn, 1999) 9.

that the plaintiff was lowered in the estimation of others: 'would the words tend to lower the plaintiff in the estimation of right-thinking members of society generally?'[7] This test is expressed in different terms depending on the jurisdiction but is the same in its general thrust across the common law jurisdictions.[8] The contemporary Australian formulation is that a statement will be defamatory if it has a tendency 'to cause ordinary decent folk in the community, taken in general, to think the less of [the person]'.[9]

Although the principal test dominates the law, it is supplemented by two other generally recognized tests. The first is almost never applied by the courts but is regularly cited as a part of the law: even in the absence of any 'moral discredit', a statement will be defamatory if 'it tends to make the plaintiff be shunned and avoided'.[10] Secondly, it may be defamatory to subject or expose a person to ridicule.[11] The ridicule test appears in the cases more often than the 'shun and avoid' test but it is still applied only occasionally. These tests effectively operate as alternatives to the principal test. They are usually argued and considered only where a plaintiff would be unable to succeed under the principal test. The three tests are usually presented together as a generally accepted statement of law about what is defamatory.

B. Problems with the current legal framework

The most immediate problem with the current framework is that the general acceptance of the tests is undermined by a widespread view that defamatory matter is difficult to define and considerable disquiet about how the law might be catalogued. In 1996, for instance, Neill LJ canvassed eight definitions that have been 'used and approved' by the English courts.[12] Professor Trindade identified five definitions of defamatory matter in a 1999 article.[13] The three tests are further flawed by their inconsistencies. Where a statement would not be defamatory under one test, the application of a different test may yield a different outcome and there is little explanation as to how such contradictions might be resolved. It might be thought that neither disagreement alone nor alternative criteria point to shortcomings so significant that the question of what is defamatory needs re-thinking,

[7] *Sim v Stretch* [1936] 2 All ER 1237, 1240 (Lord Atkin), HL.

[8] The most notable point of difference is that some jurisdictions depart from the 'general standards' requirement that the plaintiff be lowered in the eyes of the community generally, preferring instead the test that the plaintiff be lowered in the eyes of a substantial and respectable portion of the community: see Chapter 5, II.

[9] *Gardiner v John Fairfax & Sons Pty Ltd* (1942) SR(NSW) 171, 172, NSW SC FC; *Krahe v TCN Channel Nine Pty Ltd* (1986) 4 NSWLR 536, 544, NSW SC; *Farquhar v Bottom* [1980] 2 NSWLR 380, 385, NSW SC; *Boyd v Mirror Newspapers Ltd* [1980] 2 NSWLR 449, 452, NSW SC.

[10] *Youssoupoff v Metro-Goldwyn Mayer* (1934) 50 TLR 581, CA.

[11] *Boyd v Mirror Newspapers Ltd* [1980] 2 NSWLR 449, NSW SC; *Ettingshausen v Australian Consolidated Press Ltd* (1991) 23 NSWLR 443, NSW SC; *Berkoff v Burchill* [1996] 4 All ER 1008, CA.

[12] *Berkoff v Burchill* [1996] 4 All ER 1008, 1011–13, CA.

[13] F Trindade, 'When is Matter Considered "Defamatory" by the Courts?' [1999] Singapore Journal of Legal Studies 1.

but it will become clear that these difficulties are a consequence of two deep-seated problems with the legal framework. The first of these concerns the nature of reputation. The second goes to the relationship between reputation and defamation law.

The first problem is that reputation is defined internally. To the extent that defamation laws can be said to identify explicitly what constitutes reputation, they do so in a circular, self-referential manner: because defamation protects reputation, reputation is—or, by inference, must be—that which is protected by the law. There is no externally derived concept of reputation against which the appropriateness of the law might be evaluated. It is perhaps because of this that the tests for what is defamatory have endured even in the face of intuitive doubts about whether reputation (whatever it is) is really being protected. Gillooly, for example, argues that 'exclusion from society' is defamatory even though it does not require damage to a person's reputation.[14] In spite of identifying a manifest problem with the effect of the law and its relationship to the protection of reputation, Gillooly does not frame the observation as a criticism or as an issue that requires resolution. Rather, it sits simply as an observation about the way the law is structured. This is consistent with the general acceptance of the tests for what is defamatory: the legal stability has persisted in the face of clearly identified shortcomings.

Secondly, not only is it uncertain what reputation is, but the appropriate extent and manner of its protection are also uncertain. It has become apparent in recent years that the tests do not provide any clear way of resolving the defamatory capacity of imputations that concern values which are contested in a jurisdiction. This has become evident where, for example, imputations of homosexuality have arisen. Other contemporary dilemmas include statements that a person has HIV or AIDS, or that they have a mental illness. The choices faced by a court are difficult ones in an era when widespread prejudice and claims to equal rights share an uneasy coexistence. In the past it has simply been accepted by the courts that 'right-thinking' people would think the less of someone who is homosexual. Such a proposition is now highly contested in Western societies but it seems that courts can hardly ignore the reality of prejudice: there is ample evidence that a person may well suffer adverse consequences if they are thought (correctly or incorrectly) to be homosexual.[15] Do such suggestions possess a tendency to cause ordinary, right-thinking, or decent folk in the community to think the less of a person? What should the legal position be? And why should it be so?

These issues have been raised on occasion.[16] Lyrissa Barnett Lidsky addressed some of them in detail.[17] Her approach to the resolution of the problems was based

[14] M Gillooly, *The Law of Defamation in Australia & New Zealand* (1998) 44–9.

[15] G Mason, *The Spectacle of Violence: Homophobia, Gender and Knowledge* (2002); G Mason and S Tomsen (eds), *Homophobic Violence* (1997).

[16] Eg, S Walker, 'Regulating the Media: Reputation, Truth and Privacy' (1994) 19 Melbourne University Law Review 729; United Kingdom, *Report of the Committee on Defamation* (Cmnd 5909) 1975 ('The Faulks Committee Report') 15, 192–3, 256–7.

[17] LB Lidsky, 'Defamation, Reputation and the Myth of Community' (1996) 71 Washington Law Review 1.

on a claim that community is a myth and that defamatory capacity should be resolved on a public policy basis where values are contested.[18] The argument I will advance is distinctly at odds with that position. In particular, I take a very different view about the nature and role of community in defamation law. An alternative tack has been taken by Magnusson who has suggested that the determination of defamatory capacity requires a choice between the 'realism' of acknowledging the fact a person has suffered from (for example) a claim they are homosexual and contemporary 'idealism' that says sexual orientation is not a legitimate grounds for discrimination.[19] This, too, is a position that I will argue is unpersuasive. There has also been a recent Australian empirical inquiry into how people respond to contentious imputations but I will argue that an empirical analysis will not resolve the questions at hand.[20]

The best recent attempt to deal with the nature of reputation and difficult questions about what will be actionable and why is found in Jill Cottrell's critique of the supplementary tests.[21] Cottrell argues that it is difficult to say exactly what is defamatory because it is unclear exactly what reputation is: 'The truth is that the English law has not decided what the law of defamation protects and why.'[22] She works through several approaches to what is defamatory to see what the courts think they are protecting. Her analysis avoids falling into the circular approach described above because she sees the incoherence of the law as problematic. However, she ultimately sees the resolution of that incoherence as neither necessary nor worthwhile.[23] In the end, says Cottrell, 'perhaps the courts ought to abandon the search to elucidate what "reputation" is'.[24]

I hope to show that Cottrell's lack of faith is misplaced. It is neither necessary nor appropriate to abandon a search to understand what reputation is. It is not necessary because when dealing with questions about what is defamatory and why, the assumptions underlying defamation laws and the self-referential, tacit definitions of reputation become visible and problematic. It is not appropriate

[18] Ibid 9.

[19] R Magnusson, 'Freedom of Speech in Australian Defamation Law: Ridicule, Satire and Other Challenges' (2001) 9 Torts Law Journal 269, 278–80. LK Treiger-Bar-Am, 'Defamation Law in a Changing Society: The Case of *Youssoupoff v Metro-Goldwyn Mayer*' (2001) 21 LS 291, 307ff contrasts realism with moralism. Treiger-Bar-Am is discussing the 'shun and avoid' test for what is defamatory but her distinction is to the same effect as Magnusson's.

[20] R Baker, *Deciding Defamation* (2004). Importantly, Baker does not suggest that the questions can be resolved on a simple majoritarian basis. See also Communications Law Centre, *National Defamation Research Project: Submission to the Attorney-General of Australia concerning proposals for a National Defamation Law* (2004).

[21] J Cottrell, 'What Does "Defamatory" Mean? Reflections on *Berkoff v Burchill*' [1998] Tort Law Review 149.

[22] Ibid 150; also 151, 161.

[23] Ibid 155–63. Cottrell argues that the better position in the face of inconsistent authorities is to tighten the alternative tests by applying 'the right-thinking person' standard to them. This would make the ridicule test unnecessary and would qualify the 'shun and avoid' test. Judges would then quite appropriately continue to make determinations about whether reputation is harmed on an intuitive basis because that would enable courts 'to reflect what they think the views of their society to be'.

[24] Ibid 162.

because the only way to make determinations about defamatory capacity is to investigate the nature of the interest that defamation law seeks to protect. These are the reasons why the tests for what is defamatory cannot be adequately considered without inquiring into the nature of reputation.

III. Scope and Structure: An Overview of the Study

A. The scope of the study

The analysis is centred around the law in England and Australia where, even though there are defamation statutes, the common law is at the heart of the action and the legal principles and issues are the same in the relevant respects. However, this particular aspect of the cause of action—what is defamatory—is similar in almost all jurisdictions with a common law heritage, including the United States. As such, cases and literature are drawn from a range of jurisdictions.[25] Combined with the methodology that places reputation (rather than defamation) at the core of the inquiry, the legal commonality means the analysis has implications that can and will be drawn more widely.

In examining how the law has protected reputation, the analysis focuses on the tests for what is defamatory and determinations of the defamatory capacity of particular imputations. These are used as the indicators of whether and how reputation is protected by the law. It should be noted that in much of the case law the legal issue of defamatory capacity is indistinguishable from the factual issue of whether the imputation actually defamed the plaintiff. This is generally of little consequence because where the imputation is actually defamatory then the capacity speaks for itself. Similarly, although juries often play an important role in deciding whether a plaintiff has been defamed, it is the question of defamatory capacity which is important here because that determines whether an imputation will go to the jury at all. However, there are some possible concerns that need to be addressed in taking this approach.

It might be thought that for at least two reasons this is an inappropriate way to judge whether reputation is protected under the law. First, in discussing the cause of action, the only element of concern in determining actionability will be whether the imputation conveyed is defamatory of the plaintiff. So, it could be suggested that the inquiry is too narrow because a plaintiff must also prove publication, identification and that the imputations complained of were conveyed.

[25] Case law and commentary from the United States is highly pertinent, though sometimes more useful by way of contrasts than parallels. Case law from Ireland, South Africa, Canada, New Zealand, and Israel is also addressed where relevant. For wide ranging studies of how the law and practice in the US, the UK, and Australia compares, see A Kenyon, *Defamation: Comparative Law and Practice* (2006); RL Weaver *et al*, *The Right to Speak Ill: Defamation, Reputation and Free Speech* (2006).

Of course, each of these requirements has a significant effect on how reputation is and is not protected under the law. However, a presumption that all of them can be established enables the analysis to proceed on the least complicated footing and avoids issues being unnecessarily clouded. Moreover, the analysis will demonstrate the validity of this presumption by showing how the nature of reputation is such that the determination regarding defamatory matter is the legal and conceptual vehicle which is used to make critical decisions about whether reputation is or is not protected under the law. For simplicity, the question of whether words are actionable will be treated as if it turned solely on the question of whether they are capable of defaming a person. Where other elements of the cause of action are in issue then it will be made clear in the discussion.

A second objection might be that a plaintiff who establishes a cause of action may not prevail if a defence is successfully established. However, that outcome would not at all indicate that reputation is unprotected. Rather, it merely reflects the fact that defamation law takes account of interests other than reputation. Most notably, it balances the protection of reputation with freedom of speech.[26] The scope and limits of the cause of action inform the analysis of reputation because the balancing process will be—and should be—irrelevant and unnecessary unless there has been an attack on reputation in the first place.

The relationships between reputation, privacy, and defamation law are important.[27] A tort of privacy might, for example, be highly relevant to recovery for harm arising from the unwanted disclosure of a person's sexual orientation.[28] Moreover, there is a close relationship between an individual's sense of self-worth and their standing in the eyes of their community.[29] A study of privacy may enrich one's grasp of these matters but this is not the place for such a study. My objective is to clarify the nature of reputation so as to examine the law of defamation. That clarity will be best achieved by maintaining a focus on reputation.

The discussion of reputation will always refer to the reputation of a natural person. Reputation as the public perception and judgment of company behaviour is sometimes explored in the corporate or commercial contexts. This strand of the

[26] F Schauer, 'Social Foundations of the Law of Defamation: A Comparative Analysis' (1980) 1 Journal of Media Law and Practice 3.

[27] RC Post, 'The Social Foundations of Privacy: Community and Self in the Common Law Tort' (1989) 77 California Law Review 957.

[28] HE Ware, 'Celebrity, Privacy Rights and Free Speech: Recalibrating Tort Remedies for "Outed" Celebrities' (1997) 32 Harvard Civil Rights & Civil Liberties Law Review 449; DA Pollack, 'Forced out of the Closet: Sexual Orientation and the Legal Dilemma of "Outing"' (1992) 46 University of Miami Law Review 711; E Paton-Simpson, 'Private Circles and Public Squares: Invasion of Privacy by the Publication of "Private Facts"' (1998) 61 MLR 318; B Moretti, 'Outing: Justifiable or Unwarranted Invasion of Privacy? The Private Fact Tort as a Remedy for Disclosures of Sexual Orientation' (1993) 11 Cardozo Arts & Entertainment Law Journal 857. On the interest in and protection of privacy generally, see the seminal works by SD Warren and LD Brandeis, 'The Right to Privacy' (1890) 4 Harvard Law Review 193; WL Prosser, 'Privacy' (1960) 48 California Law Review 383.

[29] See Chapter 2, Part II(A)(2).

literature will not be addressed because the commodified nature of corporate or celebrity reputation and the associated proprietary interests make it very different to the reputation in its ordinary sense for a natural person. Similarly, the aspects of the law that enable a natural person to commence action regarding trade-related imputations will not be addressed.[30]

Finally, there are very substantial theoretical and historical dimensions to the study. This distinguishes it from much of the defamation literature. These matters have unfortunately received too little attention in attempts to deal with the question of what is defamatory. Strong theoretical and historical foundations are essential in order to build a base from which one can challenge—and hopefully begin to rectify—the deeply ingrained flaws and presumptions about reputation and defamation which so frustrate contemporary attempts to articulate and justify a test which is capable of protecting reputation in its modern context.

B. An overview of the study

In Part I, a theory of reputation is proposed. This provides an external point of reference which will be used in the analyses, evaluation, and re-thinking of the tests for what is defamatory which follow in Parts II and III.

1. Part I: Theorizing reputation

The point of departure in Chapter 1 is a defence of reputation, rather than defamation, as the choice of analytical category. The literature on reputation is somewhat thin but nevertheless provides a strong basis for viewing reputation as intimately related to the concept of community. A theory of reputation is proposed on this basis. Drawing on the sociology of community and the liberal-communitarian debates in political philosophy, a theoretical framework is developed within which moral judgment is the central element of reputation. At all times and in all circumstances, it is argued, the attribution of reputation is necessarily a moral activity.

Against this background, Chapter 2 considers the dominant theoretical perspectives on reputation in the legal literature. The main arguments have characterized reputation as an aspect of property or an aspect of personality. The latter has typically taken the form of honour, though Robert Post has also looked at reputation as dignity.[31] A critical analysis of the literature will show that none of these perspectives provide an adequate account of the nature of reputation. Other disciplines provide a better insight into reputation and yield some critical insights into the legal scholarship. The historical and anthropological literature on honour, especially, can be used to show how the judgments that constitute

[30] *Capital & Counties Bank Ltd v Henty* (1882) 7 AC 741, HL.

[31] RC Post, 'The Social Foundations of Defamation Law: Reputation and the Constitution' (1986) 74 California Law Review 691, 707–19.

reputation are always governed by particular criteria. A set of criteria for moral judgment can be usefully thought of as a 'moral taxonomy'. It will be argued that neither honour nor dignity is a form of reputation. Rather, they are more appropriately understood as umbrella-terms that can be associated with different types of moral taxonomies.

Together, the chapters in Part I seek to provide a coherent and cohesive account of reputation that builds upon a breadth of literature and disciplines. Moral judgment is at the core of that account. The contention is that any given jurisdiction will contain numerous communities and sub-communities that will, by definition, have different and sometimes conflicting moral taxonomies. Those taxonomies will differ not only in their substantive criteria for moral judgment, but sometimes the criteria will also be derived from different sources. That is, communities may present different justifications to defend their differing views of what constitutes the moral good. A legal framework which seeks to protect reputation must take appropriate and adequate account of the diverse substance and sources of values in contemporary Western societies.

The chapters in Parts II and III use the theory of reputation to analyse and critique the relationships between reputation and the common law of defamation. They examine the extent to which it can be said that defamation law protects reputation, the manner in which the law attempts to do so, and how the tests for what is defamatory should be re-shaped if the law is to protect reputation.

2. *Part II: History, law, and reputation*

Part II has a strong historical focus. This is important because histories of defamation have long observed that the common law is riddled with anomalies and its development exhibits little doctrinal coherence. The two chapters here try to escape the strictures of the traditional doctrinal analysis by viewing the history of defamation law through the prism of reputation.

Chapter 3 looks at the extent to which reputation was protected in the local and church courts and under the statutes of *scandalum magnatum* where defamation laws pre-dated the common law action. Chapter 4 turns to the development of the common law actions for libel and slander. Building on the analysis in Chapter 3, it considers the legacy of the Star Chamber's law of criminal libel to explain how and why the common law approached the actionability of words as it did. I argue that not until the 19th century could it really be said that defamation law functioned to protect reputation. Around that time, influenced by the distinctly modern intellectual framework of Enlightenment philosophy and science, the common law made a new claim that defamation law aimed to protect reputation and had always done so. In addition, the treatises attempted to derive general statements of legal principle from the disparate body of cases. These developments imposed on the law of defamation a historical and conceptual unity that it did not in fact have. This was to have a profound influence on the shape of the modern common law and its relationship to the protection of reputation.

3. Part III: Reputation and actionable defamation in the modern common law

Part III explores the relationships between reputation and the modern common law tests for what is defamatory. Chapter 5 examines how and to what extent reputation is protected under the principal test. It will show how the values of Christian morality gradually became entrenched in the legal standard of 'the right-thinking person' and against that backdrop then looks at how the legal framework takes account of competing and conflicting values. On the quantitative aspect of the law, it will be suggested that the Anglo-Australian test that uses the 'general standards' of the community should be discarded in favour of the American 'sectional standards' test that more effectively takes account of diversity. With respect to the qualitative dimension of the test, the chapter looks at how determinations of the defamatory capacity of imputations rely on the concept of 'the right-thinking person' in a process of 'ethical recognition' of criteria for moral judgment. Typically, the process has been most visible when the courts have refused to recognize certain views and the protection of reputation has thus been limited. The principal test and its application raise a major issue that goes directly to the way the tests for what is defamatory might be reworked to best protect reputation in morally diverse jurisdictions: if views are to be excluded on ethical grounds then there must be some foundation for the ethical choices that are made. Before these matters are addressed in detail in Chapter 8, the supplementary tests are examined.

Chapter 6 looks at the protection of reputation under the 'shun and avoid' test. It begins with a critique of the widely accepted proposition that the presence or absence of 'moral fault' is the point of distinction between the principal and supplementary tests. It is suggested that the concept of 'moral worth' is a more useful way to understand how reputation is protected under these tests. Secondly, the doctrinal foundations of the 'shun and avoid' test are explored. The analysis shows that by relying on cases decided before reputation was the focus of the common law, the modern common law has misinterpreted the significance of the early decisions. Consequently, publications have been actionable even where they do not tend to tarnish a person's reputation. The conceptual and doctrinal critiques show that the 'shun and avoid' test is partly superfluous because matters that go to reputation can be decided under the principal test, and partly inappropriate because some matters that are actionable under test are not matters regarding reputation. The test should be discarded.

Chapter 7 explores how a publication is actionable under the ridicule test and the extent to which it can be said that reputation is protected under that test. By looking at the early authorities and examining how the diminution of the plaintiff's moral worth has historically been at issue, it is possible to see that the test is unsatisfactory. Twentieth century courts misused the older cases and the test has come to protect a plaintiff's sense of self-worth rather than their reputation. The ridicule test should be removed from the legal framework. Where ridicule does tend to tarnish reputation, it may be actionable under the principal test. That is most likely to occur as a result of satire, though defences of justification and comment may serve to absolve the defendant of liability.

Chapter 8 returns to the principal test—the one satisfactory test for protecting reputation—and considers its operation where values of tradition and modernity clash by asking how, if at all, 'the right-thinking person' should form a part of the current law of defamation. The cases on imputations relating to race show an unexplained shift in the content of 'the right-thinking person'. Decisions concerning imputations that a person is homosexual are more helpful because the courts have tried on occasion to grapple with difficult questions regarding ethical recognition of marginalized values. The cases show that the traditional values which were embodied in 'the right-thinking person' now function as presumptions. There is a compelling case, it will be argued, for the common law to change so that 'the right-thinking person' is associated with inclusive liberal presumptions, so that exclusion (rather than inclusion) must be justified, and any justification must be made transparently and on sound ethical grounds.

The conclusion proposes a revised legal framework in which a single test for what is defamatory is shaped and expressed so that the common law's claim to protect reputation is most appropriately given effect.

PART I

THEORIZING REPUTATION

1

Reputation and Community: The Centrality of Moral Judgment

Without a clear sense of what reputation *is*, it will be difficult to make a judgment about the manner and extent of its protection under the law. To that end, this chapter commences the inquiry with the aim of theorizing reputation. That is, it sets out to articulate the nature of the interest that the law seeks to protect.

The selection of reputation—rather than defamation—as the analytical category for investigation is explained in section I. Section II looks at how opposing ideas of 'legal' reputation and 'real' reputation can be discerned from the literature. It proposes a definition of reputation that seeks to take account of both these approaches. That definition identifies community as the form of association upon which reputation rests. Investigating the concept of community, section III argues that moral judgment is the central feature of reputation. The analysis of community also lays the foundations for Chapter 8 where I will propose a resolution to some of the legal choices that the courts must make with respect to the scope and limits of protection for reputation. Drawing the threads of the chapter together, section IV looks at the places of moral judgment and community in legal and real reputation.

I. The Choice of Analytical Category: Reputation or Defamation?

The law of defamation and the interests it protects have typically been explained historically. However, as this section will show, the historiography of defamation limits rather than enhances an understanding of reputation.

In his seminal critique of legal history scholarship, 'Tradition and Method in Legal History', Daniel Boorstin was highly critical of the traditional approach to legal history.[1] He argued that legal history 'has been considered an alchemy for distilling legal principle' or a 'search for the data of legal principles'.[2] The past

[1] D Boorstin, 'Tradition and Method in Legal History' (1941) 54 Harvard Law Review 424.

[2] Ibid 424–5. He cites Holdsworth's *History of English Law* as the prime example of this approach: 424–8.

was viewed and reconstructed in terms of contemporary categories of contract, property, equity, and so on. Boorstin describes this approach as:

a sort of legal embryology—a search for the rudimentary forms of the 'full-grown' legal system. The present becomes the culmination of all the past, and the present forms of institutions seem to be their inevitable forms.[3]

The consequence is that 'the imagination is thus closed to the infinite possibilities of history'.[4] By keeping 'the discussion of the development of the law within the framework of the present legal vocabulary', the historian struggles to identify and appreciate the meaning of the past.[5] Boorstin says that historians can 'hope only to give the data of the past one of many possible illuminating formulations' but, calling for 'a greater self-consciousness' among legal historians, he argues that 'many possible arrangements of the data of legal history will appear as soon as one is freed from the necessity of finding in the distant past the seeds of current legal principles'.[6] He argues that the choice of analytical category is crucial to such illumination.[7]

The literature that seeks to explain the development of defamation laws and the interests they protect is dominated by the traditional approach to legal history. The contrast between the traditional approaches and the different light that might be cast by alternative analyses of the laws can be seen even in a brief review.

It has been observed that 'it has been easy to read back later doctrine into the past [and the] truism that lawyers customarily see the present in the past is well illustrated by the history of defamation'.[8] This is exemplified in Van Vechten Veeder's early-20th-century study of the 'history and theory' of defamation law which was included in the Association of American Law Schools' *Select Essays in Anglo-American Legal History*.[9] Veeder observed at some length the lack of consistency in the development of the law:

The English law of defamation is not the deliberate product of any period. It is a mass which has grown by aggregation, with very little intervention from legislation, and special and peculiar circumstances have from time to time shaped its varying course. The result is that perhaps no other branch of the law is as open to criticism for its doubts and difficulties, its meaningless and grotesque anomalies. It is, as a whole, absurd in theory, and very often mischievous in its practical operation.[10]

[3] Ibid 428–9.

[4] Ibid 429.

[5] Ibid 426. Boorstin (431–2) gives the example of contract law, arguing that a 'functional analogue' of agreement might be more instructive than a search for some practice that bears a tenuous resemblance to consideration.

[6] Ibid 434.

[7] Ibid 431–6.

[8] RH Helmholz (ed), *Select Cases on Defamation to 1600: Publications of the Selden Society, Vol 101* (1985) xii.

[9] VV Veeder, 'The History of the Law of Defamation' in *Select Essays in Anglo-American Legal History* (1909) 446.

[10] Ibid 446. More recently, WP Keeton *et al*, *Prosser and Keeton on the Law of Torts* (5th edn, 1984) 771. N Rosenberg, *Protecting the Best Men: An Interpretive History of the Law of Libel* (1986) 1, refers to Prosser but puts it more strongly when he notes the 'sheer irrationality' of the doctrines.

He then chronicled the existence and development of actions for defamation in different jurisdictions: 'The beginnings of the law of defamation among the Germanic people take us back to the first stages in the development of organised society.'[11] The approach has largely been the same in the body of literature that deals with the history of defamation law.[12] The history and theory of the law are equated: the anomalies and inconsistencies in the law defy explanation and so the history of defamation simply *is* its theory. In the absence of any internal or doctrinal logic, the only thing that can be done with the history of defamation is to recount it.

In contrast to these conventional accounts, Richard Helmholz's superb examination of defamation cases from 1222 to the end of the 15th century bears the self-awareness Boorstin pleads for when he [Helmholz] considers the inference to be drawn from historical data: '[I]t may be that we are asking questions and attempting analysis which would have puzzled the people involved.'[13] Similarly, Neil Rosenberg expressly rejects the traditional approach to legal history and presents his study of libel laws not as a work on defamation, but as an exploration of 'forces that are not distinctly legal, especially changes in political practices, in ideas of social and political order, and in the nature of American journalism'.[14] Defamation law is a part of that exploration—indeed, it is necessarily at the heart of the matter—but, in short, Rosenberg's position is that to study libel laws he will need to study more than just libel laws.

The point of thinking critically about the categories used to explore legal history is that it may at the very least lead to a richer understanding of the law, providing insights into 'the social usefulness of the various doctrines of the law, and the new uses to which old doctrines were being constantly adapted'.[15] Reputation—as the interest said to be protected by the law—will be considered as an alternative analytical category in order to pursue a richer understanding of what is and what should be defamatory. This approach escapes the self-referential presumption inherent in defamation law, commentaries and histories, that reputation is that which is protected by defamation.[16] It problematizes the concept of reputation and thus necessitates a critical and broader inquiry about the sorts of sources that assist one in understanding reputation. The choice of category has implications for the choice and use of source materials.

First, Boorstin's critique invites consideration of areas of the law other than defamation that may be instructive with respect to what reputation is and how it is relevant to legal relationships.[17] However, I will focus on defamation actions.

[11] Veeder (n 9 above) 448ff.

[12] See the Appendix for a discussion of the historical sources.

[13] Helmholz (n 8 above) lxv.

[14] Rosenberg (n 10 above) 7.

[15] Boorstin (n 1 above) 434–5.

[16] See the Introduction, II(B).

[17] Boorstin (n 1 above) 435 uses the example of looking at the category of 'agreement' in the law and suggests this may require exploring aspects of contract, criminal, property, tort, and administrative law. Where reputation is concerned it might, for instance, be productive to look at the history of laws relating to malicious prosecution and the laws of evidence, especially the operation

There are three reasons for this: contemporary defamation's claim to protect reputation makes this branch of the law worthy of inquiry in its own right; there is nothing to suggest that a review of other areas of the law is likely to yield a very different interpretation of reputation;[18] and there are other, more challenging implications that follow from selecting 'reputation' instead of defamation as the analytical category.

Secondly, although defamation laws are still the principal historical phenomena I will consider in studying reputation, they need not and will not always be considered in the traditional legal sense. Rather, one might consider (as, for instance, a historian or anthropologist might) the form and operation of defamation laws as an aspect of social and political relationships and institutions that could contribute to an understanding of reputation. Gordon cautions that the social significance of legal materials will vary depending on the circumstances; legal sources may be especially valuable where participants have:

> relatively clear access to legal decision-makers . . . ; the decision-makers pretty much share their views of what is generally desirable for the society . . . ; the rest of society shares or passively accepts the same norms as [the decision-makers] do . . .[19]

It will become clear in Chapters 3 and 4 that some defamation jurisdictions have exhibited these features and are thus capable of exposing 'the hitherto invisible ways in which the apparently most commonplace incidents of a legal order illuminate social values'.[20]

Thirdly, the selection of a 'non-legal' concept as the analytical category suggests the possibility of understanding the protected interest as a social and cultural phenomenon. Accordingly, several disciplines are used to navigate the conceptual territory between reputation and that legal framework that claims to protect it. These disciplines include sociology, philosophy, anthropology, history, and literature.

Throughout the inquiry, I will seek to demonstrate that using reputation as the analytical category provides the most coherent account of the ways that the histories, theories, and doctrines of contemporary defamation laws might inform an understanding of how those laws have come to be as they are, and how they should be.

of juries where the character of jurors and their knowledge of the parties' reputations were major features of the legal system. Works looking at reputation using laws other than defamation include BA Hanawalt, *'Of Good and Ill Repute': Gender and Social Control in Medieval England* (1998); J Kermode and G Walker (eds), *Women, Crime and the Courts in Early Modern England* (1994); LM Friedman, 'Name Robbers: Privacy, Blackmail, and Assorted Matters in Legal History' (2002) 30 Hofstra Law Review 1093.

[18] The possible exception to this is the laws of evidence relating to prior sexual history in sexual assault cases. It might be that the history, development, and reform of these laws could give rise to significant critical insights into the moral taxonomies associated with reputation; eg, S Lees, *Ruling Passions: Sexual Violence, Reputation and the Law* (1997).

[19] RW Gordon, 'J Willard Hurst and the Common Law Tradition in American Legal Historiography' (1975) 10 Law & Society Review 9, 53.

[20] Ibid 54.

II. Defining Reputation: The Literature and the Legal Framework

A. Analyses of reputation in the literature

A substantial body of literature deals with matters relevant to reputation. However, only a few works are concerned with the nature of reputation.

There is a strand of the literature that concerns defamation laws (those laws being the matter relevant to reputation) but very little defamation scholarship can be categorized as literature on reputation. The defamation literature sometimes intersects with reputation though, in most works, the intersections are not central to the authors' objectives. Over the last 15 years or so, there has been a stronger and more critical focus on how the law protects reputation, but defamation—not reputation—has still been the issue of concern.[21]

There is historical and anthropological scholarship on honour, especially as it relates to the southern United States and in Europe. The literature here addresses issues highly relevant to reputation but does so as an investigation into the nature and practices of honour rather than examining honour as a form of reputation.

The literature on reputation consists, perhaps surprisingly, of only a few key works.[22] The earliest serious investigation of reputation was Roscoe Pound's 'Interests of Personality', published in the *Harvard Law Review* in 1915.[23] Pound distinguished between social interests, public interests, and individual interests in the legal recognition of rights to personality. Unlike much of the defamation literature, Pound's main concern is not the law, but the interests it protects. George Spencer Bower's *An Actionable Code of the Law of Defamation* was published in its first edition in 1909 and revised in 1923.[24] Although principally concerned with the law of defamation, Bower also considers the definition and analysis of reputation. He looks at the inconsistencies in the law and effectively presents an

[21] LB Lidsky, 'Defamation, Reputation and the Myth of Community' (1996) 71 Washington Law Review 1; J Cottrell, 'What Does "Defamatory" Mean? Reflections on *Berkoff v Burchill*' [1998] Tort Law Review 149; LK Treiger-Bar-Am, 'Defamation Law in a Changing Society: The Case of *Youssoupoff v Metro-Goldwyn Mayer*' (2001) 21 LS 291. Other significant pieces that address the concept of reputation, but which sit more appropriately within the defamation strand of the literature are: [unattributed] 'The Community Segment in Defamation Actions: A Dissenting Essay' (1949) 58 Yale Law Journal 1387; F Trindade, 'When is Matter Considered "Defamatory" by the Courts?' [1999] Singapore Journal of Legal Studies 1; A Rigney, 'Fame and Defamation: Toward a Socio-Pragmatics' (1994) 99 Semiotica 53; F Schauer, 'Social Foundations of the Law of Defamation: A Comparative Analysis' (1980) 1 Journal of Media Law and Practice 3; Rosenberg (n 10 above). One might add to these United Kingdom, *Report of the Committee on Defamation* (Cmnd 5909, 1975).

[22] The paucity of legal scholarship on libel law, especially in the UK, was noted by Eric Barendt, 'What is the Point of Libel Law? (1999) 52 CLP 110, 110, 112. This has since been remedied to a degree—eg, Treiger-Bar-Am (n 21 above) and Cottrell (n 21 above)—but the observation certainly still applies regarding analyses of reputation.

[23] R Pound, 'Interests of Personality' (1915) 28 Harvard Law Review 343–65, 445–56.

[24] GS Bower, *A Code of the Law of Actionable Defamation* (2nd edn, 1923).

argument that defamatory matter is defined in such a way that it protects interests other than reputation.[25] FG Bailey's edited collection, *Gifts and Poison: The Politics of Reputation* was published in 1971. Anthropological studies of reputation in small European communities are linked with Bailey's own chapters on the concept of reputation, exploring what it is and how it operates.[26] Bailey's work appears to be the only major study of reputation that expressly uses the concept of reputation as its analytical category.

In the last two decades, defamation has been central to discussions of reputation. Robert Post's seminal article, 'The Social Foundations of Defamation Law' is of special interest.[27] This piece distinguished itself from other analyses because it sought to identify different conceptions of reputation. These were property, honour, and dignity. The discussion does not take the conceptual questions as far as it might, but that was not Post's aim; rather he was considering how different ideas about reputation have implicitly or explicitly underpinned defamation law. In addition to the unique nature of his inquiry, the defamation orientation of Post's analysis of reputation makes the piece especially relevant here. It provides the major point of comparison for the analysis of reputation in Chapter 2. The most important theoretical contribution since Post has come from Thomas Gibbons. Like Post, Gibbons was concerned with defamation but at the core of his project was an examination of 'the way that reputations are created'.[28] Eric Barendt has more recently offered some reflections on the nature of reputation, drawing significantly and critically on Post's work.[29]

None of these works presents itself as, per se, a theory of reputation. Absent such a theory, it seems that an attempt to theorize reputation should begin by considering a broad range of possibilities. To do this, I will use key points of dispute that can be discerned in the literature and the legal framework for defamation. These provide a sense of the scope and possibilities that need to be taken account of in developing a definition of reputation that will in turn open a suitably wide path into the breadth of literature that might be considered in theorizing reputation.

[25] Ibid 2, 253–4; on reputation more generally, 3–4, 240–58.

[26] FG Bailey (ed), *Gifts and Poison: The Politics of Reputation* (1971).

[27] R Post, 'The Social Foundations of Defamation Law: Reputation and the Constitution' (1986) 74 California Law Review 691. The same special issue of the journal included a brief piece by sociologist Robert Bellah, 'The Meaning of Reputation in American Society' (1986) 74 California Law Review 743, who argues that reputation is not so much an individual interest as a part of the common good and identifies the roles of personality and character as central to the perception and projection of reputation since the 1960s.

[28] T Gibbons, 'Defamation Reconsidered' (1996) 16 OJLS 587, 587; also T Gibbons, 'Personality Rights: The Limits of Personal Accountability' in E Barendt (ed), *Yearbook of Media and Entertainment Law, 1997/98* (1997) 53.

[29] Barendt (n 22 above) 112–18.

B. Legal and social constructs of reputation

It was observed in the Introduction that defamation law has defined reputation. The principal test for what is defamatory is whether ordinary decent or right-thinking folk would think the less of a person. Here, reputation is the view of a person that is held by ordinary decent or right-thinking folk in the community.[30] In contrast Gibbons has argued that reputation as envisaged by the common law is a distortion; it is not 'real' reputation because notional standards of judgment are applied. Defamation law neither comprehends nor protects 'real' reputation but provides only 'a forensic re-assessment of the plaintiff's socially constructed reputation'.[31] Reputation, according to Gibbons, is 'the outcome of [others'] judgments [about a person]' where 'an external assessment has been made of the person's behaviour and characteristics, and that... represents the views of a community of interests'.[32] For Gibbons, reputation is a social (rather than legal) construct. Derived from 'real' social judgment, it is an evaluation that is distinct from the artificial moral standards of the law.[33]

Because they are fundamentally opposing viewpoints, these concepts of 'legal' and 'real' reputation provide a useful starting point for theorizing reputation. To avoid closing off either proposition too soon, I will propose here a definition of reputation that accommodates both conceptions:

An individual's reputation is a social judgment of the person based upon facts which are considered relevant by a community.

This definition has four components. All lie on common ground shared by the legal and social conceptions of reputation. The last of them, community, exposes as problematic the place of moral judgment in reputation.

First, as a *judgment*, reputation is an evaluation of a person. Secondly, reputation is based on *facts*. Those facts may be something a person has done (such as accepted a bribe) or a characteristic of a person (such as their sexuality).[34] Thirdly, as a *social* judgment, reputation is a product of association. Fourthly, reputation

[30] *Sim v Stretch* [1936] 2 All ER 1237, 1240 (Lord Atkin), HL; *Gardiner v John Fairfax & Sons Pty Ltd* (1942) 42 SR(NSW) 171, 172, NSW SC FC; *Krahe v TCN Channel Nine Pty Ltd* (1986) 4 NSWLR 536, 544, NSW SC; *Farquhar v Bottom* [1980] 2 NSWLR 380, 385, NSW SC; *Boyd v Mirror Newspapers Ltd* [1980] 2 NSWLR 449, 452, NSW SC. While the English formulation refers to right-thinking members of *society* and the Australian formulation refers to ordinary, decent folk in the *community*. This distinction has not been relevant in the cases.

[31] Gibbons, 'Defamation Reconsidered' (n 28 above) 600.

[32] Ibid 589.

[33] Bower (n 24 above) 243 provided a similar definition of reputation as the collection of opinions of other people and 'the opinion of others which is the fabric of reputation may take the form of esteem, goodwill, or confidence'.

[34] Both the legal conception of reputation and Gibbons' 'real' reputation are faced with the same problem here. The facts which support a reputation may be only perceived facts. A reputation—be it 'real' or otherwise—may be based upon facts that are not in any sense true. However, that does not affect the legal and social concepts of reputation differently; both are equally vulnerable to misleading presentation or perception. What is of importance is the dependence on facts.

flows from a particular form of association: it is about what is considered relevant by a *community*. The essence of reputation lies within this last point and, as such, it requires some close consideration. An examination of the concept of community will show it to be a moral construct and, because of that, moral judgment is central and essential to both the social construct of 'real' reputation that is proposed by Gibbons and the legal construct of reputation underlying defamation law.

III. The Concept of Community

The term 'community' is often used but rarely defined. The discussion of what 'community' means has two important functions. First, as the remainder of this chapter will argue, it is the foundation for the claim that moral judgment is the key to understanding reputation. And, in turn, a grasp of reputation is essential if the deficiencies in the law regarding what is defamatory are to be remedied. Secondly, the literature on community will be especially relevant to the resolution of problems that are discussed in Chapter 8. It will help explain and prioritize some of the choices the courts must make when determining the defamatory capacity of imputations in circumstances where fundamental differences of public opinion regarding the substance and sources of values make those choices especially difficult. Such differences are apparent in much of the debate surrounding the concept and relevance of community.

The concept of community has been extensively examined in sociology and political philosophy. There is general agreement across both disciplines that it is difficult to define clearly and is susceptible to a number of uses. Elizabeth Frazer provides the most comprehensive account of this uncertainty, suggesting that the best approach to the concept of community—indeed, the only possible approach—is not to define it, but to analyse it.[35] She argues that the indeterminacy of its meaning does not prevent that meaning being discussed.[36] The corollary of this position is that it precludes any claim that one has discovered the true nature of community or conclusively defined it. As Frazer puts it, one 'is not thereafter in a position to present [the concept] as normative and authoritative'.[37]

Frazer's argument is a persuasive caution but does not proscribe an attempt to explain how the concept of community might best be understood or viewed

[35] E Frazer, *The Problems of Communitarian Politics* (1999) 60. Frazer is not the only one to provide an account of the conceptual uncertainty and ambiguity; eg, A Mason, *Community, Solidarity and Belonging: Levels of Community and their Normative Significance* (2000) 17–41; C Bell and H Newby (eds), *The Sociology of Community* (1974); N Elias, 'Towards a Theory of Communities' in Bell and Newby (eds), ibid ix–xli; M Stacey, 'The Myth of Community Studies' (1969) 20 British Journal of Sociology 134.

[36] Frazer (n 35 above) 60.

[37] Ibid 60. She illustrates her point with an example: if 'freedom' was the subject of analysis, one could not say, '"this is the concept of freedom; any usage which does not conform to this is invalid"'.

in the context of argument about or analysis of another concept (such as reputation). It only demands that any definitional claims should be understood as analytical and argumentative claims about how one *should* think about community, rather than conclusive and authoritative claims to know what community *is*. Accordingly, I will argue for a particular meaning of community in the sense that I will suggest how one might best think about 'community' when trying to understand reputation. While this is then most certainly a normative claim, it is not an authoritative claim in the sense that Frazer suggests would be invalid. It does not deny the possibility of thinking about community in other ways. It will, however, be suggested that the concept of community I propose is consistent with the analyses in the literature, including Frazer's analysis, and provides the basis for the most coherent account of reputation.

A. Community, modernity, and the individual

A major theme in the study of community is its significance as the basis for a critique of modernity. In sociology its unity is contrasted with the disintegrating effects of industrialization on traditional, small, rural communities. In political philosophy its focus on the interconnectedness of people provides a point of opposition to the individualist claims of liberal political theory.

The distinction between the modern and pre-modern world is marked by the Enlightenment of the 18th century. As well as being a period of technological change, the philosophical changes of the time reconceived the relationships between individuals, and between individuals and the state. In the pre-modern world, knowledge about how one should live—that is, ethical knowledge about what constitutes 'the good life'—was derived from the structures of tradition and, especially, religion that dominated communities. The Enlightenment was characterized by a rejection of this. The fundamental source of knowledge about the physical and human world became reason—that is, the capacity of individual human beings to know truth through independent and critical thought. The pursuit of human freedom—of liberty—was thus directed toward the individual. This philosophical revolution was seen at the time as 'the achievement by the self of its proper autonomy', liberating individuals from 'outmoded forms of social organisation'.[38]

On this view, modernity was an advance in the project of human freedom. Emancipation would come about as individuals were disentangled from the bonds and limitations of tradition. This philosophical theory became the ideal for a lived social practice in the democratic polity of America, and the technological advances of the industrial revolution which re-structured working and social life made sense in such a philosophical framework. However, these political and social changes were also the subject of great critique. To its critics, modernity was

[38] A MacIntyre, *After Virtue: A Study in Moral Theory* (2nd edn, 1984) 60.

not an advance; it was a loss. It detracted from the quality of individual life and this was in different ways identified as a consequence of the breakdown or loss of community. These themes recur throughout the sociological and philosophical debates about community.

B. 'Community' in sociology

The earliest influential study of community is the late-19th century work by Ferdinand Tönnies, *Gemeinschaft and Gesellschaft*.[39] The book was a critique of the impact of modernity, arguing that it brought about a loss because it detracted from the qualitative interactions between people. Tönnies' two concepts captured a distinction between what was translated as community ('*Gemeinschaft*') and association or society ('*Gesellschaft*'). These opposing themes and the ideas that informed Tönnies' notion of community have endured.

Gemeinschaft, says Tönnies, is an old phenomenon. It is a 'genuine, enduring life together' and 'a truly human community in its highest form'.[40] It sees the mutual affirmation of human beings through a unity of their wills in an organic manner. People are unified by kinship, locality, and friendship. These ties constitute and evoke a shared common spirit that 'gives the bond a living, lasting form'.[41] *Gemeinschaft* is where one finds the moral good. It is, however, much more than a set of values which can be identified in community life; *Gemeinschaft* actually constitutes the moral good. As Tönnies explains it: 'A young man is warned about mixing with bad society: but "bad community" makes no sense ...'[42] The moral good is transmitted through authority of age, force, and wisdom which is exercised by the superior and accepted by the subordinate. In this way, tradition supports itself both as a form and practice of social life and as the ethical good life.[43]

In contrast to community there is *Gesellschaft* which is 'life in the public sphere' in the sense that it is not the 'familiar, comfortable and exclusive' co-existence that is life in *Gemeinschaft*.[44] The 'original or natural state' of human relations is excluded in *Gesellschaft*; 'every person in [*Gesellschaft*] seeks his own advantage and acknowledges others only as long as they help to further his own ends.'[45] Society is a form of relationship between individuals that arises under conditions of modernity. It is mere association.

39 F Tönnies, *Community and Civil Society* (2001; first published in German as *Gemeinschaft und Gesellschaft*, 1887).

40 Ibid 19, 28.

41 Ibid 28–9.

42 Ibid 18.

43 Tradition in Tönnies work is heavily patriarchal: ibid 21–7. Issues of gender and power have not characterized the literature on defamation. A starting point for a feminist critique that would engage with the arguments in this book may be provided by E Frazer and N Lacey, *The Politics of Community: A Feminist Critique of the Liberal-Communitarian Debate* (1993).

44 Tönnies (n 39 above) 18.

45 Ibid 22, 64–5.

Both *Gemeinschaft* and *Gesellschaft* are forms of connection between individuals, but while the distinguishing feature of *Gemeinschaft* is an attachment with others, *Gesellschaft* is characterized by detachment from others. Tönnies' notions of community and association—and especially the idea that a recovery of life in community was essential for human well-being—have a recurring resonance in subsequent scholarship on community. These themes were manifest in Robert Bellah's project in *Habits of the Heart*.

Bellah and his co-authors set out in the early 1980s to ask Americans the questions, 'how ought we to live?' and 'who are we as Americans?' with a view to enquiring into 'how to preserve or create a morally coherent life'.[46] The research was prompted by what they saw as the conflict between on the one hand the American ethos of individualism which Alexis de Tocqueville had studied in the early-19th century and, on the other, the traditions of family life, religion, and local political participation on the other.[47] Paralleling de Tocqueville's concern that individualism 'might eventually isolate Americans from one another and undermine the conditions of freedom' that he saw as sustained by American traditions, Bellah explained his team's view:

> We are concerned that this individualism may have grown cancerous—that it may be destroying those social integuments that Tocqueville saw as moderating its more destructive potentialities, that it may be threatening the survival of freedom itself.[48]

And, in the authors' views, there was evidence of such a loss both of the ties of tradition and the conditions of freedom. This had to do with the effects of class and race, with the disintegration of the family unit, and with the diminishing connections between individuals in local communities of neighbours and friends,[49] but Bellah argued it could best be understood—and recovered—in terms of the conflict between individualism and a broader sense of community.[50] The realization of the individual's humanity and freedom would not come about through individualism, but through traditions that identify connections.[51] Bellah is not

[46] R Bellah *et al*, *Habits of the Heart: Individualism and Commitment in American Life* (Updated edn, 1996; first published 1985) xli.

[47] Ibid xlii; Alexis de Tocqueville, *Democracy in America, Vols I & II* (1945; first published in English 1835).

[48] Bellah (n 46 above) xlii.

[49] Ibid xvi. Bellah cites Robert Putnam's 'Bowling Alone: America's Declining Social Capital' (1995) 6(1) Journal of Democracy 65 as exemplary of the loss of connection. Putnam's argument was that 'features of social organisation, such as networks, norms and trust, that facilitate coordination and cooperation for mutual benefit', which he called 'social capital', were declining in America. Bellah explains Putnam's thesis and choice of title: '[B]etween 1980 and 1993 the total number of bowlers in America increased by 10 per cent, while league bowling decreased by 40 per cent. Nor, he points out, is this a trivial example: nearly 80 million Americans went bowling at least once in 1993, nearly a third more than voted in the 1994 congressional elections and roughly the same as claim to attend church regularly.' Most recently, see Putnam's book: *Bowling Alone: The Collapse and Revival of American Community* (2000).

[50] Bellah (n 46 above) ix; on individualism as a moral value, see x–xi.

[51] Ibid ix–x.

'nostalgic for an idealized past'.[52] Instead, the point was to identify and to live in a way that comprehended and enabled connections beyond the family and neighbourhood, 'affirm[ing] community as a cultural theme that calls us to wider and wider circles of loyalty, ultimately embracing that universal community of all beings....'[53]

At the heart of this cultural theme is a moral element. Like Tönnies in *Gemeinschaft and Gesellschaft*, *Habits of the Heart* sees the individualist associations of modernity as characterized by a loss of community and, as a consequence, inherently lacking the basis for a moral life that maximizes individual fulfilment. Bellah describes community as 'a group of people who are socially interdependent, who participate together in discussion and decision making, and who share certain *practices*... that both define the community and are nurtured by it'.[54] The concept of practices is central: 'Practices are shared activities that are not undertaken as a means to an end but are ethically good in themselves.'[55] Hence, in *Habits of the Heart*, 'community' is a form of association constituted by ethical connections.

The point I wish to draw from the sociology of community is that 'community' is a moral construct. A community is a group of people that see themselves united by the values that they consider they share. It is both an inclusive and an exclusive concept. Just as those who share the values are bound together and recognize their equivalent moral goodness, a failure to share those values means that one is, necessarily, not a part of the community.

This sociological understanding of community is consistent with that which emerges from contemporary debates in political philosophy. The recurring themes in both disciplines are that community is constituted by shared values and that the values which link people into a community are founded in tradition.

C. 'Community' in political philosophy

Although the liberal political philosophy of (and since) the Enlightenment was primarily concerned with the rights of individuals, the role of community has consistently appeared as a point of opposition for understanding human nature, the conditions of human freedom and the ethical principles which should guide us in living the good life. This has most recently become apparent in the communitarian critique of liberalism and the liberal responses to that critique. Although different scholars see the nature and roles of individuals and community very differently, all see the idea of community as a moral construct.

52 Ibid xi. On de Tocqueville's interpretation of America: 34–9.
53 Ibid ix, xxx.
54 Ibid 333, emphasis in original.
55 Ibid 335. The echoes of Tönnies position are clear, recalling his view that it makes no sense to talk of 'bad community'.

Before proceeding to those debates, it should be noted that the limited aims of this chapter mean that it is at this stage unnecessary to deal extensively with the political philosophy literature, but two issues that will be addressed in later chapters should be flagged at this point to indicate the boundaries of the present discussion. First, there will be a need later to inquire into the content of a community's values, especially as it relates to the contested norms that have posed difficult questions for defamation courts. Secondly, if people differ in their moral views, can they still be said to share a sense of community? The theoretical literature discussed here will underpin later arguments that seek to resolve those current legal dilemmas.

1. Liberalism and the communitarian critique

A core question for political theory is how we can know 'the good life'—the ethical life which will fulfil our humanity. For liberals, the moral life can only be known by the individual. Reason is vested in the individual and the enhancement of individual freedom will enable each person to lead the good life as they see it.[56] In the classical liberal theory of Mill, this is subject only to the harm principle—the only basis for limiting the freedom of an individual is to prevent their behaviour impinging on the freedom of other individuals.[57] Modern liberalism, most notably formulated by John Rawls in *A Theory of Justice*, refines liberal theory but maintains its essential foundations as a theory of individual liberty.[58]

In contrast to liberal theory, communitarians have argued that our moral life is constituted within and by our connections to other people. As Bell explains it,

> Whereas Rawls argues that we have a supreme interest in shaping, pursuing, and revising our own life-plans, he neglects the fact that our selves tend to be defined or constituted by various communal attachments (eg, ties to the family or to a religious tradition) so close to us that they can only be set aside at great cost, if at all.[59]

The central difference between the opposing views is that for liberals the individual is a self-constituting person. That is, the individual is able to recognize and determine the good life independently of the values of their connections with other people. For communitarians, the individual is constituted at least to some extent by those connections. As such, connections to others cannot be forgone (for individualism) without some loss to the person. This position as it has been advanced in the last two decades is known as the communitarian critique of liberalism. The most significant of the critics are Charles Taylor, Michael Walzer,

[56] M Walzer, 'The Communitarian Critique of Liberalism' (1990) 18 Political Theory 6, 16.

[57] JS Mill, *On Liberty* in A Ryan (ed), *Mill: Text, Commentaries* (1997; *On Liberty* first published 1859) 48–9.

[58] J Rawls, *A Theory of Justice* (1971).

[59] D Bell, 'Communitarianism' in EN Zalta (ed), *The Stanford Encyclopedia of Philosophy (Winter 2001 Edition)* at <http://plato.stanford.edu/archives/win2001/entries/communitarianism/> (19 November 2003) 6.

Michael Sandel, and Alasdair MacIntyre, each of whom proffered a major critique of liberalism during the 1980s.[60]

Communitarian perspectives have had two significant effects. They have on the one hand provided impetus and support for a political movement of communitarianism.[61] The stated project is to 'restore the moral voice' of communities, especially with regard to the direction of family relationships and the role of 'moral education', so that non-legal measures encourage people to 'behave more virtuously that they would otherwise'.[62]

Secondly, the theoretical critique has prompted new defences of liberalism.[63] These responses argue that the communitarians have misunderstood or misrepresented the liberal position and that liberalism can take account of the social nature of the individual without necessarily yielding ground on rights.[64] They also highlight the importance of liberalism's deontological ethics as providing a point outside the community from which internally generated community morality can be judged.[65]

The debates are especially significant where there is a conflict between the content of liberal individual rights and the moral proscriptions of a community. For instance, one strand of the debates asked whether it is defensible to prohibit consensual homosexual sex.[66] As Kadish explains it, the questions concern 'the propriety of legal prohibitions that serve to protect a community's sense of decency and regard for its traditions, even at the odds of infringing personal liberties of

[60] M Sandel, *Liberalism and the Limits of Justice* (1982); M Walzer, *Spheres of Justice: A Defense of Pluralism and Equality* (1983); C Taylor, *Sources of the Self: The Making of Modern Identity* (1989); MacIntyre (n 38 above). These authors do necessarily self-identify as communitarians.

[61] 'The Responsive Communitarian Platform: Rights and Responsibilities' in A Etzioni (ed), *Rights and the Common Good: The Communitarian Perspective* (1995) 11–23; A Etzioni, *The Spirit of Community: Rights, Responsibilities, and the Communitarian Agenda* (c1993); A Etzioni, *The New Golden Rule: Community and Morality in a Democratic Society* (1996); P Selznick, *The Communitarian Persuasion* (2002).

[62] 'The Responsive Communitarian Platform: Rights and Responsibilities' (n 61 above) 12–16; A Etzioni, 'Preface: We, the Communitarians' in A Etzioni (ed), *Rights and the Common Good* (n 61 above) iii, iii–iv.

[63] Eg, W Kymlicka, *Liberalism, Community and Culture* (1989).

[64] D Bell, *Communitarianism and its Critics* (1993); A Gutmann, 'Communitarian Critics of Liberalism' (1985) 14 Philosophy & Public Affairs 308; JR Wallach, 'Liberals, Communitarians, and the Tasks of Political Theory' (1987) 17 Political Theory 581; R Dworkin, 'Liberal Community' (1989) 77 California Law Review 479.

[65] Rawls (n 58 above) 260–3 on the 'Archimedean point'. Dworkin has argued that 'justice is our critic not our mirror': 'What Justice Isn't', *The New York Review of Books*, 14 April 1983, republished in R Dworkin, *A Matter of Principle* (1985) 214, 219. In 'Liberal Community' (n 64 above) 490, Dworkin refers to the need for 'a moral and ethical anchor' that lies outside 'conventional practice'. For a critical discussion of the debates around these themes, see Gutmann (n 64 above).

[66] See the special issue of the California Law Review: (1989) 77(3) California Law Review 475 which discussed these issues in relation to the US Supreme Court's finding in *Bowers v Hardwick* 478 US 186 (1986) that the Georgia sodomy laws were constitutionally valid. (*Bowers* was overturned in *Lawrence v Texas* 539 US 558 (2003)). Gutmann (n 64 above) 318 identifies as another example Sandel's discussion of whether a town might ban pornographic bookstores.

individuals'.[67] Here, the potentially conservative implications of a communitarian politics which seeks to reinstate the value—and values—of local communities could override claims to freedoms and rights, perhaps reversing those that are already recognized by the law. In spite of communitarian commitments to tolerance and inclusion, Amy Gutmann is, rightly, highly sceptical of the communitarian project in this regard, observing the historical tendency of established communities to engage in repression.[68]

The implications of the communitarian position will be of considerable interest later but my present concern is to examine the extent to which liberals and communitarians share the same concept of community.

2. *Common ground and disagreement*

Important though it is to both sides, the concept of 'community' is not articulated in a straightforward or consistent way in the liberal-communitarian debates.[69] However, it is possible to see a deal of common ground between the protagonists and, on that ground, community is most appropriately seen as a moral construct. It is the idea of 'moral community', in which 'individuals are conjoined by the shared understanding of social goods', that best equates with the sociological concept of community (above) and most appropriately explains how 'community' should be seen in its essence as a form of moral connection. This is especially apparent in the distinctions drawn between moral and other types of—typically, legal or political—community.[70] To a significant extent, the debates are concerned with the alignment of the political and moral communities, or the moral order of the political community.[71] In this way, understanding the concept of community turns on grasping its unifying moral dimensions. It turns on understanding the values that include and exclude to make a group of people into a community.

For communitarians, the moral nature of community is fairly clearly expressed. Alasdair MacIntyre, for example, argues that certain medieval societies were moral communities because they had strong 'shared understandings of what particular human activities were virtuous and the nature of virtue in general', and these understandings were integral to and integrated in every aspect of daily life.[72] Sandel argues that community 'is constitutive of the shared self-understandings

[67] SR Kadish, 'Foreword' (1989) 77 California Law Review 475, 475–6.

[68] Gutmann (n 64 above) 309, 319.

[69] This is so at very fundamental levels. Liberal attention is directed primarily at the individual and Bell (n 64 above) 91 notes that even within the communitarian critique there is no theory of community.

[70] Distinctions are regularly drawn between different types of communities: WA Galston, 'Community, Democracy, Philosophy: The Political Thought of Michael Walzer' (1987) 17 Political Theory 119, 120.

[71] Ibid 121 on Walzer; Dworkin (n 64 above); P Selznick, 'Dworkin's Unfinished Task' (1989) 77 California Law Review 505.

[72] MacIntyre (n 38 above) 165–80, esp 172, 178; Wallach (n 64 above) 592–3.

of the participants and embodied in their institutional arrangements'.[73] In short, a true community is by definition a moral community. Daniel Bell has argued that the term community thus makes sense as a normative ideal.[74] It is the moral significance of one's social world which he says 'sets the authoritative moral horizons within which we determine ... what's worth doing, achieving, or being'.[75]

D. The significance of understanding community

Community, I have argued, should be understood as a moral construct. This is consistent with the sociological literature and is common ground between the political theory of liberals and communitarians. As a moral construct, any reference to the community is necessarily a reference to the norms that bind people together. That is, it is a reference to the norms that constitute a group of people *as a community*. The corollary of this is that a judgment about a person's standing in that community must inevitably be a moral judgment. The combined import of these propositions is that, because it is a judgment founded in the concept of community, reputation is necessarily a moral judgment. This position will be supported and defended in section IV which looks at the place of moral judgment and community in the 'legal' and 'real' forms of reputation. Before proceeding to that analysis, it will be useful to draw attention to some of the core themes and issues that will be relevant in later chapters.

Liberalism sees principles of individualism as enhancing individual freedom and views the connections of community as encumbering that freedom. For communitarians, however, such connections are not an encumbrance. On the contrary, those connections are the essence of our humanity. Put simply, liberals disagree with the communitarian position that the moral connections of community provide the basis for justice. The communitarian preference for and ethical legitimation of 'traditional' values suggests that the continued or further marginalization of traditionally marginalized groups may be morally and politically justifiable in contemporary Western societies.[76] By contrast, liberalism has more inclusive implications, suggesting that claims to rights should override the traditional tendencies to exclude minorities. In Chapter 2, the communitarian and liberal affiliations with tradition and modernity will help explain the conceptions of reputation that have been proposed in the literature. The conflict between liberalism and communitarianism will be addressed in Chapter 8, as will the possibility of using the competing philosophical positions to formulate an approach that may help resolve some of the legal questions that arise in defamation actions.

[73] Sandel (n 60 above) 173.
[74] Bell (n 64 above) 10.
[75] Ibid 37.
[76] Gutmann (n 64 above) 309 has warned of the conservative implications of communitarianism.

IV. Reputation, Moral Judgment, and the Constitution of Community

A definition of reputation was proposed in section III. An individual's reputation, it was said, is a social judgment of the person based upon facts which are considered relevant by a community. It was suggested that the definition was consistent with both the legally derived concept of reputation implicit in the principal test for what is defamatory and Gibbons' socially constructed 'real' reputation. In particular, community was the element of association in both. Next, section III argued that community is a moral construct. The significance of that argument was that the attribution or evaluation of reputation—because it is a judgment founded in community—must necessarily and always involve a moral judgment. Now, this section looks at 'legal' and 'real' reputation to see if and how moral judgment plays a role in both. The analysis that follows will suggest that moral judgment is indeed central to both views of reputation. In doing so, it will also become apparent that the process of moral judgment presupposes a conception of community. That is, it entails a vision or understanding of who is in the community and who is not. It necessarily delineates who is included—who 'we' are—and who is excluded by the moral ties that bind people together. This constitution of community is formally visible in the legal framework and most apparent where the norms in question are not the subject of consensus.

A. 'Legal' reputation and moral judgment

In the 'legal' formulation of reputation, the centrality of moral judgment is most apparent in the determination of capacity to defame. In establishing whether a statement is defamatory of a person, the threshold inquiry is whether the statement is *capable* of being defamatory. This is not a question of fact for the jury, but a question of law for the court. The test is whether an imputation would have a tendency 'to lower the plaintiff in the estimation of right-thinking members of society generally'[77] or whether it would tend 'to cause ordinary decent folk in the community, taken in general, to think the less of [the person]'.[78] The terms 'society' and 'community' do not denote any distinction of the kind Tönnies discussed. Rather, whatever the formulation, the test relies on a conceptualization of community.

If the judge decides that the matter complained of cannot possibly tend to make ordinary decent folk think the less of a person, then no question of fact arises for a

[77] *Sim v Stretch* [1936] 2 All ER 1237, 1240 (Lord Atkin), HL.

[78] *Gardiner v John Fairfax & Sons Pty Ltd* (1942) 42 SR(NSW) 171, 172, NSW SC FC; *Krahe v TCN Channel Nine Pty Ltd* (1986) 4 NSWLR 536, 544, NSW SC; *Farquhar v Bottom* [1980] 2 NSWLR 380, 385, NSW SC; *Boyd v Mirror Newspapers Ltd* [1980] 2 NSWLR 449, 452, NSW SC.

jury to consider. No cause of action has been disclosed and the defendant will prevail. In most cases no significant problems arise for a judge with regard to the question of capacity to defame; for instance, allegations of wrongdoing or dishonesty which typify defamation actions clearly have the requisite tendency and would go to a jury. An allegation that a person is a paedophile provides a straightforward example. Paedophilia is quite clearly a behaviour that ordinary, decent folk in the community would disapprove of and a court will rightly hold that an imputation of paedophilia is capable of being defamatory. What is of most interest is that, in doing so, the court is necessarily relying on a vision of the community which excludes paedophiles and those who would approve of or tolerate paedophilia. That is, defamation laws protect individuals from slurs which allege they have engaged in behaviour that violates the norms which constitute the community.

Once an imputation is held to be capable of being defamatory, the matter goes to a jury. The jury is asked whether the imputation has a tendency to cause ordinary, decent folk in the community to think the less of a person. The jury, like the court, also envisions a certain form of community when it forms a view about what the community's norms are. In considering paedophilia they will certainly conclude that those norms frown upon paedophilia and are violated by anyone who commits such an act. Importantly, a jury finding that the imputation does not in fact have the requisite tendency would not be inconsistent with a court's finding that the imputation is *capable* of lowering the estimation in which a person is held. It is, however, crucial to recognize that the court controls what the jury can consider, thus delimiting the community boundaries which will or will not be recognized by the law.

This view of the centrality of moral judgment and the constitution of community in the cause of action is buttressed by a consideration of the common law defence of justification. If the publisher establishes the truth of the statement made about the plaintiff, she or he will prevail because the diminution of the plaintiff's reputation is justifiable. A person who is wrongly said to be a paedophile is thus protected by the courts: they will be permitted to recover and their reputation is, in Post's words, 'rehabilitated' as they are once again accorded the esteem they claimed as someone who did not violate the norms of the community.[79] On the other hand, a paedophile who is correctly identified as a paedophile will not be able to recover because they previously held a good reputation that they did not deserve.[80]

If moral judgment is central to the legal concept of reputation that inheres in the principal test for what is defamatory, what, then, is the position regarding 'real' reputation?

[79] Post (n 27 above) 713.

[80] 'The law will not permit a man to recover damages in respect of an injury to a character which he either does not, or ought not to, possess': *M'Pherson v Daniels* (1829) 10 B&C 263, 272. The complex rationales and history of the defence of truth are explored with a critical eye in R Ray, 'Truth: A Defense to Libel' (1931) 16 Minnesota Law Review 43, esp 54–61.

B. 'Real' reputation and moral judgment

Gibbons claims that, in contrast to the reputation that law protects, 'real' reputation does not distort the plaintiff's social standing. It will be recalled that he argued that it is the outcome of others' judgments about a person which constitutes the person's reputation, and that the factual underpinnings are the most important dimensions of such judgment: '[A]n external assessment has been made of the person's behaviour and characteristics, and... it represents the views of a group or a community of interests...'[81] A person's reputation is dependent upon an evaluation of the individual based upon any number of 'facts' such as the individual's behaviour, physical characteristics, class, or status. However, facts are only one dimension of the judgment that constitutes reputation. Whether reputation is viewed in a legal or social sense, facts do not on their own explain it. Even in Gibbons' formulation, reputation entails a moral judgment. This is because norms are an indispensable element of social evaluation: facts (or perceived facts) are evaluated in light of prevailing mores. In the example of paedophilia allegation, this is uncontroversial. However, where other imputations are concerned, the facts upon which an evaluation is based may give rise to a different reputation at different times or in different places. For instance, to say that a person is a communist suggests that she or he holds certain views or engages in certain behaviour (such as being a member of a political party with communist leanings). At a given time and in a given community, facts may be judged positively or negatively. This holds true for both the legal form of reputation and Gibbons' 'real' reputation.

Gibbons seeks to play down the moral dimensions of judgment, arguing that 'reputation is not necessarily, or even mainly, dependent upon moral evaluations' and that taste or preferences are more likely to be important than moral evaluation.[82] But this is misleading, for it gives the appearance that morality is either non-existent or irrelevant to judgment. Even within Gibbons' argument lies an acknowledgment that such a proposition is flawed when he makes it clear that norms do matter: '[A] reputation... is an appraisal based on the facts which are known about the person and on the social values which are considered relevant.'[83] He concedes that any given evaluation may result in a social judgment that has 'a morally questionable base, as when the mentally disordered or the financially embarrassed are shunned and avoided'.[84] There is no doubt moral judgment is an essential component of the socially derived 'real' reputation. The absence of express moral considerations (which appears to underpin Gibbons' thesis) is better interpreted as a consensus about the moral relevance of the facts, or at least that there is no meaningful dispute over the moral standards in question.

[81] Gibbons, 'Defamation Reconsidered' (n 28 above) 589. [82] Ibid 592.
[83] Ibid, references omitted. [84] Ibid 592.

C. Contested norms: The visibility of moral judgment

For the most part, the defamatory status of imputations is not an issue in litigation because the parties and the court accept that the moral standards in question are not contested in any meaningful way. However, the processes of moral judgment and the constitution of community become visible when norms are contested. This is because the principal test makes 'right-thinking' or 'decent' persons in the community the point of reference. A brief look at imputations of homosexuality will help show how this is the case.

The moral status of homosexuality is contested in Western societies. There is certainly significant discrimination against people on the grounds of homosexuality. There is, with equal certainty, a widespread acceptance of homosexuality. So, should it be said as a matter of law that an imputation of homosexuality may possess a tendency to cause ordinary, decent folk in the community to think the less of a person? Or should the imputation be legally incapable of defaming a person on the grounds that no ordinary, decent person could think the less of a person on the grounds of their sexuality?

To make a decision, the court must form a view about who the ordinary, decent, right-thinking folk are that will be the benchmark for its judgment. That is, it must form a view about what makes the people of the jurisdiction more than merely a legal or political community; it must form a view about what values bind the people in the jurisdiction together as a *moral community*. The determination necessarily requires this. The idea of a community containing anybody other than 'right-thinking' or 'decent' people makes no sense. As Bailey puts it, a community is only recognizable as a community because 'the people who belong share some idea about how things are and how things should be: they... share a definition of the good things and bad things in life'.[85] A community is a community because its members share an idea of what is 'decent', of what it is to be 'right-thinking'.

If the court holds that the statement is incapable of being defamatory, the community envisaged by the law is one that includes homosexuals and tolerant persons as ordinary, decent people whose views are to be considered the benchmark. If, on the other hand, a court holds that an imputation of homosexuality is capable of being defamatory then it is necessarily relying on a vision of the community that excludes homosexuals and those who would approve of or accept homosexuality.

In making the determination, the court engages in the practice and authorization of moral inclusion or exclusion. By this I mean that the perceived opinions, ideas, practices, or identities of people or groups of people are such that their inclusion or exclusion from the community is warranted and recognized by the common law. Post has argued that by confirming (or denying) membership in the community, defamation laws enable the resolution of such ambiguity about

[85] FG Bailey, 'Gifts and Poison' in Bailey (n 26 above) 1, 8.

inclusion and exclusion.[86] They are concerned with the 'rules of civility' which exist in a community:

> Rules of civility are the means by which society defines and maintains [the respect (and self respect) that arises from full membership in society]. Conversely, rules of civility are also the means by which society distinguishes members from non-members. Persons who are socially acceptable will be included within the forms of respect that constitute social dignity; persons who are stigmatised as deviants will be excluded.[87]

Exclusion denies the 'respect (and self-respect) which arises from full membership in society'.[88] There has been a slur upon the person's character which suggests they do not share the traditionally accepted ideas about how things are and how things should be. The inclusion/exclusion dynamic is inherent in the process of judgment and also a positive feature of it because it maintains the community's identity and status as a community.[89]

The same process operates when there is an allegation that a person is a paedophile. The court asks whether it should be said as a matter of law that an imputation of paedophilia may possess a tendency to cause ordinary, decent folk in the community to think the less of a person? Or whether the imputation should be legally incapable of defaming a person on the grounds that no ordinary, decent person could think the less of a person on the grounds that they are a paedophile? The process is less visible here because it requires no discussion. It goes without saying (quite literally!) that the imputation will be capable of defaming a person. The jurisdiction as a community agrees that paedophilia is to be detested. The processes of moral judgment and the constitution of the jurisdiction as a moral community are present in all determinations of defamatory capacity. It occurs with allegations that a person is a paedophile or that they are homosexual.

None of this answers the question of whether an imputation of homosexuality should or should not be capable of defaming a person. However, it does make it clear that the answer is in no circumstances a benign one: the process of attributing and judging reputation involves moral judgment and moral inclusion and exclusion.

Conclusion

Reputation is a social judgment of a person based upon facts which are considered relevant by a community. It concerns the evaluation of a person in a community.

[86] Post (n 27 above) 710, 712.

[87] Ibid 711.

[88] Ibid. This aspect of Post's analysis is drawn from his discussion of 'reputation as dignity' (see further, Chapter 2). As the following chapters will make clear, I am of the view that the position applies to reputation however it is conceived.

[89] Ibid 713–15.

An evaluation of a person's reputation by a community always rests upon some sense of who is—and who is not—a part of the community. It relies on a sense of what values bind people together as a community. Because community is a moral construct, moral judgment is at the heart of reputation. This is all entirely consistent with Gibbons' idea of 'real' reputation.

By conceptualizing reputation in this way, it is possible to give some content and shape to an external point of reference that might be used to evaluate the law. It starts to provide a basis on which one might judge whether and how the law does in fact protect reputation, and whether and how it might be able to do so. The complexity of reputation and its foundation in community suggests that neither of these tasks will be straightforward.

The analysis of 'legal' reputation suggests that the law as it stands can only protect ('real') reputation if the jurisdiction is in fact a genuine moral community. In all other circumstances the courts must form and express a vision of the moral ties that bind people together, constituting the jurisdiction as a moral community. This will involve moral inclusion and exclusion. This will be required in almost all circumstances because modern jurisdictions are not characterized by a breadth and depth of shared values. Individuals may be members of different communities, and may be members of sub-communities that share some values and disagree about others, and yet exist within the wider group of people that live within the bounds of any given jurisdiction. Where diversity is greatest then the choices will be hardest.

If defamation law is to meaningfully protect reputation in these circumstances then two paths need to be taken. First, it will be necessary to see how reputation is attributed in communities. Put simply, one needs to know what one is dealing with. In particular, it will be important to see how moral judgment and moral inclusion and exclusion function in the attribution of reputation because, as this chapter has argued, these matters are at the very heart of reputation. Chapter 2 will pursue that line of inquiry by looking at the conceptions of reputation that have been advanced in the literature and will draw some connections between those conceptions and the communitarian critique of liberalism. Secondly, the methods which the law uses to make words actionable as defamation—that is, the tests for what is defamatory and their application—need to be studied closely and critically, as do their relationships with reputation. The study will be occupied with this task from Chapter 3 onwards. By the end of Chapter 8, it will be possible to state the method that should be used to answer the question of whether an imputation of homosexuality should be capable of defaming a person. The literature on liberalism and communitarianism discussed in this chapter will be valuable in doing so.

2

Moral Judgment and Conceptions of Reputation

Reputation, I have argued, is based in community and, because of that, moral judgment must be central to any attempt to theorize reputation. This position differs from that which characterizes the literature on reputation, but that literature warrants attention. How, then, can the conceptions of reputation in the literature be of assistance in understanding the nature of reputation?

Generally, reputation has been explained in terms of interests and concepts that are familiar to the law. Foremost among the analyses have been works by Roscoe Pound and Robert Post. Writing in the Harvard Law Review in 1915, Pound considered how the various individual interests protected by the law might be classified.[1] He was especially concerned with the extent to which reputation was a form of property (an 'interest of substance—the individual economic life') and the extent to which it was a form or 'interest of personality', a matter of 'the individual physical and spiritual existence'.[2] Robert Post has argued that in defamation law, reputation has been conceived of as property, honour, and dignity.[3] While they are 'not the only possible concepts of reputation', Post argues that 'they have had by far the most important impact on the development of the common law of defamation'.[4] His argument in that respect is compelling and, with the respect for Post's work in the literature, there can be no question that the three conceptions of reputation warrant attention.[5] In referring to property, honour, and

[1] R Pound, 'Interests of Personality' (1915) 28 Harvard Law Review 343, 347–9.

[2] Ibid 349.

[3] RC Post, 'The Social Foundations of Defamation Law: Reputation and the Constitution' (1986) 74 California Law Review 691.

[4] Ibid 693. Perhaps the most significant alternative which could be helpful in analysing defamation and reputation is 'character'. The courts have distinguished character from reputation: *Plato Films Ltd v Speidel* [1961] 1 AC 1090, 1137–9, HL. It has also attracted attention in the literature: E Barendt, 'What is the Point of Libel Law? (1999) 52 CLP 110, 115; R Bellah, 'The Meaning of Reputation in American Society' (1986) 74 California Law Review 743, 750–1. A second concept that has been less investigated is 'integrity'. Useful starting points might be found in FH Stewart, *Honor* (1994) 51; Pound (n 1 above) 357.

[5] Post's work is without question the benchmark in contemporary commentary and critique. For instance, Thomas Gibbons refers to his analysis as 'masterful': 'Personality Rights: The Limits of Personal Accountability' in E Barendt (ed), *The Yearbook of Media and Entertainment Law, 1997/98* (1997) 53, 61. It is also the core point of theoretical reference in LB Lidsky, 'Defamation,

dignity as 'conceptions' rather than 'concepts' of reputation, I make a somewhat approximate use of Dworkin's distinction between concepts and conceptions.[6] Reputation is a concept, but the content of that concept—the conception—can be constituted in different ways.

Property (I) and personality (II) are the headings under which different conceptions of reputation will be addressed in this chapter. The former is of itself a conception of reputation. Conceptions of reputation as honour and reputation as dignity will be discussed under the latter heading. The use of headings should not be taken to mean there is a neat division between the different forms of reputation in the literature but, as this chapter will show, they are still meaningful distinctions to draw.[7]

Section I examines and rejects the proposition that reputation is a form of property. In section II, the conception of reputation as honour is eschewed in favour of a more richly rewarding inquiry into honour as a concept. Drawing on historical and anthropological work, it will be argued that honour can best be understood in terms of the 'moral taxonomies' that underpin judgments of social and self-worth in a community. The connections between social and self-worth, and between honour, reputation, and dignity, suggest that the idea of a moral taxonomy will also be a useful way to think about honour and dignity, and about reputation and its relationships to defamation law.

I. Reputation and Property

Robert Post has demonstrated very effectively that the common law has often treated reputation 'as a form of intangible property akin to goodwill'.[8] Of course, that does not mean that such treatment reflects the true nature of reputation. On the contrary, there are good reasons to reject the proposition that reputation is best conceived of as property: none of the legal foundations of the proposition, the philosophical underpinnings that give it coherence, or the material value of good standing in the community are sufficiently persuasive to see the property conception as an appropriate way to understand the nature of reputation.

A. Legal foundations

The legal foundations of the proposition that reputation is a form of property can be traced back to Pound and, especially, Bower. Pound argued that reputation

Reputation and the Myth of Community' (1996) 71 Washington Law Review 1; LK Treiger-Bar-Am, 'Defamation Law in a Changing Society: The Case of *Youssoupoff v Metro-Goldwyn Mayer*' (2001) 21 LS 291; Barendt (n 4 above).

[6] R Dworkin, *Taking Rights Seriously* (1977) 134–5; R Dworkin, *Law's Empire* (1986) 70–1.

[7] On conceptual overlap, see Pound (n 1 above) 349, 449, 451; Post (n 3 above) 693, 720–1.

[8] Post (n 3 above) 693.

and property became closely aligned because, as an action on the case, a defamation claim in the common law courts required proof of damage.[9] Bower is the more ardent exponent of the position: 'For the purposes of the civil law of defamation, reputation is regarded as a species of property.'[10] For Bower, 'the fabric of reputation' is 'the opinion of others which... may take the form of esteem, goodwill, or confidence'.[11] When the collection of individual opinions in a community is favourable, he claims that a person is said to have gained or won that opinion and is entitled to hold it as an asset.[12] In support of this, Bower relies on a series of 19th-century cases where the courts accept arguments that there is no difference between types of personal property, be they 'money or reputation', in so far as the loss of each is actionable.[13] There are several reasons why Bower's stance is unpersuasive.

First, the common law has long indicated that reputation is an interest in personality and Bower does not contest this effectively. In *Savill v Roberts*, for example, Holt CJ distinguished between damage to fame, person, and property.[14] Bower rejects this. For him, there are no distinctions between damage to fame and damage to property; they are merely different 'species of one and the same genus of rights or things which cannot be invaded without incurring civil liability'.[15] In the same paragraph, however, he makes a concession that undermines this unity:

> Reputation in many respects differs from other forms of property, and connotes certain ideas involved in the notion of 'person' or 'personality,' for it is certainly a very special and strictly personal type of asset...[16]

That is, Bower is prepared to accept that reputation is certainly not property in the same way that real or personal property is 'property'. Indeed, reputation is at the very least, an asset 'of a somewhat peculiar description'.[17] Ultimately, Bower's claim that 'it is permissible to consider these rights as assets' is not adequately supported by his own analysis.

Secondly, Bower's analysis contemplates dimensions of reputation that are inconsistent with (or at least more complex than) the idea of reputation as an asset in which its holder has a proprietary interest. For instance, he places the English ideas of 'honour' and 'fame' among the equivalents of reputation and argues that these and others acknowledge a sense of monetary value and carry the theme of

[9] Pound (n 1 above) 349–50.
[10] GS Bower, *A Code of the Law of Actionable Defamation* (2nd edn, 1923) 240.
[11] Ibid 243.
[12] Ibid 242.
[13] Ibid 240; *M'Pherson v Daniels* (1829) 10 B&C 263; *Dixon v Holden* (1869) LR 7 Eq 488.
[14] *Savill v Roberts* (1692) 12 Mod 208, 88 ER 1267. (NB: The word 'fame' is printed as 'same' in the reports, though this must be a typographical error.)
[15] Bower (n 10 above) 240. Bower includes damage to the person as the third member of the species. Pound was critical of Bower's rejection of this position.
[16] Ibid 240–1.
[17] Ibid 241.

'good name as a possession'.[18] However, in his discussion of the Latin equivalents of reputation as including 'fama' (roughly, fame) he notes that, while including pecuniary value, it 'connoted more than "reputation": to a Roman citizen it meant all that his "civitas" involved,—his whole political status ...'.[19] The problem with Bower's analysis is that he does not acknowledge that the English equivalents are just as multi-dimensional as the Latin counterparts he discusses. As I shall argue in some detail in section IV, honour (for example) involves much more than the opinions held about a person. Like fame, it may be tied up with political status and it is inherently connected to self-worth. In this sense, it is quite possible—even within Bower's analysis—to envision reputation as a much wider concept than merely the proprietary elements that are associated with one's esteem in the community.

Thirdly, as Pound notes, the haphazard development of defamation law does not justify the inference of a pattern or consistency that would support Bower's view of reputation as property.[20] Pound and Post both suggest the anomalies and inconsistencies in the case law indicate defamation laws protect more than a mere proprietary interest.[21] It seems reasonable to accept Pound's claim that even though reputation was treated as property, this occurred 'because of some inherent difficulty in securing an interest legally, and not because the interest itself is essentially one of substance'.[22]

These inconsistencies show that, even as Bower was writing, the common law was far from comfortable viewing reputation as property. However, the appeal and persistence of the idea might be attributed to its early philosophical coherence and the temporal value of good standing in the community.

B. Philosophical coherence

The conceptualization of reputation as property reflects the times in which the authors were writing. First, it was consistent with 19th-century perceptions of progress and civilization. The proposition that reputation was property was not merely evident in the common law, but was claimed to be an *appropriate* feature of it. Bower, for example, draws on the arguments in *R v Burdett* where the view was expressed that 'one of the most refined conditions at which a refined state of society can arrive, is, that a man shall have a solid property in his reputation'.[23] Recognizing reputation as a form of property did justice to the interest, reflecting human nature appropriately:

> It is one of the greatest privileges that belong to the nature of man, that he possesses a sensibility to fame and a love of glory, and that the individual, by the combination of

[18] Ibid 242.
[19] Ibid 241.
[20] Pound (n 1 above) 446.
[21] Post (n 3 above) 697, 727–30; Pound (n 1 above) 447, 449.
[22] Pound (n 1 above) 447.
[23] *R v Burdett* (1820) 4 B&Ald 95, 96, 106 ER 873, 874, cited by Bower (n 10 above) 240.

opinion and the force of character, begets in his own reputation a property more valuable than the mere materials to which the crude notions of property are first applied.[24]

At around the same time, this theme was also clear in Starkie's *Treatise on Libel and Slander*.[25] The progress from 'barbarism' and 'times of remotest antiquity' to 'a more peaceful and settled state of society', and then to 'a much later and more mature stage of civilization' was the basis for the recognition of reputation as a right that was equivalent to property and person.[26]

Secondly, a conception of reputation as property reflected the emergence of individualism in the liberal political philosophy of the late-18th century. These particular aspects of individual and society are reflected in Post's argument that the vision of a 'market society' underpins the idea of reputation as property.[27] Post argues the relationship between individualist philosophy and reputation as property is captured in Starkie's treatise. For Starkie, in this advanced state of society the 'various artificial relations' of the market meant that an individual's reputation—'gradations of rank and authority, honours and distinctions'—became a substitute for property in commercial dealings with others.[28] This dictated that 'credit and character [should have affixed to] them a value, not merely ideal, but capable of pecuniary admeasurement, and consequently recommending them as the proper objects of legal protection'.[29]

Both of these themes were evident in Pound's analysis when he argued that the protection of individual interests was a development of both law and society, where 'the progress of civilization [gave rise to many] individual interests and... the growth of law [made] men conscious of them'.[30] In this way, the philosophical currents gave a coherence to the idea derived from the cases that reputation was truly a form of property. That is, the cases made sense because of the philosophical framework in which they were decided and read. But it is appropriate to be wary of that coherence because the reverse was also true: just as philosophy made the law seem sensible, the decisions of the courts seemed consistent with nature of the world as the philosophers saw it.[31] The coherence is ultimately circular and self-supporting. But might there nevertheless be other reasons to see the property conception as a true reflection of reputation? The material value of the interest requires some consideration.

24 *R v Burdett* (1820) 4 B&Ald 95, 96, 106 ER 873, 874.

25 T Starkie, *A Treatise on the Law of Slander, Libel, Scandalum Magnatum and False Rumours* (2nd edn, 1830) v; see also (1st edn, 1813) 12 and right through to HC Folkard, *Folkard's Starkie on Slander and Libel* (6th edn, 1897) 6.

26 Starkie, 2nd edn (n 25 above) vi–viii.

27 Post (n 3 above) 695.

28 Starkie, 1st edn (n 25 above) 2; Starkie, 2nd edn (n 25 above) xxii; *Folkard's Starkie* (n 25 above) 14.

29 Starkie, 1st edn (n 25 above) 2.

30 Pound (n 1 above) 348.

31 Ibid 354.

C. The material worth of a good reputation

There is no doubt that a good reputation may in the ordinary course of events carry some material advantage. While acknowledging that not all people work at their reputations for financial gain, Bower maintains quite rightly that:

> reputation is not to be considered as 'a chimerical good,' or as merely 'the food of vanity and ambition,' but rather as 'one of the chief comforts of society,' and as a thing 'in which our worldly interests are concerned'.[32]

To that extent, it seems entirely appropriate to recognize through the remedy of pecuniary damages the loss that may accompany a diminution of reputation. However, to say that we have 'worldly interests' in reputation, and to say that the law will recognize that those interests carry material consequences is far from saying that reputation *is* property. Rather, it is simply to say that:

> Reputation is regarded by the law in the same light as that in which it is regarded by the common understanding of mankind, viz as carrying with it, if good, temporal advantages...[33]

In short, even though reputation has a temporal dimension, that does not mean it is best viewed as a form of property.

The analysis of the proposition that reputation is a form of property helps explain how and why the courts have developed and interpreted the law in a way that treats reputation *as if it were* property. But it is neither appropriate nor necessary to stretch the concept of property so far that reputation is to be a form of property simply because it carries material consequences.

The conception of reputation as property fundamentally fails to explain the nature of reputation because it does not reveal anything about it. For example (using the language of its proponents discussed above), it does not indicate how or why the opinion of others forms as it does. It does not explain why esteem, confidence, and goodwill are vested in a person. It does not tell us anything about how and why the respect and regard of one's fellows will attach to a person. All it says is that when these things are present, one's proprietary position is stronger than when they are not and when they are diminished, one's proprietary position is diminished with them. In the terms of the theory of reputation proffered in Chapter 1, the idea that reputation is a form of property does not tell us anything about the processes of moral judgment that are central to the formation of reputation.

II. Reputation and Personality

The nature of reputation is best explained within the realms of personality. Here, Pound is more persuasive when he argues that the individual has a claim 'to be

[32] Bower (n 10 above) 240, drawing on Sir Henry Fielding, 'Charge to the Grand Jury at the Westminster Sessions, 29 June 1719'. See also Starkie, 2nd edn (n 25 above) xxi; more recently, T Gibbons (n 5 above) 63.

[33] Bower (n 10 above) 243.

secured in his dignity and honor as part of his personality in a world in which one must live in society among his fellow men'.[34] The nature of reputation is best studied in these terms because the processes of moral judgment are located in social life.

I begin by sketching Robert Post's influential analysis of reputation as honour and then turn to the anthropological and historical literature to escape the limits of the traditional view of honour as an aristocratic phenomenon. The second section turns to the processes of moral judgment as they have been seen to operate in communities of honour. The third section argues that by understanding honour in terms of 'moral taxonomies' it is possible to accommodate the various insights into honour that arise in the different strands of the literature. Finally, it will be suggested that moral taxonomies enable one to make sense of the relationships between honour, dignity, and reputation.

A. The concept of honour

1. *The limits of 'reputation as honour'*

Robert Post has argued that in the common law reputation has at times been understood as honour and that this view was particularly influential 'in pre-industrial England during the formative years of defamation law'.[35] He acknowledges that honour 'has many aspects'—a point to which I shall return—but that the most important form of honour for the law was:

> a form of reputation in which an individual personally identifies with the normative characteristics of a particular social role and in return personally receives from others the regard and estimation that society accords to that role.[36]

Honour of this kind was claimed 'by virtue of the status with which society endows [the] social role'.[37] It was premised upon a 'deference society' comprised of unequal individuals in which:

> ascribed social roles are pervasive and well-established, and in which such roles provide the point of reference both for the ascription of social status and for the normative standards of personal conduct.[38]

Defamation law maintained the hierarchy of social roles in two ways, he argues. It could be:

> either as a potent method for reaffirming the importance to the whole society of the status of particular social roles, or as an instrument for the forceful imposition of such status.[39]

[34] Pound (n 1 above) 447.
[35] Post (n 3 above) 699.
[36] Ibid 699–700.
[37] Ibid 700.
[38] Ibid 700, 702. He draws here on FML Thompson, *English Landed Society in the Nineteenth Century* (1963).
[39] Post (n 3 above) 703.

The affirmative processes could be seen in the parallels:

> between the traditional common law of criminal libel and the 'Code of Honor' under which gentlemen duelists sought to 'avenge insults' and thereby achieve 'the restoration of wounded honor.'[40]

Honour, argues Post, is all encompassing, and dishonour 'is a fall from grace in the most comprehensive sense—loss of face in the community, but also loss of self and separation from the basic norms that govern human life'.[41] The value of honour, he says, 'is the value of a meaningful life'.[42]

As a thesis regarding defamation law, Post's position is persuasive. However, his analysis does not reveal as much about reputation as it might. This is because he has unreasonably limited the conceptual inquiry into honour. In Post's analysis, hierarchical honour dominates to the exclusion of other forms or dimensions of honour. Most importantly, this view of honour tends to marginalize the fact that a diverse range of ordinary people saw honour as playing a very important role in their individual and communal lives. A richer sense of honour will be of more assistance in understanding the nature of reputation.

2. *A richer sense of honour: social worth and self-worth*

Honour has mainly been studied by historians and anthropologists. Historical research has most notably examined the nature and operation of honour amongst the aristocracy of early-modern England and Europe, and the codes of honour that governed the social and political life of the upper-classes in the antebellum southern United States. Anthropological research in the last 50 years has explored the place of honour in the lives of 'ordinary' people. The cornerstone of this highly influential literature is a collection edited by Peristiany, *Honour and Shame: The Values of Mediterranean Society*.[43] The central theme of this work was that honour (and its corollary of shame) was the value that constituted and characterized a common 'Mediterranean' culture among the peoples of non-aristocratic classes in countries of the Levant, Southern Europe, and North Africa.[44] Julian Pitt-Rivers' contribution to the book is of special importance. He presented a general conceptual framework for honour which sought to account for both the traditional aristocratic honour and the sense of honour that governed political and social life across the classes.[45] Both the theses on Mediterranean culture and the conceptual framework have since been subjected to substantial critique and review but the

[40] Ibid 704.

[41] Ibid 701, quoting P Berger, B Berger, and H Kellner, *The Homeless Mind: Modernization and Consciousness* (1973) 90.

[42] Post (n 3 above) 701.

[43] JG Persitiany (ed), *Honour and Shame: The Values of Mediterranean Society* (1966). Also significant was J Campbell, *Honour, Family and Patronage* (1964).

[44] Stanley Brandes provides these labels in 'Reflections on Honor and Shame in the Mediterranean' in DD Gilmore (ed), *Honor and Shame and the Unity of the Mediterranean* (1987) 121.

[45] J Pitt-Rivers, 'Honour and Social Status' in Persitiany (ed) (n 43 above) 21.

concepts of honour developed there remain a key point of reference and debate in the literature.[46]

Central to Pitt-Rivers' account is the diversity of honour: it has 'varied within Europe from one period to another, from one region to another and above all from one class to another'.[47] Pitt-Rivers argued that studies of different cultures suggest honour is a product of several interrelated factors:

> Honour is the value of a person in his own eyes, but also in the eyes of his society. It is his estimation of his own worth, his *claim* to pride, but it is also the acknowledgment of that claim, his excellence recognised by society . . .[48]

Other definitions were provided but similar themes arise in all of them.[49] In the end, as Stewart explains, it is Pitt-Rivers' original definition which has endured and best reflects the currency of the literature.[50]

At the core of Pitt-Rivers' definition are the elements of social worth and self-worth.[51] Across the disciplines, the relationship between social worth and self-worth is seen as an intimate one.[52] Nancy Shields Kollman speaks of the 'inescapable

[46] This is especially so in anthropology: S Pink, *Women and Bullfighting: Gender, Sex and the Consumption of Tradition* (1997); FH Stewart, *Honor* (1994); U Wikan, 'Shame and Honour: A Contestable Pair' (1984) 19 *Man* 635. In history, see B Wyatt-Brown, *Southern Honor: Ethics and Behavior in the Old South* (1982); B Wyatt-Brown, *The Shaping of Southern Culture: Honor, Grace, and War, 1760s–1890s* (2001); NS Kollman, *By Honor Bound: State and Society in Early Modern Russia* (1999). A number of recent works explore the more pervasive presence of honour in England and Europe across all class boundaries and often its persistence through to more recent times. The place of gender, especially, attracts significant attention: BA Hanawalt, *'Of Good and Ill Repute': Gender and Social Control in Medieval England* (1998); RA Nye, *Masculinity and Male Codes of Honor in Modern France* (1993); P Spierenburg (ed), *Men and Violence: Gender, Honor and Rituals in Modern Europe and America* (1998).

[47] Pitt-Rivers (n 45 above) 21.

[48] Ibid, emphasis in original.

[49] For instance, Spierenburg suggests that: 'Honor has at least three layers: a person's own feeling of self-worth, this persons assessment of his or her worth in the eyes of others, and the actual opinion of others about her or him': 'Masculinity, Violence and Honor: An Introduction' in Spierenburg (ed) (n 46 above) 1, 2. See also Stewart (n 46 above) 12–13. Nye sees the essence of honour as lying in the reflective sentiment of the individual, though that sentiment is shaped by the views of others and honour is: 'not an ontological essence that men possessed by nature, but the product of an attribution process consisting of successive judgments by contemporaries about the consistency of a man's public behavior': RA Nye, 'Honor Codes' in PN Stearns (ed), *Encyclopedia of Social History* (1994) 325, 326. For a critical discussion of how the anthropological literature has failed to deal adequately with the relationship between the two elements, see Wikan (n 46 above).

[50] Stewart (n 46 above) 13.

[51] Other terms could be used. Stewart (n 46 above) 12 and 17, frames the two aspects of honour—social worth and self-worth—in slightly different terms of outer (or external) and inner (or internal) honour. Wikan (n 46 above) 642–3 uses the expressions 'social esteem' on the one hand, and 'self-respect' or self-regard on the other. In a later definition, Pitt-Rivers says honour has three components: it is 'a sentiment, a manifestation of this sentiment in conduct, and the evaluation of this conduct by others': J Pitt-Rivers, 'Honor' in DL Sills (ed), *International Encyclopedia of the Social Sciences, Volume 6* (1968) 503. Here, he identifies the evaluation by others as being one's reputation. By the 1990s, Pitt-Rivers seems to revert back to his earlier 'two aspect' position: JG Peristiany and J Pitt-Rivers, 'Introduction' in JG Peristiany and J Pitt-Rivers (eds), *Honor and Grace in Anthropology* (1992) 1, 4–5.

[52] Stewart (n 46 above) 12.

link between personal esteem and public approbation' which makes honour 'personal identity socially ratified'.[53] The anthropology and ethnography of honour quite clearly demonstrate that the opinion of other people is very important to individuals' sense of self-worth. The same point is made in the historical literature. Wyatt-Brown, for example, notes that one element 'crucial in the formulation of Southern evaluations of conduct' was that the 'opinion of others [was] an indispensable part of personal identity and [a] gauge of self-worth'.[54] The relationship between social and self-worth will be highly dependent upon its context. The substance or operation of honour will be constituted by different things in different places, at different times, and where different people are concerned.[55] Regardless of the variations, there is broadly based agreement that an individual's sense of self-worth is intimately related to how other people see them, and that means reputation *matters*.[56]

As the following sections will show, the close relationship between the components of honour mean that criteria for moral judgment that govern an individual's social worth—their reputation—are the same as those that inform the individual's sense of self-worth.

B. Honour and moral judgment

In Chapter 1, reputation was defined as a social judgment of the person based upon facts which are considered relevant by a community. The analysis in that chapter argued that such judgments—because they are founded in the concept of community—are inherently moral judgments. A community, it will be recalled, was defined as a form of moral connection; it is a group of people that see themselves united by the values that they consider they share. By looking at the history of aristocratic honour and the anthropology of honour in the Mediterranean, it is possible to see processes of moral judgment, inclusion, and exclusion at work in communities of honour. Understanding how these processes operate in honour will help explain how moral judgment functions in reputation and will provide a way of thinking about reputation that enables a comparison of the relationships between reputation and defamation across different historical and cultural contexts.

1. Aristocratic honour

The historical literature has paid special attention to duelling because, as a highly visible and formalized mode of resolving disputes, it helps explain how

[53] Kollman (n 46 above) 25–6. Kollman draws on E Goffman, *Interaction Ritual* (1967). Post (n 3 above) 708ff also draws on Goffman.

[54] Wyatt-Brown, *Southern Honor* (n 46 above) 34, 45–6.

[55] See especially Wikan (n 46 above).

[56] Barendt (n 4 above) 116–17 has argued that the point of libel law is to protect reputation because damage to reputation affects our sense of self-worth (which he calls dignity). The dignity conception of reputation is discussed below in section D.

honour played a significant part in the lives of the upper classes.[57] The duel only makes sense within the code of honour that characterized the aristocratic life. Conversely, the duel helps explain that form of honour.

Duels were fought from at least the early-16th century through until the mid-19th century in Britain, later in the South of the United States, and into the early-20th century in continental Europe.[58] The parties were always of the ruling classes. They were always men, for it was masculine honour at stake.[59] Duels were preceded by a complex process of negotiation, perhaps occurring over some months, and generally involving intermediaries who would act on behalf of the parties in the attempts to resolve a dispute over a 'point of honour' without either party losing face. The essence of a point of honour was that one party had not been treated with the respect appropriate to their social standing. Typically, this resulted from an insult. When negotiations were unsuccessful then the aggrieved party could demand 'satisfaction' through a duel. The other party could not decline without losing face, for accepting the challenge was itself a point of honour.[60]

The duel illustrates the way that honour was concerned with the boundaries of aristocratic community. To duel was to accept that both parties were—and could be—possessed of honour, and honour was, self-evidently to those involved, premised upon the superiority of the upper classes. As Andrew explains it, 'the willingness to fight a duel, as well as the recognition of being a person who was "challenge-able" defined, in great part, what it meant to be a gentleman'.[61] Wyatt-Brown argues that the principles of honour and the duel 'were the means to create and bind together a privileged group and to classify the ranks of its members

[57] Among the most significant works are: DT Andrew, 'The Code of Honour and its Critics: The Opposition to Duelling in England, 1700–1850' (1980) 5 *Social History* 409; F Billacois, *The Duel: Its Rise and Fall in Early Modern France* (1990); KS Greenberg, *Honor and Slavery* (1996); M James, 'English Politics and the Concept of Honour 1485–1642' [1978] *Past & Present Supplement* 3 1; VG Kiernan, *The Duel in European History: Honour and the Reign of Aristocracy* (1988); K McAleer, *Dueling: The Cult of Honour in Fin-De-Siècle Germany* (1994); Wyatt-Brown, *Southern Honor* (n 46 above); Wyatt-Brown, *The Shaping of Southern Culture* (n 46 above). Several contributions to Spierenburg (n 46 above) consider the complex relationships between morality, violence, ritual, and honour in a way that builds on the duelling literature.

[58] Spierenburg, 'Masculinity, Violence and Honor' (n 49 above) 16–19; Nye (n 49 above) 326. James (n 57 above) 6 suggests that the duel had in fact been fought for honour in England as early as the mid-15th century.

[59] Spierenburg, 'Masculinity, Violence and Honor' (n 49 above) 5; Billacois (n 57 above) 205.

[60] See generally, Greenberg (n 57 above) 74; Billacois (n 57 above) 205–7.

[61] Andrew (n 57 above) 415. The parties were always of equal social standing: Greenberg (n 57 above) 74; Pitt-Rivers (n 45 above) 31. As a consequence, not every insult was taken as a point of honour. An insult from a lesser man may warrant punishment, but it would not be dignified by a duel: Pitt-Rivers, ibid; Stewart (n 46 above) 67. An insult from someone on the fringes of the aristocracy would be a difficult matter. It would not do to ignore the offence, but the options were difficult. A duel would be undesirable because one's honour could never be recovered by duelling with a person of lower status: Stewart (n 46 above) 67. On the other hand, to take the insult as a point of honour would be to acknowledge the other person as your equal; to seek satisfaction through a duel would be to admit them into the 'community of honourable gentlemen': see, for example, Greenberg (n 57 above) 55, 81–2.

for the purposes of establishing order and group cohesion... Duels separated respectable gentlemen from the rest of society.'[62] The possession of honour was a prerequisite for duelling and it was derived from lineage-based social standing. Importantly, while the code of honour dictated that men of honour would fight duels, a person could not become possessed of honour simply by doing so. By giving privilege to their own lineage and attaching honourable status to their actions, the upper classes simultaneously defined and proved their honour:

> [T]he status of being honourable implied a tension between inherited status and personal quality, between 'blood' and 'virtue'. The man of honour was required to establish the innate quality of his honourable blood by his virtuous deeds...[63]

James' turn of phrase captures the duality nicely: their superiority was 'self-selecting and self-authenticating'.[64]

The group of honourable people constituted a community in every sense of the word. Their status as a community was defined and confirmed by the aristocratic values they shared. Inclusion and exclusion from the community were based on those values, as were judgments of social and self-worth. Similar processes also existed outside the aristocracy, though criteria for moral judgment were distinctly different.

2. *Honour outside the aristocracy*

Ordinary people everywhere had long seen themselves as being in possession of what they understood to be honour. There might not have been duelling but there is much evidence that people of lower classes regularly fought some form of combat based on offence against honour.[65] Similarly, the records of the civil and criminal courts in Europe, England, and the United States indicate that ordinary people took offence at matters that they saw as going to their honour.[66] It is apparent from the behaviour of people across the class spectrum that hierarchy and superiority do not adequately explain the meaning(s) of honour. The ethnographies and the theoretical frameworks in the anthropology of the Mediterranean

[62] Wyatt-Brown, *The Shaping of Southern Culture* (n 46 above) 56–7, 62. This exclusionary aspect of the code of honour was manifest also in the swearing of oaths—'only those within the circle of honor were entitled to participate' as those without honour could not pledge it in an oath: Wyatt-Brown, *Southern Honor* (n 46 above) 57.

[63] James (n 57 above) 22, drawing on Gerard Legh, *The Accedens of Armory* (1562).

[64] James (n 57 above) 22.

[65] Spierenburg, 'Masculinity, Violence and Honor' (n 49 above) 15–17, also 10; Greenberg (n 57 above) xii.

[66] This point is made by various scholars (eg, Nye (n 49 above) 326; Andrew (n 57 above) 415–16; Wyatt-Brown, *Southern Honor* (n 46 above) 43), though there have been few analyses. Wyatt-Brown has criticized the lack of attention paid to the law, though this has been remedied to some extent by works such as that by Kollman (n 46 above). The most ambitious work has been the attempts by Barbara Hanawalt to re-conceptualize the hierarchy and marginalization in medieval social relationships through an investigation of the exclusionary rituals of legal processes: Hanawalt (n 46 above) 18–34.

lay the foundations for a conceptual framework within which the complexity and diversity of honour might be better understood.

The anthropological evidence shows that honour was clearly a meaningful part of life across the social spectrum, including in the peasantry.[67] Pitt-Rivers argued that all classes possessed honour, though it operated in different ways, 'present[ing] itself in a different contextual framework to the individual according to his place in the social structure, and the differing value attached to it can be explained by this'.[68] Persitiany argued that there was a dialectic of honour and shame at the core of Mediterranean culture:

> Honour is at the apex of the pyramid of... social values and it conditions their hierarchical order... The Mediterranean people discussed in these papers are constantly called upon to use the concepts of honour and shame in order to assess their own conduct and that of their fellows.[69]

Honour and shame were 'the constituents of virtue'.[70] The sources of honour and shame in these communities lay not in class-based social standing but in the characteristics that were valued, such as honesty, loyalty, and 'the avoidance of moral turpitude in general'.[71] Honour is gained by exhibiting these characteristics and one is shamed or dishonoured by failing to do so. The most distinctive content of honour and shame—of virtue itself—was found in gender roles and relationships:

> The honour of a man and of a woman therefore imply quite different modes of conduct... [A man is obliged] to defend his honour and that of his family, a woman to conserve her purity... [A] woman who takes to physical violence or attempts to usurp the male prerogative of authority or, very much more so, sexual freedom, forfeits her shame.[72]

This sense of honour was quite distinct from the more familiar form that had long existed among the aristocracy. Pitt-Rivers argued that the opposite of aristocratic honour (which he called 'honour as precedence') was 'honour as virtue'. Aristocratic honour was reliant on hierarchy and precedence gained through a birthright or status-based admission to the upper classes. But without economic and political

[67] For example, in Pitt-Rivers' study of a rural Andalusian community, he distinguishes between 'the plebeian community' of rural workers, 'the *senoritos*' who constitute 'the upper class of the town', and 'the upper class' of the whole community which includes not only 'the aristocracy' by birth who hold the land, but also 'persons of wealth or eminence who do not belong by birth to the aristocracy': Pitt-Rivers (n 45 above) 42, 50–4, 61–4, 71.

[68] Ibid 61.

[69] JG Persitiany, 'Introduction' in Persitiany (ed) (n 43 above) 9–10. The elipsis in the phrase 'pyramid of... social values' omits the word 'temporal'. Persitiany explains (10, 17–18, note 4) that he uses the word temporal to distinguish honour and saintliness. I have omitted the word to avoid confusion between Persitiany's use of it and the sense in which it has been used earlier in this chapter to distinguish between interests of personality and property.

[70] Pitt-Rivers (n 45 above) 42.

[71] Ibid.

[72] Ibid 42–3; also Persitiany (n 69 above) 9.

power, ordinary people could not compete on the same terms with their superiors and 'their prestige relate[d] ... to a public opinion which recognize[d] virtue rather than precedence as the basis of honour'.[73]

To sum up thus far, a study of the historical and anthropological literature shows that honour, like reputation, is founded in the concept of community. Accordingly, it exhibits the features of inclusion, exclusion, and moral judgment that characterize communities. Central to every form of honour is a system of publicly acknowledged moral values that defines the membership of a community and is the point of reference for judgment within it. Pitt-Rivers observed in his later work that honour is 'at once a sentiment and an objective social fact; on the one hand, a moral state [...] and at the same time a means of representing the moral worth of others'.[74] Wyatt-Brown, for example, recognizes expressly the constitutive role of ethics:

> It cannot be too strongly emphasised that honor is not confined to any rank of society; it is the moral property of all who belong within the community, one that determines the community's own membership.[75]

The observation is echoed by Stewart, for whom the constitutive aspect is 'the right to be treated as a full or equal member of the honor group'.[76] Kollman makes a similar point:

> At root, then, honor can be seen as one of the means to define and police the boundaries of community. Honor gives community members a discourse—a rhetoric and a cultural practice—with which to shape the way they interact, to identify insiders and outsiders in a community...'[77]

The basis for the values that identify the moral good were identified in the anthropological literature as deriving either from precedence (where an individual's social and self-worth is evaluated on the basis of social standing), or virtue (where an individual's worth is evaluated on the basis of behaviour and characteristics the community regards as virtuous). The anthropology of the Mediterranean has been subjected to thorough, compelling, and productive critique, especially over the last two decades.[78] The critique has exposed deep flaws in the substantive aspects of the honour/shame paradigm, especially with respect to the understanding of gender.[79]

[73] Pitt-Rivers (n 45 above) 61.

[74] J Pitt-Rivers, 'La Maladie de l'honneur' in M Gautheron (ed), *L'honneur: image de soi ou don de soi un ideal equivoque* (1991) 21, quoted in Stewart (n 46 above) 13.

[75] Wyatt-Brown, *Southern Honor* (n 46 above) xv.

[76] Stewart (n 46 above) 54.

[77] Kollman (n 46 above) 29. See also PG Wilson, 'Reputation and Respectability: A Suggestion for Caribbean Ethnology' (1969) 4 *Man* 70, 83 note 7.

[78] Pink (n 46 above); DD Gilmore, 'Honor, Honesty, Shame: Male Status in Contemporary Andalusia' in Gilmore (ed), *Honor and Shame and the Unity of the Mediterranean* (1987) 90; Brandes (n 44 above); A Lever, 'Honour as a Red Herring' (1986) 6(3) *Critique of Anthropology* 83; Wikan (n 46 above).

[79] Pink (n 46 above); Wikan (n 46 above).

However, the conceptual framework still poses the right questions. None of the substantive criticisms of the Mediterranean anthropology undermines Pitt-Rivers' conceptual position that honour is not always determined by hierarchy. On the contrary, they highlight the possible different sources of honour. Indeed, Wikan accepts the core of Pitt-Rivers' thesis, though arguing that it has been inadequately applied:

> [Pitt-Rivers argued that], 'The social scientist is concerned with the fact and processes of recognition: how, on what grounds and by whom is the claim to honour recognized?' But it is precisely the '*processes* of recognition' to which anthropologists have not paid attention.[80]

How, then, might one address these processes in the context of diverse configurations of values that are the basis for judgments about honour in different communities? The question is a methodological one and the anthropology of the Mediterranean is, again, of considerable use. It houses a methodological tool that might help answer those questions in the context of an inquiry into both honour and reputation. That tool is a 'moral taxonomy'.

C. Ethnographies of honour as moral taxonomies

Michael Herzfeld lays out one of the most insightful critiques of the honour/shame framework. First, he is not persuaded that one can meaningfully speak of the 'Mediterranean' as 'a discrete cultural zone' because it is ethnographically diverse.[81] He is troubled by the circularity involved as the region is on the one hand geographically defined by the shared characteristic of honour/shame frameworks and, on the other, it then is claimed that the region exhibits characteristics of honour/shame frameworks.[82] The critique undermines the interpretation of the region advanced by Persitiany and Pitt-Rivers, but it does not prevent general observations being made about the nature of honour. To that end, the same diversity informs Herzfeld's second concern.

In the Mediterranean anthropology, he argues, translations of distinct local words to the terminology of honour and shame are 'unavoidably inexact' and made without reference to the contexts in which the original words are used; consequently, the honour/shame framework does not accurately comprehend the nature of social relations in these societies.[83] Herzfeld does not doubt that honour and shame are important concepts. Rather, he is concerned that they not be misused. He is especially critical of the 'false coherence' that derives from

[80] Wikan (n 46 above) 638, reference omitted, emphasis in original.
[81] M Herzfeld, 'Honour and Shame: Problems in the Comparative Analysis of Moral Systems' (1980) 15 Man 339.
[82] Ibid 340; DD Gilmore, 'Introduction: The Shame of Dishonor' in Gilmore (ed), *Honor and Shame and the Unity of the Mediterranean* (1987) 6.
[83] Herzfeld (n 81 above) 340.

'conflation [of Mediterranean values] as "honour" and "shame"'.[84] However, Herzfeld argues that the studies have managed to avoid the reductionism (reducing everything to honour and shame) 'by reporting each terminological use in its own ethnographic context'.[85] Hence, it seems Herzfeld is arguing that although the ethnographies are solid, they do not—even on their own terms—support the generalized propositions that are made about the region. He argues that what has been discussed as 'honour and shame' in the ethnographies is not usefully identified in those terms. Instead, the patterns and processes they discuss are best thought of as 'moral taxonomies':

> They have provided moral taxonomies—systems, that is, for the ranking of one's fellow citizens according to a set of ethical criteria.[86]

These taxonomies, he says, are concerned 'with the public evaluation of behaviour'.[87] Wyatt-Brown's identification of the essence of honour as moral or ethical rules resonates with Herzfeld's analysis:

> [H]onor is essentially the cluster of ethical rules, most readily found in societies of small communities, by which judgments of behavior are ratified by community consensus.[88]

Wyatt-Brown's expression provides an appropriate parallel to Herzfeld's moral taxonomy terminology and will be used in the same way here.

Herzfeld's interpretation of the anthropology of honour is persuasive and useful. First, it can accommodate both precedence and virtue as the bases upon which social and self-worth are adjudged within upper classes and non-elites. As explained above, both of these are quite clearly systems for ranking others according to ethical criteria.[89] Secondly, it recognizes the diversity between and within cultures and communities with respect to what *constitutes* precedence and virtue in different contexts. In doing so, it is able to accommodate the feminist critiques of the honour/shame paradigm. Simultaneously, it is consistent with the coterminous pursuit

84 Ibid 348. He draws the expression 'false coherence' from J Davis, 'Honour and Politics in Pisticci' [1968] *Proceedings of the Royal Anthropology Institute* 69, though is critical of Davis' argument on the substance of the debates.

85 Herzfeld (n 81 above) 340; see also Wilson (n 77 above) 82.

86 Herzfeld (n 81 above) 340.

87 Ibid 341.

88 Wyatt-Brown, *Southern Honor* (n 46 above) xv; also xix where he refers to 'moral rules'. Morality appears relevant to honour in this way elsewhere in the literature, albeit that different terminology is used. Andrew (n 57 above) 411, associates honour with 'systems of moral authority'. Lever's critique of the Mediterranean anthropology is substantially directed to grasping the value systems at work in communities: Lever (n 78 above). Similarly, Wilson's comparison of Mediterranean honour and shame with 'the moral and social values revolving around the ideas of "reputation" and "respectability"' in the Caribbean: Wilson (n 77 above) 70.

89 When in the 1990s Peristiany and Pitt-Rivers turned to symbolic and religious dimensions of honour, their approach was consistent with this accommodation of diverse and particular conceptions of honour: 'It is therefore an error to regard honor as a single constant concept rather than a conceptual field within which people find the means to express their self-esteem or their esteem for others': Persitiany and Pitt-Rivers (n 51 above) 4.

in those critiques that seeks to recognize the different and particular processes by which social and self-worth are attributed and evaluated in communities. While that suggests there are extremely diverse criteria and sources of honour, it does not preclude generalized statements being made about honour. Indeed, Wyatt-Brown's concern with the 'ethical patterns that gave coherence to the region's culture' is premised upon the ability to draw connections with respect to criteria for moral judgment and, as such, to identify groups of people as communities.[90]

From Herzfeld's critique, a general proposition can be derived: the concept of honour and its operation in different contexts can be understood through the underlying moral taxonomies that are the bases for judgments of social worth and self-worth in a community. Those moral taxonomies (or ethical rules) are comprised of the criteria for moral judgment that can be identified in and which constitute a community. Because this proposition is general and abstract, it accommodates the many and diverse ways of judging social worth and self-worth. However, that same generality and abstraction gives rise to two significant uncertainties.

First, while it might be that honour should be understood through those moral taxonomies, what of the obverse: should *every* judgment about social and self-worth that is governed by a set of ethical rules be understood as a judgment about honour?[91] This is especially pertinent because the literature has suggested dignity as an alternative way of thinking about mediations of social and self-worth.[92] Secondly, if honour is diverse and context-dependent, then is it ever possible to meaningfully discuss and draw connections between the phenomena that have traditionally fallen under the heading of honour without being limited by the constant need to couch and distinguish them with reference to their particular context(s)? In short, is it possible to speak in any generalized way about 'honour' as a concept with *content*?

Resolving these uncertainties will help make sense of the relationships between honour, dignity, and reputation. With respect to the first matter, not all mediations of social and self-worth should be understood as honour. Regarding the second, I think it is possible to give 'honour' some content that makes it useful as a term and concept of general application, and thus to speak meaningfully of various phenomena in terms of honour. To explain why requires a closer look at moral taxonomies and a return to some of the literature on community discussed

90 Wyatt-Brown, *Southern Honor* (n 46 above) xvi.

91 Stewart (n 46 above) 5–6 has asked a similar question in his study of the social relationships of the Bedouin: 'It may not be clear why some things count as honor and others do not... [If it can be said that] "the ideals or moral virtues of Bedouin society together constitute... the Bedouin code of honor" [... then...] do the ideals or moral virtues of every society constitute a code of honor, or is there something special about Bedouin ideals or moral virtues that makes them a code of honor? And, if there is, what is it?'

92 It will be recalled that Roscoe Round's view of reputation as an interest in personality used the terms honour and dignity, though not drawing any clear distinction between them. This possibility was also echoed in Post's argument that reputation has at times been understood in the courts as dignity: Post (n 3 above) 707–19.

in the first chapter. This will help considerably in the task of getting to grips with the nature of reputation and the challenges involved in its legal protection.

D. Honour, dignity, and moral taxonomies

There are two important dimensions to the moral taxonomies that underpin judgments of social worth and self-worth. First, taxonomies consist of criteria that are recognized by a community as constituting and being evidence of moral goodness or moral badness. Secondly, those criteria obtain their moral status in particular ways.

1. The substance of criteria for moral judgment

Pitt-Rivers identified certain substantive criteria for moral judgment among the lower classes of the Mediterranean. These included, for example, honesty and loyalty generally, while shyness and restraint were relevant to women and 'manliness' and authority over family were important for men.[93] Some behaviours, he argued, were seen as shameful or dishonouring in the lower classes but carried no such import for the upper classes where honour was obtained by precedence rather than virtue.[94] The importance of precedence was similarly apparent in Wyatt-Brown's sketch of the criteria for moral judgment in the American South. He describes the factors applied in the evaluation of a person's worth in communities of honour:

> Family integrity, clearly understood hierarchies of leaders and subordinates, and ascriptive features of individuals and groups are guides for those evaluations. By 'ascription' is meant such biological determinants as race and color, gender, bloodlines, physique and physical skill, age, and inherited position.[95]

The identification of criteria across classes and the precedence/virtue framework may be a generally accurate reflection of the communities that were studied, but a consideration of honour can yield far more. What I wish to draw attention to is the functional equivalence of the moral roles played by the different criteria. That equivalence is important: what matters is that moral taxonomies identify characteristics that are honourable. When viewed this way, the distinction between honour as precedence and honour as virtue collapses. That is, when considering honour in terms of moral taxonomies, one is faced with criteria that identify the moral good in a community and these criteria are, by definition, all virtues. Social and self-worth is warranted in a community when one possesses or exhibits them.

If one can identify factors—virtues—that are relevant in the attribution and recognition of social and self-worth, the second question of interest is why, then, are they virtues? What is the source of their goodness? What makes them factors

[93] Pitt-Rivers (n 45 above) 42–5.
[94] Ibid 67–71.
[95] Wyatt-Brown, *Southern Honor* (n 46 above) xv.

that, if possessed or exhibited, will make a person deserving of respect and regard? The anthropology and history of honour is not sufficient if one is to make sense of the bases or sources of criteria for moral judgment. It will be necessary to move outside that work, returning to the literature on community and the understanding of dignity which Post argued was the third concept of reputation that was apparent in defamation law. By doing so, the terms 'honour' and 'dignity' can be used to distinguish between judgments associated with moral taxonomies where criteria for moral judgment derive their ethical status from different sources.

2. *The bases or sources of criteria for moral judgment*

The anthropological studies of honour suggest that some things may be virtues because they are the characteristics of those who have social power. Honour as precedence tends to conceal the moral element because it equates social standing and moral goodness; the latter is implicit in the former and, as a result, the former will necessarily define the latter.[96] Wyatt-Brown described this in the American South where morality and hierarchy were one and the same: 'The greater the space along the moral and social continuum, the more respect due the higher, the less regard owed the lower.'[97] Or, as Pitt-Rivers puts it, '[a]uthority as political power claims always to be moral authority' and precedence is synonymous with virtue.[98] In other instances, some things are virtues for no other reason than that the community regards them as virtues. Where honour is defined by virtue, the moral dimensions of honour are a little more exposed because it begs the questions of what constitutes virtue and why. Pitt-Rivers indicates that some qualities are virtues because they are seen as 'naturally occurring', while others obtain that quality because education has taught that they are virtuous.[99] The crucial point in each case is that the ethical status of criteria in the moral taxonomies described by the Mediterranean anthropologists and in the American South derives from what might be thought of as 'tradition'. 'Tradition' is used here in the same way it was discussed in Chapter 1—that is, it refers to the dominance of cultural norms that are found in community traditions—and sits in contrast with rights-oriented principles of liberal individualism. The distinction is important and appropriate because liberal-communitarian debates document the ongoing conflict between 'traditional' values and liberal rights in struggles for political dominance in contemporary Western communities. These same debates can be used to make sense of the moral taxonomies that govern reputation in communities.

Liberal principles suggest that the ethical status of criteria for moral judgment derives not from community traditions of religion or culture, but from the individual. Liberal moral taxonomies can be usefully identified with the concept of

[96] To foreshadow the argument that follows later, the relevance of this point for both reputation and defamation is immediately apparent because honour as precedence is embodied in the statement of law regarding what is defamatory: a person's reputation will be damaged by a statement that would tend to make a decent person think the less of them.

[97] Wyatt-Brown, *Southern Honor* (n 46 above) 63.

[98] Pitt-Rivers (n 45 above) 37.

[99] Ibid 43–5.

dignity that appears in Post's work. The clearest definition of dignity that Post provides is his description of it as 'our own sense of intrinsic self-worth'.[100]

This contrast between tradition and liberalism enables a distinction to be drawn between different types of moral taxonomies that underpin judgments of social and self-worth. Where moral taxonomies are informed by traditional values then it is convenient to speak of them as being associated with honour. Where moral taxonomies are informed by liberal values then it is convenient to speak of them as being associated with dignity.[101] To discriminate between the two types of taxonomy, one can look for the presence or absence of 'ascriptive' factors in the sets of ethical criteria that are applied in judging a person. In communities dominated by tradition, ascriptive factors are among the moral virtues that determine inclusion or exclusion in the community. For example, racial or sexual identity will be one of the criteria that is very important to judgments of social worth. Typically, whiteness and heterosexuality are among the criteria of moral goodness. On other hand, liberal communities or sub-communities view ascriptive features that are constitutive of identity as being irrelevant when formulating a judgment about a person.[102] That is, for instance, a person's race or sexuality will be irrelevant to a judgment of their worth in these communities.

These distinctions help resolve the uncertainties identified at the end of section C (above): not every set of ethical rules can be said to be concerned with honour, and it is possible to speak of honour as a concept with content. And, as the conclusion below will explain, the analysis in these first two chapters provides a novel and effective way of approaching reputation and understanding the challenges involved in its legal protection.

Conclusion

The principal conceptions of reputation in the literature suggest that reputation is, variously or in combination, a form of property or personality. This chapter

[100] Post (n 3 above) 710, drawing in part on *Rosenblatt v Baer* 383 US 75, 92 (Stewart J) (concurring) (1966). This is not to say that dignity does not exist for individuals in communities governed by tradition. Rather, Post's use of dignity has an essentially modern, rights-based content that enables it to be distinguished from the more general use of dignity in the older literature.

[101] While drawing on Post's concept of dignity, I disagree significantly with him in some very significant respects. Post (n 3 above) 693 argued that each different concept of reputation 'corresponds to an implicit and discrete image of the good and well-ordered society'. If reputation takes the form of dignity, he argues (716), it 'presupposes a particular kind of society [. . . where . . .] all persons are equally eligible for inclusion in the community'. Certainly, I agree with him that dignity in the form he suggests is based on an inclusive society. However, there are two important points of distinction. First, I do not see reputation as dignity; rather, reputation is the judgment made about a person using the principles of dignity that are embodied in the conception of an inclusive society. Secondly, Post argues that the inclusive society is a communitarian society. That may be the case, but it is not likely to be so. The communitarian reliance on tradition is far more likely to result in an exclusionary community: see Chapter 1, III(D).

[102] In describing these factors as being constitutive of identity, I draw on Bell's use of 'constitutive communities': D Bell, *Communitarianism and its Critics* (1993) 93ff.

has accepted that an individual's reputation may carry material consequences, but rejected the proposition that it is a form of property. Instead, it seems appropriate to understand reputation as an interest of personality. This is not to say that reputation should be conceptually equated with either honour or dignity as it is explained in the literature. Instead, an investigation of a breadth of literature suggested that the ideas of honour and dignity are both suggestive of useful ways for thinking about reputation. In particular, the anthropological literature presented the idea of honour as a moral taxonomy. This is a most helpful tool for understanding reputation.

Judgments about the social worth of individuals—their reputations—rely upon moral taxonomies. Those taxonomies are comprised of criteria for moral judgment. They consist of publicly acknowledged virtues—the shared moral goods—that define the boundaries of a community and are the criteria against which judgments of social worth and self-worth are made within the community. Just as the liberal-communitarian debates indicate a struggle over values in contemporary Western communities, it is possible to use the terms of those debates to distinguish between types of moral taxonomies that govern reputation in those same communities. As the last section explained, some communities are governed by moral taxonomies associated with tradition and others are governed by moral taxonomies associated with liberalism. A key discriminator that can be used to distinguish between the two is the presence or absence of ascriptive values in those taxonomies. This discriminator is especially useful because ascriptive or identity-based claims to dignity—claims that one's identity should not be relevant to one's moral worth—may expose, rupture, and challenge very long-standing bases on which communities make their judgments.

When the courts are called upon to make determinations about what is defamatory, they must somehow take account of the competing moral taxonomies in the communities of a jurisdiction. The law is an indicator and reflector of moral taxonomies. On most occasions, there will be little difference between traditional and liberal moral taxonomies. However, sometimes there will be difficult issues to resolve. Those issues arise when sub-communities within the jurisdiction have different values. The decisions of the courts will determine how the jurisdiction is constituted as a moral community: those decisions will both identify and determine who is included in that moral community and who is excluded from it. They will give legal recognition and legitimacy to a moral taxonomy. In determining which values or ethical rules are to be recognized as legitimate governing values of the community, it will be appropriate to consider the bases or sources of those criteria. That is, recognition or rejection of particular criteria may be justified in terms of upholding traditional values or liberal rights.

The centrality of moral judgment and the moral taxonomies that govern reputation in communities will be of interest throughout the chapters that follow. In Part II they will be used to examine whether and how reputation has been protected by different types of defamation laws across a wide period of history and in the development of the common law. In Part III, they will be used to see whether and how the contemporary legal framework protects reputation, and to see how the law might best address the ethical challenges that must be met where jurisdictions are characterized by diverse views about the ethical rules that should govern judgments of social worth.

PART II

HISTORY, LAW, AND REPUTATION

3

Reputation and the History of Defamation

The theoretical framework in Chapters 1 and 2 sought to provide an account of the nature of reputation. It argued that reputation can best be understood through the substance and sources of the criteria for moral judgment—that is, moral taxonomies—that govern judgments of social and self-worth in communities. That framework will be used to analyse the relationships between reputation and the common law of defamation. The remaining chapters examine the extent to which it can be said that defamation law protects reputation, the manner in which the law attempts to do so, and how the tests for what is defamatory should be re-shaped if the law is to protect reputation. The point of departure is historical.

Histories of defamation are regularly recounted in the literature and have long observed that the common law is riddled with anomalies and that its development exhibits little doctrinal coherence. It is a history that should yield for legal scholars a great deal more than it has done. To escape the strictures of the traditional doctrinal analysis the history of defamation law will be viewed through the prism of reputation. This chapter aims to explain the extent to which reputation was protected—and not protected—in jurisdictions where defamation laws predated the common law action. This is important because (as Chapter 4 will show) the conceptual and doctrinal dimensions of the common law and its relationships with reputation cannot be fully understood without a grasp of the relationships between defamation and reputation in the jurisdictions that preceded it.

There are two main parts to this chapter. Section I is primarily concerned with methodology. It looks at how an inquiry into defamation actions in a range of jurisdictions might cast light upon reputation and its protection under the law. With this in mind, Section II considers how defamation actions were a part of the English legal landscape long before such claims were entertained by the common law. It examines the relationships between defamation laws and reputation: (A) in the local courts; (B) in the ecclesiastical courts; and (C) under the *scandalum magnatum* statutes. It is important to note that although defamation was actionable in each of these before the common law courts allowed recovery, the laws discussed in this chapter continued to operate with some force even after the common law action developed. (The Court of Star Chamber will be addressed in Chapter 4. Although defamation matters were probably heard there before the common law allowed recovery, the Star Chamber's work was most significant for the common law courts upon its demise in the 17th century. By that time the common law action was thoroughly entrenched.)

I. Law and Reputation

A. Relationships between law and reputation

A dialogue is involved in understanding the relationships between law and reputation. Legal actions can provide insight into communities' values and concerns, and a grasp of community values and concerns can enrich and inform an understanding of the law. The literature on honour illustrates both sides of this dialogue and suggests how law and reputation might be addressed in the history of the common law.

Findings and penalties imposed by the courts have reflected values in communities. For example, where an aristocrat killed a person in a duel he would be most likely acquitted because the matter was recognized as an affair of honour, while a peasant or worker would suffer the same punishment as any ordinary killer.[1] Greenberg has distinguished laws that sought to impose criminal punishment on duellists from laws that imposed sanctions which would matter to a man of honour, such as mutilation of the dead body or disqualifying survivors from holding public office.[2] These, he said, indicated that 'some legislators understood the nature of men of honor'.[3] But of the various scholars to address the connections between law and honour, Nancy Shields Kollman's study of honour in early modern Russia makes by far the most significant contribution.[4]

Kollman found law an especially useful source for several reasons. Honour in Russia was a socially inclusive phenomenon; all in the community were recognized as having honour, and all in the community could and might defend that honour in the courts.[5] The duel was not, until the 17th century, a part of Russian aristocratic life and so there was not the inherent European opposition between honour and law; rather the state legislated rights to sue and honour was mediated within the law.[6]

[1] P Spierenburg, 'Masculinity, Violence and Honor: An Introduction' in P Spierenburg (ed), *Men and Violence: Gender, Honor and Rituals in Modern Europe and America* (1998) 1, 11; DT Andrew, 'The Code of Honour and its Critics: The Opposition to Duelling in England, 1700–1850' (1980) 5 Social History 409, 415–16; KS Greenberg, *Honor and Slavery* (1996), 8.

[2] Greenberg, ibid 15.

[3] Ibid; also FH Stewart, *Honor* (1994) 61, 111; F Billacois, *The Duel: Its Rise and Fall in Early Modern France* (1990) 206.

[4] NS Kollman, *By Honor Bound: State and Society in Early Modern Russia* (1999). Other considerations of honour and law can be found in B Wyatt-Brown, *Southern Honor: Ethics and Behavior in the Old South* (1982) xvii–xviii (writing on the American South); Stewart (n 3 above) 1, 79 (writing on the Bedouin communities of the Arabian peninsula).

[5] Kollman, ibid, 1–2, 4.

[6] Ibid 4.

There were also none of the formalized tracts on honour that could be found in the countries of western Europe.[7] 'In the end', argues Kollman, 'we are left with legal materials as our primary sources for the study of honor in Muscovy... We must turn to court cases to define honor and trace how individuals and communities used it...'[8] While keeping in mind the limits of what can be drawn from legal resources, Kollman's use of the law in her study of honour is strongly suggestive of law's potential to inform an inquiry into reputation.

Kollman relied upon two sets of legal resources: actions by members of the landed cavalry elite who contested their assignment of service (arguing that it was not appropriate to their status) and, more relevantly here, litigation regarding insult to honour.[9] In examining the law, she was looking not simply at the institution but at 'a code of values' and 'a social discourse' that could be seen within it.[10] Her findings show how litigation provided insight into the values that characterized the communities:

> By and large, there was a common core of insulting vocabulary, which sketches out what Muscovites considered the honorable person... Of highest concern to Muscovites were allegations of unlawful behavior... Family and family reputation, and the closely related issue of sexual probity, form the second most sensitive area. Litigation... over accusations of adultery, loose morals, and the like was common... A third common concern was social standing. No matter how lowly in the social hierarchy, Muscovites objected if their social rank were insulted.[11]

The litigation suggests that the criteria for moral judgment—that is, what constituted virtue or moral goodness, or what made 'the honorable person'—tended to be an absence of criminal behaviour, an adherence to sexual probity (especially for women), and social standing of a given rank. The disputes revealed 'a shared discourse of community norms'.[12] The law simultaneously supports the interpretations provided from other sources in historical and anthropological research on honour and is itself a resource for understanding social and moral relations. So too, I will suggest, with respect to reputation. In the history of the common law of defamation, might one be able to identify the moral taxonomies of reputation in a similar way? That is part of the project in the next section, though some limitations need to be noted with respect to interpretation.

First, where aristocratic honour is concerned, the law has special limitations because honour was in its most important respects a form of moral and social regulation that was set outside the law.[13] The power-plays of the State and Church

[7] Ibid 20–1; M James, 'English Politics and the Concept of Honour 1485–1642' [1978] *Past & Present Supplement* 3 1.

[8] Kollman (n 4 above) 22–3.

[9] Ibid 1.

[10] Ibid xi.

[11] Ibid 46–7.

[12] Ibid 96.

[13] The medieval judicial order of a duel was an acknowledgment that no law could decide the point of honour: 'By granting the field, the sovereign proclaimed that he did not have the power to make a judicial decision. The Prince, or the magistrate, thus announced the limit to his powers, and defined a space beyond the law': Billacois (n 3 above) 206.

alone are enough to cast doubt upon whether one might rely upon laws and litigation as a reflection of morality or whether the substance of the legal regulation and disputes are more blatantly political in their orientation. Secondly, at the personal (rather than institutional) level of litigation, there are also interpretive difficulties with respect to why things happen and, often, exactly what happened. The expense of litigation has always been a factor that influences who is able and willing to go to court; the parties who appear in the records may not at all be a cross-section of the community and arguably it may also mean the courts are dealing only with limited types of complaints. Across all classes, the secrecy of some personal resolution may be preferred to the publicity of the courts.[14] Kollman explains that interpreting litigation in Russia was 'not as straightforward as it might seem' because:

> disputants litigated in ways that we might not expect. Litigants very frequently, for example, did not pursue cases to conclusion, or they accepted the judgment of God in coming to resolution. They frequently settled even seemingly rock-solid cases out of court. They often invoked the authority of the community in the form of witnesses, sureties, or character references in pursuing their suits.[15]

The observation seems to apply with equal force to English legal history and is echoed by Martin Ingram's analysis of the way that 16th- and 17th-century communities dealt with the law. Although it concerns prosecutions in the church courts, the patterns it observes seem more generally applicable. Ingram captures the complexity of social relationships which is too easily lost in the brief, de-contextualized and formal reports of the early courts.

> [I]t was a commonplace of the period that when local officers were called upon to name offenders they had a strong tendency to under-present or even to report that 'all is well'...Not all forms of behaviour which the law proscribed were regarded as reprehensible in the community, while the zeal of presenting officers was also restrained by neighbourly tolerance and a desire not to stir up trouble in the community by taking people to court. Hence, some matters were liable to be passed over either because they were regarded as too trivial for (or even undeserving of) legal action, or because it was felt that recourse to the law would stir up additional tensions and bitterness, threaten local harmony, and hence make the cure worse than the disease.[16]

There is no reason to see these limitations as making interpretation inherently unreliable, but they are reminders that the law may provide an outline rather than

[14] S Hughes, 'Men of Steel: Dueling, Honor, and Politics in Liberal Italy' in Spierenburg (ed) (n 1 above) 64, 66, discusses the importance of secrecy where 'highly personal matters of family honor or the honor of women' were involved. More generally, Kollman (n 4 above) 108, addresses the risks of venting the details of the dispute and of giving the defendant the opportunity to win over public opinion.

[15] Kollman (n 4 above) 95.

[16] M Ingram, *Church Courts, Sex and Marriage in England, 1570–1640* (1987) 31–2.

a comprehensive picture of reputation. Still, that outline might be of significant interpretive value, as Kollman's assessment of her own findings indicates:

> Muscovites' concerns about honor express the society's living social values. Admittedly, those values were ideals as much as living realities; they were a code to which individuals aspired and not all achieved... [Nevertheless, they] indicate the parameters within which people could live without incurring social opprobrium or official sanction.[17]

While litigation may point to ideals, it is those ideals that capture the essence of the moral taxonomies which governed the relationships of social and self-worth that constituted honour, and which might similarly inform our understanding of reputation. As a counter to the interpretive limitations, it will be useful to draw on non-legal sources to sketch the sorts of values that appeared to underpin judgments of social and self-worth in pre-19th-century England. These values will provide the point of reference for the examination of English defamation laws in Part III and then in Chapter 4.

B. Moral taxonomies in early modern England

In sketching the criteria for moral judgment in England prior to the 19th century, it is necessary to make some very substantial compromises and generalizations because there were variations in the moral taxonomies of different communities and significant changes over time.[18] However, it is sufficient to identify values and influences that are relevantly representative of the moral taxonomies because the key distinctions relating to reputation lie in the disjunctures between the historical and modern formulations of these taxonomies, rather than in their manifestation within the different historical jurisdictions and periods. Dramatic and religious works provide useful insights into the moral taxonomies of early modern England.

In *The Idea of Honour in the English Drama 1591–1700*, Barber set out to examine the meanings of honour in the 17th century through a study of 206 plays that he hoped might 'reveal something about the attitudes and the scale of values' of the time.[19] Barber argued that although honour was 'a prerogative of the gentry', the dramas indicated that a loss of self-esteem and social regard could also be keenly felt by those outside the nobility.[20] However, social and self-worth in the two classes was governed by different criteria.

Moral judgment amongst the aristocracy was characterized by things that were distinct to the aristocratic code of honour, such as: a sensitivity to injury and

[17] Kollman (n 4 above) 62. On using ideals to understand cultural mores, see M Morgan, *Manners, Morals and Class in England, 1774–1858* (1994) 2.

[18] RL Greaves, *Society and Religion in Elizabethan England* (1981); R Kelso, *The Doctrine of the English Gentleman in the Sixteenth Century* (1964; first published 1929).

[19] CL Barber, *The Idea of Honour in the English Drama 1591–1700* (1957) 11, 15, 39.

[20] Ibid 30, 102–5.

insult; not tolerating a rival in love; not being outwitted or otherwise made to lose face; insisting on one's rights; not having one's authority flouted; not performing menial tasks; and not suffering an ignominious death.[21] The lives of ordinary people, however, were governed by an ethic of essentially Christian values.[22] In spite of denominational disagreements and rationalist philosophy that was beginning to penetrate the age, there was universal agreement that the nature and content of religious truth were essentially sound.[23] People generally agreed:

> on many basic points of human conduct, such as the undesirability of theft, adultery, and murder, and the desirability of meekness, mercy and charity. It is such basic points that I shall take as the moral norm for the seventeenth century... This generalized seventeenth-century Christian standard of conduct will be referred to as 'Christian virtue'.[24]

Barber lists the content of Christian virtue as it appears in the dramas. It includes: telling the truth; keeping promises and oaths; not withdrawing from a marriage contract; obedience to civil governors; obedience to parents; not committing murder; honesty; not conniving at or encouraging unchastity; sexual continence (as opposed to the sexual virility which is valued in honour); piety; and justice, in the sense of not indulging in or conniving at bribery and corruption.[25] There was substantial overlap between the code of honour and Christian virtue. In particular, the chastity of women was important in the moral codes of all classes.[26]

Christian virtue was articulated explicitly in one of the best-known religious treatises of the time, Richard Allestree's *The Whole Duty of Man*.[27] It has been observed that with over 200,000 copies sold between 1658 and 1700, its contents 'must have been one of the most widely known sets of ideas at the time'.[28] Setting out 'the particulars required of every Christian' with respect to 'the three great branches of man's duty... to God, Our Selves and our Neighbour', Allestree identifies a core set of virtues.[29] These included piety and fidelity to God which would be demonstrated by (among other things) speaking the truth, and avoiding blasphemy, perjury, and the swearing of false oaths (ie, swearing the truth of something one knows is untrue, or swearing inconsistent oaths of promise).[30] To fulfil the duty to one's self, a person would avoid, for example, covetousness and

21 Ibid 141–3.
22 Ibid 137–8.
23 Ibid 138.
24 Ibid 138–9.
25 Ibid 143–4.
26 Ibid 300. A failure to maintain chastity and to present oneself as chaste (in terms of dress or the places one might go) would put one at risk of being held in low esteem: BA Hanawalt, *'Of Good and Ill Repute': Gender and Social Control in Medieval England* (1998).
27 R Allestree, *The Whole Duty of Man* (1726; first pub c1657).
28 K Konkola and D McCulloch, 'People of the Book: The Success of the English Reformation' (2003) 53(10) *History Today* 23, 29.
29 Allestree (n 27 above) ix, 4.
30 Ibid 99–109.

would aid themselves by adhering to temperance and chastity in their habits.[31] The duty to one's neighbours turned substantially on adherence to justice—murder, assault, theft, deceit, and slander were all to be avoided—and behaving with care for one's family and respect towards civil officials such as magistrates or pastors.[32] The maintenance of social order and class distinctions was expressly God-ordained, with 'respect due to men in regard of their ranks and qualities'.[33]

Notwithstanding the prescriptions and proscriptions of Christian ethics, some norms were more important than others in the lives of communities. Martin Ingram has pointed out that many formal and ethical rules were not observed strictly or were not the subject of consensus.[34] For example, the prohibition on Sunday work was not often enforced broadly and with any strictness.[35] Alcohol was a frequent vice that seemed to often be accepted as a part of community life.[36] There was a variety of opinion about the evils or beneficence of recreation and games such as dancing or bowling.[37] To some, they would matter greatly, while others would see nothing wrong with it and thus it seems that these things might or might not have diminished a person's standing in their community. Nevertheless, the substance of Christian ethics governed life to a large degree. The populace generally was neither overly pious nor markedly rejected Christian ethics but for the most part observed religion in some way, or took its ethics on board. Most people, argues Ingram, 'professed some degree of unspectacular orthodoxy'.[38]

Though derived from 17th-century sources, the above outline of the substantive criteria and the sources of moral knowledge captures the essence of moral taxonomies in England since as far back as the 12th century.[39]

In looking at defamation laws, it might be expected that laws which protect reputation would reflect and recognize the sets of values described in this section. A failure to reflect the values or to make actionable the words which cast slurs in respect of these matters would suggest that the law is falling short of protecting reputation. This is not to say that all the virtues of Christianity would have been adhered to or would have been taken equally seriously in communities, nor that all breaches of these morals would have found their way to the courts. (Even Allestree said Christian virtue dictated the need to let trivial breaches pass!) However, it does seem that in a general sense they can provide a useful point of comparison for considering the extent to which defamation laws protect reputation. Section II begins looking at how that might be done.

31 Ibid 162–212.
32 Ibid 213–87.
33 Ibid 281.
34 Ingram (n 16 above).
35 Ibid 99.
36 Ibid 99–100.
37 Ibid 101–4.
38 Ibid 123 and generally 30–1, 92–7.
39 A Harding, *Medieval Law and the Foundations of the State* (2002) 137; A Harding, *England in the Thirteenth Century* (1993) 220–63; F Pollock and FW Maitland, *The History of English Law Before the Time of Edward I* (2nd edn, 1968; first pub 1898) Vol 1, 40, 74–5; E Dudley, *The Tree of Commonwealth*, ed and introduction by DM Brodie (1948; first pub c1510) vii, 90–1; Hanawalt (n 26 above) xii–xiii.

II. Reputation and Defamation Outside the Common Law

The common law action for defamation was not an established feature of the legal landscape until the 16th century. However, its shape, purpose and time of arrival can only be understood in light of the earlier actions entertained in other jurisdictions. This section examines how reputation was protected outside the common law from the 12th to the 16th century. Three branches of litigation are discussed: actions for slander in the local courts; causes in the consistory of the ecclesiastical courts; and actions under the *scandalum magnatum* statutes.[40]

A. Defamation in the local courts

Until at least the 14th century the most significant venues for defamation actions were the local courts of the manors.[41] The seignorial jurisdiction of these courts was founded in the feudal relationship between the lord and his tenants, and permitted by will of the King.[42] Defamation claims were occasionally heard in other local courts—notably those of the fair[43] and the borough[44]—but it was only in the manor courts that defamation was a regular part of business.

Defamation actions invariably fell under the heading of slander. Libel was not known as a distinct wrong.[45] There was, of course, no reason for any distinction between written and oral defamation as the community was largely illiterate and written matter was not a standard part of local communication. Local

[40] A discussion of the sources is included in the Appendix.

[41] JH Baker, *An Introduction to English Legal History* (3rd edn, 1990) 495; CHS Fifoot, *History and Sources of the Common Law: Tort and Contract* (1949) 128; JA Sharpe, *Defamation and Sexual Slander in Early Modern England: The Church Courts at York (Borthwick Papers No 58)* (c1980) 5.

[42] Pollock and Maitland (n 39 above), Vol 2, 571–2; FW Maitland, *Select Pleas in Manorial and other Seignorial Courts, Vol I: Publications of the Selden Society, Vol 2* (1888) xli–lx. The manor courts dealt generally with civil matters, though some minor offences to the public peace that were (give or take) criminal in nature were also a part of regular business: Pollock and Maitland, ibid, 587–92; Maitland, ibid, xviii.

[43] Where fairs or markets were held there were courts that heard disputes between traders: C Gross, *Select Cases Concerning the Law Merchant, 1270–1638, Volume 1: Publications of the Selden Society, Vol 23* (1908). Defamation claims were presumably entertained because the casting of aspersions could have significant financial consequences for merchants. Cases in the fair courts would often be pleaded with what would be understood as special damage, it being claimed that some sort of pecuniary loss flowed from the allegation: *John of Rushbrook v Woodfool* (1293) Fair Court of St Ives (1908) 23 Selden Society 57; *Woodfool v Pors* (1295) Fair Court of St Ives (1908) 23 Selden Society 71; *Christine of Darlington v Burser* (1302) Fair Court of St Ives (1908) 23 Selden Society 85.

[44] The borough was larger than a village but smaller than a city: Pollock and Maitland (n 39 above), Vol 2, 634–88. I have not seen any defamation cases from the borough courts but there are several borough 'custumals' that indicate remedies would be provided for defamation: M Bateson, *Borough Customs, Volume I: Publications of the Selden Society, Vol 18* (1904) 78–80, 153, 181.

[45] Written defamation was not completely unknown, but it was dealt with in the same manner as spoken defamation: eg, *Henry of Swindon v Stalker* (1294) Manor of King's Ripton (1888) 2 Selden Society 116.

court slander was a civil action rather than a prosecution and the remedy was a payment of damages. It was at its core a private matter; the public interest was the prevention of breaches of the peace which could arise out of private disagreements.[46] Claims were argued in different ways. Sometimes a plaintiff said they had been 'assaulted with vile words'.[47] In other instances the action is framed as a trespass.[48] But plaintiffs often directly complained that they had been defamed, slandered, or the like.[49]

What can be made of defamation and reputation in the local court jurisdiction? First, although the remedy was a financial one, it does not appear that plaintiffs were motivated or their sensitivity to defamation enlivened by the prospect of financial gain. Instead, there were many non-pecuniary actions and this suggests that people saw their reputations as intrinsically valuable and the restoration of social and self-worth was a more deep-seated concern.[50] Pollock and Maitland noted that in early cases the award of damages would expressly take account of the shame done to the plaintiff.[51] Judgments of social and self-worth were expressed in different ways, but notably 'honour' was seen as something that was possessed by ordinary people.[52]

[46] AK Kiralfy, *Potter's Historical Introduction to English Law and its Institutions* (4th edn, 1962) 431; Fifoot (n 41 above) 126.

[47] *William of Tilney v Shearman* (1287) Fair Court of St Ives (1908) 23 Selden Society 17; *William of Houghton v Joan of Earith* (1288) Fair Court of St Ives (1908) 23 Selden Society 33; *John of Rushbrook v Woodfool* (1293) Fair Court of St Ives (1908) 23 Selden Society 57; *Woodfool v Pors* (1295) Fair Court of St Ives (1908) 23 Selden Society 71; *Christine of Darlington v Burser* (1302) Fair Court of St Ives (1908) 23 Selden Society 85.

[48] *Mor's Case* (1333) County Court of Bedford, reproduced in Fifoot (n 41 above) 139.

[49] *Reeve v Reeve & Ors* (1278) Manor of the Abbey of Ramsey (1888) 2 Selden Society 95; *Kiwel v Viner* (1290) Manor of the Abbey of Bec (1888) 2 Selden Society 36; *William (the bailiff) v John of Radclive* (1294) Honour of Broughton (1888) 2 Selden Society 82; *Grayling v Dike* (1288) Manor of King's Ripton (1888) 2 Selden Society 109; *Henry of Swindon v Stalker* (1294) Manor of King's Ripton (1888) 2 Selden Society 116; *Richard Young v Ellen, Wife of Roger Chapman* (1294) Manor of Brightwaltham (1888) 2 Selden Society 170; *Waite v Hamon* (1287) Fair Court of St Ives (1908) 23 Selden Society 13; *Walter v Adam* (1287) Fair Court of St Ives (1908) 23 Selden Society 29; *John of Tooting v Woodfool* (1302) Fair Court of St Ives (1908) 23 Selden Society 84. See also Custumals of Preston, cap 40, 48 (12th century); Ipswich, cap 73 (1291); Torksey, cap 16, 17 (c1345): Bateson (n 44 above) 78–9.

[50] F Carr, 'The English Law of Defamation, Part I', (1902) 18 LQR 255, 265–6.

[51] Pollock and Maitland (n 39 above) Vol 2, 537. In defamation, this was most apparent in the fair court where the remedy was sometimes expressly stated as being for 'damage and dishonour': *Thomas of London v Maud, Wife of John Woodfull* (1275) Fair Court of St Ives (1888) 2 Selden Society 143; *Waite v Hamon* (1287) Fair Court of St Ives (1908) 23 Selden Society 13; *John of Tooting v Woodfool* (1302) Fair Court of St Ives (1908) 23 Selden Society 84. In other instances, reference to honour or dishonour was explicit: *William of Houghton v Joan of Earith* (1288) Fair Court of St Ives (1908) 23 Selden Society 33. There was also reference to honour in cases which were not strictly defamation actions: *Hugh of Swinford v Tanner* (1287) Fair Court of St Ives (1908) 23 Selden Society 13; *Pollard v Nicholas* (1288) Fair Court of St Ives (1908) 23 Selden Society 35. Though the practice of expressly asking for compensation for disgrace seems to have died out in the first half of the 13th century, Pollock and Maitland, ibid, argue that it continued to be relevant to compensation.

[52] Eg, Ipswich Custumal, cap 73 (1291): Bateson (n 44 above) 78–9.

Secondly, the types of values that are evident in the disputes are unsurprising and generally correspond to or are at least not in conflict with the sorts of criteria for reputation that could be seen clearly in the 17th century. It seems that most local court matters concerned allegations of dishonesty and theft.[53] In the fair courts the dishonesty might have been concerned with business dealings.[54] While sexual slander fell for the most part in the domain of the church courts (as the next section will discuss), being called a whore was actionable in the local courts.[55] Individuals seemed to clearly know and to agree on what would damage one's worth and standing. That is, they all understood and acknowledged their community's criteria for moral judgment. This might be inferred from the absence of any principles, criteria, or categories that set out what made something defamatory of a person. It was enough to state that one had been defamed. Moreover, there seems to have been no dispute or debate about what sort of comment constituted an actionable slur.

Might it then be said that with a view to keeping the public peace, the local courts protected reputation through their defamation laws (albeit with limited attention to slander of a sexual kind which was principally attended to by the church courts)? For at least two reasons, one should be cautious about concluding that this was the case. First, the range of matters that came before the courts seems remarkably small. Communities are complex places and it seems inconceivable that reputation would be attributed on such a narrow range of criteria as appeared in the cases. It is probably better to see the local courts as a venue which dealt with matters that had a significant impact on reputation. Secondly, the hearing of an action and its conclusion with an award of damages should not necessarily be seen as the essence of the medieval defamation suit. It certainly seems to have been a meaningful process. In Carr's picturesque explanation, the local courts were effective because 'the plaintiff was known, and his smirched reputation was cleansed in the ears of those very persons in whose presence he

[53] The cases selected for the Selden Society publications suggest that such allegations were the most frequent to come before the court. Typical of these cases is *Grayling v Dyke* (1288) Manor of King's Ripton (1888) 2 Selden Society 109; *Henry of Swindon v Stalker* (1294) Manor Court of King's Ripton (1888) 2 Selden Society 116; *Kiwel v Viner* (1290) Manor of the Abbey of Bec (1888) 2 Selden Society 36; *William of Tilney v Shearman* (1287) Fair Court of St Ives 23 Selden Society 17; *William (the bailiff) v John of Radclive* (1294) Honour of Broughton (1888) 2 Selden Society 82; *Moses v Ayulf* (1249) Manor of the Abbey of Bec (1888) 2 Selden Society 19; *John of Tooting v Woodfool* (1302) Fair Court of St Ives (1908) 23 Selden Society 84; *Mor's Case* (1333) County Court of Bedford, reproduced in Fifoot (n 41 above) 139.

[54] *Woodfool v Pors* (1295) Fair Court of St Ives (1908) 23 Selden Society 71; *John of Rushbrook v Woodfool* (1293) Fair Court of St Ives (1908) 23 Selden Society 57; *Waite v Hamon* (1287) Fair Court of St Ives (1908) 23 Selden Society 13; *Walter v Adam* (1287) Fair Court of St Ives (1908) 23 Selden Society 29; *William of Houghton v Joan of Earith* (1288) Fair Court of St Ives (1908) 23 Selden Society 33.

[55] *Thomas of London v Maud, Wife of John Woodfull* (1275) Fair Court of St Ives (1888) 2 Selden Society 143; *Christine of Darlington v Burser* (1302) Fair Court of St Ives (1908) 23 Selden Society 85; *Bindebere v Bolay* (1321) Court of the Bishop of Ely at Littleport (1890) 4 Selden Society 133.

had been reviled'.[56] However, Davies and Fouracre explain that going to court was just one aspect of settling disputes in the pre-conquest era, and it sat within a much larger framework of motivations, processes, and relationships that enabled disputes to be waged and settled in a community.[57] Though the legal process was unquestionably important in community life, the tendency by Carr and others to mark the legal action as the point of dispute resolution and justice may not be entirely accurate.

In all, it seems that reputation was protected by the local courts, but only as it was affected by the most significant of criteria for moral judgment, and perhaps as part of a much broader dispute resolution framework than the legal literature would suggest.

B. Defamation in the ecclesiastical courts

Ecclesiastical courts were established in England following the Norman conquest, taking their authority from William I who settled upon the church pleas 'which belonged to the government of souls' and those that related to 'episcopal laws'.[58] Each diocese had a court called the Consistory and during the 13th century these became important venues for hearing defamation matters among the lower and middle classes.

As the ability of the church to regulate peoples' behaviour posed a significant threat to the monarch's power, the Crown set out to restrict the church's jurisdiction. The statute of *Circumspecte Agatis* in 1286 directed judges in the common law courts not to punish clergy who heard matters that were 'purely spiritual, that is concerning corrections which prelates impose for mortal sin, namely for fornications, adulteries and such like'.[59] It affirmed the practice that defamation pleas would be heard in the church courts only when 'money is not claimed [and] the action is for the correction of a sin'.[60] These formal restrictions appear substantial but the church court archives have revealed that ecclesiastical courts were very active and significant through to the mid-17th century, especially where

[56] Carr (n 50 above) 263; also Pollock and Maitland (n 39 above) Vol II, 538.

[57] W Davies and P Fouracre (eds), *The Settlement of Disputes in Early Medieval Europe* (1986) 232–8. Some cases also suggest that the parties saw keeping the peace as more important than prevailing in litigation: *Moses v Ayulf* (1249) Manor of the Abbey of Bec (1888) 2 Selden Society 19; *Richard Young v Ellen, Wife of Roger Chapman* (1294) Manor of Brightwaltham (1888) 2 Selden Society 170.

[58] Kiralfy (n 46 above) 222, reference omitted.

[59] 'The writ "*Circumspecte agatis*", June–July 1286' in H Rothwell (ed), *English Historical Documents, Vol III 1189–1327* (1975) 462, 463; EB Graves, 'Circumspect Agatis' (1928) 43 *English Historical Review* 1.

[60] 'The writ "*Circumspecte agatis*", June–July 1286', ibid, 462. If a claim for damages was entertained by the church courts then a common law writ of prohibition could be issued to stop the action. See also *Statute of the Writ of Consultation*, 18 Edw I (1290) and 1 Edw III, stat 2, c. 11 (1327).

defamation was concerned.[61] The literature also suggests that the church courts were probably quite effective in punishing a defendant and restoring a plaintiff's good name in their community.[62] Their importance for several centuries cannot be understated.

Defamation fell within the purview of the church because it was a sin. It was a part of the penal jurisdiction of the church, 'exercised alike against clergy and laity for the good of their souls'.[63] Two important consequences flowed from its sinful status: the focus was on the defendant who spoke ill of a person rather than on the person who was the subject of allegations, and, like all sinners, the consequence for the defendant was that they would have to do penance. Actions were governed by a much more coherent and cohesive body of law than that which was found in the local courts. There was an identifiable, generalized test for defamation in the form of the 1227 constitution of the Council of Oxford:

> We excommunicate all those who, for the sake of hatred, profit, or favour, or for whatever cause maliciously impute a crime to any person who is not of ill fame among good and serious men, by means of which at least purgation is awarded to him or he is harmed in some other manner.[64]

The church saw itself as having a broad jurisdiction. A 'crime' was anything prohibited by either canon or secular laws, and no temporal harm was required.[65] The church itself could set proceedings in motion, or the target of the slur could subject their accuser to the procedures of the court for the sin of slander—a sin that could not be (or was not in practice) defended by a claim that the allegation was true.[66]

[61] RH Helmholz, 'Canonical Defamation in Medieval England' (1971) 15 *American Journal of Legal History* 255; Ingram (n 16 above); Sharpe (n 41 above); CA Haigh, 'Slander and the Church Courts in the Sixteenth Century' (1975) 78 *Transactions of the Lancashire and Cheshire Antiquarian Society* 1; SM Waddams, *Sexual Slander in Nineteenth-Century England: Defamation in the Ecclesiastical Courts, 1815–1855* (2000). The jurisdiction of the church courts began to decline seriously from 1641 when its powers of corporal punishment were removed by statute: 16 Charles I, c 11 (1640). The post-Restoration reinstatement of the church courts in 1662 left them devoid of substantial powers: Carr (n 50 above) 269–70. Ecclesiastical defamation actions fell away steadily during the 18th century but were still to be found until the power of the courts to hear them was formally terminated by statute: 18 & 19 Vic, c 41 (1855): *An Act for Abolishing the Jurisdiction of the Ecclesiastical Courts of England and Wales in Suits for Defamation*.

[62] Helmholz (n 61 above) 264–7; Sharpe (n 41 above) 15.

[63] Kiralfy (n 46 above) 216; VV Veeder, 'The History and Theory of Defamation Law I' (1903) 3 Columbia Law Review 546, 550. The sinful nature of defamation is explained by Allestree (n 27 above) 260ff: 'we are not to lessen or impair [our neighbour's credit] by any means, particularly not by false reports.' This included not spreading word of things that one was unsure about, not making false reports to authorities, and slandering neither publicly or by 'whispering' to one person at a time.

[64] Translation by Helmholz (n 61 above) 256. Other dioceses adopted resolutions in the same form: ibid.

[65] Helmholz (n 61 above) 257–60; Ingram (n 16 above) 51–2, 293.

[66] See Ingram (n 16 above) 293–5; Helmholz (n 61 above) 257–63. Helmholz argues that although truth was technically not a defence, the records of litigation show that the falsity of the allegation was always mentioned and concludes that it was mostly false allegations that were

The church was highly influential in shaping and enforcing the values that comprised the moral taxonomies of early modern England. Throughout Europe, the Church exercised as much influence over individuals and institutions as did the governments of the states.[67] The values of Christianity were not only reflected in the content of defamation actions, but also enforced by the defamation laws and procedures of the church courts. Both aspects of the relationship are important.

First, ecclesiastical defamation actions in the 16th and 17th centuries revolved around allegations of sexual sin. Theft and dishonesty allegations were also heard by the church courts but sexual slander dominates. In the church courts at York, over 150 of 200 cases from the 1590s and 1690s concerned matters that related broadly to sexual probity.[68] Of Ingram's 349 cases in Salisbury from 1570–1640, around 90 per cent were sexual slander.[69] In Haigh's study of the courts at Chester almost all defamation cases concerned sexual matters.[70] Certainly, the patterns reflect the Christian ethic of the time, especially with regard to the virtues of female chastity.[71] Around 60–70 per cent of sexual slander plaintiffs were women.[72] Reputation with respect to sexual probity had substantial consequences, especially for women; it could affect their opportunities for marriage, result in humiliation and ostracism, put them in danger of physical violence from the community, or render them liable to prosecution in the church or common law courts.[73] The slurs that characterized defamation actions in the church courts parallel and complement those found in the local courts, suggesting again the prevalence of sexual purity and honesty as core virtues in communities.

Secondly, even though the law may have functioned to protect reputation, the substance and procedure of ecclesiastical law were intimately connected to the church's exercise of social control. The control dimension of the law is reflected first in the benchmark standard of 'good and serious men'. It was by definition acceptable under the law to speak ill of a person who was not of good fame 'among good and serious men'. The meaning of the phrase 'good and serious men' is never discussed in the literature or cases, but there is never any doubt expressed about

regularly taken to the courts and truth was at times argued as a defence: RH Helmholz (ed), *Select Cases on Defamation to 1600: Publications of the Selden Society, Vol 101* (1985) xxx–xxxii.

67 Veeder (n 63 above) 550; Carr (n 50 above) 268; Ingram (n 16 above) 303.

68 Sharpe (n 41 above) 10.

69 Ingram (n 16 above) 301. The repeated patterns are consistent with the observations made regarding older works. Carr (n 50 above) 270–1 states that in the collection of ecclesiastical proceedings compiled by Archdeacon Hale covering the period 1475–1610, there are 700 cases which total between 5 and 6 per cent of the complete collection and the majority of these concern 'lapses from sexual morality'.

70 Haigh (n 61 above) 2–3.

71 Allestree (n 27 above) 173–4.

72 Ingram (n 16 above) 302; LR Poos, 'Sex, Lies and the Church Courts of Pre-Reformation England' (1995) 25 *Journal of Interdisciplinary History* 585, 594; Sharpe (n 41 above) 10. Around half of the defamers were also women: Poos, ibid, 596.

73 Ingram (n 16 above) 304–14; Haigh (n 61 above) 6–8.

what it might mean.[74] Those who were thought of as 'of no account' or 'not of good fame' included the 'underclass [of the poor and lawbreakers] who would rendezvous in taverns and other gathering places'.[75] Exclusion served to maintain the social order. Hanawalt notes that the processes of marginalization in medieval England 'were as important in establishing boundaries as were those that elevated and enclosed the space around the elite'.[76] Social control and exclusion are based on the equating of social standing and moral goodness; that is, power defines virtue. While there is much to indicate that the church saw the community—and the community saw itself—as generally inclusive, the constitutive nature of the ethical rules is evident here: those who were not of good fame were not to be recognized as a part of the community, they were not entitled like others to the protection of the church law.[77]

The protection of reputation was also intimately connected to social control through the penance of public confession that was usually imposed in defamation actions. The confession in *Mitford v Shaw* illustrates not only the nature of the punishment but also the reasons why it attracted the attention of the courts. The element of social control is at least as evident as the aspects of sin:

> I acknowledge that thus to slander my Christian brother is an heinous offence, first towards God, who hath straightly forbidden it in his holy laws, accounting it to be a kind of murdering of my neighbour, and threatening to punish it with hellfire and the loss of the kingdom of heaven. Also the Queen's laws . . . Again, my unruly tongue, if it were not punished, it would not only set more of you on fire, but it would bolden others to do the like.[78]

With slander being a sin that carried very earthly punishments, the Ecclesiastical jurisdiction held great sway over the behaviour of individuals in so far as they chose to comment upon their neighbours.

Defamation in the ecclesiastical jurisdiction shows that reputation was judged against accepted norms of good and right behaviour. Those norms were the standards of good and serious men, defined implicitly by a combination of social and religious power. However, it does not seem appropriate to extrapolate from what

[74] Though Helmholz, *Selden Society* (n 66 above) xxvi–xli, divides the ecclesiastical test into its elements he does not deal at all with this part of the constitution, presumably because he does not see any doubt about what would and would not have reduced one in the esteem of good and serious men. The phrase 'good and grave men' is used without equivocation in *Austin v Laybrooke* (1416) Canterbury Consistory, reproduced in AKR Kiralfy, *A Source Book of English Law* (1957) 393.

[75] Hanawalt (n 26 above) 18, references omitted.

[76] Ibid 24.

[77] The inclusive sense of community is especially indicated by the fact that individuals from across the class spectrum were parties in ecclesiastical actions. Sharpe (n 41 above) 17 found that the plaintiffs, witnesses, and defendants were 'the rural middling sort: tradesmen, shopkeepers, yeomen, artisans, and the wives of members of these occupational groups', and there was evidence that 'even lower social groups' might also be plaintiffs or witnesses.

[78] *Mitford v Shaw* (1569–70) Durham Consistory, 21 Surtees Society Publications, CXLIII, 106, reproduced in Kiralfy (n 74 above) 399–401. Generally on social control, see Ingram (n 16 above) 3, 53–4, 334–8; Haigh (n 61 above) 9.

is in the cases and say that reputation was protected by either the local courts, the church courts, or a combination of both.[79] This is because what is *absent* from the cases is also of interest. It will be recalled that matters such as working on Sundays, drinking, dancing, and games were the subject of diverse opinion. Such behaviour would have certainly had an effect on people's standing in the eyes of others. But none of these matters seem to appear in the cases. That could be because they were not technically actionable, though certainly alcohol and Sunday work were both formally prohibited. It could be because 'good and grave men' may differ on the egregiousness of the sins. But it certainly suggests that reputation was protected in only a very narrow sense. The criteria for moral judgment that were recognized as actionable by and in the church courts were only the most fundamental of the many criteria relevant to evaluations of social and self-worth.

C. *Scandalum magnatum*: defamation and the great men of the realm

Shortly after Edward I ascended the throne in 1272, a new statute made it a criminal offence to slander the 'great men of the realm':

> Forasmuch as there have been oftentimes found in the country devisors of tales, whereby discord or occasion of discord, hath many times arisen between the King and his People or Great Men of this Realm; for the damage that hath and may thereof ensue; it is commanded, that from henceforth none be so hardy as to tell or publish any false news or tales, whereby discord or occasion of discord or slander may grow between the King and his People or, the Great Men of the Realm; and he that doth so, shall be taken and kept in prison, until he hath brought him into the Court which was the first author of the tale.[80]

The statute was re-enacted again in 1388 with the punishment unspecified and the King's Council—rather than the common law courts—being the body that would dispense justice.[81]

These were the statutes of *scandalum magnatum*. Though used only sporadically and falling into desuetude in the 1700s, they remained in force until the late 19th century.[82] The statutes are widely seen as part of the history of defamation law.[83] What do the laws and the associated litigation reveal about reputation? In

[79] This is at odds with the orthodox claim by Veeder that, 'Early in the middle ages reputation was amply protected in England by the combined secular and spiritual authorities': VV Veeder, 'The History of the Law of Defamation' in *Select Essays in Anglo-American Legal History* (1909) 446, 447; Veeder (n 63 above) 546–7.

[80] 3 Edward I, c 34 (1275) *Statute of Westminster the First*. The 'great men of the realm' were later defined as 'Prelates, Dukes, Earls, Barons and other Nobles and Great Men of the Realm [and also] the Chancellor, Treasurer, Clerk of the Privy Seal, Steward of the King's House, Justices of the one bench or of the other [and] other Great Officers of the Realm': 2 Richard II, c 5 (1378).

[81] 12 Richard II, c 11 (1388).

[82] The *Statute Law Revision Act* (1887) repealed disused legislation.

[83] T Starkie, *A Treatise on the Law of Slander, Libel, Scandalum Magnatum and False Rumours* (1813) 14; Veeder (n 63 above) 554; cf Fifoot (n 41 above) 129 who describes it as 'little more than a historical curiosity'.

short, they exemplify the presence of aristocratic honour in the law and illustrate the constitutive and exclusive functions of the criteria by which the nobility judged their self-worth and the social worth of their peers. This can be seen principally in the rationales for the early enactments, and the reasons why the laws endured until the 18th century.

The character of the statute was to be reinterpreted over time. It seems the laws were originally intended to quell dissent across the social spectrum and make critics of the Crown or the nobility liable to punishment, though there is little evidence of prosecutions.[84] During the later 15th century it became the basis for slander actions by the nobility.[85] By 1677, the Court of King's Bench in *Lord Townsend v Dr Hughes* proposed the theory that the statutes were designed from the start to keep the peace and prevent nobles taking up arms.[86] It was said in the *Townsend* case that the statutes aimed to prevent nobles taking up arms to defend their honour because:

> revenge did not usually end up in private quarrels; they took parties, engaged their friends, their tenants and servants on their side, and by such means made great factions in the Commonwealth; by reason whereof the whole kingdom was often in a flame, and the Government as often in danger of being subverted...[87]

To offend the law, words did not need to import 'a great scandal in themselves' but extended to 'even such things as savoured of any contempt of their persons, and as such brought them into disgrace with the Commons, for hereby they took occasion of provocation and revenge'.[88] Cases began to appear more regularly from the later 1500s as the King's Council in the Court of Star Chamber actively sought to suppress criticism of government and to bring all, including the nobles, under the power of the law.[89] It was not, however, until much later that the records show a willingness of the nobles to use *scandalum magnatum* instead of violence to reclaim their honour, and though it is widely conceded that the statutes were not completely successful, a marked upsurge of civil cases in the latter half of the 17th century is of interest. It suggests that these laws performed an unusual function with respect to protecting reputation.

[84] Kiralfy (n 46 above) 432; Veeder (n 63 above) 554; TF Plucknett, *A Concise History of the Common Law* (3rd edn, 1940) 429–30; Carr (n 50 above) 261. The additions under Richard II occurred around the time of the Peasants' Revolt of 1381 when political rhymes and songs were a significant public voice. The lack of prosecutions is difficult to explain, though until the Court of Star Chamber was formalized in 1487 it might be expected that there would be no records.

[85] Opinion is divided over whether the civil action was available from the Act's inception. There are three suggestions identifiable in the literature: (1) the statute had both civil and criminal dimensions from its enactment; (2) the first civil action was in 1497 but there may have been earlier actions; (3) the civil action developed in the mid-16th century. Plucknett, ibid 430, observed that 'there is very little evidence of the working of these statutes during the middle ages' and this seems still to stand.

[86] *Lord Townsend v Dr Hughes* (1677) 2 Mod 150, 156, 86 ER 994, 997–8.

[87] Ibid.

[88] Ibid, though cf the dissent of Atkins J, 161–2, 1000.

[89] W Holdsworth, *A History of English Law in Sixteen Volumes* (3rd edn, 1945) Vol 5, 199–201.

There were more *scandalum magnatum* actions between 1660 and 1700 than at any other period in English history.[90] Drawing especially on Lawrence Stone's *The Crisis of the Aristocracy* to set the law in its context, Lassiter claims that there were two particular spurs behind the rise of the action.[91] The first of these was the challenge to the social, economic, and political power of the nobility that was posed by a rising mercantile class.

> The statutes of *scandalum magnatum* perpetuated in law a distinction between peers and commoners which was in fact becoming obscured at the upper levels of English society... [T]he gap was closing. Over the sixteenth century, nobles suffered a loss of much of their military and political power, primarily at the hands of the crown, and a loss of land and income at the hands of lesser members of the landed classes, largely because of inflation and their own lavish overspending... [T]he immediate result was an alarming erosion of the social and economic barrier which separated peers (*nobilitas major*) from gentry (*nobilitas minor*) and along with it the deference which had once been the most gratifying proof of its existence.[92]

In this context, the civil action for *scandalum magnatum*:

> signified a reaction on the part of individual peers to the loss of respect and an attempt by the legal system itself to compensate for that loss by awarding damages and punishing those guilty of disrespect... [M]ore than simply providing an alternative to aristocratic violence, [the action] became a way of reinforcing—albeit artificially—old and weakening social boundaries.[93]

The second spur was the political machinations of the post-Restoration struggle for sovereignty between the monarch and the Parliament. The peers sought 'to assert regained privileges as a reminder to their inferiors that the old order truly had been restored'.[94]

Lassiter's argument is particularly interesting and persuasive for two reasons. First, the rise of the mercantile class has also been suggested to have influenced the expansion of the action on the case for words in the common law courts.[95] In addition, Lovell also identifies the Crown's interest in suppressing 'criticism of its policies by newer middle-class men, who did not hold to the traditional view that

[90] JC Lassiter, 'Defamation of Peers: The Rise and Decline of the Action for *Scandalum Magnatum*, 1497–1773' (1978) 22 American Journal of Legal History 216, 219.

[91] L Stone, *The Crisis of the Aristocracy, 1558–1641* (1965).

[92] Lassiter (n 90 above) 219–20.

[93] Ibid 220.

[94] Ibid 223–4. The aim this time was more overtly political with both Tory and Whig claims for heavy damages—as much as £100, 000—being brought 'not so much in hopes of recovery as in hopes of seeing the defendants jailed or ruined financially': ibid 225–30. Lassiter tentatively suggests (233–4) that the action ultimately declined following the later recovery of class superiority.

[95] Baker has identified the economic change in the first half of the 16th century as an important factor in legal developments and includes the emergent merchant class as being among the most significant elements in the process: JH Baker, *The Reports of Sir John Spelman, Volume II: Publications of the Selden Society, Vol 94* (1977) 47–50. See further, Chapter 4, II, (A).

government was ordained of God'.[96] Secondly, the use of the courts to challenge the rising classes is both consistent with and representative of the very idea of honour which the peerage, in Lassiter's argument, was seeking to claim and assert in the late 1600s. Among the peers, there was a revived interest in duelling with each other.[97] However, a duel would not be suitable between a peer and a member of the rising classes. By using the *scandalum magnatum* action to resolve disputes, a plaintiff identified himself as one of the 'great men of the realm' and, by dealing with the defendant on terms of law rather than terms of honour, refused to acknowledge the defendant as an equal. Such an interpretation of the cases is consistent with conjecture in the defamation literature.[98] The proposition that the nobility sought to re-assert its status in the later 17th century is certainly consistent with Barber's observations that the gentry tended to deliberately cut themselves off to define and demonstrate their honour.[99] It is probably incorrect to see the opposing currents of using the courts and duelling as an either/or choice; to do so would be to try to impose on the nobility a unity of views that simply did not exist. There seems no reason to think that duelling and *scandalum magnatum* actions did not rise at the same time, with both patterns being indicators of the same reclamation of status by the aristocracy.

The statutes and actions for *scandalum magnatum* illustrate the way the reputations of the 'great men of the realm' were valued, and show how they themselves determined that value. The aristocracy both drew and demonstrated its moral worth and legitimacy through its power to rule over the lower classes. The laws of *scandalum magnatum* functioned to protect reputation, but not in the same way defamation laws did. This is because they were neither intended nor used to provide for the resolution of disputes about matters of reputation *within* a community. On the contrary, they were used to distinguish one community from another, while matters of social and self-worth within the aristocratic community were resolved under principles of honour. Those principles tended to exclude the operation of law. The patterns of use of *scandalum magnatum* actions reflect the same sentiments that were exemplified by the revival of duelling. There was:

> an upper-class desire to have a kind of a class-justice outside the law courts, which were in the hands of people who were not always of gentle birth... [They] disregard the legal code of the rest of society as something beneath their notice... Bowers cites one of them as writing: 'Since no one shall judge of honour but him who has it, the judges of civil courts (who are base in their origin) are unfitted for the duty.'[100]

[96] CR Lovell, 'The "Reception" of Defamation by the Common Law' (1962) 15 Vanderbilt Law Review 1051, 1059.

[97] Barber (n 19 above) 274–5; Billacois (n 3 above) 207.

[98] See Carr (n 50 above) 272; Veeder (n 63 above) 554.

[99] Barber (n 19 above) 268, 274–5; also Stone (n 91 above) at 242–50.

[100] Barber (n 19 above) 274–5, quoting F Bowers, *Elizabethan Revenge Tragedy 1587–1642* (1940) 33.

The nobility and the lower classes were never to be judged by the same standards or in the same manner. In the end, it seems difficult to view *scandalum magnatum* statutes as laws that protected reputation.

Conclusion

The history of post-conquest England can richly inform an understanding of reputation and its protection under the law with respect to, first, the moral taxonomies of the times and, secondly, the effect and rationale of defamation laws.

The criteria for moral judgment in early modern England were God-ordained across the class spectrum. For most people, the moral good was dictated by the Christian values which were reinforced by the spiritual and temporal laws. Honesty, temperance of habits, and sexual probity—all broadly defined—were seen as virtues that made for a morally good person. For the nobility, their superiority in the world was a natural and divinely willed state of affairs. The aristocratic code of honour valued the response to insult and male sexual virility differently, but in many respects the substantive values of early modern English morality were widely applicable and constant for a long period of time. The fundamentals of the moral order were stable and uncontested by any argument that good and grave men could not or did not think the less of one for the behaviour that was at issue in the cases. It would be a long time before this would change.

Reputation was meaningfully, though narrowly, protected in the local and church courts. The law was very limited in its scope. People were only protected from slurs that concerned what might be thought of as the moral bedrock of reputation. Other slurs that would undoubtedly have affected reputations did not come before the courts. Individuals certainly saw intrinsic value in their reputations, but the rationales behind the legal protection were essentially instrumental; it served to keep the peace in communities and maintain the wider social, political, and moral order.

This was the background against which the common law courts began to entertain actions in the 16th century. Christianity was naturally virtuous and the aristocracy naturally superior. Where the law was concerned, it would have been clearly apparent to the judges and to all in the communities of the time that not everything that affected social standing would come before the courts. Defamation laws maintained peace and order. It might be expected that these themes would be reflected in the common law. Indeed, it would be remarkable if they were not.

4

The Development of the Common Law Actions

Chapter 3 undertook an exploration of reputation and the history of defamation in jurisdictions outside the common law, suggesting that it would help explain the relationships between law and reputation under the common law. With that in mind, this chapter turns to the development of the common law actions for defamation. It aims to explain how and why the common law approached the actionability of words as it did, and to examine the relationships between defamation and reputation that played a fundamental role in shaping the development and nature of the modern actions for libel and slander.

Section I looks at the early common law. It focuses on the way that only certain forms of words were actionable and these were not connected or underpinned by any clear conceptual or doctrinal rationale. Later, influenced by the Star Chamber's law of criminal libel, the common law action for written defamation became more broadly based and was founded upon a generalized principle that made damage to reputation actionable. In section II it will be suggested that this shift marks the birth of the modern law of defamation because it sat within the distinctly modern intellectual framework of Enlightenment philosophy and science. By looking at the 19th century treatises it is possible to see, first, a new claim that the common law protected reputation and, secondly, attempts to derive general statements of legal principle from the disparate body of cases. These developments were to have a profound influence on the shape of the modern common law and its relationship to the protection of reputation. The conclusion will address a number of matters raised in this and the preceding chapters, identifying some themes of particular significance for an examination of the contemporary tests for what is defamatory.

I. Reputation and Defamation Under the Early Common Law

A. The rise of the King's justice: the common law to 1648

From the late 12th century, the King's common law courts—the Court of Common Pleas and the Court of King's Bench—dealt with an extensive range of civil actions but defamation was not meaningfully among them until the 1530s.[1] There is neither certainty nor agreement about why these courts were for so long reluctant to provide a remedy for defamation or why the position eventually changed. Most of the literature suggests that the limits placed on the ecclesiastical jurisdiction left an unsatisfactory gap that had to be addressed because a plaintiff who had been defamed with respect to a temporal matter would be prevented from succeeding in the church courts, but had no action available under the common law.[2] It has also been suggested that emergent commerce may have been a particularly important influence on the courts' willingness to allow an action.[3] Helmholz's research, however, led him to make the interesting observation that the absence of a common law remedy was just one aspect of a wider absence of temporal remedies. During the 15th century, there was no common law remedy and few cases in the local courts. Defamation became almost exclusively an ecclesiastical action, suggesting there were important cultural changes in the significance of reputation; attention was focused on the sinning speaker rather than the target of the slur.[4] It seems reputation recovered its temporal significance in the 16th century—the common law courts recognized an action on the case for defamation and cases reappeared in the local courts.[5] Even if reputation did not have pecuniary consequences (though it may well have done), it appears to have been seen as a matter that affected people's lives in their communities and thus it was appropriate for the common law courts to entertain defamation claims.

[1] A discussion of the historical sources can be found in the Appendix.

[2] TF Plucknett, *A Concise History of the Common Law* (3rd edn, 1940) 434–7; W Holdsworth, 'Defamation in the Sixteenth and Seventeenth Centuries, II' (1924) 40 LQR 397, 398–404; VV Veeder, 'The History and Theory of Defamation Law, I' (1903) 3 Columbia Law Review 546, 556–60; F Carr, 'The English Law of Defamation, I & II' (1902) 18 LQR 255, 267–73, 388–9; JH Baker, *The Reports of Sir John Spelman, Volume II: Publications of the Selden Society, Vol 94* (1977) 238–42; CHS Fifoot, *History and Sources of the Common Law: Tort and Contract* (1949) 127–9; AKR Kiralfy, *Potter's Historical Introduction to English Law and its Institutions* (4th edn, 1962) 431–4; SFC Milsom, *Historical Foundations of the Common Law* (1969) 334–9.

[3] CR Lovell, 'The "Reception" of Defamation by the Common Law' (1962) 15 Vanderbilt Law Review 1051, 1058–9; Baker (n 2 above) 51–2. Baker thinks it more likely that when the Court of King's Bench was losing business in the early 16th century, it sought to make itself more appealing to litigants by adopting flexible procedures (that did not rely on writs) and demonstrating a willingness to embrace new remedies in various areas of the law, though most especially in its expansion of the action on the case: ibid 53–63.

[4] Along these lines, RH Helmholz (ed), *Select Cases on Defamation to 1600: Publications of the Selden Society, Vol 10* (1985) lxiii, argues that the 15th century saw a gradually changing appreciation of physical and intangible wrongs, agreeing with Baker's interpretation in JH Baker, *An Introduction to English Legal History* (2nd edn, 1979) 364, (3rd edn, 1990), 495.

[5] Helmholz (n 4 above) lxv. Although Helmholz gives most weight to the changing views on reputation when he tries to ascertain the reason for the change, he raises other possibilities (at lxi–lxii), each of which he argues has some evidence in its favour but opposing factors make none of them sufficiently convincing. They include: (1) the development of a legal principle that special damage must be proved, and thus defamation became a more difficult action; (2) there was a tacit agreement with the Church about jurisdictional boundaries; and (3) there was a cultural shift in which writing became more important, and thus spoken words (which had dominated defamation actions) became less significant.

However, that does not mean that the common law judges either set out to protect reputation or did in fact protect it.

The action on the case for words developed slowly and gradually, reflecting a widespread uncertainty about the nature and availability of the new remedy.[6] It was clear that an allegation must have been communicated to a third party, but difficult to tell exactly what sorts of words would be actionable. Here, ecclesiastical law appears to have been especially influential.[7] Like the church courts, the common law seemed generally to require the defendant to have made an imputation that the plaintiff had committed a secular crime.[8] However, the plea rolls also contained allegations of non-secular crimes and behaviour that was not criminal at all.[9] In all, there seemed no particular logic to the decisions; judges, lawyers, and reporters alike were often puzzled by the distinctions about what was and was not actionable.[10] The first sign of some clearly discernable patterns regarding actionability were to be found in John March's *Actions for Slaunder*, published in 1648.

March set out to provide, in the words of his subtitle: 'a methodical collection under certain grounds and heads of what words are actionable in the law, and what not?'[11] He argued that 'a general rule' of four parts identified when words would be actionable:

> [S]candalous words which touch or concern a man in his life, liberty or member, or any corporall punishment; or which scandall a man in his office or place of trust, or in his calling or function by which he gaines his living, or which tend to the slandering of his title, or his advancement, or preferment, or any other particular damage; or lastly which charge a man to have any dangerous infectious disease;[sic] by reason of which he ought to be separated by the law from the society of men: all such words are actionable.[12]

Today's categories of common law slander are recognizable within March's rule:

- the imputation of a crime;
- the imputation of a loathsome disease;
- the imputation of professional unfitness or misconduct;
- an imputation that did not fall within the above categories but nevertheless caused special damage to the plaintiff.[13]

[6] Ibid lxix, lxxii, lxxv–lxxxii. See, for example, *Boughton v The Bishop of Coventry & Lichfield* (1583) 1 And 119, discussed by Helmholz, ibid cii.

[7] Ibid lxxvi, lxv. Baker is inclined to attribute more significance to the common law precedents but still sees ecclesiastical law as highly influential: JH Baker, *An Introduction to English Legal History* (3rd edn, 1990) 497.

[8] Baker (n 2 above) 243; M Ingram, *Church Courts, Sex and Marriage in England, 1570–1640* (1987) 298.

[9] Helmholz (n 4 above) lxxvii.

[10] Ibid xcv, xcvii, lxxv–lxxxii, lxxviii, cii.

[11] J March, *Actions for Slaunder and Arbitrements* (Rev'd edn, 1674; first pub 1648).

[12] Ibid 8. It was the early textbook writers rather than the courts that categorized the imputations in this manner. See also W Sheppard, *Action Upon the Case for Slander* (1662).

[13] P Milmo and WVH Rogers, *Gatley on Libel and Slander* (10th edn, 2004) [4.1]–[4.21], [5.1]–[5.10]. March's statement includes slander of title but in the modern common law this is

Quite clearly, some things which were actionable in the common law courts were matters that went to reputation as it would have been understood in early modern England. But the courts did not use damage to reputation as the criterion for actionability and, moreover, there are good reasons to conclude that actionability was not in practice based on the protection of reputation. That is, the virtues that constituted moral goodness were not the point of reference for determining whether a slur would be actionable at common law. This is evident in at least three ways.

First, there are matters that were significant criteria for moral judgment but which were not actionable at common law. Actionability was dependent upon the imputation falling within the requisite categories of case. The most striking of these was that law did not as a general rule allow recovery where allegations went to sexual probity unless they were of a criminal nature or accompanied by temporal damage (such as a lost opportunity to marry), though sexual probity was a matter at the heart of moral judgment in early modern England. There were also other instances. For example, a statement that a person was 'forsworn' would be actionable if it was said to convey an imputation that the plaintiff had committed perjury in court (a criminal offence), but not actionable outside those circumstances.[14] Allegations of behaviour that was at odds with the moral norms of the community might greatly lower a person in the estimation of the community, but that would not make the words actionable.

Secondly, the categories of actionable words were not founded upon criteria of moral judgment about social and self-worth. This is most apparent with respect to imputations concerning diseases. Not every disease imputation would be actionable. The imputation would have to concern a 'loathsome disease'. Originally this meant syphilis; an allegation that the plaintiff had 'the French pox' was actionable whereas an allegation of 'the pox' was seen to refer to smallpox and was thus not actionable. Later leprosy became actionable as well, though it was accepted that, like smallpox, there was no moral fault involved on the part of the plaintiff, and perhaps not even a negative moral judgment.[15] It was, however, never quite clear even to the lawyers of the time why the words were actionable:

> Three overlapping reasons were suggested in the course of argument and decision: the words suggested a corrupt and criminal life, the words could cut the plaintiff off from society just as a criminal would be, and the words easily caused actual loss.[16]

generally discussed separately and viewed as an example of the tort of malicious falsehood rather than defamation: *Gatley* [20.2], [20.14]–[20.15].

[14] *Holt v Scholefield* (1796) 6 TR 691, 101 ER 775, cf *Smale v Hammon* (1610) 1 Bulstrode 40, 80 ER 743. To be 'forsworn' was to swear on an oath and then either lie or swear something to the contrary on another oath. There is no doubt that, in any context, a person's reputation would suffer if they did so, regardless of whether it constituted perjury; Richard Allestree's *The Whole Duty of Man* (1726) 100–2, expressly stated that to do so was to dishonour God.

[15] Helmholz (n 4 above) xcvii.

[16] Ibid.

It is not possible to infer that there is some allegation of moral wrongdoing that makes a disease-related statement actionable. But nor is it possible to infer that the moral aspersion is irrelevant. In the end, says Helmholz:

> The category remains something of a mystery today. Why *were* the words actionable at a time when the judges were regularly requiring the imputation of a crime?... [After the actionability of leprosy and syphilis] the category took on a life of its own. We do not know.[17]

The disease imputations are thus not suggestive of any conscious rationale that actionability should be based on the protection of reputation.

Thirdly, if an imputation fell outside the categories then proof of damage was required. This makes it difficult to conclude that the rules for actionability were designed to protect individuals' social worth and standing. It is true that damage alone was not grounds for a claim, but the courts did not use anything that resembled a clear test to determine the circumstances in which words that caused damage would be actionable. At most, the defamatory import was framed in terms of the plaintiff being of good repute 'among good and grave men' and lowered such that he could not deal with 'honest folk'.[18] This is not grounds to infer that the common law was protecting reputation because, even where words satisfied that reputational dimension, they would not be actionable without proof of damage.

The common law to the mid-17th century did not set out to protect reputation as the community understood it, nor did it in fact do so. Undoubtedly, the King's Bench judges appreciated that an individual's social standing could be harmed in many ways and they would have been aware of the long history of actionable defamation in other courts. But they could not and did not protect reputation in their own jurisdiction. At most, it can be said that the common law provided a remedy for at least some defamations that clearly affected reputation.

B. The influence of the Star Chamber on the common law

In the mid-17th century, words were actionable at common law if they fell into any of the categories March had set out. The courts had not distinguished between written and spoken defamation but around this time were confronted with the question of whether they should. The question arose because in 1606 the King's Council, sitting as the Court of Star Chamber, had developed a criminal law of libel that applied only to written defamation. This was to have a profound effect on the modern laws of civil defamation and, especially, the relationship between common law and the protection of reputation. To understand these developments it is necessary to first explain the work of the Star Chamber.[19]

[17] Ibid. Emphasis in original.
[18] Baker (n 2 above) 246.
[19] For a discussion of the historical sources see the Appendix.

1. *The Case de Libellis Famosis*

The Court of Star Chamber was so called because the room in which it met had a ceiling 'decked with images of starres gilted'.[20] Following its formal constitution in 1487, the Star Chamber (as it has become known) functioned for some decades as a respected court.[21] However, as an arm of Council and once described as a 'court of criminal equity', it was not like any other court.[22]

> The law applied was based on the common law; but the procedure of the court enabled it to disregard many of those technical common law rules which rendered the administration of the criminal law ineffective. The judges of the court did not hesitate to develop and expand the principles of the criminal law in a way in which no common law judge would have dared to attempt.[23]

Drawing on Continental law and jurisprudence, the Star Chamber adopted the medieval European distinction between 'ordinary' and 'extraordinary' procedure.[24] In Europe, the latter permitted torture, and the extraordinary gradually became the ordinary. Holdsworth argues that in Europe there was:

> popular acquiescence in this procedure in the fact that, 'the people, emerging from the anarchy of the Middle Ages and from the great wars against the English . . . felt above all else the need of security and peace. The new Ordinances furnished a better assurance than any other law for the repression of crime.'[25]

It was unsurprising that elements of the Continental system should be copied because there was widespread dissatisfaction with the state of the English legal

[20] Sir Thomas Smith, *De Republica Anglorum* (c 1565, first pub 1583) as extracted in M Evans and I Jack, *Sources of English Legal and Constitutional History* (1984) 260–1. The 'Starred Chamber' was built in 1348 and Council began meeting there prior to the close of the 14th century: AT Carter, *A History of English Legal Institutions* (4th edn, 1910) 137.

[21] The Court was formally constituted in 1487 by the statute '*Pro Camera Stellata*' 3 Hen VII, c 1, though the Council had acted judicially for some time before that: IS Leadem (ed), *Select Cases Before the King's Council in the Star Chamber commonly called the Court of Star Chamber, 1477–1509, Vol 16* (1902/03) ix–lxxi; CG Bayne, *Select Cases in the Council of Henry VII: Publications of the Selden Society, Vol 75* (1958). This seems consistent with the emergent judicial character of the Star Chamber as Baker sees it when he suggests that the Star Chamber became 'an established feature of the legal system' until the mid–1500s, and was like 'a regular court of civil jurisdiction' during Wolsey's tenure as Chancellor (1515–1529): Baker (n 2 above) 70–1. It had been observed that the Court was in its earlier years often seen as making a positive contribution to English justice. Bacon was even moved to describe it as 'one of the sagest and noblest institutions in the country': Carter (n 20 above) 152; W Holdsworth, *A History of English Law in Sixteen Volumes* (3rd edn, 1945) Vol 5, 166. The Court even heard some actions for defamation, though this was less a development of defamation law than a political incursion on the jurisdiction of the church courts: *Vale v Broke* (1493) 16 Selden Society 38; *Donyngton v Broke* (1493) 16 Selden Society 40; *Smyth v Broke* (1493) 16 Selden Society 41; Leadem, ibid cxxxii.

[22] F Holt, *The Law of Libel* (1812) 27; Holdsworth (n 21 above) 163; Veeder (n 2 above) 563; Lovell (n 3 above) 1060.

[23] Holdsworth (n 21 above) 163–4, references omitted.

[24] Ibid 173.

[25] Ibid 176, referring to and citing Esmein's analysis: A Esmein, 'La Maxime Princeps Legibus Solutus dans est l'ancien droit public francais' in P Vinogradoff (ed), *Essays in Legal History* (1913) 166.

system and 'all classes agreed that a stern criminal law was necessary to insure the safety of the state, and the security of life and property'.[26]

Continental procedure could not be imported into the common law. English procedure and its protections for the accused had been strengthened in the 12th and 13th centuries and were resilient in the face of 16th-century pressures.[27] But the Court of Star Chamber was in a different position to the common law courts: because it was an arm of the King's Council, it could exercise the Crown prerogative. It did so, adopting extraordinary processes on the basis that the political circumstances were extraordinary.[28] Those circumstances without doubt included the ever-increasing spread of pamphlets that criticized the Government.[29] Moreover, just as the extraordinary prerogative power could justify 'dispens[ing] with the ordinary rules of procedure' so it could dispense with 'the ordinary rules of law' and 'make an order according to the necessity and nature of the thing itself'.[30] In 1606 the Court considered whether the (by that time deceased) John Archbishop of Canterbury was guilty of a crime by criticizing in verse Richard Bishop of Canterbury. Able to dispose of the ordinary rules of law, the Council (in the form of the Court) created a new law of criminal libel.

Prosecuted by Coke as Attorney-General, and reported by him as *The Case de Libellis Famosis*, the Star Chamber determined that it was an 'infamous libel' when 'an epigram, rhime, or other writing is composed or published to the scandal or contumely of another, by which his fame and dignity may be prejudiced'.[31] Regardless of whether its target is living or dead, any person who published or repeated the libel 'ought to be severely punished'.[32] The Court did state that libels rob 'a man of his good name, which ought to be more precious to him than his life'.[33] This was not, however, a law that was concerned with the protection of reputation. At best, one can infer that the court agreed in the popular view that people do and should value their reputations, but it says little more.

The purpose of the law was, first, the protection of the public peace, preventing a libelled person or their family taking revenge and it aimed to subordinate

[26] Holdsworth (n 21 above) 195. In particular, juries were seen as unreliable and vulnerable to corruption and intimidation: ibid 177; Bayne (n 21 above) lxii–lxiv.

[27] Holdsworth (n 21 above) 177.

[28] Ibid 178. There was a degree of disquiet about the expansion of the powers: Baker (n 2 above) 70–4; Holdsworth (n 21 above) 186. Moreover, while the Continental system had some protection for the accused in its procedures of proof where torture was concerned, such principles 'were not so strictly applied here as on the continent; and that led to a capriciousness in the use of torture which Selden notes as peculiar to the English practice': Holdsworth (n 21 above) 187.

[29] JR Fisher, 'A Chapter in the History of the Law of Libel' (1894) 10 LQR 158, 161–2; Lovell, (n 3 above) 1060–1; Carr (n 2 above) 392–3; Veeder (n 2 above) 561–2; Plucknett (n 2 above) 441–2.

[30] Holdsworth (n 21 above) 187, citing in part from Hawarde's *Les Reportes del Cases in Camera Stellata* which covers cases from 1593–1609.

[31] *de Libellis Famosis* (1606) 5 Co Rep 125a, 125b, 77 ER 250, 251, Star Ch.

[32] Ibid. The strict application of libel law was among the key reasons why the Star Chamber became hated.

[33] Ibid.

all people to the King's authority.[34] Secondly, the new law was justifiable because it maintained the political order, suppressing criticism of the state by punishing libels 'against a magistrate or public person'.[35] Even if the individual had died, it made no difference because 'the libeller traduces and slanders the State and Government, which dies not'.[36]

The terminology '*libellis famosis*' is part of the Roman law dealing with defamation, but there was no reference to the substance of the Roman laws. Had there been, it would have been apparent that the Star Chamber was not relying on Roman law for anything more than window dressing. Roman law protected reputation under the delict of injuria.[37] The *Digest* of Justinian records that 'whatever one do or say to bring another into disrepute' will be actionable.[38] It was irrelevant whether the defamation was written or spoken.[39] The seriousness of the matter and the quantum of damages turned on the particular incident and degree of the insult it carried.[40] The action for injuria was the principal means of legal redress for defamation in Roman law. The Roman *De Libellis Famosis* law was something quite different again, being exclusively concerned with anonymous written defamations.[41] The Star Chamber,

[34] Ibid 125a–125b, 251; *Lord Darcy of the North v Gervase Markham* (1616) Hob 120, 121, 80 ER 270, 270 Star Ch.

[35] *de Libellis Famosis* (1606) 5 Co Rep 125a, 125a, 77 ER 250, 251 Star Ch.

[36] Ibid. The public peace and political order justifications were also supplemented with references to several biblical passages to support the claim that libel 'is an offence against the law of God': 125b–126a, 251–2. This religious support serves little express purpose, other than perhaps bolstering the case for this new law.

[37] 'Injuria' was a category of wrongs that constituted insult, or contumely: *Digest* 47.10.1.2. The translations differ slightly. T Mommsen (ed), *The Digest of Justinian* (1985) 771a, translates injuria as 'wrong' and continues, '"wrong" is the designation for contumely'. Scott uses 'injury' for injuria, and then 'specifically, an injury is defined to be an insult': SP Scott, *The Civil Law* (c1977) Vol 10, 307. De Zulueta describes *contumelia* succinctly as 'an affront to another's self-respect or reputation': F De Zulueta (ed and trans), *The Institutes of Gaius: Part II—Commentary* (1953) 218. Traditionally, in the years of the Republic, injuria provided a remedy only for physical assaults but the scope of the delict expanded in the second century of the Empire and the *Institutes of Gaius* (cAD 160) record defamation as actionable injuria: *Institutes of Gaius* 3.2.C.2.220; see also De Zulueta, ibid 217. Generally on injuria and defamation, see M de Villiers, 'The Roman Law of Defamation' (1918) 34 LQR 412.

[38] *Digest* 47.10.15.27. The *Digest* recounts numerous ways to do this and they include 'writ[ing] a lampoon or sing[ing] something detrimental to another's honour' (47.10.15.27), but it was also possible to insult a person by, for example, dressing inappropriately (47.10.15.27), or refusing to let them use public baths, or sit in a theatre seat (47.10.13.7). Generally, the action was a civil one, though a criminal prosecution could also be pursued: *Institutes* 4.4.10.

[39] *Digest* 47.10.15.27; *Institutes* 4.4.1; *Institutes of Gaius* 3.2.C.2.220.

[40] This would involve a consideration of the parties involved; in particular, 'the assessment of damages for contumely is increased or diminished according to rank or dignity and probity of life': *Institutes* 4.4.7.

[41] *Libellis famosis* was first recorded around AD 313 but it appears in decrees regularly through the 4th century and is detailed in the *Theodosian Code* (AD 438) 9.34.1–9.34.10: 'If at any time defamatory writings should be found, those persons about whose deeds or names they contain shall suffer no calumny therefrom, but rather, the author of the writing shall be sought, and when he is found, he shall be compelled with all severity to prove those statements which he believed should be made public. He shall not, however, be released from punishment, even if he should prove anything': 9.34.1. The *Code* indicated that persons with accusations to make should do so publicly through the criminal prosecution system, rather than by 'insidious and secret writing': 9.34.3,

however, concerned with the suppression of political pamphlets, criminalized all written libels regardless of their authorship status.[42]

The Star Chamber's use of *libellis famosis* was almost certainly in bad faith. Burdick notes Coke's 'contempt' for Roman Law as well his 'slight' knowledge of it.[43] If Coke was contemptuous of the Roman laws in his prosecution of the case then the judgment in 1606 shows no signs of it. Moreover, it seems disingenuous to think the disparity between the legal positions can be explained by a flawed grasp of the source. Further, the political practice of Rome was robust and the laws of defamation not used oppressively:

> the abuse of men in public life was common. But there is little evidence that the lampooning of public figures resulted in much litigation. If you were in the public eye, it would not be good form to sue everyone who was defaming you—a certain amount of abuse was to be expected and tolerated in public life, then as now.[44]

The Star Chamber saw the place of political criticism quite differently. It is quite clear that the Star Chamber did not incorporate Roman law into English law and its use was in important respects little more than a facade for justifying the exercise of political power.

The Star Chamber effectively created its own law with respect to written defamation, merely giving it a title that suggested some legitimacy in its origins. The new law was starkly different from that which had emerged in the common law courts where actionability was dependent upon a slur falling within categories of actionable words. The law of criminal libel was dependent upon a generalized conception of reputation and that would soon place the common law courts in a remarkable position.

2. *Thorley v Kerry and the legacy of the Star Chamber*

When the Court of Star Chamber was abolished in 1641 its jurisdiction passed to the common law courts.[45] The criminal law of libel was adopted by the King's Bench, which soon extended its jurisdiction to create the common law offences of blasphemous and obscene libel.[46] With respect to the civil law, Holdsworth argues

9.34.4, 9.34.7. Further, anyone who repeats the libels will also be liable to prosecution: 9.34.9. A person who does not immediately destroy any libel will be punished, even if they stumble across the libel unwittingly: 9.34.9. To this, Justinian's *Codex* at 9.36.1 adds: 'Where anyone having a view to his own duty or to the preservation of the public safety mentions the name of the culprit, and states with his own mouth what he thought reprehensible in the libel aforesaid, let him be under no apprehensions, for if the truth should be established by his assertions, he will be entitled to the greatest praise, as well as to a reward ... If, however, he should not be able to prove the truth of his statements, he shall be punished with death.'

42 Generally, Fisher (n 29 above) 159–60; Veeder (n 2 above) 563–7.

43 WL Burdick, *The Principles of Roman Law and Their Relation to Modern Law* (1938) 85–6.

44 A Borkowksi, *Textbook on Roman Law* (1994) 324.

45 16 Charles I, c 10 (1640).

46 *R v Beare* (1698) 1 Ld Raym 414, 91 ER 1175; 2 Salkeld 417, 91 ER 363 (criminal libel); *R v Sedley* (1663) 17 St Tr 155 (obscenity); *Taylor's case* (1676) 1 Ventris 293, 86 ER 189 (blasphemy).

that two questions arose. First, could the criminal offence of libel be regarded as a tort? Second, if it was a tort, then would it be actionable per se or would it require proof of damage?[47] It took 170 years to get a definitive answer.

The first case to consider the question was *King v Lake* in 1668.[48] Here, Hale CB held that an action would lie for libel and proof of damage was not required because written words 'contain[ed] more malice' than spoken words. Several 18th century cases took the same view, while the commentaries of the time were divided as to whether this was in fact the law.[49] Any doubt was put to rest when *Thorley v Kerry* was decided in 1812. Chief Justice Mansfield delivered the judgment of the court that reluctantly affirmed the distinction between libel and slander in civil actions.[50]

> I cannot, upon principle, make any difference between words written and words spoken, as to the right which arises on them of bringing an action... But the distinction has been made between written and spoken slander as far back as [the mid-late 1600s], and the difference has been recognised by the Courts for at least a century back... [and] has been established by some of the greatest names known to the law... [W]e cannot, in opposition to [the cases], venture to lay down at this day, that no action can be maintained for any words written, for which an action could not be maintained if they were spoken... If the matter were for the first time to be decided at this day, I should have not hesitation in saying, that no action could be maintained for written scandal which could not be maintained for the words if they had been spoken.[51]

As unappealing as he found it, the Lord Chief Justice confirmed that words which would not be actionable if spoken might well be actionable when written. So, under what circumstances would written words be actionable?

The test was not to be based on the categories of actionable slander that already existed. Instead, actionability would follow the Star Chamber's approach and turn on a general principle. The criminal test was effectively transported into the civil action: written words were actionable as libel when they contained 'that sort of imputation which is calculated to vilify a man, and bring him, as the books say, into hatred, contempt, and ridicule'.[52] This had the effect of making actionability turn on a general sense of harm to reputation. The phrase, 'hatred, contempt and

47 W Holdsworth, 'Defamation in the Sixteenth and Seventeenth Centuries, III' (1925) 41 LQR 13, 14.

48 *King v Lake* (1668) Hadres 470, 145 ER 552.

49 *Austin v Culpepper* (1683) Skinner 123, 90 ER 57; 2 Show 313, 314, 89 ER 960, 960; *Harman v Delany* (1731) Fitz-G 253, 94 ER 743; 2 Strange 898, 93 ER 925 though this case appears to have been decided on the basis that the imputation went to the plaintiff's trade; *Villers v Monsley* (1769) 2 Wils 403, 404, 95 ER 886, 887 (Gould J), KB. On commentaries, see Fifoot (n 2 above) 132–3.

50 *Thorley v Lord Kerry* (1812) 4 Taunt 355, 13 Rev Rep 626, Exch.

51 Ibid 364–6, 634–6.

52 Ibid 364, 634. Different phrases were used in argument. For example, it was argued (356, 627) that to allege the plaintiff was a writer of anonymous letters would injure him in his 'good name, fame and credit' and that he would be brought into 'public scandal, infamy and disgrace with and amongst all his neighbours, and other good and worthy subjects of this kingdom'. It was also argued (362, 632) that an action could be maintained on the grounds of 'disgrace and discredit'.

ridicule' was well-recognized at least as early as 1716 when Hawkins' *Pleas of the Crown* used it to define criminal libel.[53] Further, the seriousness of written defamation was not attributable to any greater malice. Rather, libel was an action on the case: written words were actionable because they caused damage, and damage would be presumed to flow from all written defamatory words.[54]

A brief review of the law makes it plain that this was a major change. Until 1648 the common law had allowed recovery for certain statements, written or spoken, but without a clear rationale as to why. Certainly, it could not have been said to have been allowed on the grounds that reputation was being protected because far too many matters were not actionable. Although the actionability of spoken words would always be dependent upon these narrow, category-based rules, the demise of the Star Chamber left much uncertainty with respect to the actionability of written words.[55] The resolution of that uncertainty in *Thorley v Kerry* should be seen as marking the start of the modern common law of defamation under which libel and slander became fundamentally different torts. It is the point at which the common law can be said to allow recovery for written defamation on a general, principled basis, viz, the protection of reputation. But, important as it is, this alone does not explain the common law's contemporary claim to protect reputation. *Thorley v Kerry* is a watershed in the legal protection of reputation not only because of the judgment's text but because it was underpinned by distinctly modern conceptual foundations.

II. The Common Law's Claim to Protect Reputation

The significance of the change in *Thorley v Kerry* can only really be seen by looking at how the intellectual context of the time shaped the way the law was understood. There was a notable change in the relationship between defamation and reputation in the late 1700s. This became entrenched in the law and jurisprudence of defamation over the course of the century that followed. Of the various texts and treatises, three will be of great assistance here.[56] The key works on defamation were Thomas Starkie's *Treatise on Slander and Libel* which was first published in England in 1813, again in 1830, was annotated several times for American editions during the mid-19th century, and then revised by Henry Coleman Folkard over five editions from 1869–1908.[57] John Townshend's

[53] W Hawkins, *A Treatise of the Pleas of the Crown* (1716) 193.

[54] *Thorley v Lord Kerry* (1812) 4 Taunt 355, 366; 13 Rev Rep 626, 636, Exch.

[55] *Austin v Culpepper* (1683) Skinner 123, 124, 90 ER 57, 58; 2 show 313, 89 ER 960; *Onslow v Horne* (1771) 3 Wils KB 177, 186, 95 ER 999, 1003–4 (de Grey LCJ); *Holt v Scholefield* (1796) 6 TR 691, 694, 101 ER 775, 776–7 (Lawrence J).

[56] See the Appendix for a discussion of the sources.

[57] T Starkie, *A Treatise on the Law of Slander, Libel, Scandalum Magnatum and False Rumours* (1813); (2nd edn, 1830); HC Folkard, *The Law of Slander & Libel, founded upon the Treatise of the late Thomas Starkie* ['*Folkard's Starkie on Slander and Libel*'] (3rd edn, 1869); (4th edn, 1876); (5th

A Treatise on the Wrongs called Slander and Libel was first published in 1868 with a further three editions, the last being published in 1890.[58] Blake Odgers' *Digest of the Law of Libel and Slander* was first published in 1881 and ran through six editions to 1929.[59]

Three themes in this literature are important: (A) the claim that individuals had a right to reputation and that that right was protected by defamation law; (B) the rise of scientific method in legal analysis; and (C) the relationship between the claim that the law protects reputation and the development of several statements about what was defamatory. In isolation, none of these determined either the shape of the modern common law or its relationship to reputation. Together, they are indispensable in accounting for both of those matters.

A. A conceptual shift: the intrinsic value of reputation

At around the same time *Thorley v Kerry* was decided, it became apparent that the common law was not merely functioning to allow recovery on a broader reputation-based test for actionability, but the rationale for actionability had also fundamentally changed: the raison d'etre for the tort of defamation became the protection of reputation, rather than the maintenance of public peace or social order as it had been in the past. The conceptual shift is illustrated in the treatises of the early-19th century.

Blackstone's Commentaries had in 1783 identified reputation as an 'absolute' right that affected the personal security of individuals, though the categories of actionable words were still identified narrowly.[60] The *Commentaries* would, of course, have been a major influence on the way that courts and textbook writers would have seen the relationships between reputation and law.[61] Presumably following Blackstone, Holt's *The Law of Libel* (1812) stated that 'rights of personal security apply to character and reputation' and their 'protection... most immediately falls within the common law'.[62] Starkie (1813) argued that society had progressed to a state of civilization such that all the honours and distinctions that constituted reputation were 'the proper objects of legal protection'.[63] This theme

edn, 1876); (6th edn, 1897); (7th edn, 1908). Details of American editions can be found in the list of references.

[58] J Townshend, *A Treatise on the Wrongs called Slander and Libel* (1868); (2nd edn, 1872); (3rd edn, 1877); (4th edn, 1890).

[59] WB Odgers, *A Digest of the Law of Libel and Slander* (1881); (2nd edn, 1887); (3rd edn, 1896); (4th edn, 1905); (5th edn, 1912); (6th edn, 1929).

[60] W Blackstone, *Commentaries on the Laws of England* (9th edn, 1783) Vol 3, 119, 123–5.

[61] Boorstin observed that Blackstone's influence in America was remarkable: 'In the history of American institutions, no other book—except the Bible—has played so great a role as Blackstone's *Commentaries on the Laws of England*': D Boorstin, *Mysterious Science of the Law* (1941) cited in G Himmelfarb, *Marriage and Morals Among the Victorians* (1986) 108–10.

[62] Holt (n 22 above) 3.

[63] Starkie 1st edn (n 57 above) 1–2.

was expanded in the 'Preliminary Discourse' that became a part of subsequent editions where Starkie claimed that the laws of a civilized society must consider defamation:

> not merely as an insult to feelings of dignity, which must be repressed for the sake of public peace, but [must] regard reputation as a civil right... [standing] on the same footing with his right to the enjoyment of life, liberty, health, property and all the comforts and advantages which appertain to a state of civil society...[64]

These themes were a reflection of Enlightenment philosophy and politics that saw the identification and protection of individual rights as a characteristic of the advances brought about by modernity and civilization.[65]

A broader protection of reputation would also have made sociological sense. The statement (or 'discovery') of a general principle on which defamation law rested also coincided with industrialization that characterized what Tönnies had identified as the collapse of communities.[66] The sense of reputation which governed life in small face-to-face communities of early modern England would be different from that which operated in an urbanized, industrialized nation where printing and mass communication had become a part of life for the population. Just as widespread printing had prompted the legislature and the courts to impose more oppressive regulation and criminal punishment of blasphemous, obscene, and seditious libel, damage to private reputations could also be far greater in the modern age.

The claim that the protection of reputation was the rationale behind defamation law became the theoretical cornerstone upon which the modern law would be built. By the end of the 19th century, the reputation rationale is axiomatic and features in any number of the texts.[67] Odgers begins his work with the statement:

> No man may disparage or destroy the reputation of another. Every man has a right to have his good name maintained unimpaired.[68]

Clerk and Lindsell put it similarly:

> The right of each man... to the unimpaired possession of his reputation and good name is recognised by the law.[69]

[64] Starkie 2nd edn (n 57 above) viii, xxii.

[65] See Chapter 2, I(B).

[66] See Chapter 1, III(B).

[67] F Burdick, *The Law of Torts* (1906) 291; (3rd edn, 1913) 328; (4th edn, 1926) 349; JCH Flood, *A Treatise on the Law Concerning Libel and Slander* (1880) 23; TM Cooley, *A Treatise on the Law of Torts or the Wrongs which arise Independently of Contract* (3rd edn, 1906) 35; Folkard's *Starkie on Slander and Libel* 4th edn (n 57 above) 98.

[68] Odgers, 3rd edn (n 59 above) 1.

[69] JF Clerk and WHB Lindsell, *The Law of Torts* (6th edn, 1912) 594. They do not draw any distinction between 'reputation' and 'good name'.

By the sixth edition of Folkard's *Starkie*, there was an element of historical revisionism in the assertion of the relationship between law and reputation:

> By the common law of England, reputation is acknowledged as an inherent personal right: the character and good fame of individuals are placed under protection... Character and reputation are... absolute individual rights, and have always been recognised as such.[70]

The problem was that this was untrue. As we have seen, the common law had not recognized reputation as a right until the early-19th century. Words were actionable not because individuals had a right to their reputations, but for instrumental reasons that largely served the interests of those in power. Moreover, the scope of actionable defamation had historically been very limited both outside and, until *Thorley v Kerry*, within the common law. But the force of the intellectual current was inescapable. The protection of reputation would now be the rhetorical touchstone for the law's development. After 1812, the legal protection of reputation was no longer a strategy for maintaining the social order, the spiritual order, or the public peace. Rather, reputations were seen as inherently valuable and the law *would* protect reputation because it *should* protect reputation.

B. Scientific method and defamation law

Enlightenment philosophy was characterized by scientism, wherein the methodology of the sciences was applied to the humanities. The application of scientific method to defamation law helps explain the nature of the relationship between law and reputation that would come to characterize the modern legal framework.

1. The rise of scientific method

In *Tort Law in America: An Intellectual History*, Edward White looked at how intellectual history influenced the development of tort law as a discipline, discussing how this was so and why it mattered.[71] White argued that tort law took shape as a discipline because it was identified as a discrete area of law by 19th century 'lawyer-intellectuals' influenced by the ideas of the Enlightenment. The scientific method which was the path to the discovery of knowledge about the physical world was also applied to the humanities. Scientism, as it is called, was especially influential in legal scholarship:

> In general, post-Civil War 'Victorian' intellectuals were interested in restoring the sense of order and unity that had characterized eighteenth century thought, but they rejected efforts to derive order and unity from 'mythologic' religious principles. In the quarter century after the war, these intellectuals were particularly concerned with 'conceptualization'—the transformation of data into comprehensive theories of potentially universal

[70] Folkard's *Starkie on Slander and Libel* 6th edn (n 57 above) 1.
[71] E White, *Tort Law in America: An Intellectual History* (Expanded edn 2003; first pub 1980).

applicability. The source of unity was to be methodological: the 'scientific' ordering of knowledge. As the sociologist Lester Ward put it: '[T]he origination and distribution of knowledge [could] no longer be left to chance and nature,' but were 'to be systematized and erected into true arts.'[72]

White argues that this approach underpinned the classification of a diverse set of legal actions under the heading of tort law, beginning with the first treatise by Francis Hilliard in 1859 and the first course in tort law in 1870.[73] The general project of legal scholarship around this time was to 'derive and articulate theoretical justifications for the working rules of law that had current acceptance'.[74] The law of slander and libel was not White's concern—he mentions it only in passing—but there is much to suggest that the same scientific influence took hold much earlier in defamation law.

Enlightenment scientism can be identified in treatises from the early 1800s. Francis Holt defended criminal libel laws in *The Law of Libel* (1812).[75] The laws, he said, were founded upon reason and, having had a 'long and uninterrupted course of practice as found in every text book, digest, or institute of our best writers', had been a feature of laws since 'time immemorial'.[76] Richard Mence's 1824 rejoinder of the same name was grounded explicitly in 'the science of law' when he set out to refute Holt's argument and damn his 'high pretensions to philosophical and scientific acquirement'.[77] In 1830, Starkie explains his intellectual allegiance when he lauds the power of reason and identifies himself as working within a philosophical tradition in which knowledge is:

> preserved, accumulated, and transmitted to distant regions and to all ages; by the aid of which, the wise and the learned, though locally distant, may unite in the service of science, and availing themselves of the labours of past generations, accomplish magnificent triumphs in the cause of reason and truth...[78]

The effect of the scientific influence can best be illustrated by contrasting the different approaches taken in the 17th century works by March and Sheppard and the approaches taken in the 19th-century works.

March and Sheppard both identified slander as a problem that plagued their society. With a view to limiting the extent of slander, each wanted to provide a guide to what was and was not actionable. Sheppard explained his project:

> Among the abounding iniquity of this age, the iniquity of the tongue, that little member, set on fire by hell, is not the least. And among the evils of the tongue, is there any more

[72] Ibid 6, references omitted.

[73] Ibid 3; F Hilliard, *The Law of Torts or Private Wrongs* (1859).

[74] White (n 71 above) 4.

[75] Holt (n 22 above). His exposition was an assault on 'the liberty of the press' in favour of restrictions 'which are necessary to the preservation of the state': 45, 46.

[76] Ibid 33, 44–5.

[77] R Mence, *The Law of Libel* (1824) 15.

[78] Starkie 2nd edn (n 57 above) iii.

pernicious and deadly, and yet more common and epidemical than backbiting and slander?... [This] disease, so deeply-rooted, and over-spreading, calls for the application of the remedy, which our Law doth abundantly furnish us withall. And hence it is, I have been encouraged to ingage in this work, which is nothing else but a naked and methodical collection of the remedies prescribed by the law against this malady.[79]

The full title and what follows on the front page of March's *Actions for Slaunder* indicate a similar motivation and aim:

Actions for Slaunder, or A Methodicall Collection under certain Grounds and Heads, of what words are actionable in the Law, and what not?

A Treatise of very great use and consequence to all men, especially in these time, wherein actions for Slaunder are more common, and do much more abound than in times past; And when the malice of men so much increases, well may their tongue want a directory.[80]

Their method was to compile a 'directory' or catalogue of the words that were actionable. Sheppard, for example, dealt in different chapters with slander relating to treason, murder, witchcraft, theft, perjury, forgery, and so on.[81] The later works had a quite different orientation.

The 19th-century treatises set about gathering the disparate cases into general principles. This is expressly identified as the object of the works. Odgers, for example, explains:

[A]n attempt has been made to state the law on each point in the form of an abstract proposition, the decided cases being cited in smaller type merely as illustrations of that abstract proposition... It would be of but little use to place all these decisions before the reader and leave him to draw his own conclusions. A huge collection of reported cases piled one on top of the other is not a legal treatise, any more than a pile of bricks is a house.[82]

Townshend's approach was more theoretically driven, built around the idea that the body of cases on defamation comprised 'the law as applicable to nearly all the wrongs which may be effected by means of language'.[83] The cases had to that time been treated 'less scientifically' than those in other areas of the law.[84] His project was stated clearly and broadly:

[M]y aim has been to elicit the true rule of decision on some leading points in the law of libel, and present them with more distinctness than had been theretofore attempted.[85]

[79] Sheppard (n 12 above), Preface 'To The Reader'.
[80] March (n 11 above), title and frontispiece.
[81] Sheppard (n 12 above).
[82] Odgers (n 59 above), 'Preface to the First Edition', reprinted in 3rd edn, viii. The smaller works did not set out to do this; for instance, GW Cooke, *A Treatise on the Law of Defamation* (1844) 1–6, selected different cases that used different tests or seemed to determine actionability on different grounds without identifying general principles.
[83] Townshend 4th edn (n 58 above) 8, generally 1–9.
[84] Ibid 9.
[85] Ibid v, where in his 'Preface to the Third Edition' he explains the goals of all editions of his work.

He 'desire[d] not merely to collect, epitomize and classify under appropriate titles, the reported adjudications, but to probe the subject to its core and unfold the principles which it involves'.[86] Townshend argued that with the application of scientific method he could uncover the true nature of the law and dispel the erroneous view that libel law had 'features so exceptional as to render inapplicable those general principles which govern other branches of legal science'.[87]

In the course of this, there was a remarkable unity imposed on to this branch of law. By the time Folkard writes the commentary for the sixth edition of *Starkie* in 1897, the learned men have triumphed:

> At a very early period in the history of the English law... libel had only very narrow limits, and not the same precision it acquired in the days of liberty and science... [W]hen printing came into use, and afterwards advanced with giant strides throughout the land, it became more and more apparent that the law of libel was founded in reason and justice: and thus, step by step, as learning and science progressed, so the law of defamation spread its wholesome influence.[88]

When Folkard's seventh edition was published in 1908, this had reached an almost bizarre zenith:

> The law of Defamation, in so far as it is founded upon the Common Law of the land, is one of the most scientific branches of the English law...[89]

So, what did this scientific method yield with respect to the principles regarding actionability?

2. *The law as it was stated in the treatises*

The defamation treatises of the 19th century exemplify White's point that knowledge was assumed 'to be complex and infinite but capable of orderly classification and analysis through the use of proper methodological techniques'.[90] Attempts at orderly classification were at the heart of the works. This cannot have been easy when there was great uncertainty and imprecision in the courts with respect to just what would make something defamatory.[91] Still, the texts generally tried to explain concisely what would be defamatory even if, in Bigelow's words, '[t]he chief practical difficulty with libel is that it lacks a sharp definition'.[92] The

[86] Ibid 9.
[87] Ibid.
[88] Folkard's *Starkie on Slander and Libel* 6th edn (n 57 above) 1
[89] Folkard's *Starkie on Slander and Libel* 7th edn (n 57 above) v.
[90] White (n 71 above) 21, generally 20–62.
[91] For example, the pleadings in *Cook v Ward* (1830) 6 Bing 409, 130 ER 1338 seemed to try to cover every possible angle, arguing that the publication contrived 'to injure the said Plaintiff in his said good name, fame, credit, respectability and reputation, and to bring him into public scandal, infamy, ridicule, contempt, and disgrace, with and among all his neighbours and other good and worthy subjects of this realm, and to vex, harass, oppress, impoverish, and wholly ruin the said Plaintiff...'
[92] MM Bigelow, *The Law of Torts* (2nd English edn, 1903) 138.

treatises exhibited a range of opinion about what the general principles were that governed what was defamatory and about how the decided cases related to the general principles.

Odgers' approach is representative. He begins with something that looks like a general, if imprecise, statement of principle comprised of several phrases:

> In cases of libel, any words will be deemed defamatory which appreciably injure the reputation of another, which make men think worse of him. All words which expose the plaintiff to hatred, contempt, ridicule or obloquy, ... or cause him to be shunned and avoided by his neighbours are libellous ... And so too are all words which hold the plaintiff up to contempt, hatred, scorn, or ridicule, and which, by thus engendering an evil opinion of him in the minds of right-thinking men, tend to deprive him of friendly intercourse and society.[93]

Generality could not be avoided, he said, because 'it appears to be impossible to define a libel with any greater precision or lucidity. I proceed at once therefore to give instances.'[94] And with that, he turns to the cases and lists over 60 examples of actionable words.[95]

For Townshend as well, the scientific goal was frustrated by the diversity of the cases. In his first edition, Townshend identified 19 different general phrases that had been used to explain what would make a statement defamatory.[96] By the fourth edition there was still no definition, but there were 20 general phrases and he had 'subjoin[ed] some specimens of the attempts to define libel' in a three-page footnote.[97] The best of these, he thought (somewhat unhelpfully), was the proposition that libel was 'defamation without legal excuse'.[98]

Some of the clearest examples of uncertainty about the relationship between the cases and the general principles can be seen in the evolution of Addison's *Treatise on the Law of Torts*. The first edition in 1860 defined as libellous a publication:

> holding up a plaintiff to publick [sic] hatred, contempt, or ridicule, or having a tendency to make him feared, or his society shunned and avoided ...[99]

Addison then goes on to provide examples of the cases from which the general principles are derived.[100] In the fourth edition in 1874, the author added to the statement of general principles that a publication 'imputing insanity to the plaintiff' would be libellous.[101] This was not provided as an example of the general principles, but as a separate statement of principle. In the next edition in 1879,

[93] Odgers 3rd edn (n 59 above) 18.
[94] Ibid 19.
[95] Ibid 19–23.
[96] Townshend 1st edn (n 58 above) 187–8.
[97] Townshend 4th edn (n 58 above) 203–4, 17–20.
[98] Ibid 17.
[99] CG Addison, *Wrongs and their Remedies* (1860) 579.
[100] Ibid.
[101] CG Addison, *Wrongs and their Remedies* (4th edn, 1873) 776.

the explanation was different again: the decision on insanity had been removed as a principle and the general statement was now that a publication would be libellous if it 'expose[d] any person to hatred, contempt, ridicule, or obloquy, or which causes him to be shunned or avoided'.[102]

These attempts to classify the law were the subject of some criticism on the grounds that a correctly conducted scientific analysis of the cases showed that the rules governing defamation did not constitute a cohesive body of law. Mence had already criticized Holt on the grounds that the law of libel was 'not properly a system... to be systematized'.[103] Townshend's work was reviewed in 1871 by Nicholas St John Green, whom White describes as one of the leading 'conceptualists' of the era and heavily committed to the scientific approach in law.[104] Green praised Townshend's philosophical approach, but argued that there were no principles in defamation law; it was impossible to 'classify under general principles a branch of the law which... does not admit of such classification'.[105]

The criticisms were to no avail. The texts continued to propose statements of general principle. The 'hatred, contempt, or ridicule' formulation of the test was always at the core of the principles stated in the books, and by the mid-1800s was accepted as being the essence of the test for libel in both England and America.[106] The decisions which showed that words could be actionable even when they did not quite sit comfortably within that principle were duly recorded and, in various ways, drawn into a framework that attempted to derive and order legal principles from a morass of case law. These statements of principle were accompanied by the axiom that defamation law protected reputation. Ultimately, the treatises very successfully imposed on the law an order and a rationale that it did not historically have. The relationship between that order and rationale will help explain how the modern common law took shape as it did.

C. Shaping the modern common law

The rationale behind defamation law was said to be the protection of reputation. This is what made the collection of cases a body of law from which general legal principles could be derived. However, when the authors stated tests for what

[102] Ibid, 5th edn, 149; 8th edn, 191. See also LC Innes, *The Principles of the Law of Torts* (1891) 168: 'a statement [is one] which tends to damage the reputation of [another] and expose him to public hatred, contempt, and ridicule'.

[103] Mence (n 77 above) 16.

[104] White (n 71 above) 6–7.

[105] NStJ Green, 'Slander and Libel' (1871) 6 American Law Review 593, 612–13.

[106] In the United States, see Hilliard (n 73 above) 254: to be libellous a publication must tend 'to injure one's reputation in the common estimation of mankind, to throw contumely or reflect shame and disgrace upon him, or hold him up as an object of hatred, scorn, ridicule, and contempt ... [or] which is calculated to make him infamous, odious or ridiculous'. This statement drew on the language of the cases, including *Mayrant v Richardson* 1 Nott & McCord 347; 9 Am Dec 707 (SC Ct App, 1818); *Fonville v McNease* Dudley Law 303; 31 Am Dec 556 (SC Ct App, 1838).

was defamatory they did not measure them against the rationale. Instead, it was *precedent* that constituted and that would reveal the general principles of actionability in defamation law. This was a product of the methodology they applied to the law. White explains that the value of legal principles for the conceptualists was 'their effectiveness as working analytical guidelines'.[107] The principles were thus derived from the decided cases and provided a guide for those who had to work with the law. As Green described it, and the italics are his: 'The latest decided cases upon this subject *make the law*.'[108] Thus, it is not appropriate to see the statements of law in the texts as 'reflexive' principles that present analysis and propose on that basis a point of reference that should guide a court in making decisions. Rather, they are explanatory or 'reflective' principles that aim to capture and reflect the law as it is. In that sense, they served a useful purpose for lawyers and publishers.[109] But they did not explain or inquire into how it was that the law protected reputation, nor did they suggest that the rationale should guide the determination of principles or cases in the courts.

The following chapters will explore in detail the way the courts determined actionability but it will be helpful to foreshadow the discussion. Like the textbook writers, the courts did not rely on an express consideration of reputation either. Again, it was precedent that was the point of reference for determining whether words would be actionable. However, the courts were in a distinctly different position than the jurists. Whereas the jurists' task of putting order into the law meant that treatises provided an overview of what would be defamatory, the courts did not need to bring the law together as a coherent whole. Rather, courts could to some extent pick and choose the authority on which they wanted to rely. They might use the general test, relying on an intuitive sense of whether a person had been brought into 'hatred, contempt, or ridicule'. As the following chapters will show, it would later be sufficient if the publication possessed a tendency to lower a person in the estimation of right-thinking members of society generally. Alternatively, courts could and would rely on the line of category-based cases that had been decided before the 'hatred, contempt, or ridicule' test was established as the general basis for actionability. This would be quite legitimate because the prevailing theory was that reputation had *always* been protected by the law.

Neither the courts nor the legal writers found it necessary to examine or resolve conflicting decisions. It was simply the case that there were different grounds on which words might be actionable: the courts applied them and the texts recorded them in some meaningful order. Over time, this left judges a remarkable freedom to make findings that an imputation was defamatory because, as the treatises

[107] White (n 71 above) 7.

[108] Green (n 106 above) 612.

[109] For example, H Fraser, *Principles and Practice of the Law of Libel and Slander* (1893) Preface to the First Edition: 'The object of this work is to present the Principles and Practice of the Law of Libel and Slander in a concise form; and . . . it is hoped that the book may prove useful to the Legal Profession.'

make so clear, there were a number of phrases and cases that a court might rely upon to decide that words were actionable. What emerged were parallel lines of authority in the law: each test sat alongside the others and was used as need be. When the third edition of *Halsbury's Laws of England* was published in 1958 it stated the tests in the way they are still understood today:

> A statement is defamatory... [if] it is calculated to lower him in the estimation of right-thinking members of the community or to cause him to be shunned or avoided or expose him to hatred, contempt, or ridicule...[110]

The chapters in Part III will explain and examine in some depth the development of this trio of 'lowering the estimation' (the principal test for what is defamatory), 'shun and avoid', and 'ridicule' (the alternative tests), looking throughout at the relationship between reputation and the law.

Conclusion

This and the previous chapters have covered a fairly wide range of matters. It will be useful at this point to draw some of the themes together.

The criteria for moral judgment that characterized life in early modern England which were discussed in Chapter 3 are just as evident in the rise of the common law actions for defamation. The cases reflected the same fundamental values that had characterized litigation in the local and church courts since the 13th century. There is certainly nothing to indicate that imputations of dishonesty, intemperance of habits, or sexual impropriety which had for 700 years affected judgments about social and self-worth would no longer continue to do so in either England or the United States. These traditional Christian values will continue to be of interest in forthcoming chapters, especially with regard to their endurance in the face of Enlightenment rationality and their significance for the way the modern common law protected reputation.

The way that the law protected reputation changed dramatically as the common law developed, at least where written communication was concerned. As the restrictive category-based approach to actionability was replaced by the generalized 'hatred, contempt, or ridicule' test, a wider range of imputations became actionable than had traditionally been the case. Written imputations of unchastity or dishonesty that were not previously actionable (when spoken and written words were treated alike) would now be actionable because they would bring a person into hatred, ridicule, or contempt. But, as this chapter explained, what gave the law its modern complexion was the new rationale that underpinned it. The proposition that defamation law protected reputation—and that it had always done so—was the result of an assertion that sprang from 18th-century Enlightenment

[110] *Halsbury's Laws of England* (3rd edn, 1958) Vol 24, 19.

philosophy. In the 19th century scientistic search for legal foundations it became the unifying principle that would make sense of several centuries of defamation law. The claim that reputation had always been protected was a fiction. That is clear when it is viewed in light of the relationships between law and reputation in the history of defamation outside the common law (Chapter 3) and in the early common law action (discussed in section II of this chapter).

The analysis in these chapters may undermine the foundations of the modern law's claim to protect reputation but it does not by any means displace the present substance of that claim. However artificial the rationale may be in its origins, it should be seen as being a very real and meaningful justification for the law today. By the end of the 19th century, it was agreed by judges, scholars, and lawyers that the rationale of the defamation action was the protection of reputation. In this way, the proposition that reputation is protected by defamation law has become the only appropriate basis for making sense of the law. Although it might not in the past have been used as a guide to determining the tests for actionability and their application, it is highly appropriate that it should be used in that way now. And that is the task that will occupy the remaining chapters where the tests for what is defamatory are analysed with a view to establishing how and to what extent they protect reputation, and how they might be reformed to meet that goal to the best effect. This use of reputation as the point of reference for evaluating the law is one of the particularly novel aspects of the approach taken in this book. It also means that the chapters to follow will frequently return to the historical and conceptual matters discussed so far. Three implications flow from this chapter that provide a guide to what might be of special interest when looking at the modern law, its development, and its relationship with reputation.

First, cases decided prior to *Thorley v Kerry* should be viewed with care and caution in the modern law. Actionability in these cases was determined using the narrow, category-based laws and was informed by a quite different rationale to that which characterizes the modern general principle regarding actionability.

Secondly, a process of legal dialogue might be anticipated. While on the one hand the generalized statement of legal principle will inform discussions about whether certain imputations are actionable, there will on the other hand be imputations that, when considered, will present challenges for the statement of principle. The courts will be forced on some occasions to ask if the statement of law is suitable for protecting reputation. This dialogue is both legitimate and essential because of the law's claim that the tort of libel protects individuals against slurs on their reputations. What will make the contemporary dialogue distinct is the upheaval in the moral taxonomies that govern reputation in Western liberal democracies. As Chapter 2 discussed, the shift from Christian tradition to liberal rights marked the latter half of the 20th century.

Thirdly, with a generalized test for what is defamatory and the claim that reputation is protected by the law, it might be expected that the modern common law of defamation will provide a more valuable resource for understanding the moral taxonomies that govern reputation than the narrowly cast pre-19th century defamation laws. This is enhanced by the common concerns of English, Australian, and American jurisdictions where the courts are grappling with similar issues relating to the criteria for moral judgment. In particular, it might be thought that any dialogue surrounding the statements of legal principle will be especially useful. In the past, the substance and actionability of complaints of defamation provided an indication of a community's moral taxonomy. While the substance of pleaded imputations may still identify the criteria for moral judgment in a community, the statement of legal principle will begin to indicate the *sources* of those criteria. This will become especially evident where the law states that the views of the 'right-thinking' or 'decent' person are the benchmark for what is defamatory. Here, the ethical dominance of Christian tradition will be evident and sitting in marked opposition to contemporary liberal values. Where there are uncertainties about actionability or the reasons for it, the dialogue compels questions to be asked and answered with respect to whether and why the criteria for moral judgment should be recognized by the law, and how the law should respond to ruptures in moral taxonomies.

PART III

REPUTATION AND ACTIONABLE DEFAMATION IN THE MODERN COMMON LAW

5

Protecting Reputation: The Principal Test for What is Defamatory

The chapters in Parts I and II set about explaining the nature of reputation and its place in the conceptual and doctrinal development of the common law of defamation. The claim that defamation law protects reputation is a relatively recent one but has become the objective against which the contemporary legal framework must be evaluated. I turn now to that evaluation.

The following chapters consider the relationships between reputation and the modern common law tests for what is defamatory. This chapter examines how and to what extent reputation is protected under the principal test. Chapters 6 and 7 will consider the protection of reputation under the supplementary tests of 'shun and avoid' and 'ridicule'. Chapter 8 will look at how the existing forms of protection and the limits upon them might best be shaped, expressed, and applied to most appropriately protect reputation.

In this chapter, section I looks at the central and longstanding place that moral judgment has occupied in the principal test for what is defamatory. By examining the actionability of particular imputations and general statements of legal principle, it is possible to see how the legal standard of judgment gradually acquired a particular content, that being the traditional values of Christian morality. Sections II and III then look at how the legal framework takes account of competing and conflicting values in a jurisdiction. Section II addresses the quantitative dimension of diversity and it will be suggested that the American 'sectional standards' test is to be preferred to the Anglo-Australian law that looks to the 'general standards' of the community. Section III moves to the substance of the views held in a jurisdiction. It looks at how qualitative distinctions have been drawn between different moral taxonomies to limit the legal protection of reputation in particular ways. Here, it will be suggested that determinations of defamatory capacity depend upon processes of 'ethical recognition' of criteria for moral judgment. These processes will be of particular interest because they will be essential for understanding the supplementary tests (in Chapters 6 and 7) and for examining the clash between the moral taxonomies of tradition and modernity that has become visible in recent years and which will be addressed in Chapter 8.

I. The Centrality of Moral Judgment in the Principal Test

It was explained in Chapter 4 that after *Thorley v Kerry* the principal test for what is defamatory was whether a publication had a tendency to bring the plaintiff into hatred, contempt, or ridicule.[1] Since that time, moral judgment has been central to determinations of whether words will be actionable as defamation. Its operation and effect can be seen in the ways the law has, first, applied certain criteria for moral judgment and, secondly, articulated the standards by which defamatory capacity is to be adjudicated.

A. The early application of the 'hatred, contempt, or ridicule' test

It was argued in Chapter 2 that the moral taxonomies of reputation involve publicly acknowledged systems of moral or ethical rules. Actions in court constitute and reflect that public acknowledgment. The statements and the conclusions in the cases indicate how the parties and the courts understood reputation.

Throughout the 19th century the 'hatred, contempt, or ridicule' test was the general principle that governed what was defamatory. *Parmiter v Coupland* is most often cited as authority for the test. There, Parke B stated that:

> A publication, without justification or lawful excuse, which is calculated to injure the reputation of another, by exposing him to hatred, contempt, or ridicule, is a libel.[2]

Both before and after *Parmiter*, the cases decided under the principle are repeatedly concerned with allegations of moral wrongdoing. It is the moral wrongness of the alleged behaviour that makes the words actionable. This aspect of the reasoning is usually unstated. For instance, an allegation that a person has committed a serious crime simply does not require a court to engage in any discussion of whether an ethical rule of the community has been breached. Sometimes, however, there is an express discussion of the wrongful nature of the behaviour and the presence of moral judgment is explicit in the determination of actionability.

In several early-19th century cases the courts explain that the old category-based rules regarding actionability do not apply and it is not necessary to impute criminal behaviour to a plaintiff. In these cases the moral rules of the community are clearly apparent as a governing principle of both reputation and defamation. Serious imputations such as deceptive or oppressive conduct caused the courts no difficulty at all.[3] Such allegations were libellous because they 'had a tendency [to bring the plaintiff] into hatred, contempt, or ridicule' or injure the plaintiff 'in

1 *Thorley v Lord Kerry* (1812) 4 Taunt 355, 364, 13 Rev Rep 626, 634, Exch; see Chapter 4 I(B)(2).

2 *Parmiter v Coupland* (1840) 6 M&W 105, 108 (Alderson and Gurney BB agreeing), Exch.

3 *M'Gregor v Thwaites* (1824) 3 B&C 24, 107 ER 643; *Woodard v Dowsing* (1828) 2 Man & Ry 74; *Robertson v M'Dougall* (1828) 4 Bing 670, 130 ER 927.

his good name, fame and credit'.[4] The more expansive moral dimensions of the new general principle were clear in *Robeson* where *Thorley v Kerry* was held to be authority for the proposition that:

> in a libel any tendency to bring a party into contempt or ridicule is actionable, and, in general, any charge of immoral conduct, although in matters not punishable by law.[5]

Accordingly, the defendant newspaper's statement that a Catholic archbishop offered a Protestant minister a large sum of money to entice him to become a Catholic priest was defamatory because it reflected poorly 'on the moral conduct of the archbishop'.[6]

Allegations of immoral behaviour were actionable in all manner of circumstances and sometimes the substance of the criteria for moral judgment was reflected in judicial comment. A publication that suggested the plaintiff was ungrateful was said in *Cox v Lee* to have charged 'a moral offence':

> as opprobrious as any that can be made... [N]o one can deny it who considered in what light [ingratitude] is regarded by poets and moralists, who are the mirrors and exponents of the universal feelings and judgments of mankind.[7]

The presence of upper-class values was apparent in the early-19th century cases. In *Clement v Chivis*, for instance, it was held that a letter was libellous when it said simply that the plaintiff, a coach driver, had insulted some passengers. Applying the *Thorley v Kerry* test, the court found it was 'a very serious and contumelious imputation, clearly calculated to bring the plaintiff into contempt by some persons, and hatred by others'.[8] Here, there is evidence of the substance of the moral taxonomy that informed the court. It is quite clear that when the defendant stated that the plaintiff had insulted the two ladies and the gentleman, he was saying that the plaintiff had done something significantly wrong. The coachman was clearly claiming and was acknowledged to be a morally good person because he had not insulted anyone. He knew how he should treat his passengers. Even the defendant's argument in *Clement v Chivis* accepted these premises. There was no suggestion that people would not be contemptuous of the coachman if he had in fact done what was alleged.

Cases like these expose clearly the relevance of moral judgment in determinations of actionability under the original formulation of the principal test. Moral judgment was not discussed in all decisions but that does not mean it was irrelevant. Rather, it means that in the general run of cases there was nothing remarkable

4 *M'Gregor v Thwaites* (1824) 3 B&C 24, 33, 107 ER 643, 647 (Bayley J); *Robertson v M'Dougall* (1828) 4 Bing 670, 672–4, 130 ER 927, 928–9; *Woodard v Dowsing* (1828) 2 Man & Ry 74.

5 *Archbishop of Tuam v Robeson* (1828) 5 Bing 17, 21, 130 ER 965, 967.

6 Ibid.

7 *Cox v Lee* (1869) LR 4 Exch 284, 290 (Bramwell B), 291 (Channell B), 291 (Pigott B). On the moral significance of conduct see also *Hoare v Silverlock* (1848) 12 QB 624, 116 ER 1004; *Hearne v Stowell* (1840) 12 Ad & El 719, 113 ER 986.

8 *Clement v Chivis* (1829) 9 B&C 172, 175–6.

about the moral status of alleged behaviour; there was simply no doubt that an imputation was generally viewed as immoral and would indeed affect a community's evaluation of a plaintiff's social worth. The immorality of the alleged behaviour is what makes the words actionable. And there was, as we shall see, little doubt about what was and was not immoral behaviour.

B. Articulating the standards of judgment: 'The right-thinking person'

The centrality of moral judgment was evident not only in determinations of actionability, but also in the judicial articulation of the standards that were to be applied in making those determinations. This was most apparent in the re-working of the principal test for what is defamatory.

The 'hatred, contempt, or ridicule' test had been confirmed as the touchstone of liability in both England and the United States from around 1840.[9] However, the courts were troubled by imputations that did not seem to expose a plaintiff to hatred, contempt, or ridicule as such, but which nonetheless seemed to impact negatively on the plaintiff's worth in the eyes of the community. This would have mattered—if only intuitively—because of the rationale that defamation law protected reputation. This was reflected in the variable ways that the law was expressed in the cases.

Decisions had not always appeared to require that the plaintiff be viewed with such vitriol as the terms 'hatred' or 'contempt' might suggest. As early as 1693 the view had been expressed that it was sufficient 'if the defendant induces an ill opinion to be had of the plaintiff'.[10] In *Fray v Fray*, it was held that imputations 'which may tend to lower the plaintiff in the estimation of others' were capable of being defamatory.[11] In *Tolley v Fry* it was suggested that it would be enough if the words 'disparaged' the plaintiff or brought him into 'dislike'.[12] This lesser degree of opprobrium had been recognized in at least some of the texts and the encyclopedias for some time. The second edition of *Halsbury's Laws of England* is ambivalent about the standard, stating that 'hatred, contempt, or ridicule' would be satisfied if the imputation tended to lower the plaintiff in peoples' estimation or 'induced them to entertain an ill opinion of him'.[13]

This trend was formalized when the House of Lords decided *Sim v Stretch* in 1936. Lord Atkin's tentative restatement of the law remains today the principal test for what is defamatory.

[9] See Chapter 4, II(B)(2).

[10] *Cropp v Tilney* (1693) 3 Salk 225, 91 ER 791.

[11] *Fray v Fray* (1864) 17 CB (NS) 603, 605, 144 ER 241, 242 (Erle CJ), CP. The lower threshold is expressed differently but is equally clear in *Homer v Taunton* (1860) 5 H&N 661, 157 ER 1344, Exch; *O'Brien v Clement* (1846) 15 M&W 435, 153 ER 435.

[12] *Tolley v JS Fry & Sons Ltd* [1930] 1 KB 467, 479 (Greer LJ), CA.

[13] *Halsbury's Laws of England* (2nd edn, 1936) Vol 20, 397, references omitted; also, H Fraser, *Principles of the Law of Libel and Slander* (6th edn, 1925) 1; cf PH Winfield, *A Text-book of the Law of Tort* (1937) 256 which maintained the 'hatred, contempt, or ridicule' test.

> Judges and textbook writers alike have found difficulty in defining with precision the word 'defamatory.' The conventional phrase exposing the plaintiff to hatred, ridicule and contempt is probably too narrow... I do not intend to ask your Lordships to lay down a formal definition, but after collating the opinions of many authorities I propose in the present case the test: would the words tend to lower the plaintiff in the estimation of right-thinking members of society generally?[14]

The first point of this was that it formally lowered the threshold of what it would take to establish that a publication was defamatory. It is probably best viewed as capturing the thrust of the existing test with language that more accurately reflected that test's application. Thus, since *Sim v Stretch* it has been unnecessary to argue that the plaintiff was exposed to hatred, to ridicule, or to contempt by a publication. Instead, it has been sufficient that the imputation had a tendency to lessen the esteem in which the plaintiff is held.

Secondly, *Sim v Stretch* expressly takes account of moral judgment by identifying a standard against which behaviour will be adjudged as morally right or wrong. That standard is the view of 'right-thinking members of society generally'. There has been some contention over whether right-thinking means decent and respectable, or whether it means rational and logical.[15] In effect it means both, with the different qualities applicable to different questions. As a logical being, the 'right-thinking' person certainly refers to a standard of rationality which should be applied to the ordinary reasonable reader in determining whether a particular publication conveys the pleaded imputations.[16] But as the history of the case law suggests, the expression 'right-thinking' clearly carries with it a standard of morality.[17] This is also captured in the phrase used in New South Wales, where the standard is that of the 'ordinary *decent* person'.[18]

Thirdly, Lord Atkin's statement of law seemed to represent a slightly different type of moral taxonomy than the aristocratic one that underpinned *Clement v Chivis*. Though it is difficult to see it as being fundamentally different, the language on its face articulates a vision of the community and its values that was

[14] *Sim v Stretch* [1936] 2 All ER 1237, 1240, HL. It took some years for this to settle as the principal test. The Court of Appeal quickly adopted it (*Holdsworth Ltd v Associated Newspapers Ltd* [1937] 3 All ER 872, CA) but the treatises displayed great uncertainty about the relationship between the cases and the general principles. For instance, Clerk and Lindsell adhered to the traditional 'hatred, contempt, or ridicule' formula for a long time, identifying Lord Atkin's statement as an indicator of whether the 'hatred, contempt or ridicule' test was satisfied rather than as a discrete and distinct test for whether an imputation is defamatory: *The Law of Torts* (9th edn, 1937) 574–5. By the 11th edn (1954) 728–9, the *Sim v Stretch* test sits a little more independently from the traditional test. Certainly, however, Lord Atkin's test was clearly viewed as the principal test by 1958: *Halsbury's Laws of England* (3rd edn, 1958), Vol 24, 19.

[15] *Slayter v Daily Telegraph Newspaper Co Ltd* (1908) 6 CLR 1, 7 (Griffith CJ).

[16] *Amalgamated Television Services Pty Ltd v Marsden* (1998) 43 NSWLR 158, 165 (Hunt CJ at CL, Mason P and Handley JA agreeing), NSW CA.

[17] This was quite clearly accepted by Bower as well-established and appropriate: GS Bower, *A Code of the Law of Actionable Defamation* (2nd edn, 1923) 252–3.

[18] *Gardiner v John Fairfax & Sons Pty Ltd* (1942) 42 SR(NSW) 171, 172, NSW SC FC, emphasis added.

somewhat broader. It also suggests that changes in values should be and would be reflected by the law. The move from aristocratic values as guiding actionability had been evident in *Clay v Roberts* where it was suggested that '[t]here is a distinction between imputing what is merely a breach of conventional etiquette, and what is illegal, mischievous, or sinful—between, in fact, matters of taste and matters of crime'.[19] Lord Atkin reflected on this and made a similar observation that 'exhibitions of bad manners or discourtesy' should not 'be placed on the same level as attacks on character [and] treated as actionable wrongs'.[20] This was significant because it characterized as minor the very things of appearance that aristocratic values would have seen as important indicators of social worth.

In articulating the standards to be applied, Lord Atkin called attention to the moral judgment associated with reputation which had always been present in the 'hatred, contempt, or ridicule' test. His Lordship exposed the moral foundations of actionability and provided the terms in which they might be discussed. But this still left much unclear. Who exactly were the 'right-thinking members of society generally', and what were their views?

C. Moral taxonomies and the principal test

The values of 'right-thinking members of society' were not the values of any concrete, identifiable group of people. Rather, they were a set of values that existed as an idea which embodied the dominant and public sense of the moral good. That idea might be called 'the right-thinking person'. However, to say it is 'an idea' is not to say it was a myth or a fiction. On the contrary, it was an idea of great substance. It is helpful here to draw on the language Edward Said uses to explain 'the Orient' and 'Orientalism'.[21] To speak of a 'right-thinking person' was to speak of 'an idea that has a history and a tradition of thought, imagery and vocabulary that have given it reality and presence'.[22] Like the Orient, it 'would be wrong to conclude that ["the right-thinking person"] was *essentially* an idea, or a creation with no corresponding reality'.[23] And, like Orientalism, one ought not assume that 'the right-thinking person' is 'nothing more than a structure of lies or myths which, were the truth about them to be told, would simply blow away'.[24] The phrase clearly made sense to those who used it and that was to be

19 *Clay v Roberts* (1863) 8 Law Times (NS) 397, 398, Exch.

20 *Sim v Stretch* [1936] 2 All ER 1237, 1242, HL.

21 E Said, *Orientalism: Western Conceptions of the Orient* (1991; first pub 1978).

22 Ibid 5.

23 Ibid, emphasis in original.

24 Ibid 6. The richness of the cultural structures and processes cannot be understated and any number of intellectual, political, and cultural currents and interests that could be seen to provide a context in which the idea of 'the right-thinking person' was very much a material reality that made moral and intellectual sense. Among the more significant themes that may be useful are civility and civilization: see, for example, N Elias, *The Civilizing Process* (Rev edn 2000; first pub 1939); G Gong, *The Standard of Civilisation in International Society* (1994). Themes of sex and gender may also be a useful way to understand the concept: see, for example, JA Mangan

expected because it drew on a deep reserve of history and culture, encapsulating and reinforcing a set of criteria for moral judgment that can be found in the earlier moral traditions of Christianity.

The criteria for moral judgment that characterized life in early modern England were evident in the rise of the common law actions for defamation and continued to prevail in the 19th and early-20th centuries. How was it that the values of Christian tradition survived the rationalism of the Enlightenment and continued to be the moral bedrock of social and political life in England and the United States? The processes by which this occurred need some attention because they help explain how the modern law of defamation has protected reputation and the particular standards it has applied in doing so. In turn, this illuminates some of the problems that arise in evaluating and reformulating the tests for what is defamatory.

The main works I draw on in this section are DH Meyer's account of the content and influence of 19th-century American moral philosophy, *The Instructed Conscience: The Shaping of the American National Ethic*, and the works on English intellectual history by Gertrude Himmelfarb.[25] Similar patterns underlie the endurance of Christian values on both sides of the Atlantic.[26]

1. Moral taxonomies in the 19th century

Traditionally, as Meyer explains it, 'behind the rules of conduct stood the eternal law of God'.[27] The 'question of the authenticity and legitimacy of traditional moral values' posed a major intellectual and social problem for the philosophical revolution of the Enlightenment, characterized as it was by the rejection of religion as the source of moral authority.[28] This problem was resolved in the first half of the 19th century by the theory that science and religion were unified. Christian morality was a 'divinely prescribed set of rules' that could be 'either revealed or rationally apprehended'.[29] Philosophical and moral education thus aimed:

> to accommodate the old to the new—to adapt the western tradition of Christian morals to the demands of a new and changing world... It was the task of the academic moralists to see to it that the traditional rules of virtue were not forgotten. [They] sought to offer a philosophical restatement of fundamental moral truths—truths that they regarded as eternal and unchanging. [They] were determined to... show that science proved the truths of religion and morality.[30]

and J Walvin (eds), *Manliness and Morality: Middle-class Masculinity in Britain and America, 1800–1940* (1987).

25 DH Meyer, *The Instructed Conscience: The Shaping of the American National Ethic* (1972); G Himmelfarb, *Victorian Minds* (1968); G Himmelfarb, *Marriage and Morals Among the Victorians* (1986).

26 This section provides little more than a sketch of a complex phenomenon on which there is a wealth of literature. For a critical discussion of that complexity, see FM Turner, *Contesting Cultural Authority: Essays in Victorian Intellectual Life* (1993).

27 Meyer (n 25 above) 89.

28 Meyer (n 25 above) 109

29 Meyer (n 25 above) 90.

30 Meyer (n 25 above) xiii, 11, 22, 26.

Similarly, Himmelfarb explains that Enlightenment science in England 'did not mean to challenge the pre-eminence of religion'; instead, 'the advancement of science could only contribute to the advancement of religion'.[31]

By the late 1800s, this position had become less appealing. Philosophically, the posited theoretical unity of science and religion fell away sharply, especially after Darwin's *On the Origins of Species* in 1859.[32] Sociologically and intuitively, the new complex, urbanized societies did not lend themselves to traditional, narrow, prescriptive moralism.[33] By this time, however, the moralists had done their job well. While philosophical thought would yield, the values that governed lives would persist. The substance of the criteria for moral judgment would go unchanged.

The age was one of change, uncertainty, and instability in many respects. While the religious foundations may have been undermined, traditional values were re-cast as moralism to provide certainty and stability.[34] The behaviour that moralism dictated performed an important function in modern societies by 'providing a foundation for mutual trust in the context of anonymous interactions'.[35] The same pattern was evident in America where a secular morality replaced religious dogma:

> [M]orality, both theoretical and practical, offered the nineteenth century that kind of common ground for affirmation and conduct that had once been provided by religious doctrine and practical piety... [The moral philosophers] harness[ed] and transform[ed] the energies of American evangelicalism... In combining pietism and public moralism, the Victorian Americans, intending to both inspire the heart and to shape and construct the public conscience, produced an... official moral code.[36]

Himmelfarb explains that the English, 'feeling guilty about the loss of their religious faith, suspecting that that loss might expose them to the temptations of immorality and the perils of nihilism... were determined to make of morality a substitute for religion'.[37] In many respects, then, it was quite possible to reject religious belief and see science as 'entirely compatible with the most rigorous and conventional morality'.[38]

American moralism was more 'elaborately delineated and widely promulgated' than its English counterpart, but the values of the two dictated similar, traditional standards of behaviour:

[31] Himmelfarb, *Marriage and Morals Among the Victorians* (n 25 above) 55.

[32] Meyer (n 25 above) 128–9; C Darwin, *On the Origin of Species* (1859).

[33] Meyer (n 25 above) 129–31.

[34] See M Morgan, *Manners, Morals and Class in England, 1774–1858* (1994) esp 59–86; Meyer (n 25 above) 136–7.

[35] Morgan (n 34 above) 84, 104.

[36] Meyer (n 25 above) 137–8.

[37] Himmelfarb, *Marriage and Morals Among the Victorians* (n 25 above) 21, 303. The intellectual dimensions of Victorian moralism have been explored well by S Collini, *Public Moralists: Political Thought and Intellectual Life in Britain* (1991) esp 90–118.

[38] Himmelfarb, *Marriage and Morals Among the Victorians* (n 25 above) 27.

The theoretical apparatus offered... the consolations of philosophy, while the moral rules it sustained provided the security of an established code of conduct.[39]

The effect of 19th century moral philosophy, argues Meyer, was that it 'helped cultivate and justify what may be called an American moral idiom' and 'long after the justification had been forgotten the moral idiom would remain—challenged, to be sure, but never relinquished'.[40]

The Victorian idea of virtue performed a similar culturally and nationally unifying function in England where, remarkably, it crossed class boundaries. As Himmelfarb describes its effect:

the great accomplishment of the evangelical ethic [was] the diffusion of what might otherwise have been a purely middle-class ethic... [It saw] the acceptance of a single moral code by the entire population. [T]he moral consensus was never so complete.[41]

It was this degree of consensus that made it tenable to see the polity as a community unified by a commitment to traditional values.

2. *Traditional values and the legal framework*

The survival of traditional Christian values was simultaneously reflected in the law and reinforced by it. Generally, these values were implicit in the common law. As Holt put it in 1812, 'it is a principle of our common law that everyone shall be presumed to know the duties of morality'.[42] Specifically, they were at the very heart of the moral taxonomies which governed reputation in communities and were the point of reference upon which the law relied when determining actionability in defamation. The political, social, and legal dominance of the upper classes ensured that, as in the past, the moral order was contiguous with the social order. Lord Atkin's statement of legal principle in *Sim v Stretch* reflected the moral taxonomies of the 19th century. Well into the 20th century, 'the right-thinking person' was the heir and standard bearer of the values of Christian tradition and Victorian moralism.

The statement and application of 'the right-thinking person' standard was exemplified in the enduring social and legal attitudes to sex. Few cases illustrate this as well as the 1943 decision in *Garbett*.[43] In this case, it was argued that a publication had implied that the plaintiff photographer was either displaying,

[39] Meyer (n 25 above) 141.

[40] Meyer (n 25 above) 143.

[41] Himmelfarb, *Victorian Minds* (n 25 above) 283, 311. See also G Himmelfarb, *The De-Moralization of Society: from Victorian Virtues to Modern Values* (1995) 30–1; Himmelfarb, *Marriage and Morals Among the Victorians* (n 25 above) 74. However, this should not be taken to suggest a simple uniformity. The intellectual and cultural landscape of Victorian England was complex: H Grisewood (ed), *Ideas and Beliefs of the Victorians: An Historic Revaluation of the Victorian Age* (1949); FML Thompson, *The Rise of Respectable Society: A Social History of Victorian Britain, 1830–1900* (1988).

[42] F Holt, *The Law of Libel* (1812) 35.

[43] *Garbett v Hazell, Watson & Viney Ltd* [1943] 2 All ER 359, CA.

selling, or procuring pornographic pictures. If this imputation had been conveyed (and the court found that it was) then there was no doubt that it would be defamatory and the Court of Appeal had little hesitation in stating its view that such imputations were most egregious.[44] These attitudes also had very real effects as a standard of public morality:

> The immediate result was that [the plaintiff] was shunned by those who knew him. They used to call him by his christian [sic] name and then they changed within a week of the publication and called him 'Smutty'... [He] had carried on a flower shop in previous years [but did no trade] as a result of the libel.[45]

To adopt the phrase used by Goddard LJ, the Court of Appeal saw an imputation of peddling 'this sort of muck' as one of the greatest of moral wrongs that could be imputed to a person.[46] During the course of the 20th century, attitudes to sex were considered in various defamation cases and the insights they yield into the relationships between law and reputation will be addressed in several places below.[47]

To the extent that 'the right-thinking person' represented a moral taxonomy where traditional values constituted the criteria for moral judgment, it was for a long time the cause of little controversy. Traditional and modern values were not essentially divergent, even if they derived their authority from different sources of Christian virtue, Victorian moralism, or modern secular philosophy. For the most part there was no disagreement about whether an imputation would satisfy the test. That is, the values which would be the point of reference were familiar, acknowledged, and agreed upon in jurisdictions. But this was not always to be the case. Modern societies were increasingly characterized by cultural, social, economic, and political complexity and diversity. The values that governed life in communities changed and, accordingly, the moral taxonomies that governed the attribution and evaluation of reputation also changed and diversified. This would present the courts with some difficult choices.

Diverse moral taxonomies are in many respects a distinctly late-modern phenomenon. However, the legal strategies available for the resolution of the problems they raise have developed over the last hundred years or so where on a number of occasions an imputation has arisen which will lower a person's esteem with some people in a jurisdiction, may have no effect on many, and may even raise an individual's standing with others. The next two parts of this chapter look at the legal mechanisms that have been employed to manage these challenges. They can be

[44] Ibid 360 (Scott LJ).
[45] Ibid.
[46] Ibid 361.
[47] See especially the discussion of *Random House Australia Pty Ltd v Costello & Abbott* (1999) 167 ALR 224, FCA in this chapter at II(A); the discussion of *Youssoupoff v Metro-Goldwyn Mayer* (1934) 50 TLR 581, CA, in Chapter 6, II; and the discussion of homosexuality cases in Chapter 8, II.

explored using two lines of inquiry—one quantitative, one qualitative.[48] First, to what extent and how does the legal framework take account of the degree of variation in moral taxonomies in a jurisdiction? Secondly, to what extent and how does the legal framework take account of the substantive content of different moral taxonomies in a jurisdiction? Both questions have prompted different and sometimes inconsistent responses from the courts, and both are of much assistance in understanding how the law navigates the moral taxonomies of reputation in the formulation and application of the principal test. Such an understanding will be essential if the legal framework is to cope with modern liberal claims to rights and equality that are at odds with the moral taxonomies of tradition.

II. Competing Moral Taxonomies in a Jurisdiction

Two approaches have been used to identify the standards that will be applied when determining actionability: the 'general standards' and 'sectional standards' approaches.

A. The general standards approach

The English test uses 'right-thinking persons generally' as the point of reference for determining actionability. This rests on the premises that the jurisdiction constitutes a community and that general standards of opinion exist with respect to criteria for moral judgment in the jurisdiction. The Court of Appeal explained in *Tolley v Fry* that words:

> must tend to disparage [a person] in the eyes of the average sensible citizen. Words are not actionable as defamation, however much they may damage a man in the eyes of a section of the community, unless they also amount to disparagement of his reputation in the eyes of right-thinking men generally.[49]

In Australia, the courts have expressed this test in terms of 'ordinary decent folk in the community, taken in general' and, as the High Court confirmed in *Lamb*, this means actionability:

> depends upon . . . the standards, moral or social, by which they evaluate the imputation they understand to have been made. They are taken to share a moral or social standard by which to judge the defamatory character of that imputation. . . . The defamatory nature of an imputation is ascertained by reference to general community standards, not by reference to sectional attitudes.[50]

[48] The use of qualitative and quantitative to identify the distinction seems to have first appeared in the unattributed piece, 'The Community Segment in Defamation Actions: A Dissenting Essay' (1949) 58 Yale Law Journal 1387.

[49] *Tolley v JS Fry & Sons Ltd* [1930] 1 KB 467, 479 (Greer LJ), CA. *Miller v David* (1874) LR 9 CP 118 is cited in support of this proposition but *Miller* said no such thing.

[50] *Reader's Digest Services Pty Ltd v Lamb* (1982) 150 CLR 500, 506–7 (Brennan J; Gibbs CJ, Stephen and Wilson JJ agreeing).

The court does not explain in any way whether there is a distinction between 'moral' and 'social' standards. The terms are best understood as referring to the criteria for moral judgment.[51]

The use of a general standards approach has had two significant effects. First, courts have had to proceed on the basis that there is a unity of opinion about the defamatory quality of a particular imputation even when this is clearly not the case.[52] Secondly, the general standards approach has carried the content of traditional values into the contemporary common law. Certainly, the common law has been able to accommodate some changes in the criteria for moral judgment in a jurisdiction, accepting that 'public opinion as to what is defamatory changes with the times'.[53] However, the courts have been slow to acknowledge changes in criteria for moral judgment which have resulted from the decline of traditional values as a dominant aspect of life in the jurisdiction. Both of these aspects of the general standards test—a unanimity of opinion and the maintenance of traditional values—are illustrated in *Random House v Costello & Abbott*.[54]

Costello & Abbott was one of Australia's most publicized defamation cases. There were four plaintiffs. Two were Members of the House of Representatives and key figures in the Federal Government that had been in power since 1996. Peter Costello was the Treasurer and Tony Abbott was a Parliamentary Secretary. The other two plaintiffs were their wives. They all complained they had been defamed in a book published by the defendant in 1997 which included the following passage:

> Abbott and Costello . . . they [were] both in the Right Wing of the Labor Party till the one woman fucked both of them and married one of them and inducted them into the Young Liberals.[55]

The trial judge found the book conveyed the following imputations that were defamatory of the plaintiffs:

> Mr Costello's and Mr Abbott's political commitment was so shallow that, in return for sexual favours, they were willing to abandon their principles . . . . [;] Mrs Costello and Mrs Abbott were guilty of unchastity . . . [; and] Mrs Costello and Mrs Abbott, by virtue of having married their husbands, were to be suspected of being people of such low moral

[51] It might be argued that the court intended to draw some distinction between matters of morality and matters of opinion. However, these ultimately come down to criteria for moral judgment: see Chapter 1, IV(B).

[52] Compare, eg, *Murphy & Ors v Plasterers Society & Ors* [1949] SASR 98, Sth Aust SC with *Myroft v Sleight* (1921) 90 LJ(KB) 883 where the courts considered how the community would view people who worked during a strike. For further discussion of *Myroft* see below III(C)(2).

[53] *Cameron v Consolidated Press Ltd* [1940] SR (SA) 372, 377 (Angas Parsons J), Sth Aust SC; *Slazengers Ltd v Gibbs & Co* (1916) 33 TLR 35, 36, Ch.

[54] *Random House Australia Pty Ltd v Costello & Abbott* (1999) 167 ALR 224, FCA.

[55] Ibid 251 (Drummond J). Both women were able to claim because the publication did not make it clear which of them was being referred to.

standards that they were even prepared to use sexual relations to get others to change their political allegiance…[56]

The defendants argued that the imputation of the women's unchastity was incapable of defaming them because ordinary, decent folk in the community, taken in general, would not have thought the less of them for being unchaste. The action was tried without a jury so the determination of law (that the imputation was capable of defaming the plaintiffs) was implicit in the finding of fact that the plaintiff was defamed:

Although…the imputation…only refers to two episodes of premarital sex[,] I have no difficulty in accepting that as an allegation of unchastity…[W]hile to say that society condemns such behaviour is perhaps to put too high a point on it, it would…be regarded, if not with derision or contempt, then, at least, with disappointment…The degree of offence, outrage, derision or contempt will vary. To some persons, it would be highly offensive, even outrageous, that a woman would be guilty of lack of chastity. Others might take the view that such conduct, while not ideal, is fairly commonplace. There would be some, perhaps, who would adopt the slogan, 'if it feels good, do it' and applaud such conduct. However, I have to abide by my view of the attitude, not of persons at either extreme, but of the ordinary reasonable reader generally. Even given the Labor bias likely among readers of the author's works, there is every reason to suppose that such persons would predominantly adhere to what Mr Alfred Doolittle in *My Fair Lady*…described as 'middle class morality'. Those persons would find nothing in the context of the anecdote to take away the view that the 'woman' had behaved immorally, surrendering her chastity not only to her future husband but also to another person.[57]

The entrenched Victorian moralism of 'the right-thinking person' had to be displaced by the defendant. Justice Higgins was not persuaded that it had been.

The defendants appealed. The Federal Court dealt with the matter by finding that the trial judge had understood the libel of 'unchastity' as being not simply a lack of chastity arising from 'an inference of pre-marital sex', but allegations of the 'much grosser sexual misconduct' of 'manipulative use of sexual favours' that constituted 'loose or shameless sexual conduct'.[58] On this basis, it was held that Higgins J had correctly decided the imputation was capable of defaming the plaintiffs. This strategy enabled the appellate court to avoid deciding whether the ordinary, decent folk of the Australian Capital Territory, taken in general, would have thought the less of a woman for engaging in pre-marital sex. However, given their reliance on the manipulation imputation, it might be inferred that the court

[56] Ibid 229 (Beaumont J), referring to the trial judgment in the Supreme Court of the Australian Capital Territory in *Costello & Abbott v Random House Australia Pty Ltd* [1999] ACTSC 13, [29]–[59].

[57] *Costello & Abbott v Random House Australia Pty Ltd* [1999] ACTSC 13, [49], [100], [103]–[105] (Higgins J); cited in *Random House Australia Pty Ltd v Costello & Abbott* (1999) 167 ALR 224, 236–7 (Beaumont J), FCA.

[58] *Random House Australia Pty Ltd v Costello & Abbott* (1999) 167 ALR 224, 257–8 (Drummond J); 237 (Beaumont J), FCA.

would have been reluctant to find that a simple imputation of pre-marital sex was capable of being defamatory. It seems they thought so few people would think the less of the plaintiffs for such behaviour that it could not be said those were the views of the community generally.

The issues were therefore ultimately resolved on the basis that opinions had changed markedly with respect to some aspects of women's sexual activity; the community generally used to think one thing, and now it generally thought differently. The problem at trial and on appeal is that the reasoning must posit the existence of 'general' views on the issues. The sharper and more apparent the diversity of opinions in a jurisdiction, the less satisfactory that reasoning will be: the general standards approach cannot sensibly accommodate opinions which are so diverse that it is inappropriate to say that there are 'general' attitudes about criteria for moral judgment in the jurisdiction. The sectional standards approach is better able to acknowledge and accommodate the existence of diverse moral taxonomies in a jurisdiction.

B. The sectional standards approach

The most significant instance of a divisive issue was addressed by the New South Wales Court of Appeal in *Hepburn v TCN Channel Nine* where it had been alleged, among other things, that the plaintiff doctor was 'an abortionist'.[59] It was held that an imputation that the plaintiff had performed lawful abortions could be capable of defaming her, though the reasoning departed significantly from the general standards test prescribed by the High Court in *Lamb*. Remarkably, nowhere in the decision is there a reference to the *Lamb* case.

Justice Hutley (with whom Priestley JA agreed on this point) found it a 'startling' proposition that the imputation could not be defamatory.[60] He did not advert to the general standards test for actionability, but stated simply that:

> As any abortion is regarded as wicked by a substantial part of the population on moral grounds, to say of a person that he is an abortionist may bring him into hatred, ridicule or contempt of ordinary, reasonable people.[61]

The effect of this was that Hutley JA applied a sectional standards test. This is clear enough from the use of 'substantial' as the benchmark in the judgment. Justice Glass endeavoured to explain the reasoning more carefully. He began by identifying 'the existence in the community of a deep factional divide on the issue of abortion' and observed that the imputation a doctor had performed lawful abortions 'would excite both approbation and disapprobation in different sections of the community the difference of opinion'.[62] Given this division, he asks, 'How

[59] *Hepburn v TCN Channel Nine Pty Ltd* [1983] 2 NSWLR 682, NSW CA.
[60] Ibid 686 (Hutley JA), 695 (Priestley JA).
[61] Ibid 686 (Hutley JA).
[62] Ibid 693 (Glass JA).

does the law of defamation accommodate these discrepant social attitudes?'[63] He finds different strands of authority:

There is a body of English authority which suggests that the standard of opinion is that of 'right-thinking people generally'. The corollary to this proposition was that an imputation of conduct which disparaged the plaintiff only in the eyes of a limited class was not defamatory.[64] In the United States, on the other hand, an imputation can be defamatory if it injures a man in the eyes of 'a considerable and respectable class in the community' though it only be a minority ...[65]

In Australia, he does not see that there is 'any binding pronouncement of the High Court' and draws a tenuous link between the question at hand and *Slayter v Daily Telegraph* where he says that:

Griffith CJ disapproved of the use of the term 'right thinking' unless it were to be equated with a reader of fair average intelligence. I take this to be a rejection of the notion that a moral consensus exists upon what constitutes creditable or discreditable behaviour.[66]

This is an inappropriate reading of *Slayter*; that case was concerned with the conveying of imputations and should be interpreted in that light.[67] Nevertheless, given his view of *Slayter*, Glass JA then states that the law as he sees it:

requires that regard should be paid to actual community attitudes, right or wrong... I would hold that it is proper for the law of defamation to recognize that there are many subjects in a pluralist society upon which contradictory attitudes exist...and that it would be futile for the judges to arbitrate between them...Consistency in my view requires that a man can justly complain that words, which lower him in the estimation of an appreciable and reputable section of the community, were published to members of it, even though those same words might exalt him to the level of a hero in other quarters.[68]

The court effectively adopted the American approach. As expressed in the *Second Restatement of Torts*, a statement is defamatory if it would tend to prejudice the plaintiff 'in the eyes of a substantial and respectable minority'.[69] Using 'sectional

[63] Ibid.

[64] Justice Glass's statement in this sentence is correct, but he cites as authority for this proposition the cases of *Byrne v Deane* [1937] 1 KB 818,CA, *Myroft v Sleight* (1921) 90 LJ(KB) 883, and *Clay v Roberts* (1863) 8 Law Times (NS) 397, Exch. The first two are not authority for that proposition; as discussed below, they are concerned with the qualitative element of the test, not the quantitative aspect that Glass JA is discussing. *Clay* is more appropriate authority—it is at least consistent with the statement.

[65] *Hepburn v TCN Channel Nine Pty Ltd* [1983] 2 NSWLR 682, 693 (Glass JA), NSW CA, cases and citations omitted.

[66] Ibid.

[67] See above n 15ff and accompanying text. It might be argued that the breadth of readers who have 'fair average intelligence' will no doubt display a diversity of moral views, but it stretches the judgment in *Slayter* too far to suggest the case could be authority for that proposition.

[68] *Hepburn v TCN Channel Nine Pty Ltd* [1983] 2 NSWLR 682, 693–4 (Glass JA), NSW CA. In the first sentence of this extracted quote, Glass JA is summarizing the position taken by G Fricke, 'The Criterion of Defamation' (1958) 32 Australian Law Journal 7.

[69] *Second Restatement of the Law of Torts*, § 559.

attitudes' as the moral benchmark allows a broader range of matters to be actionable because it does not require that the words tend to lower the plaintiff in the estimation of people generally. It merely requires that the imputation has a tendency to expose the plaintiff to the opprobrium of a certain portion of people in the jurisdiction.

C. Adopting a sectional standards test

The decision in *Hepburn* was appropriate. Sectional standards are a more realistic way to consider the defamatory quality of a statement because they allow the law to recognize the diversity of moral taxonomies in a jurisdiction. The general standard of *Readers' Digest v Lamb* should be reconsidered by Australian courts, especially given the cultural diversity that characterizes Australian society and many local communities.

A reconsideration of the general standards approach may seem on its face to be something of an upheaval in Australian law, but it might well be argued that it is not a radical step. Certainly, it is possible to argue that *Lamb* does not set a precedent that precludes it in all situations. The High Court stated in *Lamb* that 'the defamatory nature of an imputation is ascertained by reference to general community standards, not by reference to sectional attitudes'.[70] However, the statement of law was made by way of dismissing the relevance of 'the attitude of particular groups of (*sic*) classes'—in that case, journalists—rather than widespread differences within the jurisdiction at large.[71] Though *Lamb* was not mentioned in *Hepburn*, it seems that it must be on this basis that Glass JA in *Hepburn* appropriately found that there was no 'binding pronouncement of the High Court' and the court was free to apply a sectional standards analysis where there was a difference of opinion between 'appreciable' sections of the community.[72] Alternatively, it could have been argued that *Lamb* dealt with an issue related to honesty (an issue on which it was tenable to claim that the 'community generally' shared a view). On this approach, it could be argued *Lamb* would not be applicable in *Hepburn* because it was impossible to say that there was a general view on abortion in the community. On either line of argument, there is room to adopt a sectional standards approach in the law where opinion is divided more or less evenly. Where a minority view is not widely held then the adoption of a sectional standards approach would require a significant change in the common law. With the exception of *Hepburn*, there are no Australian or English decisions that I have been able to locate that apply a sectional standards approach. The English Court of Appeal noted in 2001 that the question 'may need to be addressed at some stage in the future' because contemporary social diversity means that 'the

[70] *Reader's Digest Services Pty Ltd v Lamb* (1982) 150 CLR 500, 506–7 (Brennan J).

[71] Ibid. Note that the phrasing seems slightly odd; it should have perhaps been intended to read 'or classes' rather than 'of classes'.

[72] *Hepburn v TCN Channel Nine Pty Ltd* [1983] 2 NSWLR 682, 694 (Glass JA), NSW CA.

reputation of a person within his own racial or religious community may be damaged by a statement which would not be regarded as damaging by society at large'.[73] The United States law provides a working example of the sectional standards approach in operation, but it would be a big leap for Australian law if applied in circumstances where a view was held by only a small group of people.

It is appropriate for a moment to consider the lower quantitative threshold of the sectional standards test. The terms 'substantial' or 'appreciable' suggest that some views might be so *insubstantial* that they do not warrant recognition. Generally, this has not been in issue in the cases and it is not clear what will constitute such an insubstantial minority that an imputation will not be actionable.[74] It would seem, however, that a group could be numerically small but still 'substantial' for the purposes of the test. It is not impossible to envision a group of several hundred people living communally with, for instance, ultra-strict and uncommon Christian-based religious beliefs where a member might claim to have been defamed by a statement that they had breached an ethical norm of the group that is not at all common to the wider society. For instance, if the group believed that one should read the bible every day of the week then a member might claim to have been defamed by a statement that she had not read from the bible every day of the previous week. The damage to reputation would not necessarily be trivial, and the essence of Christian morality is well accepted by the law. This could be a substantial imposition on freedom of speech and it may be appropriate to reconsider the defences available to a publisher to alleviate the more expansive reach of actionable defamation, but if the law is to protect reputation in a liberal jurisdiction then such a publication should be actionable. However, the quantitative threshold of actionability is not usually an issue even in jurisdictions where the sectional standards test applies.

The acceptance of sectional attitudes in the jurisdiction would at the very least be a recognition of the fact that diverse moral taxonomies are present in contemporary societies. However, this does not require that the views of all groups in a jurisdiction must be equally acknowledged by the law. There must be limits—and they are addressed through the qualitative dimension of the principal test.

[73] *Arab News Network & Soumar Al Assad v Jihad al Khazen and Al Hayat Publications Pty Ltd* [2001] EWCA Civ 118; [2001] EWCA Civ 1229, [30] (Keene LJ; Chadwick and Peter Gibson LJJ agreeing).

[74] The issue was flagged in the unattributed note, 'With How Many People Must a Writing have a Tendency to Disgrace the Plaintiff to be Actionable' (1909) 58 University of Pennsylvania Law Review 44. The only relevant case seems to be *Fairley v Peekskill Star Corporation* 83 A 2d 294 (NY SC App Div, 1981) where the court rejected the plaintiff's claim that he had been defamed by a statement that he was 'a social scientist'. It was held that 'the peculiarities of taste found in eccentric groups' could not be the relevant point of reference, even if 'among certain segments of the population a social scientist designation might be considered unflattering'. WP Keeton *et al*, *Prosser and Keeton on the Law of Torts* (5th edn, 1984) 778 note 92, cite *Galveston Tribune v Guisti* 134 SW 239 and *Guisti v Galveston Tribune* 150 SW 874 (Texas, 1912) as relevant to the issue of a group 'so small as to be negligible' but that is inappropriate as discussion in the cases turned on what imputations were conveyed.

D. The qualitative question

In *Hepburn*, Glass JA stated that in determining actionability the law should and will pay regard to 'community attitudes, right or wrong'.[75] This was incorrect. This is not at all what the law does. Under both the general and sectional standards approaches, the principal test for what is defamatory has a vitally important qualitative element. In the Anglo-Australian formulation, it is the 'right-thinking' or 'decent' members of the community that indicate the presence of qualitative limits. The American sectional standards test is referable not merely to a substantial section of the community (or an 'appreciable' section, as Glass JA put it), but also requires that that section be 'respectable' (or 'reputable'). The inevitability of a qualitative limit was neatly stated by Hand J in *Grant v Readers' Digest*. Accepting that the law was clear that the 'right-thinking' benchmark meant that some views would be excluded from consideration, he held that 'it is fairly plain that there must come a point where that is true'.[76]

Whatever label is applied—'right-thinking', 'decent', 'respectable', or 'reputable'—the language of the test clearly suggests there is a moral benchmark that means some views will not be taken into account when determining actionability because they are qualitatively unacceptable to the court. This aspect of the law requires close consideration.

III. The Ethical Recognition of Criteria for Moral Judgment

Whenever a question of actionability is decided the courts use 'the right-thinking person' to apply certain views and values as moral benchmarks, recognizing them as proper considerations in assessing whether harm to reputation should be actionable. Mostly, the issue of ethical recognition (as I will call it) is uncontentious and uncontested. That is, there is usually no disagreement about whether an imputation would affect the esteem in which a plaintiff is held by at least a substantial segment of the jurisdiction, and no disagreement that the court should recognize the tendency to lower the plaintiff's standing by finding the words to be actionable as defamation. Sometimes, however, recognition is contested. A defendant will argue that even though the plaintiff's standing may be affected among some people, the court should find the words not to be actionable because the imputation would not tend to make right-thinking or decent or respectable folk in the community think the less of the plaintiff. This section of the chapter examines how ethical recognition operates in the law. To do so, it turns to the 'informing' cases where plaintiffs have sued for imputations that they have provided state authorities with information about crimes and criminals. It is in

[75] *Hepburn v TCN Channel Nine Pty Ltd* [1983] 2 NSWLR 682, 694, NSW CA.
[76] *Grant v Readers Digest Association Inc* 151 F 2d 733, 735 (2nd Cir, 1945).

these cases that the principles and processes of ethical recognition have been most clearly established and implemented.

A. The limiting function of ethical recognition

Ethical recognition is a process by which criteria for moral judgment are judicially approved as appropriate considerations in the determination of actionability. It establishes and uses moral boundaries to mark out how and to what extent reputation will be protected by the law. A court's refusal to recognize a criterion for moral judgment has limited the extent to which reputation is protected by the law.

Because reputation is a concept founded in community, ethical recognition also has inclusionary and exclusionary functions. The refusal of recognition has an exclusionary function with respect to the constitution of the jurisdiction as a moral community: where the court refuses to recognize certain values as legitimate and acceptable considerations to take into account when determining the actionability of words, it is relying on and giving shape to a vision of the jurisdiction as a moral community that excludes those who hold the values in question. Conversely, the acknowledgement of values through the act of recognition serves to *include* those people in the moral community that is the jurisdiction.

Because ethical recognition is largely uncontentious, it generally goes unnoticed. When recognition has been refused and the legal protection of reputation limited then the operation of the principles is exposed. The informing cases can be used to explore how the courts have both recognized and refused to recognize criteria for moral judgment. The refusal of recognition is addressed first (in section B) because the issues are at their clearest in those circumstances. Section C will then look at how the ethical status of informing has on some occasions been seen as warranting recognition in the common law. Before proceeding to these matters it is necessary to clarify the legal position in the United States.

It has been suggested by Prosser and Keeton that 'the right-thinking person' does not occupy a place in American defamation law:

> It has sometimes been said that these must be 'right-thinking people'; but this seems clearly wrong, since the court cannot be called upon to make a definitive pronouncement upon whether the views of different segments of the community are right or wrong, sound, or morally justifiable.[77]

This claim is incorrect. There may not be a *definitive* pronouncement, if by this they mean a final pronouncement which cannot change, but the determination of actionability in the US courts clearly requires a judicial statement about the acceptability and respectability of criteria for moral judgment. The *Second Restatement of Torts* states the test: a statement is defamatory if it would tend to

[77] Keeton *et al* (n 74 above) 777.

prejudice the plaintiff 'in the eyes of a substantial and respectable minority'.[78] The criterion of respectability is further clarified in the *Restatement*:

> The fact that a communication tends to prejudice another in the eyes of even a substantial group is not enough if the group is one whose standards are so anti-social that it is not proper for the courts to recognise them.[79]

It is not the case, as Prosser and Keeton argue, that the United States courts do not use the standard of 'right-thinking people'. Rather, it is that they do not use the standard of right-thinking people *generally* which ostensibly applies in Australia and England. But it is quite clear that there is a threshold point at which some views will not be recognized by the courts as respectable or decent and such views will not provide the benchmark against which an evaluation of reputation can be made.

The claim that American determinations do not rely on processes of ethical recognition might be thought to obtain some support from decisions regarding imputations that a person holds an objectionable political belief. The numerous cases where a person has successfully sued over an imputation that they are a communist have been particularly important.[80] However, these decisions need to be read carefully.

Grant v Reader's Digest is the leading decision.[81] As noted above, Hand J made it clear that there was a point where views and values would be refused recognition on the grounds that they were ethically unacceptable. However, he held this did not apply to the case at hand where the plaintiff complained he had been defamed by an allegation he was associated with the Communist Party.

> We do not believe... that we need say whether 'right-thinking' people would harbor [feelings of scorn, aversion or hostility] toward a lawyer, because he had been an agent for the Communist Party, or was a sympathizer with its aims and means. It is enough if there be some, as there certainly are, who would feel so, even though they would be 'wrong thinking' people if they did.[82]

[78] *Second Restatement of the Law of Torts*, § 559.

[79] Ibid.

[80] *Levy v Gelber* 25 NYS 2d 148 (NY, 1941); *Boudin v Tishman* 35 NYS 2d 760 (NY SC App Div, 1942); *Grant v Readers Digest Association Inc* 151 F 2d 733 at 735 (2nd Cir, 1945); *Mencher v Chesley* 63 NYS 2d 108 (NY SC App Div, 1946); *Mencher v Chesley* 75 NE 2d 257 (NY, 1947); *Herrmann v Newark Morning Ledger* 138 A 2d 61 (NJ, 1958); *Herrmann v Newark Morning Ledger* 110 A 2d 529 (NJ SC App, 1958). Cf *Garriga v Richfield* 20 NYS 2d 544 (NY, 1940) where the plaintiff was unsuccessful.

[81] *Grant v Readers Digest Association Inc* 151 F 2d 733 (2nd Cir, 1945). Of the previous decisions, *Garriga v Richfield* 20 NYS 2d 544 (NY, 1940), stands alone in holding that even though such an imputation may well cause the plaintiff to be lowered in the estimation of others, it was nonetheless incapable of defaming a plaintiff. Finding that it could not be defamatory to identify a person as a member of any political party, the reasoning of Pecora J turned principally on the importance of freedom of political speech and association in a democracy. This was soon ignored and the issue became one that was concerned merely with the estimation in which a person was held: see *Levy v Gelber* 25 NYS 2d 148 (NY, 1941); *Boudin v Tishman* 35 NYS 2d 760 (NY SC App Div, 1942).

[82] *Grant v Readers Digest Association Inc* 151 F 2d 733, 735 (2nd Cir, 1945).

The proposition that the views of 'wrong-thinking' people should be recognized seems on its face to be inconsistent with the claim that views may be excluded on ethical grounds. However, 'wrong-thinking' in this instance is better seen as merely meaning that the views in question may not be widely accepted—they may even be illogical or irrational—but they are *not* views that (to use terminology that would became familiar soon after *Grant* was decided) are so anti-social that the court should not recognize them. Unfortunately, the United States courts did not see this clearly.

The decision of the Superior Court of New Jersey in *Hermann v Newark Morning Ledger* provides a good example of the United States courts' approach: even though 'right-thinking' views are said not to be the benchmark, the cases still allow for views to be excluded on ethical grounds. In *Hermann*, the court held that American law:

> is not concerned, within broad limits, with whether the segment of the public which thinks odiously of the plaintiff... is 'right-thinking'. It is sufficient that it be 'substantial' and 'respectable'... As stated by Prosser, 'The American courts have taken a more realistic view, recognizing that the plaintiff may suffer real damage if he is lowered in the esteem of any substantial and respectable group, even though it be a minority one, with ideas that are not necessarily reasonable'... We must take public opinion and mental reactions as we find them in living society, not as one might visualize them in a Utopia. For this purpose, 'society is to be taken as it is, with its recognized prejudices, without determining whether they are well-founded in reason or justice'.[83]

However, this does not fully explain the court's view. The position taken is that:

> public views and reactions may not be soundly founded in aseptic logic and may be charged by current high feeling in respect to the threat of Communism [but that] cannot justify the court in disregarding them as 'evil-minded' or 'clearly anti-social'...'[84]

The last passage is of critical importance: the reasoning in *Hermann*, like that in *Grant*, contemplates an ethical limit to actionability. It is simply that the limit does not arise on the facts in *Hermann*. Robert Cardon got it wrong when he summarized the approach of the New York courts in a similar case.[85] Cardon said that actionability 'seem[s] to depend on how strong a sentiment exists, *rightly or wrongly*, in the community at the time the charge is made'.[86] This is incorrect: it *does* matter to the courts whether the views are 'right' or 'wrong'.

The political belief cases do not suggest that processes of ethical recognition are irrelevant in American law. At most they indicate a willingness to acknowledge different opinions exist in communities and a reluctance to deny recovery on the

[83] *Herrmann v Newark Morning Ledger* 110 A 2d 529, 531–2 (NJ SC App, 1958), in part citing *Van Wiginton v Pulitzer Publishing Co* 218 F 795, 796 (1914).
[84] *Herrmann v Newark Morning Ledger* 110 A 2d 529, 532 (NJ SC App, 1958).
[85] RL Cardon, 'Libel and Slander—Charge of Communism as Libel' (1947) 45 Michigan Law Review 518 discussing *Mencher v Chesley* 75 NE 2d 257 (NY, 1947).
[86] Ibid 518, emphasis added.

grounds that views are irrational or perhaps arise from some prejudices.[87] As the informing cases will show, ethical recognition is very much a part of the American legal framework.

B. The refusal of recognition in the informing cases

The informing cases have been a regular feature of defamation actions in several jurisdictions and a number of reported cases address the issue. Surprisingly, there has been little scholarly analysis of the decisions. A short but insightful piece by Graham Fricke in the *Australian Law Journal* in 1958 and a more substantial discussion of the case law by Daniel More in 1988 are the only works of note.[88] These will be helpful but it is the cases that provide the relevant raw material. The leading informing cases are *Byrne v Deane* in England and *Connelly v McKay* in the United States.[89] The decisions can be outlined briefly.

The appellant defendants in *Byrne* were the proprietors of a golf club where police confiscated two gambling machines. Just how the police became aware of the machines was never established but the following day a brief doggerel 'poem' was placed on the wall where the machines had stood. The defendants did not place the poem there but they were aware of it and let it remain there. The plaintiff, Edmund Byrne, was a member of the club. Byrne claimed that the poem imputed that he:

> had reported to the police the presence of the said machines upon the said premises, that he was guilty of underhand disloyalty to the defendants and his fellow members of the said club and that by reason of the said facts his conduct was deserving of the gravest censure, that he was a person devoid of all true sporting spirit, and further that he was a person unfit for other members of the club to associate with and should be ostracised by them.[90]

The defendants argued it could not be defamatory to call a person an informer because right-thinking members of society generally would not think the less of a person for such behaviour.[91] In addition, they relied on *Mawe v Pigott* where it had been said in 1869 that the imputation was not actionable.[92] The plaintiff's

[87] At the opposite end of the spectrum, it has been argued that it is defamatory to say of a person that they hold extreme right-wing political views. Although it was held not to be defamatory in *Washburn v Wright* 261 Cal App 2d 789 (Cal Ct App, 1968), the decision is unhelpful because the law was not approached correctly.

[88] Fricke (n 68 above); D More, 'Informers Defamation and Public Policy' (1989) 19 Georgia Journal of International and Comparative Law 503.

[89] *Byrne v Deane* [1937] 1 KB 818, CA; *Connelly v McKay* 28 NYS 2d 327 (NY SC, 1941).

[90] *Byrne v Deane* [1937] 1 KB 818, 832 (Slesser LJ).

[91] Ibid 827 in argument citing *Sim v Stretch* [1936] 2 All ER 1237, 1240, HL as authority. This position was consistent, they claimed, with the principles stated in *Myroft v Sleight* (1921) 90 LJ(KB) 883 where 'ordinary, just and reasonable citizens' were the benchmark.

[92] *Byrne v Deane* [1937] 1 KB 818, 822–3 in argument citing *Mawe v Pigott* (1869) 4 Ir R (CL) 54, 62, CP.

reply was that 'the sting of the libel... is that it alleges that the plaintiff has been disloyal to the fellow members of the club'.[93] The plaintiff also relied on two 19th century Scottish cases where informing imputations were held to be actionable.[94] The Court of Appeal held for the defendants, finding that the material published was not capable of defaming the plaintiff.

In the United States, *Connelly v McKay* was decided in the Supreme Court of New York in 1941.[95] Connelly operated a service station and motel. His main clients were interstate truck drivers. He alleged that McKay had defamed him and caused him to lose business. Connelly claimed that McKay had told drivers that he (Connelly) had passed information to the regulatory body about drivers who were violating rules regarding the number of hours worked continuously without rest.[96] It was held by Deyo J that the words allegedly spoken 'cannot under any circumstances be held defamatory' because they do not suggest reprehensible behaviour that would degrade the plaintiff's character.[97] Judge Deyo held that it could not be actionable to allege a person had done 'an act both legal and praiseworthy', even if it caused loss to the plaintiff.[98]

The main rationale behind both decisions concerns the ethical status of the values that would see a person's reputation damaged by an imputation of informing. There has also in some cases been a supplementary policy dimension underpinning the finding that the imputation is not actionable. This has been framed around reasons of state security. These can be considered in turn.

1. *The positive ethical status of informing*

In making a determination about actionability the court in *Byrne v Deane* relied on what they saw as the standards of 'the right-thinking person'. Lord Justice Slesser, for example, held that:

> [T]o say or allege of a man... that he has reported certain acts, wrongful in law, to the police, cannot possibly be said to be defamatory of him in the minds of the general public.
>
> We have to consider in this connection the *arbitrium boni*, the view which would be taken by the ordinary good and worthy subject of the King, and I have assigned to myself no other criterion than what a good and worthy subject of the King would think of some person of whom it had been said that he had put the law into motion against wrongdoers, in considering that such a good and worthy subject would not consider such an allegation in itself to be defamatory.[99]

[93] *Byrne v Deane* [1937] 1 KB 818, 825 in argument.
[94] *Graham v Roy* (1851) 13 Session Cases 634; *Winn v Quillan* [1899] 2 Session Cases 322. The report of the argument does not show the plaintiff made submissions as to the correctness or otherwise of the 'right-thinking' standard argued by the appellants.
[95] *Connelly v McKay* 28 NYS 2d 327 (NY SC, 1941).
[96] Ibid 328.
[97] Ibid 329, drawing in part on *Terwilliger v Wands* 17 NY 54 (NY, 1858).
[98] *Connelly v McKay* 28 NYS 2d 327, 329–0 (NY SC, 1941), citing *Hallock v Miller* 2 Barb 630 (1848).
[99] *Byrne v Deane* [1937] 1 KB 818, 832–3 (Slesser LJ).

Lord Justice Slesser disposes of the early Scots cases by declaring them to be illogical; one simply cannot be defamed with an allegation that they are promoting the interest of the law.[100] 'The right-thinking person' as the appropriate standard permeates the majority judgments. The reasoning does not allow for any suggestion that one could be a good and worthy subject of the King and still think the less of a person for being an informer. The possibility that the appropriate standard may be that of public opinion regardless of 'rightness' is not entertained at any point in the case.

Fricke argues that Slesser LJ uses the entire general public as his benchmark and wrongly attributes to it a general approval of informers.[101] This is not a convincing interpretation of the judgment. The 'reality' of the plaintiff's unpopularity is barely acknowledged by the court. Moreover, if that was Slesser's approach then it implies the decision would have been different if it could have been said that the public generally *disapproved* of informers. That was never going to be the outcome. It is quite clear from the judgment that even if Slesser LJ thought that the community disapproved of informers, he would not have recognized such a view as an appropriate basis for determining actionability. This much is clear from the reference to 'good and worthy subjects of the King' and the court's reliance on *Mawe v Pigott*.[102]

The defendant in *Mawe v Pigott* had claimed that the plaintiff, a priest named Mawe, had stated that he (Mawe) would watch men who fought for 'the cause of Ireland' and would inform the authorities of their illegal behaviour so that they would be prosecuted. The plaintiff denied he had made any such statement and sued for libel. Finding for the defendant, the court stated its reasoning:

> [The plaintiff] argued that amongst certain classes who were either themselves criminal, or who sympathized with crime, it would expose a person to great odium to represent him as an informer or a prosecutor, or otherwise aiding in the detection of crime; that is quite true, but we cannot be called upon to adopt that standard. The very circumstances which will make a person be regarded with disfavour by the criminal classes will raise his character in the estimation of right-thinking men. We can only regard the estimation in which a man is held by society generally...[103]

The judgment discloses both quantitative and ethical dimensions to the refusal to recognize certain values and views. The quantitative element lies in the court's designation of the criminal classes as distinguishable from 'society generally' and, thus, as a minority. But this was not the reason why the particular views would

[100] Ibid 833–4 (Slesser LJ). He notes also that being an informer is 'protected by the law and recognised, and in certain cases [is] productive of reward': 834. There is some irony in this as the motivation of reward was among the reasons why the Scots courts found the imputation *was* actionable: *Graham v Roy* (1851) 13 Session Cases 634; *Winn v Quillan* [1899] 2 Session Cases 322.

[101] Fricke (n 88 above) 12.

[102] *Byrne v Deane* [1937] 1 KB 818, 822–3 in argument, 833 (Slesser LJ); *Mawe v Pigott* (1869) 4 Ir R (CL) 54, CP.

[103] *Mawe v Pigott* (1869) 4 Ir R (CL) 54, 62, CP.

not be recognized.[104] The ethical dimension of the reasoning is its *sine qua non* because the court defines the criminal classes as the opposite of right-thinking, and it is *that*—rather than the number of people in the class—which makes them distinguishable from the 'right-thinking members of society generally' who constitute the benchmark for judging actionability.

The principles in *Byrne* have been applied in this way to informing cases in South Africa and Australia.[105] There was one additional issue that arose solely in *Byrne*: should it matter how serious the alleged criminal offence was? It was suggested this may be relevant because right-thinking members of society generally are inclined to think differently about informers depending on what crime is at issue. That is, it was suggested that the courts should recognize moral taxonomies under which a person's reputation would be diminished if they informed the police about a minor crime. Neither Slesser LJ nor Greene LJ was prepared to draw a distinction between informing the authorities about serious and trivial crimes; the imputation would simply be incapable of defaming a person.[106]

The reasoning in the American cases has proceeded a little differently but the ethical status of the criteria for judgment has been similarly important. The court in *Connelly* accepted that a substantial segment of the community views informers unfavourably but refused to recognize those views and values on the grounds of their unacceptable ethical status:

> It is true that informers are not always held in too high esteem, and violators of the law might have good cause to shun one who engaged in such practice, but, nevertheless, such acts cannot constitute a foundation upon which to build an action for slander. 'The fact that a communication tends to prejudice another in the eyes of even a substantial group is not enough if the group is one whose standards are so anti-social that it is not proper for the courts to recognise them.'[107]

The court thus accepts that there are enough 'violators of the law' that they form a substantial group and would satisfy the quantitative dimensions of the test for actionability. The refusal of recognition is clearly founded in the 'respectable' arm of the test and, as such, it is clearly a refusal of ethical recognition. *Connelly* has been applied at regular intervals and there has been no divergence from it.[108] This includes circumstances where the imputation of informing has been made against prisoners who, as a consequence, have found themselves at particular risk of harm.[109]

[104] Cf Fricke (n 88 above) 9.

[105] *Prinsloo v SA Associated Newspapers Ltd* [1959] 2 South African LR 693, 695; *Blair v Mirror Newspapers Ltd* [1970] 2 NSWLR 604, 6067, NSW CA.

[106] *Byrne v Deane* [1937] 1 KB 818, 834 (Greene LJ), 843 (Slesser LJ).

[107] *Connelly v McKay* 28 NYS 2d 327, 329 (NY SC, 1941), quoting the first *Restatement of the Law of Torts*, § 559.

[108] *Rose v Borenstein* 119 NYS 2d 288 (NY City Ct, 1953); *Danais v Fakis* 261 A 2d 529 (Del, 1969); *Agnant v Shakur & Ors* 30 F Supp 2d 420 (US Dist Ct, 1998).

[109] *Saunders v Board of Directors, WHYY-TV (Channel 12)* 382 A 2d 257 (Del, 1978); *Burrascano v Levi* 452 F Supp 1066 (Dist Md, 1978).

To sum up, the leading cases leave no doubt that processes of ethical recognition are integral to determinations of what is actionable. The right-thinking (or respectable) person is the conceptual tool the law uses to recognize or refuse to recognize values in determining actionability. There may be some room in the reasoning to allow for degrees of distinction in informing imputations, based on the crimes concerned, but as it stands at present, the courts refuse to recognize any values that hold informers in poor esteem regardless of the quantity of people who may see informing as behaviour relevant to forming a negative moral judgment about a person.

2. *The place of public policy considerations*

There is a second strand of reasoning in *Connelly* that is not present in *Byrne*: *Connelly* has a public policy element. It is not clearly distinguished or separated from the ethical status question but follows immediately on from the ethical status rationale as Deyo J continues in the same paragraph:

> To hold otherwise would be contrary to the public interest, in that it would penalise the law-abiding citizen and give comfort to the law violator. It would impede law enforcement for the benefit of the anti-social.[110]

This aspect of the reasoning turns on the hindering of law enforcement which would arise if it were defamatory to say that a person has informed the authorities of a crime. This is quite clearly grounded in public policy concerns. It is distinct from the moral rightness or wrongness of informing the authorities that an illegal activity has occurred. This has implications of interest. It means that a court could hold that there has been damage to reputation that is deserving of ethical recognition *but* actionability will be denied for policy reasons. In *Connelly*, however, this is not what happened. The limitation on the legal protection of reputation occurred because the court refused on ethical grounds to recognize elements of a moral taxonomy.

The policy issues have been most effectively explored by the Supreme Court of Israel in the 1976 case of *Shaha v Dardiryan*.[111] *Shaha* has only been reported in Hebrew but has been addressed in English by Daniel More and the following relies on his discussion.[112] The case concerned an allegation that a Jordanian cleric had informed and collaborated with Israeli authorities. News reports from the region continue to bear out More's observation that collaborators are at risk of being killed: 'Like dozens of suspected collaborators, Mohammed Darigme... was dragged into the main square of his village by armed militants, and then machine-gunned to

[110] *Connelly v McKay* 28 NYS 2d 327, 329 (NY SC, 1941). In *Burrascano v Levi* 452 F Supp 1066, 1072–3 (Dist Md, 1978), the reasoning followed *Connelly* quite closely, picking up both the ethical exclusion and the public policy strands behind that decision. *Burrascano* was affirmed by the US Court of Appeals though no opinion was published: *Burrascano v US Attorney General* 612 F 2d 1306 (5th Cir, 1979).

[111] *Shaha v Dardiryan* ca 466/83, PD 39 (4) 734 (1985), Israel SC.

[112] More (n 88 above).

death.'[113] It may be that the importance of the political circumstances prompted a more careful analysis than has occurred in other cases.

At trial, the District Court of Jerusalem applied the general standards test and held that the imputation was incapable of being defamatory because the norms that prevailed in Israel would be the relevant benchmark, and there could be no recognition of 'those who oppose these norms and even deny the right of that community to exist'.[114] The Supreme Court of Israel unanimously held that the imputation was incapable of being defamatory. Justice Levin effectively adopted a general standards approach, while Elton and Ben-Porath JJ both held that the test is a sectional standards one.[115]

The nuances of the decision lie in the use of policy. Justice Levin took a similar path to the Court of Appeal in *Byrne v Deane*, finding that 'every reasonable person' would see collaboration in pursuit of the rule of law and security as commendable, and did so on the grounds that:

> As a matter of judicial policy, it is impossible and inconceivable that an Israeli court will determine that a collaboration with the government of Israel and its policy is an activity that should be regarded, under certain circumstances, as defaming the collaborator... A person who collaborates with the government of Israel for the realisation of these goals [of law and order, respect for life, and security] or enjoys its protection for that reason will not be regarded as doing something wrong just because his activities are regarded disfavorably by the enemies of the State who disagree with its policy in the occupied territories and with its right to rule and operate there.[116]

In this, Levin J identifies the valuing of the state and its security as one of the ethical rules that bind the people of Israel into a community. This represents a blend of public policy and ethical status rationales. Arguably, it makes explicit what was implicit in the reasoning in *Byrne*: the state is the embodiment of the moral good. The values of people who would undermine it should not be recognized by the courts. Unfortunately, this resolves very little in the end. It does not consider, for example, the possibility that there might be degrees of dissent and protest which are founded in discontent and there may be a wide range of opinion about whether one does or should think the less of a person for engaging in such practices. One is ultimately left, again, with ethical choices to make.

A less expansive position was taken by Ben-Porath J in *Shaha*. She was willing to accept that the sectional standards principle meant that an allegation of collaboration could be actionable, but policy reasons meant that it would only be actionable where the plaintiff was a citizen of both Israel and a friendly foreign state, and had collaborated with Israeli authorities to the detriment of the foreign

[113] 'Abbas Hands Over Fate of Death Row Prisoners to Grand Mufti', *AM* (ABC Radio, 10 March 2005) at <http://www.abc.net.au/am/content/2005/s1320021.htm> (10 March 2005).

[114] More (n 88 above) 505. I am quoting More's words, not the text of the judgment.

[115] Ibid 506–7.

[116] Ibid 506, quoting *Shaha v Dardiryan* ca 466/83, PD 39 (4) 734, 739 (Levin J) (1985), Israel SC.

state's interests. Policy meant that an informing or collaboration allegation would not, however, be actionable where the plaintiff was a citizen of a state hostile to Israel.[117] Similarly, Elton J thought that there was room to accommodate a diversity of views in determinations of actionability, but also thought the state interest must prevail and the imputation could not be actionable in the circumstances in *Shaha*.[118] This approach is quite different to that taken by Levin J. In effect, the court *will* grant ethical recognition to the moral taxonomies under which a person would think the less of an informer. Actionability is nullified because there is an overriding or fundamentally inconsistent state interest.

The decision by two members of the court in *Shaha* is an exception in the informing cases. They recognized criteria for moral judgment but refused on policy grounds to find the imputation actionable. In all other circumstances, the recognition has been refused on ethical grounds. Just why 'the right-thinking person' would not think the less of someone for assisting the authorities is not really explained in the cases. The decision of Levin J provides one explanation but the moral claim that decent people would not think the less of an informer is merely an assertion in other cases. That assertion might be better understood by considering it in contrast to the cases where the courts *have* recognized the views of those who think the less of informers and, consequently, found the imputation of informing to be actionable.

C. Recognition in the informing cases

There is a body of case law that has found imputations of informing to be actionable as defamation. Two 19th century Scots cases provide the earliest point of opposition to the mainstream of the case law but they are not especially helpful because, although acknowledging that an informer 'is by no means a popular character', neither provides a meaningful explanation of what gives the imputation its defamatory quality.[119] More useful for exploring the recognition of the negative ethical status of informing are the cases concerning citizens of the Republic of Ireland and the Irish diaspora where, as in the Middle East, an allegation of informing carries a special obloquy. These are the subject of the first part of this section. The second part looks at how imputations have been characterized in different ways to appeal to the criteria for moral judgment that will most readily be recognized by the courts.

1. *The negative ethical status of informing*

The earliest explanation of how an informing allegation was especially significant for the Irish can be found in *Winn v Quillan*.[120] An Irishman living in Glasgow

[117] Ibid 508, quoting *Shaha v Dardiryan* ca 466/83, PD 39 (4) 734, 747 (Ben-Porath J) (1985), Israel SC.

[118] Ibid 509.

[119] *Kennedy v Allan* (1848) 10 Session Cases 1293; *Graham v Roy* (1851) 13 Session Cases 634.

[120] *Winn v Quillan* [1899] 2 Session Cases 322.

had accused one of his countrymen of being an informer. The plaintiff argued that amongst the Irish this was:

an opprobrious, degrading and calumnious epithet, applicable to a person of a base and treacherous disposition, and who is regarded by his fellow Irishmen and others as a person unworthy of trust, and capable of committing base and treacherous actions, and disreputable motives, to the Crown or its executive. [He] is regarded, especially by Irishmen, as a person to be treated as an outcast from society, and to be shunned and boycotted, and as a person whom no one should transact business with, or be on terms of friendship with.[121]

The court held the imputation to be actionable. However, other than noting the 'grave consequences' for the plaintiff, no reasoning was provided.[122] Nonetheless, the case is still instructive because it starts to suggest there is a cultural significance attached to informing amongst the Irish that is not present in the same way in, for example, English or American cultures. This theme was a key issue when *Berry v Irish Times* was decided in 1973.

The informing question in *Berry* was framed in a slightly unusual way because the appellate court was asked to decide a different question than that which had confronted other courts. In the general run of cases, a defendant publisher has asked the court to find that the imputation of informing is incapable of defaming a person. That is, a court is usually asked to declare as a matter of law that the imputation is not defamatory. In *Berry*, however, the trial judge had applied a sectional standards test and found the imputation was capable of being defamatory, and allowed the imputation to go to a jury. The problem that plaintiff faced was that the jury subsequently found he had not in fact been defamed by the allegation.[123] So, to circumvent the jury decision, the plaintiff then asked the appellate court to declare as a matter of law that an imputation of informing *is* defamatory.

By a majority of 3:2 the Supreme Court refused to say that the imputation was defamatory as a matter of law. None of the five judges took issue with the proposition that the imputation was capable of defaming of a person. There was a clear acceptance that the imputation had a special effect because of the national context of Irish political life and history. The plaintiff, for example, claimed he had been especially upset by the publication, stating that he could:

think of nothing more ugly, more horrible in this life than to be called an informer. It has a peculiarly nauseating effect in Irish life.[124]

As FitzGerald J pointed out in his dissent, the published description of the plaintiff as a 'Felon-setter' and that the statement that he 'Helped jail republicans in England':

were not words in respect of which one has to have recourse to a dictionary to know what they meant to an Irishman; they were equivalent to calling him a traitor.[125]

[121] Ibid 323.
[122] Ibid 324–5 (Lord Justice-Clerk, Lord Trayner, and Lord Moncrieff; Lord Young dissenting).
[123] It appears to be something of a perverse verdict with the jury apparently taking the view the plaintiff was in fact an informer and thus did not deserve to succeed in the action.
[124] *Berry v Irish Times Ltd* [1973] IR 368, 380 (McLoughlin J), Ireland SC.
[125] Ibid 378 (FitzGerald J).

Informing and treachery here are caught up with the national sense of self. To call someone an informer carries with it a whole complex of imputations that take on meaning because the criteria for moral judgment reflect a shared political and cultural history by which the people see themselves *as* a people. The ethical rules of at least a section of the jurisdiction are recognized by the courts, acknowledged as legitimate moral ties, the existence of which enables the people in the jurisdiction to see themselves as a community.

2. *The character of the publication: informing, disloyalty, and treachery*

The moral connections that were recognized in *Berry* have been raised in other cases. The plaintiff's strategy has been to characterize the publication in terms of imputations other than informing so that a court will more readily accept it as capable of being defamatory. This has largely been unsuccessful in the informing cases but the decisions still show how important the characterization is.

The Court of King's Bench in *Myroft v Sleight* had to determine whether it could be defamatory to say of a trade unionist that, after voting in favour of a strike that he had crossed picket lines and worked.[126] The court noted that unionists and anti-unionists would hold very different views on this, but the general standard of the community was the benchmark.[127] It was held that the imputation was not capable of defaming a person in the eyes of 'ordinary, just, and reasonable citizens' because it only imputed the valuable qualities of 'independence of thought or courage or opinion or speech or manliness of action'.[128] However, the court thought that a separate imputation arose which was defamatory according to general community standards:

> [A] charge of trickery or underhand disloyalty or of hypocrisy is a very different matter. Such a charge... is as defamatory of a trade unionist as it is of any other man. All men, whatever their political or economic opinions, would deprecate bad faith and secret treachery in any post or status.[129]

In *Byrne v Deane* the court rejected the argument that the publication was actionable because it suggested the plaintiff was treacherous and disloyal to his fellow club members.[130] The court took the view that the pleaded imputations came down to the single

[126] *Myroft v Sleight* (1921) 90 LJ(KB) 883.

[127] Ibid 885–7, quoting GS Bower, *A Code of the Law of Actionable Defamation* (1st edn, 1909) 4, 287, and following *Mawe v Pigott* (1869) 4 Ir R (CL) 54, CP.

[128] Ibid 886–7.

[129] Ibid 887. Although the plaintiff succeeded in persuading the court in this regard, he was still unsuccessful. As a slander action, he had to prove that the imputation was raised against him in an office of a trade unionist (he could not), or it was defamatory as determined then he had to prove special damage. He was unable to prove damage and thus could not recover.

[130] Lord Justice Greer was sympathetic to the argument but his judgment is terribly confused. It is ostensibly a dissent but is ultimately not a dissent at all. After Slesser and Greene LJJ have delivered their judgments, Greer LJ (840–2) adds two paragraphs 'in order to prevent any misconstruction of my judgment' which agree expressly (840–1) with the proposition that an imputation of informing could not be defamatory.

allegation that the plaintiff had reported to the police the presence of the machines; all other objections to the plaintiff followed from this.[131]

The most significant consideration of the characterization of informing in American courts is found in *Westby v Madison Newspapers*.[132] The defendant newspaper claimed the plaintiffs were being paid by federal authorities to spy on their neighbours, who were allegedly engaged in 'political activism'. The Westbys contended the article suggested they were 'deceitful and dishonest, that they betray their neighbours and friends and cannot be trusted or confided in, that they lack integrity, and that they are stool pigeons'.[133] It implied they were 'contemptible, dishonest double-crossers'.[134] The newspaper argued the article was:

> nothing more than a report that the Westbys were cooperating with responsible officials performing a lawful function; that the key words 'spy' and 'paid informants' are consistent with the unobjectionable, indeed laudable efforts of the Westbys, or any other citizens, to aid the police.[135]

The plaintiffs succeeded. The allegation they were paid negated the assertion that the Westbys were good citizens and instead labelled them 'as mercenary opportunists, violating the trust of their neighbors...'[136] The informing cases were distinguished as dealing with circumstances where the information concerned 'actual lawbreakers' whereas this allegation was about monitoring people who were neither criminals nor suspects.[137]

The approach to dual characterization in *Myroft* has not been extended to the informing cases. That is, characterization in the sense discussed above can be distinguished from the more familiar inquiry about what imputations are conveyed by a publication. The process of characterization is itself an ethical one and is a form of ethical recognition. This is apparent from the jurisdictional difference in the significance of saying that a person is an informer. *Byrne* and *Westby* both suggest that the courts are generally unwilling to let any imputation of disloyalty or treachery render actionable a publication that suggests the plaintiff has been a police informant. Even if it was accepted that such a publication gave rise to a disloyalty imputation, the publication will not generally be actionable because the courts effectively refuse to recognize moral taxonomies that do not have the interests of the state as the more significant of the two competing ethical norms. In the Irish contexts, however, the ethical rules that constitute the jurisdiction and the people as a moral community are quite different. Unlike disloyalty in *Byrne*, the alleged treachery in *Berry* is committed towards the Irish nation—a group that has a much greater moral significance than a golf club—and the courts recognized that. Similarly, the Israeli court in *Shaha* was willing to recognize the negative ethical status of the imputation in Jerusalem. There,

[131] *Byrne v Deane* [1937] 1 KB 818, 832 (Slesser LJ), 839 (Greene LJ), CA.
[132] *Westby v Madison Newspapers* 295 NW 2d 691 (Wis, 1977).
[133] Ibid 692. [134] Ibid.
[135] Ibid 693. [136] Ibid 694. [137] Ibid.

an allegation of informing was qualitatively different; it constituted national, cultural, and religious treachery.

Conclusion

In the modern common law of defamation, it is clear that moral judgment is an important and persistent factor in the principal test for what is defamatory. There is variation in the way that the law takes account of moral judgment but—whether expressed in terms of the right-thinking or decent or respectable person—the standards of judgment are in every instance a function and mediation of the concept of community within the jurisdiction in question. Together, the centrality of moral judgment and community as the point of reference mean that it is appropriate to view the principal test as a law which protects reputation. Certainly, this element of the modern legal framework for determining actionability is fundamentally different from that which existed prior to the 19th century. It has moved well beyond the restrictive category-based tests for actionability and offers instead a broad and general protection for reputation. There are, however, some qualifications that need to be made in grasping the extent and manner of the legal protection of reputation under the principal test. Most importantly, the scope of the legal protection is limited. Not all harm to reputation will be actionable under the principal test. The law contemplates and enforces a difference between reputation as it is attributed and evaluated in communities, and reputation that will receive legal protection.

There are two main legal mechanisms that are used to limit protection. The first of these works on a quantitative basis where Anglo-Australian law dictates that the standards to be applied by the law are those of the community in general. As section III of the chapter argued, this is inappropriate. A sectional standards approach is to be preferred. The possibility of adopting that approach should not simply be dismissed on the apparent basis that *Readers Digest v Lamb* precludes it under the doctrine of precedent. As I have suggested, precedent does not preclude it. There is no doctrinal obstruction to a sectional standards approach in at least some circumstances. This approach is preferable because it acknowledges the existence of diverse moral taxonomies within a jurisdiction.

The second limit is explicitly normative. When conflicting and competing criteria for moral judgment exist in a jurisdiction then there must be limits on the legal protection of reputation. Jurisdictions are not inherently coterminous with communities. The determination of actionability thus involves what I have called the ethical recognition of criteria for moral judgment. The courts must form a sense of what makes the jurisdiction a community and conflicting ethical rules cannot always be recognized simultaneously. The recognition of criteria for moral judgment—and the consequent constitution of the community—results in inclusion and exclusion from the moral community of the jurisdiction. Those who are excluded from the moral community are people whose values the courts refuse to recognize.

These are the processes that the law uses in protecting reputation and in limiting that protection. They are processes which have been imbued with content over the course of the modern law's development. The moral taxonomies that have been recognized by the common law are for the most part those of Christian tradition and Victorian moralism. 'The right-thinking person' (or respectable person) has long embodied what are seen as traditional values. Both the processes and the content they carry are of great significance for coming to grips with questions about how reputation can best be protected under the law. The principal test and its application raise a major issue that goes directly to the way the tests for what is defamatory might be reworked to best protect reputation in morally diverse jurisdictions: if views are to be excluded on ethical grounds—which they are—then there must be some justification for the ethical choices that are made.

It is clear that ethical recognition is not an empirical matter in defamation law. The ethical status of a view is not dependent upon its prevalence in the jurisdiction. The mere fact that a view is widely held will not of itself imbue it with a positive moral status such that the courts will deem it worthy of recognition. This is important because it suggests that even if reputation is determined by the reality of community opinion, its legal protection is determined on a different basis. That is, the courts appeal to an ethical benchmark that is independent of majority opinion. These ethical choices will be subjected to further analysis in Chapter 8, especially with respect to the way that contemporary moral diversity has seen a change in the substantive criteria for moral judgment and the sources that legitimate the criteria of any given moral taxonomy.

Before these matters are considered, it is necessary to look at the protection of reputation under the other tests for what is defamatory: the 'shun and avoid' test (Chapter 6) and the ridicule test (Chapter 7). Each of these is no less important than the principal test for understanding the manner and extent of the legal protection of reputation as governed by the tests for what is defamatory.

6

The 'Shun and Avoid' Test as the Basis for Actionability

Chapter 5 established that moral judgment is central to the determination of actionability under the principal test for what is defamatory and argued that reputation is protected under that arm of the law. I turn now to the supplementary tests for what is defamatory and the extent to which it can be said that reputation is protected under these tests.

This chapter begins by looking in section I at the proposition that the supplementary tests are distinguished from the principal test because words can be actionable under the supplementary tests even though they do not suggest that the plaintiff has been at fault. This distinction is said to be supported by authority that goes back to the time before the common law's claim to protect reputation was firmly established. The analysis of the 'shun and avoid' test is structured around these two themes of moral fault and precedent. The moral fault distinction is considered in section II by examining how imputations regarding female chastity have been actionable under the 'shun and avoid' test. It will be suggested that the distinction clouds rather than clarifies the manner and extent to which reputation is protected under the test. A focus on moral worth will be more useful in establishing how reputation is protected and the limits of that protection. Section III moves to the role played by precedent in the operation and articulation of the 'shun and avoid' test. The doctrinal foundations of the test are said to lie in the early cases on disease and insanity imputations. A close look at these lines of authority casts doubt upon that. The analysis in this chapter suggests that, if defamation law is to protect reputation, the inadequacy of the moral fault distinction and the misconceived interpretation of precedent point to the need for a substantial revision of the place the 'shun and avoid' test occupies in the contemporary legal framework.

The second of the supplementary tests, ridicule, will be discussed in Chapter 7.

I. Distinguishing Between the Principal and Supplementary Tests

A. The statements of law

Three leading 20th century cases provide clear statements of the supplementary tests. One of the most authoritative recent statements was made by Neill LJ in

Berkoff v Burchill. After sketching a collection of definitions of defamatory matter from the 19th and 20th centuries, Neill LJ concluded that:

> words may be defamatory, even though they [do not] impute disgraceful conduct to the plaintiff... if they hold him up to contempt, scorn or ridicule or tend to exclude him from society.[1]

Secondly, in the Supreme Court of New South Wales, Hunt J in *Boyd v Mirror Newspapers Ltd* stated the principal test of 'lowering the estimation' and then explained the alternative tests:

> At common law, in general, an imputation, to be defamatory of the plaintiff, must be disparaging of him... I say that this is 'in general' the position, as the common law also recognizes as defamatory an imputation which, although not disparaging, tends to make other persons 'shun or avoid' the plaintiff..., as well as an imputation that displays the plaintiff in a ridiculous light, notwithstanding the absence of any moral blame on his part...[2]

Boyd is regularly cited in the Australian texts and cases, and was noted in *Berkoff* as an indicator of the Australian position.[3] Thirdly, the decision in *Youssoupoff v Metro-Goldwyn Mayer*, which was relied upon by both Neill LJ and Hunt J, draws the distinction in a similar manner though with slightly different language again and, relevantly for this chapter, only with reference to the 'shun and avoid' test:

> Not only is the matter defamatory if it brings the plaintiff into hatred, ridicule or contempt by reason of some moral discredit on her part, but also if it tends to make the plaintiff be shunned avoided and that without any moral discredit on her part. It is for that reason that persons who have been alleged to have been insane, or to be suffering from certain diseases, and other cases where no direct moral responsibility could be placed upon them, have been held to be entitled to bring an action to protect their reputation and their honour.[4]

Two issues in these statements of law are highly significant for understanding the relationships between the tests and is essential for explaining the extent and manner of the legal protection of reputation under both the 'shun and avoid' and ridicule tests.

B. The moral fault distinction and lines of authority

First, the conceptual distinction between the principal and supplementary tests can be understood as turning on moral fault. The more recent cases indicate that,

[1] *Berkoff v Burchill* [1996] 4 All ER 1008, 1013 (Neill LJ), CA.

[2] *Boyd v Mirror Newspapers Ltd* [1980] 2 NSWLR 449, 453, NSW SC.

[3] *Berkoff v Burchill* [1996] 4 All ER 1008, 1020 (Phillips LJ), CA; D Butler and S Rodrick, *Australian Media Law* (2nd edn, 2004) [2.110]; S Walker, *Media Law: Commentary & Materials* (2000) 133–7; M Gillooly, *The Law of Defamation in Australia & New Zealand* (1998) 47; R Watterson, 'What is Defamatory Today?' (1993) 67 Australian Law Journal 811, 819–21.

[4] *Youssoupoff v Metro-Goldwyn Mayer* (1934) 50 TLR 581, 587 (Slesser LJ), CA.

to be actionable, a publication need not suggest the plaintiff has engaged in any 'disgraceful conduct' (*Berkoff*) or bears any 'moral blame' (*Boyd*) with respect to what is said of them. This indicates the interpretation that has been placed on the use of 'moral discredit' as the distinction arose in *Youssoupoff*.[5] Separately and together, the cases indicate that a publication can be actionable even though it does not suggest the plaintiff has engaged in any morally blameworthy behaviour. The moral fault distinction as it concerns the 'shun and avoid' test will be examined in section III by looking at imputations related to chastity. That discussion will inform the Chapter 7 analysis of the protection of reputation under the ridicule test.

Secondly, the three leading cases highlight the role precedent has played in shaping the rules of actionability. In *Berkoff*, cases from the late-17th century and mid-18th century were identified as longstanding authority for the ridicule and 'shun and avoid' tests respectively.[6] And where *Boyd* relies on *Youssoupoff*, *Youssoupoff* draws on a longer line of cases. As Slesser LJ explained it, the 'shun and avoid' test was directly traceable to earlier cases where 'persons who have been alleged to have been insane, or to be suffering from certain diseases, and other cases where no direct moral responsibility could be placed upon them' could commence defamation actions.[7] The place of moral fault in the contemporary law is thus closely connected to its place in the older cases. These lines of authority need some investigation to see how, if at all, they support the now accepted proposition that moral fault is irrelevant to actionability under the 'shun and avoid' test. Further, it will be necessary to look at the scope of actionability under these authorities and whether it is consistent with the protection of reputation. These inquiries will be the subject of section IV which looks at the disease and insanity threads that Slesser LJ cited as authority in *Youssoupoff*. Chapter 7 will address the lines of authority that are said to support the ridicule test.

Youssoupoff is an especially significant decision because it is the standard authority for the existence and form of the contemporary 'shun and avoid' test.[8]

[5] The moral fault distinction has been observed in the literature. Prompted by the decision in *Berkoff v Burchill*, Jill Cottrell has considered the question of how the supplementary tests sit in comparison to the principal test. Her core question is, 'Can one be defamed by statements which impute no blame?': J Cottrell, 'What Does "Defamatory" Mean? Reflections on *Berkoff v Burchill*' [1998] Tort Law Review 149, 154. She frames the question this way in light of the Faulks Committee's conclusion that the law ought not to make actionable 'the case of a person being shunned or avoided by society as a result of an allegation which imputes no moral blame': 154 citing United Kingdom, *Report of the Committee on Defamation* (Cmnd 5909, 1975) ('The Faulks Committee Report') App V, [7]. Unsurprisingly, Cottrell answers her question in the affirmative. However, as this chapter shall argue, the question itself tends to draw attention away from more important issues.

[6] *Berkoff v Burchill* [1996] 4 All ER 1008, 1014 (Neill LJ), CA, referring to *Mason v Jennings* [1680] Raym Sir T 401, 83 ER 209; *Cropp v Tilney* (1693) 3 Salk 225, 91 ER 791; *Villers v Monsley* (1769) 2 Wils 403, 95 ER 886, KB.

[7] *Youssoupoff v Metro-Goldwyn Mayer* (1934) 50 TLR 581, 588 (Slesser LJ), CA.

[8] P Milmo and WVH Rogers, *Gatley on Libel and Slander* (10th edn, 2004) [1.5]; Gillooly (n 3 above) 49; Butler and Rodrick (n 3 above) [2.110]; Walker (n 3 above) 133; *Boyd v Mirror Newspapers Ltd* [1980] 2 NSWLR 449, 453, NSW SC.

The statement of law it contains is the basis for claims that moral fault is irrelevant to determinations of actionability under the 'shun and avoid' test. Moreover, it lays claim to interpreting the decisions that preceded it and it has subsequently become the lens through which those earlier decisions have been viewed.

II. A Critique of the Moral Fault Distinction

Imputations regarding the chastity of women have for centuries been the subject of defamation actions. Although verbal imputations of unchastity were not actionable at common law under the strictly limited categories of slander, the courts readily acknowledged that casting aspersions on a woman's chastity would damage her reputation.[9] In the 19th century, parliaments expanded those categories with legislation that made 'words which impute unchastity to any girl or woman' actionable without proof of special damage.[10]

Written imputations of unchastity posed no problems for the courts because (as Chapter 4 explained) written defamation was subject to the general libel test of 'hatred, contempt, or ridicule'. There was never any doubt that slurs on a woman's chastity would satisfy that test or the 'lowering the estimation' test that succeeded it. Only with *Costello & Abbott* was a challenge to that position seriously considered by the courts.[11] The law consistently reflected traditional moral taxonomies under which communities expected women to protect their sexual purity and would frown upon a woman who did not. But what was the position where a publication alleged that a woman's chastity had been violated, but did so without any suggestion that she was responsible for that violation? This was the issue that faced the English courts in *Youssoupoff v Metro-Goldwyn-Mayer*.[12]

A. *Youssoupoff*: Chastity and 'moral discredit'

The MGM film, *Rasputin, The Mad Monk,* gave rise to one of the most famous libel actions in British legal history. Princess Youssoupoff claimed that the film had falsely depicted her as having been either seduced or raped by Rasputin.[13] The trial judge directed the jury that it was defamatory to say of a person anything that would bring them into hatred, contempt, or ridicule, or, because the case law shows actionability to have a broader foundation than that, anything that 'causes them to

[9] *Wharton v Brook* (1669) 1 Ventr 21, 21, 86 ER 15, 15 (Twisden J); *Ayre v Craven* (1834) 2 Ad & El 2, 3–4, 111 ER 1, 2; *Albrecht v Patterson [No 1]* (1886) 12 VLR 597, Vic SC; *Albrecht v Patterson [No 2]* (1886) 12 VLR 821, 826 (Higginbotham CJ), 826–8 (Williams and Webb JJA), Vic SC FC.

[10] *An Act to Amend the Law of Slander 1865* (Sth Aust), s 2; *Wrongs Act 1890* (Vic), s 7; *Slander of Women Act 1891* (UK), ss 54 and 55 Vic c51; *Slander of Women Act 1900* (West Aust).

[11] See Chapter 5, II(A).

[12] *Youssoupoff v Metro-Goldwyn Mayer* (1934) 50 TLR 581, CA.

[13] Ibid 582 (Scrutton LJ).

be shunned or avoided' will also be defamatory.[14] The jury awarded her £25,000 damages.[15] The defendants appealed.

Among the issues in the Court of Appeal was the (then very open) question of whether potential defamation in a film was to be treated as slander or libel. Approaching it as slander, Scrutton LJ understood the defendant's argument to be that although an imputation of unchastity was actionable per se under statute, the plaintiff could not succeed here because an imputation of rape did not imply any unchastity. This proposition was summarily dismissed with a curt expression of judicial derision: 'I really have no language to express my opinion of this argument'.[16]

The defendant's argument was seen by Greer LJ and Slesser LJ as a complaint about the jury direction on libel. The trial judge had said that for a publisher to say of a woman 'that she has been either seduced or ravished by such a villain as Rasputin is, of course, the worst and most vile libel that could be imagined'.[17] The defendant complained that this was wrong in law because it instructed the jury to treat imputations of rape and seduction the same way. The defendant's contention was that different damages would have been appropriate depending on whether the jury thought the film had implied rape or seduction. The seduction imputation would warrant a greater award of damages because it suggested a willing participation and thus impugned the Princess's character more seriously.[18]

Lord Justice Greer did not discuss the defendant's argument, but made it clear that he saw the imputation of rape as capable of being defamatory.[19] Lord Justice Slesser considered the issue more closely. He saw the imputation as defamatory whether or not the Princess was alleged to have been 'the more or the less moral' because:

> Not only is the matter defamatory if it brings the plaintiff into hatred, ridicule, or contempt by reason of some moral discredit on her part, but also if it tends to make the plaintiff be shunned and avoided and that without any moral discredit on her part.[20]

The absence of 'moral discredit' did not prevent her reputation being tarnished:

> One may, I think, take judicial notice of the fact that a lady of whom it has been said that she has been ravished, albeit against her will, has suffered in social reputation and in opportunities of receiving respectful consideration from the world. It is to shut one's eyes to realities to make these nice distinctions . . .[21]

With respect to damages, Slesser LJ thought it was not essential that the jury consider 'the precise manner in which she has been despoiled of her innocence

[14] Ibid 584 (Scrutton LJ).
[15] Ibid 582 (Scrutton LJ).
[16] Ibid 584 (Scrutton LJ).
[17] Ibid 586 (Greer LJ), quoting the trial judge.
[18] Ibid 586 (Greer LJ), 588 (Slesser LJ).
[19] Ibid 585–6 (Greer LJ).
[20] Ibid 587 (Slesser LJ).
[21] Ibid.

and virginity'; they could award a large sum on the grounds that rape was the imputation.[22] The point, in the end, was that the Princess had been 'defamed in her sexual purity' regardless of whether it had been seduction or rape that was implied.[23]

The use of 'moral discredit' in the reasoning warrants closer consideration because it helps explain how the court saw the imputation affecting the plaintiff's reputation.

B. Moral discredit, moral fault, and moral worth

The most thorough analysis of *Youssoupoff* has been undertaken by Leslie Kim Treiger-Bar-Am.[24] As she points out, there is no doubt that in the 1930s a woman who had been raped would be held in lower regard by the community.[25] The question of how that was considered in defamation was much less clear. In discussing how the Lord Justices reach their conclusion, Treiger-Bar-Am characterizes the court's view of the relationship between sexual impurity and immorality as follows:

> [The rape victim] is tainted with sexual impurity, and hence, as purity entails moral worth or value, with immorality... Scrutton LJ and Slesser LJ slip from using the term 'raped' to the term 'ravished'. The definition of the latter term includes the meaning 'allured', thus bearing the implications of seduction and consent, and therefore immorality... *Immorality* is at some level attributed to the woman because of the loss of sexual *purity*, regardless of the cause of that loss... [The judges] associated a loss of sexual purity, even through rape, with immorality.[26]

Her contention is that the judges 'imbue[d] the standard with hints of moral blameworthiness' because they saw the allegation of rape as an allegation that the victim was 'guilty of sexual misconduct'.[27] That is, she argues that the court saw a rape victim as morally blameworthy. The problem with this analysis is that the text of the case—especially the observation that there was no moral discredit on the plaintiff's part—suggests that the court thought the loss of sexual purity was not reducible to blame. Treiger-Bar-Am acknowledges this in her use of terms such as 'immorality' and 'moral worth or value' (and not simply 'moral blameworthiness') to discuss the loss of sexual purity. However, she tries to fit the reasoning into the two legal categories that more recent decisions have used

[22] Ibid 588 (Slesser LJ).

[23] Ibid 587 (Slesser LJ).

[24] LK Treiger-Bar-Am, 'Defamation Law in a Changing Society: The Case of *Youssoupoff v Metro-Goldwyn Mayer*' (2001) 21 LS 291.

[25] Ibid 307, citing J Lewis, *Women in England 1870–1950: Sexual Divisions and Social Change* (1984).

[26] Ibid 306, emphasis in original.

[27] Ibid 306, 309–12. A similar argument is run in PH Winfield, *Youssoupoff v Metro-Goldwyn Mayer* (Casenote) (1935) 51 LQR 281, 282.

to discuss *Youssoupoff*. Those discussions rely on a simple opposition based on the moral fault distinction: there are circumstances where a plaintiff bears moral fault, as against circumstances where a plaintiff bears no moral fault.[28] Retaining these as the only analytical choices, she inappropriately and unnecessarily places the court's view of rape in the former category.

The court did not attribute blameworthiness to the victim. On the contrary, the point was that the publication was actionable even in the absence of blame. The moral fault distinction is inappropriate because it presumes that one's standing in the community will be favourable in the absence of any morally blameworthy behaviour. And the court in *Youssoupoff* did not proceed on that basis; it had a more nuanced sense of how the status of 'immorality' could be acquired. *Youssoupoff* shows that the court thought that female sexual purity could be lost either with or without any fault on a woman's part. A woman's reputation could be disparaged by allegations that she has been sexually promiscuous, but it could also be disparaged by imputations that suggested she had been engaged in or subjected to some kind of sexual act, regardless of her own conduct, will, or volition. 'Blameworthiness', then, does not adequately capture the spectrum of criteria for moral judgment that the court perceives and recognizes. A negative moral judgment may be made on the basis of the plaintiff's own morally egregious conduct, and sometimes on the basis of the morally egregious conduct of another.

The intellectual and moral reasoning in *Youssoupoff* is also at work in the American case of *Snyder v New York Press Co Ltd* where the plaintiff claimed the publication was actionable under the ridicule test.[29] Though this digresses from the 'shun and avoid' test for a moment, it is helpful to observe how the distinction operates in the same way across both the supplementary tests. The defendant newspaper in *Snyder* published a story about a process server who entered the female plaintiff's home and inadvertently saw the plaintiff in the bath. The court held that the article had:

> a direct tendency to subject the plaintiff to unfavorable comment, to diminish her respectability, to abridge her comfort and enjoyment, and to expose her to public ridicule, such as provokes contempt, not merely such as may be sportive and thoughtless.[30]

The phrase and idea of 'respectability' denotes the presence and relevance of a moral sensibility. The reasoning shows how the court saw the place of moral judgment in actionability:

> An article may be libelous, though it does not impute immoral conduct. The whole tenor of this article is to ridicule the plaintiff. It has a direct tendency to lower her in the estimation of the community, though it may not charge immoral conduct, or impute immoral character.[31]

[28] This distinction is maintained throughout Trieger-Bar-Am's argument: for example, 318: 'The *Youssoupoff* standard should, then, be interpreted to reflect moral blameworthiness...'

[29] *Snyder v New York Press Co Ltd* 121 NY Supp 944 (NY SC App Div, 1910).

[30] Ibid 945 (Miller J; Ingraham PJ, Laughlin, Clarke, and Scott JJ concurring).

[31] Ibid 946.

As in *Youssoupoff*, the plaintiff's respectability is diminished without the plaintiff bearing any responsibility for the immoral occurrence.

An individual's reputation is a social judgment of the person based upon facts which are considered relevant by a community.[32] Mostly, the relevant facts will be those over which the plaintiff has control, but this is not always the situation. The chastity cases illustrate that a person's moral worth may be diminished by either their choice to engage in behaviour that is socially frowned upon (which I have referred to as 'moral fault') or by their being affected by someone else's behaviour or by being caught in circumstances that are frowned upon. The latter might be called 'immoral association'.[33] The moral fault distinction identified in the leading cases is neither a helpful nor an appropriate tool for understanding the scope of the legal protection of reputation under the shun and avoid test because one's reputation can be damaged either with or without moral fault. In sum, it was not the *absence* of moral *fault* that was determinative of actionability, but the *diminution* of moral *worth*. That diminution may flow from something for which the plaintiff bears responsibility, or it may flow from some other circumstance. Those circumstances or facts will depend on the moral taxonomies that govern reputation in a community.

In finding the imputation of rape capable of being defamatory, the court recognized a particular set of criteria for moral judgment as legitimate concerns in the evaluation of reputation. Those criteria included the loss of sexual purity, however caused. The criteria were a part of the same moral taxonomies of Christian tradition and Victorian moralism that were apparent in the application of the principal test. The application of the 'shun and avoid' test in *Youssoupoff* thus entailed the same process of ethical recognition. That parallel prompts an important question: if (like the principal test) the application of the 'shun and avoid' test involves ethical recognition, is it also the case that (like the principal test) ethical recognition can be refused under the 'shun and avoid' test?

C. Ethical recognition in the 'shun and avoid' test

It might be thought that the 'shun and avoid' test does not contemplate the refusal of ethical recognition and is thus fundamentally different from the principal test. This is because the standard of judgment in the principal test was encapsulated in the idea of 'the right-thinking person', and that phrase has not generally been

[32] See Chapter 1, II(B).

[33] *Cary v Allen* 39 Wis 481 (Wis, 1876) provides an excellent example of this. A publication had claimed the female plaintiff had 'gone away with or had appointed a time and place to meet a man' who had been involved in a major fraud. The article did not impute 'any sexual immorality or criminal charge' to the plaintiff. The court found it was still defamatory because the man in question 'it was alleged, had committed forgery, had been guilty of frauds, had betrayed his friends, had deserted his family; who was, in short, a man of such character that no respectable woman could associate with him anywhere without social degradation; or without, as the books say, bringing her into hatred, contempt and ridicule': 488 (Cole J).

associated with the 'shun and avoid' test. In particular, it was absent from the court's consideration of actionability in *Youssoupoff*.

This absence is at least partly intuitive. The lingering Victorian morality meant that while 'the right-thinking person' might have had sympathy or pity for a woman who had been raped, the Lord Justices understood that a rape victim would not be regarded with the same respect as other women.[34] The fact the plaintiff was a royal and thus inherently deserving of respect could only have compounded that intuition. The recognition of these values endured. The New South Wales Supreme Court described and adopted the import of the reasoning 50 years later in *Krahe*. After noting that a plaintiff could be defamed even though they were 'not at fault', it was explained that an imputation of rape was defamatory because 'when a woman is raped, she has been dishonoured in the same sense of being the subject of shame or disgrace'.[35]

The defamatory capacity of a rape imputation was stated without comment in *Boyd*, but there has since been much to suggest that the criteria for moral judgment have altered in the later part of the 20th century. Values have changed. The intrinsically violent and violating nature of rape is recognized and overwhelmingly deplored in Western society. Judicial intuition about the moral worth of the victim has reflected that change. Lord Justice Phillips in *Berkoff*, and Levine J in the 1998 New South Wales case of *Galea* both expressed the view (in obiter) that an imputation of rape would be incapable of being defamatory.[36]

Judicial discomfort with *Youssoupoff* has also caused the courts to reflect upon and articulate the place of ethical recognition in the 'shun and avoid' test. In particular, the courts have had to consider whether the principles of ethical recognition apply as they do in the principal test, or whether the 'shun and avoid' test is different. That is to say, the question has been: to determine whether a publication is actionable does one ask whether the imputation would make right-thinking people shun and avoid the plaintiff? Or does one simply ask whether the plaintiff would be shunned and avoided without consideration of whether the values of those who would treat her that way are values that should be recognized by the law? In more recent decisions, such as *Galea* and *Berkoff*, 'the right-thinking person' standard has been an express element of the 'shun and avoid' test.[37] In *Galea*, for example, Levine J asked whether the imputation he was dealing with was capable of making the 'ordinary, right thinking member of the community ... shun and avoid the plaintiff'.[38] The re-statement of the test in the last decade has

[34] There were some observations at the time that a rape victim would be an object of sympathy or pity rather than lose esteem in the usual way associated with a defamatory imputation: WTS Stallybrass, *Salmond's Law of Torts* (9th edn, 1936) 399; WL Prosser, *Handbook of The Law of Torts* (1941) 780. Neither suggested the imputation should not be actionable.

[35] *Krahe v TCN Channel Nine Pty Ltd* (1986) 4 NSWLR 536, 546, NSW SC.

[36] *Berkoff v Burchill* [1996] 4 All ER 1008, 1020–1 (Phillips LJ), CA; *Galea v Amalgamated Television Services Pty Ltd* (NSW SC, 20 February 1998) 12–14.

[37] Ibid.

[38] *Galea v Amalgamated Television Services Pty Ltd* (NSW SC, 20 February 1998) 6, 12–14.

been appropriate: ethical recognition is as much a part of the 'shun and avoid' test as it is a part of the principal test. As such, recognition may be refused with the effect of limiting the legal protection of reputation.

There is a second reason why 'the right-thinking person' standard was absent from *Youssoupoff*. The court took the view that there was a line of authority which indicated that, under the 'shun and avoid' test, imputations could be actionable even where the publication did not prompt a negative moral judgment of the plaintiff. Hence, if words which did *not* damage reputation could be actionable then the corollary was that it would be illogical to limit the scope of actionability where reputation *was* damaged. Section III will show that this interpretation of the authorities cannot be justified.

III. Lines of Authority: Disease and Insanity

The proposition that a person could be defamed by a statement that tended to make them shunned and avoided had been recognized long before the English courts relied upon it in *Youssoupoff*.[39] Lord Justice Slesser in *Youssoupoff* identified the source of the phrase:

> [P]ersons who have been alleged to have been insane, or to be suffering from certain diseases, and other cases where no direct moral responsibility could be placed upon them, have been held to be entitled to bring an action to protect their reputation and their honour.[40]

By looking at the disease and insanity cases the relationship between defamation and reputation under the 'shun and avoid' test can be more fully explained.

A. Disease: The influence of slander on libel

To what extent do the disease cases support the proposition that the 'shun and avoid' test dictates that words should be actionable even in the absence of an imputation that tends to prompt a negative moral judgment of the plaintiff? To answer this requires a return to the history of defamation. Where disease is concerned, the test for what is defamatory in libel actions can be traced back to, in particular, the decision in *Villers v Monsley* in 1769 and to slander cases prior to that time.[41]

1. Written allegations of disease in the 18th century

The plaintiff in *Villers v Monsley* complained of a written imputation that he suffered from 'the itch'.[42] The Court of King's Bench agreed that this would not be

[39] Eg, CG Addison, *Wrongs and their Remedies, being a Treatise on the Law of Torts* (1860) 579 included the phrase in his definition of libellous words.

[40] *Youssoupoff v Metro-Goldwyn Mayer* (1934) 50 TLR 581, 587 (Slesser LJ), CA.

[41] *Villers v Monsley* (1769) 2 Wils 403, 95 ER 886, KB.

[42] Ibid.

actionable as slander if it was merely spoken.[43] As a written allegation, however, it was asked to consider the defendant's argument that:

> the itch is a distemper to which every family is liable; to have it is no crime, nor does it bring any disgrace upon a man, for it may be innocently caught or taken by infection; the small pox, or a putrid fever, are much worse distempers; the itch is not so detestable or so contagious as either of them, for it is not communicated by the air, but by contact or putting on a glove, or the clothes of one who has the itch, and although it be an infectious distemper, yet it implies no offence in the person having it, and therefore no action will lie for saying or writing that a man has got the itch. It is not like saying or writing that a man has got the leprosy, or is a leper, for which an action upon the case will lie, because a leper shall be removed from the society of men... although it be a natural infirmity.[44]

This argument was rejected and the publication was held to be actionable. Why? The test would be whether the publication 'renders [the plaintiff] ridiculous, or tends to hinder mankind from associating or having intercourse with him'.[45] Justice Bathurst used similar terminology: 'publishing any thing which renders a man ridiculous is actionable; and whether the itch be occasioned by a man's fault or misfortune, it is a cruel charge, and renders him both ridiculous and miserable, by being kept out of all company'.[46] This is echoed by Gould J who held that a statement will be libellous if it 'cuts a man off from society', which seems to be an incident of a statement that 'renders him ridiculous'.[47]

The court appears to accept that a suggestion that a person has a disease does not necessarily imply any wrongdoing on their part. The first consequence of *Villers v Monsley* was that personal moral fault on the part of the plaintiff would not be required for an imputation to be actionable. Secondly, the case suggests that words can be actionable as defamation even though they do not impute any diminution in a person's moral worth. It is the fact that people may not associate with the plaintiff that makes the words actionable. They are actionable in these circumstances not *because* they damage a person's reputation. They are actionable in spite of the fact that they do *not* damage a person's reputation. To see why this comes about, it is helpful to view the questions in the light of the legal position as the court would have seen it at the time.

Two things would have been uppermost in the minds of the judges. First, they were well aware that, even if not *all* disease imputations were actionable as slander, verbal allegations of sexual diseases and some non-sexual disease were actionable as slander. Secondly, the judges would have been aware that written defamation would be more easily actionable than spoken defamation. There was also a general sense by at least 1716 that written defamation would be

43 Ibid 404 (Bathurst J and Gould J).
44 Ibid 403.
45 Ibid 404 (Wilmot CJ; Clive J agreeing).
46 Ibid 404 (Bathurst J).
47 Ibid 404 (Gould J).

actionable if it tended to bring the plaintiff into hatred, contempt, or ridicule.[48] On the face of it, then, it would have seemed a non-sequitur to hold that a written disease imputation was not actionable. After all, libel was intended to expand actionability, not to narrow it.[49] The problem that the courts did not grapple with was that the basis for actionability in written defamation was different than the basis for actionability in spoken defamation. In spoken defamation it was dependent upon one of the set categories being satisfied. In written defamation, it depended upon whether the plaintiff's reputation had been damaged in the sense that they were exposed to hatred, contempt, or ridicule and that seemed to involve some sense of disgrace. The court's reasoning *should* have led them to the conclusion that the publication was not actionable because, as they pointed out, it did not damage the plaintiff's reputation in the requisite sense. Instead, they expanded the scope of actionable words by relying on the general expansion of actionability when defamation was written rather than spoken, and justified it with reference to the disease category of actionable slander which (as Chapter 4 explained) was not founded upon damage to reputation.

2. *Disease imputations after* Villers v Monsley

It might be possible to consider the decision in *Villers v Monsley* as acceptable in 1769 because the law had not then settled on any fixed rationale or test for defamation. Moreover, the general claim that defamation law protected reputation was not as established as it would be in the early 1800s. But after *Thorley v Kerry* in 1812, and certainly after *Parmiter v Coupland* was decided in 1840, it should not have been acceptable to view *Villers v Monsley* as good law with respect to the actionability of written imputations that a person suffered from a disease. So, how did the courts deal with such actions? The short answer is: they didn't! Somewhat remarkably, the issue has not arisen for consideration.

There have been no cases since *Villers* where a plaintiff has argued they have been defamed on the grounds of a written statement that suggests she or he has a disease. Pollock's *Law of Torts* noted that there was only one disease case at all in the 19th century.[50] That case, *Bloodworth v Gray*, was an action for slander where the plaintiff relied on the 1788 slander case of *Carslake v Mapledoram*.[51] The question in *Carslake* was whether it was actionable to say that a person had in the past suffered from a disease but that they did not presently do so. Though

[48] The Star Chamber had long ago articulated the evils of libel and the trend of the civil cases since *King v Lake* in 1670 had made it seem for a century that written defamation was more serious than spoken defamation. See Chapter 4, I(B).

[49] See Chapter 4, I(B).

[50] F Pollock, *The Law of Torts* (10th edn, 1916) 255; (14th edn, 1939) 194.

[51] *Bloodworth v Gray* (1844) 7 Man & G 334, 135 ER 140; *Carslake v Mapledoram* (1788) 2 Term Rep 473, 100 ER 255.

there is no reference at all to *Villers*, the court in *Carslake* seems to have adopted the interpretation of actionability that was used in *Villers*:

> The reason why the making of such a charge is actionable, is because the having a contagious disorder renders the person an improper member of society; but there is no reason why the company of a person who has had a contagious disorder [in the past] should be avoided [when they no longer have it]; and therefore such a charge is not actionable.[52]

The entirety of the judgment in *Bloodworth* states that: 'This case falls within the principles of the old authorities.'[53] In the United States, *Villasenor v Villasenor* proceeded on the basis that the imputation of a 'loathsome disease' would be actionable as slander, though no imputation had been conveyed in the circumstances.[54] In the 20th century, there do not seem to have been any libel cases on point in Australia or England.[55]

What, then, do the disease cases say about the 'shun and avoid' test and the protection of reputation? There has only been one case that has considered written allegations that the plaintiff has a disease. That case is *Villers v Monsley*, and indicates that words may be actionable in the absence of any diminution of moral worth at all. It says that a disease imputation can be actionable even if the publication does not imply that there was morally blameworthy behaviour, and even if it does not imply that any one else's behaviour or any of the circumstances would result in a diminution of the plaintiff's moral worth.[56] As such, the principle in

[52] *Carslake v Mapledoram* (1788) 2 Term Rep 473, 475, 100 ER 255, 256 (Buller J).

[53] *Bloodworth v Gray* (1844) 7 Man & G 334, 334, 135 ER 140, 140 (Tindal CJ stating the opinion of the court).

[54] *Villasenor v Villasenor* 911 SW 2d 411 (1995) (Civ App, TX). In *Plumley v Landmark Chevrolet Inc* 122 F 3d 308 (5th Cir, 1997), the plaintiff revealed that he had AIDS and was called a 'fucking faggot'. In the subsequent slander action, he successfully argued that the abuse implied he had committed the crime of sodomy and the statement was thus actionable as slander. There was no discussion at all as to whether an imputation that the plaintiff had HIV or AIDS would be actionable. The Ohio Court of Appeals in *Retterer v Whirlpool Corporation* 677 NE 2d 417 (Ohio Ct App, 1996) considered a defamation action in the circumstances of workplace harassment where an employee argued that police 'caution' tape across a bathroom referred to him having AIDS. The court concluded that the plaintiff had not been defamed as no defamatory words were published to a third party (423) and no imputation was conveyed (424). The Court's lack of regard for innuendo is of some concern but, nonetheless, on their reasoning the actionability of a written statement alleging disease did not need to be and was not considered in any way.

[55] In *Henry v TVW Enterprises Ltd* (1990) 3 WAR 474, West Aust SC, a television broadcast stated that the plaintiff had Hepatitis B but the defamation action did not allege he had been defamed for that reason. Instead, the imputation was characterized as one that the plaintiff dentist had failed to warn his patients that he had an infectious disease and possibly exposed his patients to contraction of that disease: 478.

[56] It might be thought that I have unwisely taken at face value the court's acceptance of the proposition that the plaintiff's moral worth was undiminished by the allegation in the case. However, it should not be problematic because it means that the analysis in this section has proceeded on the assumptions most favourable to an expansive interpretation of *Villers*. If the assumption is inappropriate then the argument is stronger because it means that *Villers v Monsley* provides absolutely no support for the proposition that words can be actionable when they do not detract from a person's reputation.

Villers may make words actionable but it does not protect reputation. That is because it is not concerned with facts that are relevant to a community's judgment about a person. Instead, actionability comes about because the principle relies on the slander cases which were not themselves based on the protection of reputation; actionability was instead determined on the basis of a technically applied category of words, the rationale for which was very uncertain. To the extent that the current legal position relies on *Villers*, it is incorrect.

B. The uncertain moral status of insanity

Decisions relating to imputations of insanity were the second line of authority that Slesser LJ relied upon to support the application of the 'shun and avoid' test in *Youssoupoff*.

1. The insanity cases

An imputation of insanity first appears in *Mayrant v Richardson*, an 1818 American decision.[57] The South Carolina Court of Appeals took the view that this was not defamatory. The court began by noting the observation in *Villers v Monsley* that 'words written and published are actionable, which if spoken would furnish no ground of action', and accepted it as a correct statement of the legal position.[58] However, where the *Villers* court looked (incorrectly) to the slander cases on disease, the *Mayrant* court looked (correctly) at the general test for libel. Accordingly, it was held in *Mayrant* that if words were to be actionable as written defamation then they would have to satisfy the following requirements:

> [T]hey must be such as, in the common estimation of mankind, are calculated to reflect shame or disgrace upon the person they are spoken of, or hold him up as an object of hatred, ridicule or contempt.[59]

Applying this to the insanity imputation, Nott J delivered the opinion of the court:

> There is nothing of that sort contained in these publications. They barely express an opinion that the plaintiff's mind had been affected by disease. That was a misfortune and not a fault. It might have been calculated to excite compassion, but not hatred, ridicule, or contempt... The private character has not been attacked, the moral conduct impeached... There has been no imputation calculated to render the plaintiff an object of contempt or ridicule, or to lessen him in the estimation of his fellow-citizens.[60]

[57] *Mayrant v Richardson* 1 Nott & McCord 347; 9 Am Dec 707 (SC Ct App, 1818).
[58] Ibid 708.
[59] Ibid.
[60] Ibid 708, 711.

This well-reasoned decision has not been followed in the United States.[61] *Mayrant* is not referred to in Australia or England where, instead, the tendency has been to rely on the English case of *Morgan v Lingen*.[62]

Morgan v Lingen is the decision most frequently cited as authority for the proposition that it has been held to be defamatory to say of a person that they are insane, and is generally cited as an example of the 'shun and avoid' test.[63] The defendant, a doctor, wrote to a friend of the plaintiff's saying that the plaintiff was delusional and paranoid. Baron Martin directed the jury in the following terms: A 'statement in writing that a lady's mind is affected, and that seriously, is without explanation *prima facie* a libel.'[64] This is the total of his reasoning on the point. There is not a word in the judgment to suggest why he thought the statement libellous. There is nothing to suggest that Martin B was applying anything other than the (then) principal test of 'hatred, contempt, or ridicule' and there is no indication about whether he thought the imputation did or did not carry a sense of disgrace or a diminution of moral worth typically associated with attacks on reputation. With so little to rely on, it is odd to cite the decision (as Slesser LJ did in *Youssoupoff*) as authority for a discrete 'shun and avoid' test.

There are several cases after *Morgan* where an imputation of insanity has been held to be defamatory, but in almost all these instances there has been no discussion about why it is defamatory and mostly, as in *Morgan*, there has been no indication that the proposition was contested.[65] In the absence of judicial explanation, the treatises on defamation provide an alternative avenue for understanding the rationale behind the decisions.

2. *The place of the insanity cases in the legal framework*

In the treatises of the 19th and early-20th centuries the insanity cases were classified in different ways, suggesting there was great uncertainty about just what it was that made an imputation of insanity defamatory and how, if at all, it tarnished a person's reputation.

[61] *Mayrant* was noted in *Totten v Sun Printing & Publishing Assoc* 190 F 289 (NY Circuit Ct, 1901) but the court there held that 'the weight of authority and reason' dictated that the imputation was defamatory. Unfortunately, the authorities were not cited and the reasons not explained.

[62] *Morgan v Lingen* (1863) 8 LT 800.

[63] *Gatley on Libel and Slander* (n 8 above) [2.6]; Butler and Rodrick, *Australian Media Law* (n 3 above) [2.110].

[64] *Morgan v Lingen* (1863) 8 LT 800, 801.

[65] In the US: *Seip v Deshler* 170 Pa 334; 32 A 1032 at 1033 (Pa, 1895); *Lawson v Morning Journal Association* 32 AD 71; 52 NY Supp 484 (NY SC App Div, 1898) where a defence of truth was argued; *Wemple v Delano* 187 Misc 710; 65 NYS 2d 322 (NY SC, 1946). In the UK: *Hodson v Pare* [1899] 1 QB 455, CA where it was unsuccessfully argued it was not defamatory. In Australia: *Justin v Associated Newspapers Ltd* [1967] 1 NSWR 61, NSW CA; *Livingstone-Thomas v Associated Newspapers Ltd* [1969] 1 NSWR 771, NSW CA. In New Zealand a jury found the imputation was not defamatory of a plaintiff, though Burrows has cautioned that it is still capable of being defamatory in that country: *Hall v Fourth Estate Holdings Ltd* (HC Auckland, c2003, CP 476/00) cited and discussed in J Burrows, 'Media Law' (2004) 4 New Zealand Law Review 787.

One of the earliest of the tort writers, Addison, seems to have found it difficult to make sense of the decision in *Morgan*. In 1860, prior to *Morgan*, his definition of libellous words was:

> Every publication in writing, holding up a plaintiff to publick [sic] hatred, contempt, or ridicule, or having a tendency to make him feared, or his society shunned and avoided, is a libel.[66]

In 1874, an addition was made:

> Every publication in writing, *imputing insanity to the plaintiff*, or holding him up to public hatred, contempt, or ridicule, or having a tendency to make him feared, or his society shunned and avoided, is a libel.[67]

Insanity is accommodated as a *sui generis* test for actionability, suggesting he thought the defamatory capacity of the imputation was inconsistent with liability on the other grounds.

From the turn of the century through until the late 1930s Clerk and Lindsell also saw the actionability of insanity imputations as being inconsistent with the general principles of defamation. A publication would be generally actionable if it imputed a serious departure 'from the accepted rules of right-feeling, good conduct, and prudence' because such departures were either hateful or contemptible.[68] Other than ridicule, which could 'be incurred through accidental circumstances', imputations would not be actionable in the absence of moral blame.[69] For this reason, they argued that an imputation of insanity—'rather a subject of pity than any harsher feeling'—would not of itself be actionable.[70] This position was taken in spite of the decision in *Morgan*. Not until the ninth edition (published after the decision in *Youssoupoff* and with reference to that case) did they write that an imputation could be defamatory even though it suggested no 'moral turpitude' on the plaintiff's part, conceding that insanity could be actionable even though it was a subject of pity.[71]

Fraser's works in the 1890s identify defamatory material as that which is 'injurious to the reputation', by which he means it is 'of a disparaging nature,—anything which exposes the plaintiff to hatred, contempt, ridicule, or obloquy, or causes him to be shunned or avoided…'.[72] The cases, including the finding that an imputation of insanity is defamatory, are then explained as being consistent with this definition.[73]

[66] CG Addison, *Wrongs and their Remedies* (1st edn, 1860) 579.

[67] CG Addison, *Wrongs and their Remedies* (4th edn, 1873) 777, emphasis added.

[68] JF Clerk and WHB Lindsell, *The Law of Torts* (6th edn, 1912) 596, 598; (7th edn, 1921) 549–50; (8th edn, 1929) 500–1; (9th edn, 1937) 575–7.

[69] Ibid.

[70] Ibid (6th edn, 1912) 598–9; (7th edn, 1921) 551; (8th edn, 1929) 502; (9th edn, 1937) 578.

[71] Ibid (9th edn, 1937) 577.

[72] H Fraser, *Principles and Practice of the Law of Libel and Slander* (1893) 1; later editions use the same formulation, though omit 'obloquy'.

[73] Ibid 2; (2nd edn, 1897) 1–2; (3rd edn, 1901) 6; (4th edn, 1908) 6–7; (5th edn, 1917) 10; (6th edn, 1925) 10–11.

There is no elaboration on the meaning of 'disparaging', but Fraser clearly thought insanity imputations were defamatory because they disparaged the plaintiff. This is different from the position taken by Addison and Clerk and Lindsell under which the imputation seemed not to be disparaging, but was defamatory nonetheless.

Thomas Cooley's American *Treatise on the Law of Torts* stated that a publication libels a plaintiff if it:

> Renders him contemptible or ridiculous in public estimation, or exposes him to public hatred, ridicule or contempt, *or hinders virtuous men from associating with him.*[74]

Cooley argues that a 'moral [or] legal wrong' or breach of the 'moral code' must be attributed to the plaintiff for the imputation to be libellous. In the course of this, he has no quarrel with the decisions of the courts that had held an insanity imputation to be libellous:

> [S]ince the belief that one is not in his right mind has a natural tendency to withdraw from him the association of his fellows, to publish of one that he is insane, and a fit person to be sent to the lunatic asylum, is libellous.[75]

The decisions and Cooley's view of them suggest that imputations of insanity had a negative effect on a person's moral worth. That is, the fact that 'virtuous men' would not associate with an insane person indicated that the insane person was not seen to be virtuous in the same way as other people. For Cooley, as for Fraser, the insanity imputation did in fact carry the requisite disgrace that had been denied in *Mayrant*.

Just as *Youssoupoff* suggested that a diminution of moral worth could result from some kind of immoral association, the insanity cases suggest the possibility that there is another way that moral worth may be diminished. There is no need for moral fault, nor even for immoral association. Instead, it seems that at least some authors thought moral worth could be diminished by what might be thought of as an 'ascriptive moral inferiority'. In common with the ascriptive or identity-based factors Wyatt-Brown discusses in his study of honour, it is a factor over which neither the plaintiff nor anyone else has any control.[76] The plaintiff's health or (dis)ability becomes a factor which diminishes their moral and social worth in the eyes of the community.

Youssoupoff represents substantial judicial creativity. The texts suggest that there was disagreement and uncertainty about why insanity imputations had been held to be defamatory and at least some of the writers seemed to think

[74] TM Cooley, *A Treatise on the Law of Torts or the Wrongs which arise Independently of Contract* (3rd edn, 1906) 401, emphasis added. This statement seems to have been taken from the Supreme Court of Errors of Connecticut: *Lindley v Horton* 27 Conn 58, 61 (Hinman J delivering the opinion of the court) (Conn, 1858). The definition was subsequently used regularly in several American states and continues to be cited.

[75] Ibid 403, citing as examples *Perkins v Mitchell* 31 Barb 461 (NY, 1860) and *Lawson v Morning Journal Association* 32 App Div 71; 52 NY Supp 484 (NY SC App Div, 1898).

[76] See Chapter 2, II(D)(1).

actionability was inconsistent with the legal principles. The texts do not support the claim by Slesser LJ that insanity imputations were defamatory because they had a tendency to make the plaintiff shunned and avoided even though there was no suggestion of moral discredit (whether that term is understood narrowly as meaning moral fault or more broadly as a diminution in moral worth). The case law is similarly unpersuasive. Only one decision, *Mayrant*, is at all reasoned and that came down on the side of the defendant. There is nothing in the other cases to support Slesser's position.

Conclusion

The courts have distinguished the supplementary tests from the principal test for what is defamatory on the grounds that a publication can be actionable under the former without imputing any moral fault to the plaintiff. This distinction is an inappropriate and inadequate tool for understanding reputation and defamation. The broader concept of 'moral worth' is a better way to think about how reputations are harmed and how the law protects them under the supplementary tests. A person's moral worth may be diminished by the fact that they have engaged in some morally blameworthy behaviour ('moral fault'), or by the fact that they have been subjected to some kind of behaviour or circumstance that is regarded by the community as morally repugnant ('immoral association'), or—possibly—on the grounds that they have a characteristic that is regarded by the community as constituting an 'ascriptive moral inferiority'. This last factor will be of further interest in Chapter 8.

The analysis in this chapter suggests that words will only be actionable under the 'shun and avoid' test when the publication tends to produce a negative moral judgment of the plaintiff (ie, where it tends to diminish the plaintiff's moral worth). With the possible exception of *Villers v Monsley*, the disease and insanity cases do not suggest otherwise. I have argued that *Villers* should be disregarded. Even at the time *Villers* was decided there were good reasons not to use the slander cases to guide the decisions on disease imputations in libel cases and now, long after the protection of reputation has become the clear object of the law, they should carry no weight at all. Disease imputations should not be actionable as libel unless the publication imputes something that tends to diminish the plaintiff's moral worth. Similarly, the suggestions in *Youssoupoff* that insanity cases were decided on a 'shun and avoid' basis and that moral discredit is irrelevant to actionability do not stand up to scrutiny.

The recent trend towards appending 'the right-thinking person' standard to the 'shun and avoid' test is a correct step in stating the law. It makes explicit the moral judgment that was present in *Youssoupoff*, without requiring that there be any moral fault on the plaintiff's part. If the 'shun and avoid' test is used to determine actionability, 'the right-thinking person' standard should be explicitly stated as a part of it. This means, of course, that ethical recognition and the possibility of its refusal would apply to the 'shun and avoid' test just as they apply to the principal test.

On this analysis, the test could arguably be revised to render a publication actionable if it has a tendency to make right-thinking persons in the community shun and avoid the plaintiff. However, this would not be a satisfactory test for actionability. Compare it with the principal test under which a publication will be actionable if it has a tendency to make right-thinking persons in the community think the less of the plaintiff. There is an important difference between these expressions. Consider, for example, the question of whether an imputation that a person has a contagious disease might be actionable. It might be that a right-thinking person will shun and avoid someone with a contagious disease and not think the less of them in any way at all. The publication would be actionable under the revised 'shun and avoid' test on the grounds that there it tends to prompt particular *behaviour* by right-thinking people. That tendency should not make a publication actionable because it does not rely on an indicator that relates to reputation. Reputation, it will be recalled, is the *judgment* made about a person. Only if behaviour is prompted or accompanied by a negative judgment can it be said that the publication has a tendency to damage the person's reputation. Otherwise, what has occurred may be harm in the form of the loss of association, but that is not of itself reputational harm. It should not be actionable as defamation if the purpose of defamation law is to protect reputation.

The consequence of this is that the shun and avoid test should not be applied except in so far as it makes actionable publications which tend to prompt a negative judgment of the plaintiff. This makes the shun and avoid test and the principal test indistinguishable, with the single exception that the former has a higher threshold than the latter which merely requires that the imputation tends to lower the estimation of the plaintiff. Thus, anything actionable under the correctly conceived supplementary test would also be actionable under the principal test, and hence the shun and avoid test is superfluous. The shun and avoid test should be discarded. Any imputations that might be actionable under it can be determined more appropriately under the principal test, without a confusion or conflation of behaviour and judgment as indicators of a tendency to harm reputation.

When the idea of moral worth is applied to the case law associated with the shun and avoid test, it helps throw light upon the moral taxonomies that govern reputation and indicates that moral judgment and processes of ethical recognition are as much at work here as they are in the principal test when the law protects reputation. Consequently, some of the unresolved issues relating to the principal test remain unresolved. There are important and unanswered questions about the processes of ethical recognition and how the law is to take account of diverse moral taxonomies. There are still questions about the appropriate scope and limits of the legal protection of reputation. These will be examined in Chapter 8. Before that inquiry, Chapter 7 will examine the second of the supplementary tests.

7

The Ridicule Test as the Basis for Actionability

This chapter examines how a publication is actionable as defamation under the ridicule test and the extent to which it can be said that reputation is protected under that test. As in Chapter 6, the moral fault critique and the lines of authority on which the current law relies will be important. However, where the 'shun and avoid' cases could be categorized according to the imputations in issue, the ridicule cases do not for the most part lend themselves to this kind of classification because there is a diversity of factual scenarios and little consistency in the reasoning. There is no established path of analysis in the cases or the literature. Indeed, there have been few attempts to reconcile what often seem to be disparate approaches and sometimes conflicting legal principles.[1] The longstanding lack of clarity and certainty in the rationale behind the test, especially with respect to the relationship between ridicule and reputation, and the often questionable reliance on precedent suggest that the ridicule test is best examined chronologically.

Section I considers the formation of the ridicule test from 1680–1936. While it was quickly accepted that ridicule could found a defamation action, there was no clear sense of why or in what circumstances it could do so. Over time, the test came to have a wide scope and much room for flexibility in its application. Section II examines the American attempt to discern and articulate some rationale for the test in 1936 in *Burton v Crowell*. This marked an expansion of the law as publications would be actionable when they damaged a plaintiff's sense of self-worth regardless of whether their reputation was affected. Section III looks at how the reasoning in *Burton* became a settled part of the law in the later part of the 20th century. Section IV turns to what has become the most contentious aspect of the law where ridicule of the plaintiff is in issue: the actionability of satire.[2]

[1] Some attempts have been made in: *Berkoff v Burchill* [1996] 4 All ER 1008, CA; *Ettingshausen v Australian Consolidated Press Ltd* (1991) 23 NSWLR 443, NSW SC; J Cottrell, 'What Does "Defamatory" Mean? Reflections on *Berkoff v Burchill*' [1998] Tort Law Review 149; R Magnusson, 'Freedom of Speech in Australian Defamation Law: Ridicule, Satire and Other Challenges' (2001) 9 Torts Law Journal 269.

[2] It will be presumed that all publications discussed constitute more than 'vulgar abuse', which is not actionable as defamation: *Mundey v Askin* [1982] 2 NSWLR 369, NSW CA. The actionability of abusive words is addressed in: J Wade, 'Tort Liability for Abusive and Insulting Words'

I. Formation: The Origins and Early Application of the Test

The ridicule test was formed in two stages. The first consists of the cases decided during the 17th and 18th centuries when the common law had not settled on clear principles of libel law. The second stage is found in cases decided from 1827–1936. The courts during this period could confidently assert that a person who had been ridiculed would *prima facie* have an actionable case in defamation, though there was little certainty about just what it was that made the publication actionable. The test's formation helps explain the background of protection of reputation against which the test would expand in 1936, and will show how these older cases were concerned with the protection of reputation in a way that has not been recognized in the contemporary cases.

A. The earliest decisions: *Mason, Cropp,* and *Villers*

The first indication that a person held up to ridicule could have an actionable claim in defamation is found in 1680. In *Mason v Jennings*, a coachman sued a passenger for defamation because the passenger 'rode Skimmington' on the coach so as to ridicule the coachman.[3] To ride Skimmington was to face backwards while sitting on a horse and it was understood that a person riding this way had been beaten by his wife. The single-paragraph judgment in *Mason* states only that this was defamatory of the plaintiff. There is no indication as to why it was defamatory. The case does not at all suggest that moral judgment is irrelevant to actionability where ridicule is concerned. On the contrary, the better view is that in 1680 a man who would be beaten by his wife was to be viewed as a lesser man than others and a negative moral judgment of him was warranted. The ridicule that followed such an imputation was really evidence of the plaintiff's lowered esteem in the community. Although the facts may have been novel as the basis for a claim, there is no indication that the court in *Mason* saw itself making a determination that was remarkable.

Thirteen years later, *Mason* was cited in *Cropp v Tilney*.[4] *Cropp* was not itself a case involving ridicule. The fact that riding Skimmington could be actionable was used as authority for the proposition that words could be actionable without a 'scandalous' imputation arising: it would be enough 'if the defendant induces an ill opinion to be had of the plaintiff, or to make him contemptible and ridiculous'.[5] As discussed in Chapter 4, Hawkins' *Pleas of the Crown* in 1716 provided

(1950–51) 4 Vanderbilt Law Review 63; PR Handford, 'Tort Liability for Threatening or Insulting Words' (1976) 54 Canadian Bar Review 563.

[3] *Mason v Jennings* [1680] Raym Sir T 401, 83 ER 209.

[4] *Cropp v Tilney* (1693) 3 Salk 225, 91 ER 791.

[5] Ibid 226. *Mason v Jennings* was not referred to by name but is clearly the case the court had in mind.

the first statement of 'hatred, contempt, or ridicule' as the test for what is defamatory. It can only be conjecture, but it would seem reasonable to surmise that Hawkins' phrase took its form in part because of the decisions in *Mason* and *Cropp*. This is important because it means that there is nothing in the original expression of the traditional test that suggests moral judgment would ever be irrelevant to a determination of actionability. That is, the 'hatred, contempt, or ridicule' test reflected the case law, and all the case law involved imputations that prompted a negative evaluation of the plaintiff's moral worth. This changed in 1769 when the Court of King's Bench decided *Villers v Monsley*, a case that continues to be cited today.[6]

The plaintiff in *Villers* had been accused of having a disease—'the itch', which could be caught inadvertently by contact with the clothes of an infected person—and the court held the publication was actionable, even though the imputation did not 'bring any disgrace upon a man'.[7] In the course of its determination the court noted the actionability of ridicule:

> I have no doubt at present but that the writing and publishing [of] any thing which renders a man ridiculous is actionable…[8]

No authority is cited for this statement of law. There was also a suggestion that the imputation in the case exposed the plaintiff to ridicule:

> whether the itch be occasioned by a man's fault or misfortune, it is a cruel charge, and renders him both ridiculous and miserable, by being kept out of all company…[9]

That position conflates and confuses the ridicule and disease bases of actionability. The former stemmed from the emergent 'hatred, contempt, or ridicule' formulation that made written slurs on reputation actionable, while the latter stemmed from the slander categories under which spoken disease imputations were actionable. There is no doubt that the court had some trouble with ascertaining or articulating exactly what it was that made the statement defamatory and it is impossible to know exactly what the court thought about the law. Indeed, it seems difficult to establish precisely what the judges meant when they said the imputation rendered the plaintiff ridiculous. Although the case is not in substance a ridicule case but (as argued in the previous chapter) is better seen as one where the publication alleged the plaintiff suffered a disease, it is possible to see why the case came to occupy an important place in the ridicule test.

First, the court certainly accepted that ridicule could be the basis for actionability. That acceptance would be consistent with *Mason*, *Cropp*, and the recognition of ridicule in Hawkins' *Pleas of the Crown*, and the court would have been aware of each of these. Secondly, because disease imputations were actionable as

[6] *Berkoff v Burchill* [1996] 4 All ER 1008, 1014 (Neill LJ), CA.
[7] *Villers v Monsley* (1769) 2 Wils 403, 95 ER 886, KB; see Chapter 6, V(A)(1).
[8] Ibid 404 (Bathurst J), 404 (Gould J).
[9] Ibid 404 (Wilmot LCJ).

slander regardless of whether they tended to prompt a negative moral judgment of the plaintiff, the conflation in *Villers* gives the impression that a statement exposing the plaintiff to ridicule will be actionable even if it does not prompt a negative moral judgment. In this way, the reasoning thus permits later courts to interpret the law to allow a wider range of publications to be actionable than would be the case if a negative moral judgment was required. This was a very significant step because it meant that courts in future ridicule cases did not need to distinguish between, on the one hand, the fact that the publication ridiculed the plaintiff or tended to expose them to ridicule and, on the other, a publication's tendency to prompt a negative moral judgment of the plaintiff. This flexibility would come to dominate the interpretation and application of the ridicule test.

Even once the protection of reputation became the stated rationale for defamation law in the early 19th century, there was little attempt to deal with the possibility that ridicule may not detract from one's reputation and what consequences that might have for determining actionability. Instead, the cases were soon characterized by the absence of a clearly articulated and consistent rationale for why ridicule is actionable.

B. From the 19th to the 20th century

Villers v Monsley was used as authority for a ridicule test in *Levi v Milne* in 1827.[10] In the following hundred or so years there are around seven other reported cases where plaintiffs claimed they were defamed because they were exposed to ridicule. They succeeded on all occasions but one.

Although the publication in *Levi v Milne* ridiculed the plaintiff, actionability was not clearly decided on that basis. Levi, the plaintiff, was a sheriff's officer who went to the house of a person he was trying to locate for the purposes of serving a writ. There, he found a woman in bed and quickly ran from the house. He was sued for trespass and had to pay damages. Milne published a magazine that included in one issue an eight-verse doggerel poem that humorously recounted the story and made fun of Levi. Levi sued Milne for libel, eventually succeeding on appeal.

Justice Park's position captures the general agreement that the law was:

> as laid down by Wilmot J, Bathurst J, and the rest of the Court, in *Villers v Monsley*, and as it has always been held,—that whatever is published of a man tending to make him ridiculous, or to prevent others from associating with him, is a libel . . .[11]

Presumably, *Mason v Jennings* was the sort of decision that Park J had in mind when he said 'it had always been held' that ridicule could be defamatory. The proposition that loss of association was relevant presumably flowed from the

[10] *Levi v Milne* (1827) 4 Bing 195, 130 ER 743.
[11] Ibid 200, 745 (Park J), citation omitted.

slander cases on disease. In the instance at hand, it was said to be libellous to publish a work 'holding [the plaintiff] up in the most ridiculous light'.[12] The case is not a straightforward application of this principle because the publication cast a slur on the plaintiff's performance as a sheriff's officer and involved disrespect for the courts and their officers.[13] It is nevertheless clear that the court thought the publication conveyed an imputation that diminished Levi's standing in the eyes of his community. This occurred either by virtue of the slur on Levi's ability to perform his job properly, or in the suggestion of unmanly fright he took at the sight of the naked woman.

Cook v Ward was decided soon after *Levi* and the appellate judges clearly accepted that words which exposed the plaintiff to ridicule could be actionable.[14] The plaintiff, Cook, had told a group of friends about an occasion where he had been in a public house and was mistaken for a hangman. The defendant newspaper had published this story and the plaintiff found himself ridiculed in his community and excluded from his circle of friends.[15] The defendant argued there was nothing in the publication that could have made the plaintiff the object of ridicule and any ridicule suffered was a consequence of the plaintiff having told the story in the first place. The court found for the plaintiff on the grounds that 'there is a great difference between a man's telling a ludicrous story of himself to a circle of his own acquaintances, and a publication of it to all the world through the medium of a newspaper'.[16]

A not dissimilar situation arose in *Dolby v Newnes* where the defendant newspaper published a transcript of an 'after-dinner speech' that had ridiculed the plaintiff.[17] What is of interest is that the publication could be actionable whether or not it was true because when a speech originally made to a small, private group was published to the general public, it infringed 'that honest liberty of private life and... that sense of dignity and propriety which were among the most cherished qualities of the people of this country'.[18] The jury awarded damages 50 times greater than those the plaintiff had claimed.[19]

In *Dunlop Rubber Co Ltd v Dunlop* an Irish resident sought an injunction to prevent the distribution in Ireland of advertising material which included a caricature of his image, complaining that the material 'expose[d] him to public ridicule or contempt by misrepresenting his appearance or costume'.[20] The decision was concerned with other issues but it was accepted by the House of Lords

[12] Ibid 199, 745 (Best CJ), 200–1, 745–6 (Burrough J); cf Park and Gasalee JJ who both found the publication libellous but did not state what it was that made the publication satisfy the test.

[13] Ibid.

[14] *Cook v Ward* (1830) 6 Bing 409, 130 ER 1338.

[15] Ibid 410–11.

[16] Ibid 415–16 (Tindal CJ, with the court concurring).

[17] *Dolby v Newnes* (1887) 3 TLR 393, QB.

[18] Ibid 394.

[19] Ibid.

[20] *Dunlop Rubber Co Ltd v Dunlop* [1921] 1 AC 367, 370 (Lord Birkenhead LC), HL.

that the publication 'was at least capable of carrying a defamatory meaning'.[21] Though often cited in the texts, the case is ultimately of little assistance because no explanation or analysis was provided.[22]

Two American ridicule cases were decided in the early-20th century.[23] The defendant newspaper in *Snyder v New York Press Co Ltd* recounted the story of a process server inadvertently walking in on the plaintiff while she was in the bath.[24] As the previous chapter explained, the plaintiff's reputation was damaged because of the immoral association involved and that, it seemed, was why the publication was actionable.[25] In the second case, *Zbyszko v New York American Inc*, the plaintiff complained that when the defendant published an article on the scientific theory of evolution, it had defamed him by placing a picture of him next to one of a gorilla with the caption, 'Stanislaus Zbyszko, the Wrestler, Not Fundamentally Different from the Gorilla in Physique'.[26] The court stated that publication tended 'to disgrace the plaintiff and bring him into ridicule and contempt'. It was noted that under the law:

> It is not necessary that words impute disgraceful conduct to the plaintiff. If they render him contemptible or ridiculous, he is equally entitled to redress.[27]

The article in *Zbyszko* conveyed an imputation the plaintiff was animal-like and somehow less than human. It did not attribute any flaw for which the plaintiff was somehow responsible, but it still seemed to suggest that the plaintiff was a lesser person than others even though he bore no moral responsibility for carrying that lesser status.

C. The legal position by the 1930s

It will be recalled that Parke B confirmed the 'hatred, contempt, or ridicule' test for defamatory matter in 1840. While the third arm of that statement reflected the decided cases, there was certainly no coherent, logical approach to the proposition that ridicule could be actionable as defamation. Little changed in the decades that followed. Nevertheless, some general observations might still be made about the significance of the case law as it stood in the 1930s.

21 Ibid 370 (Lord Birkenhead LC), 374, 375 (Atkinson and Moulton LJJ agreeing).

22 For example, P Milmo and WVH Rogers, *Gatley on Libel and Slander* (10th edn, 2004) [2.2], [2.4]; M Gillooly, *The Law of Defamation in Australia & New Zealand* (1998) 48.

23 An earlier American decision recites the acceptance of the ridicule test though on the facts it was unnecessary to apply it: *Stewart v Swift Specific Company* 76 Georgia 280 (Ga, 1886). *Swift* relied on *Villers v Monsley* (1769) 2 Wils 403, 95 ER 886, KB and *Cook v Ward* (1830) 6 Bing 409, 130 ER 1338 (among others) but does not itself appear to be cited in the later American ridicule cases.

24 *Snyder v New York Press Co Ltd* 121 NY Supp 944 (NY SC App Div, 1910); see Chapter 6, II(B).

25 On immoral association see Chapter 6, II(B).

26 *Zbyszko v New York American Inc* 239 NY Supp 411 (NY SC App Div, 1930).

27 Ibid.

First, moral judgment was relevant to almost all the determinations of actionability where ridicule was the substance of the complaint. In *Mason*, *Levi*, *Cook*, *Dolby*, *Zbyszko*, and *Snyder* the exposure to ridicule was actionable because it detracted somehow from the plaintiff's social standing because the publication imputed some moral fault or some immoral association, or perhaps in *Zbyszko* it was some ascriptive moral inferiority.[28] That is, in each of these cases it seems that the publication had the tendency to convey an imputation that went (negatively) to a matter on which a community would base its judgments of a person and thus lower the plaintiff in the estimation of his or her community. Only in *Villers* was it said that the allegation did not carry any disgrace. As such, it is appropriate to characterize the ridicule arm of the test as one that traditionally functioned to protect reputation. However, in no cases was the law explicitly examined or applied with a view to ensuring that was the case. Rather, it looks like a more intuitive process based on a general sense that it was unacceptable to publish some things about a person, even if they were true.

This prompts a second observation: it seems that the truth of a statement will be irrelevant where ridicule is the basis for actionability. In *Levi* and *Cook* there was no doubt that the information published was true but the courts expressed no concern about that. Instead, the decisions apparently proceeded on the footing that it would not matter whether the publications were true. This seems to place ridicule in a very different position from the principal test and the 'shun and avoid' test where truth had long been a defence to defamation. Why is this position taken? It seems from *Cook* and *Dolby* that there was a judicial willingness to use defamation law to protect a plaintiff's privacy. In effect, the courts recognized that certain facts were relevant to reputation but refused to permit general disclosure of those facts without the plaintiff's consent. It seems from the cases that publishers were denied the possibility of arguing a defence. This is inconsistent with the general availability of the justification defence and suggests instead that the courts were willing to allow a plaintiff to retain a reputation that (as the expression goes) they did not necessarily deserve. The court is not protecting reputation. The court is protecting the plaintiff's sense of self-worth, which may be diminished by the disclosure of private facts, whether or not those facts would prompt a negative moral judgment of the plaintiff.

[28] I am reluctant to classify *Dunlop* because there is no discussion of why the publications were defamatory. However, it is plausible that the plaintiff could be thought to bear some moral fault for having allowed himself to be made to look like a fool. That inference might be drawn because, as the inventor of the pneumatic tyre which the Dunlop company produced and with the company bearing his name, the ordinary reasonable reader might well think that he has allowed himself to be abused, manipulated, exploited, duped, or hoodwinked by the company with which he had such a close association and that he should have known better. In *Cook* it is difficult to tell whether the disgrace followed from some sense that the plaintiff's behaviour was of itself morally blameworthy, or whether some immoral association was attributed to the fact of what had happened to him at the hotel, or whether the disgrace arose because the event had been made public. It does, however, seem clear that the plaintiff's moral standing was diminished. The refusal to associate with him was not analogous to the refusal to associate with a person infected with a contagious disease.

The position was made more complex in 1926 when the English Court of Appeal decided *Emerson v Grimsby Times* in favour of the defendant.[29] Here, the plaintiff sued a newspaper over its report of his wedding. The paper mistakenly printed an article about the wedding the day before the ceremony occurred. The paper had reported that the plaintiff was on his honeymoon on a day when he was in fact at work.[30] His workmates ridiculed him. The court's reasoning is not entirely clear but it effectively stated that no cause of action arose because the article was not defamatory. Lord Justice Bankes thought no imputation could be conveyed that would provide grounds for subjecting the plaintiff to ridicule because the paper had obviously made a mistake.[31] To Warrington LJ: 'It was absurd to think that [the article] . . . should entitle him to say that he was thereby held up to ridicule and contempt.'[32] It was presumably irrelevant that the plaintiff was in fact ridiculed because there was nothing about the text of the article that of itself held him up to ridicule. Lord Atkin reluctantly concurred in the decision, but was inclined to think that in the circumstances the article could have been defamatory.[33]

What should be made of the case? The court was clearly applying some limit to the ridicule test for actionability, but the nature of that limit is very unclear. Four possibilities come to mind. On one view, trivial matters would not be actionable and the plaintiff failed because he suffered an insignificant degree of ridicule. Alternatively, actionability may depend on the manner in which the publication holds a plaintiff up to ridicule. Here, the publication did not do so on its face. Of course, that would seem to inappropriately remove innuendo from the interpretation of the work, and obviously the plaintiff's workmates drew the requisite innuendo. A third interpretation might be that the absence of any intention to ridicule the plaintiff was relevant, at least in so far as a clear error demonstrates a lack of intent to ridicule and thus prevents a defamatory imputation being conveyed. That is, the reader would not see the publication as casting aspersions on the plaintiff because there has clearly been a mistake. A fourth view might be that ridicule would not be actionable where it did not impute to the plaintiff any moral fault or immoral association. That is, *Emerson* is distinct among the ridicule cases because there is no suggestion that the plaintiff is somehow diminished in the eyes of the community. This is, at least in part, based upon the presumption that the ordinary reasonable reader would have realised that the newspaper had made an error.

The sum effect of the cases was that the wide scope for actionability opened up by *Villers v Monsley* remained a part of the common law by the 1930s. The cases after *Villers* did not restrict this scope because there was no clear or comparative

[29] *Emerson v Grimsby Times & Telegraph Company Ltd* (1926) 42 TLR 238, CA.
[30] Ibid 239 (Bankes LJ).
[31] Ibid 239 (Bankes LJ).
[32] Ibid 239 (Warrington LJ).
[33] Ibid 239 (Atkin LJ).

explanation of why ridicule should be actionable, nor was it precisely clear how the test was to be applied. In particular, it was not clear whether the form of publication was at the heart of actionability or whether (as in *Emerson* and perhaps *Zbyszko*) it was the substantive imputation conveyed by a publication. Mostly, the cases were characterised by a combination of the two: the publication was in a form that somehow poked fun at or ridiculed the plaintiff and had a substance that somehow conveyed an imputation that would prompt a negative judgment of the plaintiff (eg, *Mason*, *Levi*, *Cook*, *Dolby*, or *Snyder*). *Emerson* indicated that there were limits to actionability, but there was little certainty about what those limits were or the rationale behind them. Against this background, *Burton v Crowell Publishing Company* was to mark a turning point when in 1936 the United States Court of Appeals for the 2nd Circuit attempted to identify some coherent principles.

II. Expansion: from Social Worth to Self-Worth

Burton v Crowell sits with *Sim v Stretch* and *Youssoupoff* as having shaped the contemporary law of defamation. It was the first thoroughly reasoned decision on ridicule as the test for what is defamatory. Delivering the opinion of the court, Judge Learned Hand's explanation of how a plaintiff's reputation could be affected by ridicule would be crucial because the publication did not convey any imputations that might have lowered the plaintiff in the estimation of the community.

The plaintiff in *Burton* was a jockey who participated in an advertising campaign for the Camel brand of cigarettes. He was photographed holding a saddle and the resulting picture showed the straps of the saddle hanging between his legs, but they appeared to be attached to the jockey rather than the saddle. The result was a 'ribald' image of the plaintiff and combined with the caption under the next photograph—'Get a lift with a Camel'—it made the photograph 'grotesque, monstrous and obscene'.[34] The court rejected the plaintiff's claim that the advertisement depicted him as being 'physically deformed and mentally perverted' because the image was clearly an inadvertent 'optical illusion'.[35] However, the court did find that 'it exposed the plaintiff to overwhelming ridicule': the image 'made of the plaintiff a preposterously ridiculous spectacle; and the obvious mistake only added to the amusement'.[36]

Was a publication of this kind actionable? Considering a range of authorities from England and the United States, Hand J was unsure:

> Literally, therefore, the injury falls within the accepted rubric; it exposes the sufferer to 'ridicule' and 'contempt'. Nevertheless, we have not been able to find very much in the

[34] *Burton v Crowell* 82 F 2d 154, 154 (2nd Cir, 1936).
[35] Ibid 154–5.
[36] Ibid 155.

books that is on point, for although it has long been recognized that pictures may be libels, and in some cases they have been caricatures, in nearly all they have impugned the plaintiff at least by implication, directly or indirectly uttering some falsehood about him.[37]

This statement does not quite accurately reflect the case law. Certainly, cases like *Dolby* and *Cook* do not fit the statement. The plaintiffs there were indeed impugned, but not by falsehood. Nonetheless, Hand J continues and examines the authorities to see whether ridicule can be defamatory in the absence of any impugning of the plaintiff's moral worth. The reasoning is troubling in some important respects.

First, he turns to cases that were not concerned with ridicule and notes there are numerous instances where there is no slur on a person's 'moral qualities' and yet the words have been actionable.[38] Such cases, it is said, have concerned imputations that a person is insane, or is a negro, or is poor.[39] This view of the case law is flawed. The insanity cases have already been addressed above, where it was noted that they were not decided on the basis that moral qualities were irrelevant. The next chapter will discuss the race cases and show they were very much concerned with a person's moral qualities.[40] The proposition that moral judgment did not matter in the poverty cases is unconvincing. These determinations generally relied on the 'shun and avoid' test which was argued in Chapter 6 to be an unpersuasive, ill-supported line of authority.[41] In all, when Hand J asserts that there is a line of authority where moral judgment has been irrelevant, he is in error.

Secondly, Hand J looks at cases where ridicule has been the basis for actionability. He notes that not all ridicule is actionable and finds that the cases suggest that 'a man must not be too thin-skinned or a self-important prig' and that ridicule will not be actionable when 'only a morbid person would not laugh [it] off'.[42] A publication would be actionable only if it exposed the plaintiff 'to more than trivial ridicule'.[43] On the facts in *Burton* he thought that 'the [plaintiff's] mortification, however ill-deserved, was a very substantial grievance'.[44] The problem with this observation is that Hand J does not explain the *nature* of the grievance. There is no question that the plaintiff was exposed to ridicule, and undoubtedly he would be angered and upset by that, but that does not mean the plaintiff's grievance concerns his reputation.

[37] Ibid.
[38] Ibid.
[39] Ibid.
[40] See Chapter 8, I(B).
[41] *Burton v Crowell* 82 F 2d 154 (2nd Cir, 1936) cites *Moffatt v Cauldwell* 3 Hun 26 (c1880). See *Katapodis v The Brooklyn Spectator* 38 NE 2d 112 (NY Ct App, 1941) for a better interpretation of *Moffatt*. In particular, the court in *Katapodis* notes that Townshend had viewed *Moffatt* and poverty imputations as an application of the 'shun and avoid' test: J Townshend, *A Treatise on the Wrongs called Slander and Libel* (4th edn, 1890) 220.
[42] *Burton v Crowell* 82 F 2d 154, 155 (2nd Cir, 1936).
[43] Ibid 156.
[44] Ibid 155–6.

Judge Hand maintains that exposure to ridicule such as that suffered by the plaintiff 'affects a man's reputation, if by that is meant his position in the minds of others; the association so established may be beyond repair; he may become known indefinitely as the absurd victim of this unhappy mischance'.[45] This is unsatisfactory. Although it may cause others to laugh at the plaintiff's expense, it is not clear how that fact alone—'being known indefinitely as the absurd victim of the unhappy mischance'—affects a person's worth or moral standing in the eyes of the others. This gap in the explanation is important because unless the plaintiff's standing is affected then it cannot be said that their reputation has been damaged. Later, the connection is argued in a little more detail:

> It seems to us that in principle there should be no doubt [that ridicule can be actionable as defamation]. The gravamen of the wrong in defamation is not so much the injury to reputation, measured by the opinions of others, as the feelings, that is, the repulsion or the light esteem, which those opinions engender.[46]

This means it does not matter whether the publication tended to prompt a negative moral judgment of the plaintiff. It is unhelpful to say it is the 'feelings' of the community that matter because nothing on the facts indicates repulsion or light esteem. It is true that the publication might tend to prompt the community to *behave* in certain ways, but that is not to the point unless those behaviours are accompanied by an ill opinion of the plaintiff. Judge Hand is expanding the law substantially. What becomes the criteria for actionability is not the feelings of the community, but the feelings of the plaintiff. He makes the plaintiff's sense of self-worth an interest that is to be protected under defamation laws. It is for this reason that the threshold test refers to the thickness of the plaintiff's skin; actionability is not about the community's feelings, but about the plaintiff's feelings. The law often takes account of the effect on a plaintiff's sense of self-worth when it is diminished as a result of an attack on their reputation.[47] But the rationale in *Burton* does not require this. It makes harm to self-worth actionable independently of the community's judgment of the plaintiff's social worth.

The effect of *Burton* was that it widened even further the scope of actionable publications under the ridicule test. This is noticeable when *Burton* is viewed in light of the earlier cases. First, all the actionable claims prior to the 1930s involved a negative moral judgment about the plaintiff, which was consistent with the protection of reputation. There had been no judicial statement saying whether such a tendency was or was not required for actionability. *Burton* effectively made that statement: there would be no need for the publication to tend to result in a negative moral evaluation of the plaintiff. Secondly, *Burton* confirmed that the truth of a publication was irrelevant where ridicule was in issue. Judge Hand rightly

45 Ibid 155.

46 Ibid 156.

47 *Carson v John Fairfax & Sons Ltd* (1993) 178 CLR 44, 60 (Mason CJ, Deane, Dawson and Gaudron JJ); *Crampton v Nugawela* (1996) 41 NSWLR 176, 190–2 (Mahoney A-CJ), NSW CA.

held that it would be 'a non sequitur to argue that whenever truth is not a defense there can be no libel'.[48] This makes sense—for many non-factual things might damage a person's reputation—but it ensured that the form of the publication rather than its substance would be sufficient to found an action. Thirdly, as I have argued above, *Burton* confirmed the tendency to protect the plaintiff's self-worth, rather than their reputation.

The expansion in *Burton* was inappropriate. It used a rationale under which publications could be actionable as defamation even though they did not have a tendency to damage the plaintiff's reputation. In the later part of the 20th century this rationale and the historical line of ridicule decisions combined to influence the contemporary application of the ridicule test.

III. Settlement: the Focus on Form, the Protection of Self-Worth, and the Failure to Explain the Connection Between Ridicule and Reputation

A. Decline and revival

If the law reports are any guide, plaintiffs did not rely on the ridicule test for some time after *Burton*, even though that decision left a deal of room to do so. Neither the major texts nor the leading decisions refer to ridicule cases decided between 1936 and 1980. Still, it was never suggested that the test had been abolished by the *Sim v Stretch* formula, nor that it had fallen into desuetude. *Halsbury's Laws of England* continued to identify it as a part of the law.[49] It might be argued that the expansive scope of the law had a chilling effect on publication, but the more likely reason is that the new 'lowering the estimation' formulation of the principal test was broad enough to take account of aspersions that fell short of hatred or contempt. As such, there would have been no need to rely on the old formulation of the test and argue that ridicule was the basis for the action.[50]

The ridicule test was revived in the New South Wales Supreme Court in 1980. In *Boyd v Mirror Newspapers Ltd* a rugby league footballer had been heavily criticized in an article headlined, 'Boyd is Fat, Slow and Predictable'.[51] Part of the plaintiff's case was unremarkable, arguing that the article in its entirety conveyed imputations that he was at fault for allowing his weight to increase and his fitness to deteriorate. However, one aspect of the argument was unusual. The journalist had described the plaintiff footballer as overweight and offered his impressions

[48] *Burton v Crowell* 82 F 2d 154, 156 (2nd Cir, 1936).

[49] *Halsbury's Laws of England* (3rd edn, 1958) Vol 24, [40]; (4th edn, 1978, 1997) Vol 28 [42].

[50] Eg, in *Gardiner v John Fairfax & Sons Pty Ltd* (1942) 42 SR(NSW) 171, NSW SC FC it was accepted that a scathing book review ridiculed the plaintiff but the court proceeded on the basis of the review's capacity to cause ordinary decent folk to think the less of the plaintiff:.

[51] *Boyd v Mirror Newspapers Ltd* [1980] 2 NSWLR 449, NSW SC.

of the team's entry to the playing field: 'As the player wearing No. 9 jersey for the Sea Eagles waddled into the sunshine, I couldn't believe it was Les Boyd.'[52] Justice Hunt accepted the plaintiff's argument that this was capable of defaming him because it suggested he 'was so fat as to appear ridiculous as he came on the field to play a first grade rugby league match'.[53] The definition of ridicule as Hunt J expressed it, and counsel agreed, was that 'ridiculous' means 'deserving to be laughed at or absurd'.[54] There was little explanation or analysis of the test. Citing *Cook*, *Dunlop*, *Burton*, and *Zbyszko*, Hunt J simply held that an imputation will be defamatory if it 'displays the plaintiff in a ridiculous light, notwithstanding the absence of any moral blame on his part'.[55] In the simple step of finding the article had a defamatory capacity on this basis, Hunt J awakened a dormant test.

B. Ridicule in the absence of moral fault or immoral association

The first claims to arise after *Boyd* paralleled the action in *Burton* as plaintiffs claimed they had been made to appear ridiculous and argued the publication was actionable even in the absence of any suggestion that there was some moral fault or immoral association on the their part. These cases have fallen into two categories. First, two New South Wales Supreme Court cases found that photographs of naked plaintiffs were actionable.[56] Secondly, the English Court of Appeal in *Berkoff v Burchill* held that it could be defamatory to poke fun at the plaintiff in writing.[57] Like *Burton*, each of these cases suggests that the ridicule test may render a publication actionable even if it does not affect reputation.

1. The photograph cases

In *Ettingshausen v Australian Consolidated Press Ltd* a rugby league footballer sued over the publication of a picture of him, naked, in the showers after a game.[58] The photograph was taken when the Australian team was accompanied on its tour of England by a journalist and photographer. All the team members were aware of their presence and the fact they were writing for publication. Two imputations were pleaded. First, that 'the plaintiff deliberately permitted a photograph to be taken of him with his genitals exposed for the purposes of reproduction in a publication with a widespread readership'; and, secondly, that 'the plaintiff is a person whose genitals have been exposed to the readers of the defendant's magazine "HQ", a publication with a widespread readership'.[59] The first imputation was cast in terms of the principal test, it being argued that people would think

[52] Ibid 451. [53] Ibid 452.
[54] Ibid 453. [55] Ibid.
[56] *Ettingshausen v Australian Consolidated Press Ltd* (1991) 23 NSWLR 443, NSW SC; *Obermann v ACP Publishing Pty Ltd* [2001] NSWSC 1022.
[57] *Berkoff v Burchill* [1996] 4 All ER 1008, CA.
[58] *Ettingshausen v Australian Consolidated Press Ltd* (1991) 23 NSWLR 443, NSW SC.
[59] Ibid 445.

the less of the plaintiff for such behaviour. The second imputation was argued on the grounds that 'as a result of the exposure of his genitals, he has been held up (or exposed) to ridicule'.[60]

Justice Hunt held that the third limb of the *Parmiter v Coupland* 'hatred, contempt, or ridicule' formulation was the basis of the ridicule test and observed that although 'some of the older cases provide examples of defamation by exposing the plaintiff to ridicule, ... there is little discussion in them of the principle involved'.[61] He turned to *Burton v Crowell* for an explanation of the test and after quoting from the case at some length he applied the principle from that case to Ettingshausen's claim in the following terms: 'the publication of this imputation is in my view capable of subjecting the entirely blameless plaintiff to a more than trivial degree of ridicule'.[62] Other than quoting *Burton*, there was no explanation of how exposure to ridicule affected the plaintiff's reputation.

This uncritical adoption of the *Burton* rationale made the protection of the plaintiff's self-worth—rather than the protection of his or her reputation—a fixture of the contemporary law.[63] This adoption of *Burton* was later approved and applied in *Obermann* where a magazine photograph of an Olympian water polo player's breasts was held to be capable of defaming the plaintiff.[64] This finding stood in spite of the statement by Levine J that:

> The tort of defamation, if successfully actionable, provides a remedy by way of damages for a person injured in that person's good name or reputation. It is not a remedy for a mere offence against personal dignity, good taste or an intrusion into a person's privacy.[65]

Justice Levine does not explain how a publication can be defamatory in the absence of any diminution of the plaintiff's reputation. He simply adopts *Ettingshausen*, quoting at length the passage in that case that adopted *Burton*.[66] There is no explanation of how the exposure to ridicule does more than embarrass, offend, or maybe humiliate the plaintiff.

It might be argued that the publication of a photograph would in fact diminish the plaintiff's standing in the eyes of the community. On this view, the connection between the publication and reputation is not related to the exposure to ridicule, but to the plaintiff being (immorally) associated with a magazine that was at least moderately pornographic. But this would require an application of the principal test and a view that the community's criteria for moral judgment saw such an occurrence as a fact that was relevant to the social judgment of the plaintiff.

[60] Ibid 447. An oddity of Ettingshausen's case was his claim that he was made to look ridiculous. The photograph was so grainy that his penis could barely be discerned and the the article praised Ettingshausen as being 'built like a Greek God'.

[61] Ibid 448.

[62] Ibid 448–9.

[63] Ibid.

[64] *Obermann v ACP Publishing Pty Ltd* [2001] NSWSC 1022 [40].

[65] Ibid [16].

[66] Ibid [37].

This seems a difficult argument to make in contemporary times, especially when the magazine did not suggest the plaintiff was a willing participant or had even consented to publication. As a result, if the principal test could not be satisfied and if the ridicule test is unconvincing as one that protects reputation then the plaintiff would be left without an action. This makes sense because the plaintiff's reputation has not apparently been damaged.

The second point to arise from the photograph cases is that contemporary courts have not applied an explicit process of ethical recognition to the ridicule test. In particular, the test was not applied with reference to the standards of right-thinking persons. Discussion of this issue is generally absent from the cases. Cottrell has suggested that it would raise problems because it might force a conclusion that right-thinking people, by definition, do not ridicule others in the community.[67] I am not sure that conclusion necessarily follows. It seems not unreasonable to think that ethical recognition is implicit in the reasoning, at least in so far as the courts would be willing to exclude some views in determining whether a publication has the requisite defamatory capacity. For example, if a plaintiff complained that she or he had somehow been depicted as a police officer and that would expose them to ridicule then the court would certainly consider 'the right-thinking person' standard just as it did in the informing cases.[68] Ethical recognition processes are at work but in this case they are focusing on whether the court should allow recovery for the hurt or humiliation felt by the plaintiff (the sense of self-worth) rather than for a diminution of the estimation in which he or she is held. What distinguishes *Ettingshausen* and *Obermann* is that they allowed recovery for the former.

Thirdly, the photograph cases call attention to the defence of justification. Although not strictly a matter of actionability, it indicates the importance of the fact that ridicule is generally actionable on the form of the publication rather than its substance. So, when the plaintiff in *Obermann* pleaded that her breasts had been exposed in the magazine, justification at common law would merely require proof of the fact of publication.[69] The defendant could not succeed in *Ettingshausen* or *Obermann* because the statutory defence of justification required the defendant to also establish that the publication was in the public interest. The upshot of this is that if the publication is actionable because of the form it takes and the defendant argues a justification defence at common law then the defendant must inevitably succeed because they have in fact done what the plaintiff complains of.

The photograph cases adhere to the *Burton* principles and rationale. They do not explain the connection between actionability and reputation any further than

[67] Cottrell (n 1 above) 157.

[68] See Chapter 5, III.

[69] *Obermann v ACP Publishing Pty Ltd* [2001] NSWSC 1022 [38]. Similar conclusions have been reached in Canada: *Hollinsworth v TV Group Ltd* [1996] CanLII 2379 [9] (BC SC); *Hollinsworth v BCTV* [1998] CanLII 6527 [20] (BC CA).

Hand J did. The second circumstance where the test has recently been applied has concerned written statements that plaintiffs claimed held them up to ridicule. These cases did not refer to *Burton* but the reasoning in the decisions was to the same effect.

2. *The written cases*

In what appears to be the first English ridicule case since *Emerson*, the Court of Appeal considered the nature of the test and its application in *Berkoff v Burchill*.[70] The plaintiff, Stephen Berkoff, is an actor and director who sued over statements in two 1995 film reviews. Neither was reviewing Berkoff's work. Burchill wrote that 'film directors, from Hitchcock to Berkoff are notoriously hideous-looking people' and later described the monster in a film version of *Frankenstein* as 'scarred and primeval', observing that 'it looks a lot like Stephen Berkoff, only marginally better-looking'.[71] Berkoff claimed that these statements implied he was 'hideously ugly' and, as such, tended to expose him to ridicule and/or would tend to cause people to shun and avoid him.[72] In a split decision, the Court of Appeal held that the imputation was capable of defaming the plaintiff.

The leading judgment was that of Neill LJ. He began by identifying a collection of definitions of defamatory matter, including those from *Parmiter v Coupland*, *Sim v Stretch*, and *Youssoupoff*, reaching the conclusion that the combined import of them was that:

> words may be defamatory, even though they [do not] impute disgraceful conduct to the plaintiff... if they hold him up to contempt scorn or ridicule or tend to exclude him from society. On the other hand insults which do not diminish a man's standing among other people do not found an action for libel or slander. The exact borderline may often be difficult to define.[73]

The problem with stating the test in this way is that it sets up an opposition between ridicule (which is actionable) and the absence of reduced standing (which is not actionable). The statement thus presumes that ridicule at some point becomes so great that it diminishes standing. This 'borderline' idea suggests that the two lie on the same continuum with some forms of communication falling on the actionable side of the line and some (such as insults) on the other side. As I have argued above, this is not a presumption that stands up to scrutiny; there has not been a persuasive explanation that ridicule is necessarily connected to the diminution of standing. That is, it might be that a person is held up to ridicule but that should not be the reason why a publication is actionable unless there is something about the publication that tends to reduce the plaintiff's standing.

[70] *Berkoff v Burchill* [1996] 4 All ER 1008, CA. There is a reference in *Berkoff* to an unreported judgment, *Winiard v Tatler Publishing Company Ltd* (CA, 16 July 1991), where ridicule might have been relevant but that case appears to have been decided using the principal test.

[71] *Berkoff v Burchill* [1996] 4 All ER 1008, 1010 (Neill LJ), CA.

[72] Ibid.

[73] Ibid 1013 (Neill LJ).

Secondly, Neill LJ examines the decided cases for guidance, quoting from several though not explaining how the cases are relevant or how they are to be reconciled. He really provides only a chronology of cases which state that ridicule has long given rise to actionable defamation and indicate that words have been actionable even though they do not suggest any moral wrongdoing or blame on the plaintiff's part. Somewhat curiously, while the American decision of *Zbyszko* was cited, *Burton* was not. The rationale from *Burton* was, however, very much present in Neill's mind because he noted the Supreme Court of Canada's unanimous view in *Manning v Hill* that defamation law 'serves the equally or perhaps more fundamentally important purpose of fostering our self-image and sense of self-worth'.[74] This may be so where the effect on self-worth follows from damage to reputation, but in so far as the protection of self-worth is seen as a goal of defamation law regardless of the impact on reputation then the Canadian court has seriously misstated the purpose of defamation law. However, the *Manning v Hill* view is not an inaccurate observation of the ridicule cases because, as *Burton* and *Ettingshausen* show, the law has indeed protected self-worth independently of reputation.

Thirdly, Neill LJ deals with the arguments advanced by counsel. The defendant argued that *Sim v Stretch* distinguishes between statements that constitute 'bad manners or discourtesy' which should not be defamatory and 'attacks on character' which constitute an injury to reputation and should be defamatory, and submitted that Burchill's publication fell into the first category.[75] Neill LJ agrees with this, but concludes that the publication may be defamatory 'because it affects in an adverse manner the attitude of other people towards [the plaintiff]'.[76] The problem with this is that Neill LJ does not show how it is that the statement about the plaintiff affects his reputation. As such, the reasoning is flawed in the same way as that in *Burton*, *Ettingshausen,* and *Obermann*.

Ultimately, Neill LJ finds that the words may be defamatory on either the principal test or on the ridicule test, and somehow these are connected with Berkoff's profession:

> [A] jury [could] conclude that . . . the remarks about Mr Berkoff gave the impression that he was not merely physically unattractive in appearance but actually repulsive. It seems to me that to say this of someone in the public eye who makes his living, in part at least, as an actor, is capable of lowering his standing in the estimation of the public and of making him an object of ridicule.[77]

This finding is inadequate in its statement of the principal test because 'the public' is not the legal point of reference. It is not enough to ask whether the publication

[74] *Manning v Hill* (1995) 126 DLR 4th 129, 162, Can SC; *Berkoff v Burchill* [1996] 4 All ER 1008, 1017 (Neill LJ), CA.
[75] *Berkoff v Burchill* [1996] 4 All ER 1008, 1017 (Neill LJ), CA.
[76] Ibid 1018 (Neill LJ).
[77] Ibid.

would adversely affect the attitude of others towards the plaintiff. The principal test asks what the effect would be on right-thinking members of society. It is uncertain whether the courts would say that no right-thinking person would think the less of a person for his looks.[78] So, Neill's finding can be sustained only on the grounds that the ridicule test is satisfied, and even then only on the presumption that the ridicule test is not referable to the right-thinking person.

The second judgment for the plaintiff was delivered by Phillips LJ. On the question of when ridicule will provide the basis for an action, he finds the law 'is too elusive to encapsulate in any definition'.[79] He does not quarrel with the proposition that ridicule can be the basis for finding that words are defamatory, but he thinks the form that words take will be important when determining actionability. It is not enough, he says, to suggest a person is ugly. The circumstances and words used will matter:

> There are many ways of indicating that a person is hideously ugly, ranging from a simple statement of opinion to that effect, which I feel could never be defamatory, to words plainly intended to convey that message by way of ridicule.[80]

He saw Ms Burchill's work as an example of the latter.[81] The problem here is the same as that in Neill's judgment; the focus is on the form of the publication—the way the message is conveyed—and there is no explanation of how the form of the publication affects a person's moral standing in the community.

Lord Justice Millett delivered a dissenting opinion in *Berkoff*. He saw the comments as 'an attack on [Berkoff's] appearance, not on his reputation', which he defined as 'a man's standing in the world'.[82] He found that although the intention may have been to ridicule Mr Berkoff, he did not think:

> they made him look ridiculous or lowered his reputation in the eyes of ordinary people . . . It is one thing to ridicule a man; it is another to expose him to ridicule.[83]

As to when ridicule becomes defamation, he differs from the majority only in his determination on the facts:

> The line between mockery and defamation may sometimes be difficult to draw. When it is it should be left to the jury to draw it . . . I am not persuaded that the present case could properly be put on the wrong side of the line.[84]

Lord Justice Millett's reasoning is as flawed as that of the majority judgments because he sees defamation as constituted by the harshness of the mockery, with one factor of relevance being whether the plaintiff is merely being ridiculed by an

[78] Cf ibid 1020–1 (Phillips LJ); see below, n 85 and accompanying text.
[79] Ibid 1021 (Phillips LJ).
[80] Ibid.
[81] Ibid.
[82] Ibid 1019 (Millett LJ).
[83] Ibid 1019–20 (Millett LJ).
[84] Ibid 1019 (Millett LJ).

author, as opposed to being held up to the ridicule of others. This, again, confuses the form of the publication with its substance.

The effect of *Berkoff* is that it privileges the protection of self-worth which underpinned *Burton* and which was highlighted in *Manning v Hill.* But while a plaintiffs' feelings may be hurt by harsh ridicule, it does not mean their standing in the community will be diminished. At no point in *Berkoff* is it explained how the latter follows from the former. Standing can only be diminished if the publication somehow raises something that tends to prompt a re-evaluation of the plaintiff's social worth. It is quite possible that a publication which ridicules might in fact do that, but it needs to be explained how that is so. In *Berkoff's* case that could only arise if a community's substantive criteria for moral judgment included the ascriptive factor of physical appearance. Lord Justice Phillips was prepared to accept that this might have been so when he considered the shun and avoid test: '[I]t is, perhaps, just possible to think of a right-minded person shunning one of his fellow men because of a subjective distaste for his features'.[85] Even that is a statement about the community's behaviour rather than the moral judgment of the plaintiff. On the facts here, however, it was not possible 'that a right-minded person would shun another merely because a third party had expressed distaste for that other person's features'.[86] But this reasoning was not applied to the ridicule test.

Berkoff was relied upon by the Court of Appeal in *Norman v Future Publishing Ltd* as authority for the proposition that ridicule can be defamatory.[87] The court held that an author's intention would affect the meaning conveyed by a publication. Overall, even though a small section of the article in *Norman* related a tale (that was untrue) where the plaintiff opera singer was said to have made a self-deprecating remark in jest, the publication overall was intended to be and was in fact highly complimentary to her. The court held it could not be said that it exposed the plaintiff to ridicule.[88] This approach is at odds with *Burton v Crowell* where intention was irrelevant.

In all, the shape of the modern law has been substantially influenced by the shift in rationale that was observed in *Burton*. Most importantly, the ridicule test has operated to protect a plaintiff's self-worth rather than their reputation. This effect has been recognized uncritically in the courts with a consequent reliance on the form of the publication rather than its substance when determining actionability. The result has been a significant and unjustifiable departure from the idea that the action for defamation is a tort to protect reputation. While *Norman* is little more than a postscript to the major cases, the view that intent is relevant is interesting. The expansive potential of the ridicule test may make publications actionable in circumstances where the author's intent is fundamental to the messages conveyed by a publication. Satire is the most important instance of this.

[85] Ibid 1020 (Phillips LJ).
[86] Ibid 1021 (Phillips LJ).
[87] *Norman v Future Publishing Ltd* [1998] EWCA Civ 1800.
[88] Ibid (Hirst LJ, Peter Gibson LJ; May LJ agreeing).

IV. Satire and Actionability Under the Ridicule Test

Defamation laws have been subjected to critique in Australia in recent years following two successful actions relating to works that satirized or intentionally ridiculed a person and their beliefs. The decisions were not based on the ridicule arm of defamation law but the critics are right to be concerned because satire relies on ridicule for much of its force. As a consequence, satire is particularly vulnerable to defamation actions. This section examines the actionability of satire by looking at how the cases were decided, how they might have been decided had the ridicule test been applied, and how the critics have dealt with the issues that arise.

A. The *Hanson* case

The satire case that has attracted most attention in Australia is *Hanson v Australian Broadcasting Corporation*.[89] Pauline Hanson was a right-wing, populist elected to the federal Parliament in 1996. The following year, a song titled *(I'm a) Backdoor Man* by a performer calling himself 'Pauline Pantsdown', was broadcast widely on the defendant's radio station. The performer was Simon Hunt. At public appearances he dressed in 'drag', mimicking and mocking Hanson. The work was comprised of recorded snippets of Hanson's speeches, pasted together and set to dance music. The cutting and pasting was clearly apparent upon hearing the song. The resulting lyrics were somewhat absurd. They included, for example, the following:

> I like trees and I like shrubs and plants and trees and shrubs and plants but I've put the fence up now so that can't get in—yeh. Please explain me me, please me me, please explain. Poor Pauline Poor Pauline I'm a tory and indeed, Pauline and her family. I'm a backdoor man. I'm very proud of it. I'm a backdoor man. I'm homosexual and I'm back here. This is a circular driveway...
>
> I'm a backdoor man for the Ku Klux Klan with a very horrendous plan. I'm a very caring potato.[90]

Hanson sought an injunction to prevent its broadcast. She argued the song would convey to the ordinary reasonable reader the impression that she was and was proud to be a paedophile; homosexual; prostitute; and person who engaged in unnatural sexual practices including anal sex with members of the Ku Klux Klan. The broadcaster argued the song would not be taken by listeners as a serious literal statement of fact because of the obvious absurdity, clear manipulation of the speeches, and because each broadcast was prefaced with an announcement

[89] *Hanson v Australian Broadcasting Corporation* (Qld SC, 1 September 1997); aff'd *Australian Broadcasting Corporation v Hanson* (Qld CA, 28 September 1998); special leave to appeal to the High Court was denied: *Australian Broadcasting Corporation v Hanson* (HCA, 24 June 1999).

[90] Ibid 2–3.

that the words were not to be treated seriously. The ordinary reasonable reader, it argued, would understand the work as 'alluding in a satirical or ironic sense to the respondent's conservative political views'.[91] Hanson's interlocutory application succeeded and was then affirmed by the Court of Appeal, with all judges agreeing the song was so clearly defamatory of her that any jury verdict to the contrary would be overturned by an appellate court as unreasonable.[92]

The decision has rightly been criticized on the grounds that the court's view of the ordinary reasonable reader's interpretation of the song was, frankly, bizarre. Handsley and Davis argue that the courts took 'an approach which overlook[ed] completely the song's satirical nature' and that 'the many considerations which pointed to a meaning other than the literal one were given no weight'.[93] One of the most important considerations was, in Magnusson's words, that 'it was certainly arguable that the "literal" imputations Hanson pleaded . . . were so extravagant, or "over the top" that they were not, in fact, conveyed'.[94]

The approach in *Hanson* can be contrasted with that taken in *Brander v Ryan*. In *Brander* the leader of a right-wing, anti-immigration political party sued a local newspaper over an editorial piece that criticized him in a manner that ridiculed him heavily.[95] It was a sarcastic rather than satirical piece:

> It's Little Mikey and the big bad racists. How did little Mikey Brander get to be the leader of the racist gang National Action? Did he beat all the other, bigger NA chaps in a peeing contest or something? It's hard to imagine how you can piddle higher than everyone else if you sit down to take a pee.[96]

The plaintiff argued that the piece conveyed factual imputations that the plaintiff was effeminate or homosexual.[97] The Full Court of the South Australian Supreme Court held that the ordinary reasonable reader would have understood from the text that the author's intention was to ridicule the plaintiff and only a 'forced interpretation' would yield the conclusion that such imputations were conveyed.[98]

Magnusson argues that when determining what imputations are conveyed by satire, the law should take account of the author's intentions or attribute to the

[91] Ibid 6.

[92] Ibid 4–7.

[93] E Handsley and G Davis, 'Defamation and Satire: *Hanson v Australian Broadcasting Corporation*' (2000) 9 Torts Law Journal 1, 9. See also R Magnusson, 'Freedom of Speech in Australian Defamation Law: Ridicule, Satire and Other Challenges' (2001) 9 Torts Law Journal 269, 283–4; T Fitzgerald, 'Telling the Truth, Laughing' (1999) 92 Media Information Australia 11; J Eisenberg, 'Sex, Satire and "Middle-Class Morality": Reflections on Some Recent Defamation Cases' (1999) 92 Media Information Australia 19, 25–6.

[94] Magnusson, ibid 284; S Hunt, '"(I'm a) Back Door Man": An Essay for the Australian Broadcasting Corporation' (2000) 4(4) *Perfect Beat* 29, 32–3.

[95] *Brander v Ryan & Messenger Press Pty Ltd* [2000] SASC 2 (12 January 2000) (Sth Aust SC, Wicks J) ('*Brander v Ryan*, Supreme Court'); [2001] Aust Torts Rep ¶81-953 (21 December 2000) (Sth Aust SC (FC), Lander, Prior and Bleeby JJ) ('*Brander v Ryan*, Full Court').

[96] *Brander v Ryan*, Supreme Court ibid [18].

[97] *Brander v Ryan*, Full Court (n 95 above) [80] (Lander J; Prior and Bleby JJ agreeing).

[98] Ibid [77]–[88].

ordinary reasonable reader a greater capacity to understand satire.[99] He is correct that the courts need a better appreciation of satire (at least based on *Hanson*) but there are no legal obstacles preventing that. The test for whether an imputation is conveyed is more than capable of accommodating an appreciation of satire and should in fact do so:

> The ordinary reasonable reader (or listener or viewer) is a person of fair average intelligence... who is neither perverse... nor morbid or suspicious of mind... nor avid for scandal... That person does not live in an ivory tower but can and does read between the lines in light of that person's general knowledge and experience of worldly affairs.[100]

Similarly, to the extent that the author's intent can be interpreted by the reader, the standard test seems able to accommodate that. *Emerson*, for example, was a case where there was a clear absence of intent to convey any untrue imputations and the courts saw that as relevant to determining the imputations conveyed.[101]

The criticisms of *Hanson* should be heeded. The application of the standard test should have yielded a conclusion that the ordinary reasonable reader would have understood 'Backdoor Man' to be a satirical work that did not impute any of the things the plaintiff claimed it did.[102] This, however, is not the end of the matter. Actionability under the principal test is one thing. The vulnerability of satire to action under the ridicule test is another matter. Would the song have been actionable on the grounds it held the plaintiff up to ridicule? This possibility is not considered by any of Handsley and Davis, Eisenberg, or Fitzgerald.[103] Magnusson looks at the statement of law for the ridicule test and, although he does not examine how it might apply on the facts of Hanson, it is the most substantial critique in the literature. The following sections look at Magnusson's critique of the law and the application of the ridicule test to satire.

B. Applying the ridicule test to the *Hanson* facts

Brander v Ryan helps show how a work might be interpreted for the purpose of the ridicule test. There, Lander J stated the law in now familiar terms:

> [T]here is authority for the proposition that to hold a plaintiff up to ridicule, even in the absence of moral blameworthiness, is actionable as a defamation. It would be appropriate to follow that authority... [A] publication may be defamatory of a plaintiff even where it imputes no moral discredit or blameworthiness to the plaintiff, if the article holds the plaintiff up to ridicule or contempt...[104]

[99] Magnusson (n 93 above) 290–1. A better judicial appreciation of satire can be found in *Buckstaff v Viall* 84 Wis 129; 54 NW 111 (Wis, 1893).

[100] *Amalgamated Television Services Pty Ltd v Marsden* (1998) 43 NSWLR 158, 165, NSW CA.

[101] *Emerson v Grimsby Times & Telephone Company Ltd* (1926) 42 TLR 238, CA; see above n 29ff and accompanying text.

[102] Magnusson (n 93 above) 283–4; Handsley and Davis (n 93 above) 9.

[103] Handsley and Davis (n 93 above); Fitzgerald (n 93 above); Eisenberg (n 93 above).

[104] *Brander v Ryan*, Full Court (n 95 above) [79].

On the facts, he thought the publication could have been actionable:

> [T]his article does hold the plaintiff up to ridicule. The whole text of the article [belittles] the plaintiff and the article does that by reference to the plaintiff being 'little', 'growth hormones', 'sitting down to pee', 'bowel movements', '[Mikey out the front doing the splits in a] green leotard', his 'mum [who tucks him into bed with a hot mug of Horlicks]' and being an 'annoying little brat'.[105]

The form of the publication would have made it actionable under the ridicule test, even without factual imputations arising.[106] Using this as a guide, how might 'Backdoor Man' have fared under the ridicule test?

Given that the test is concerned with the form of the publication, the essence of the plaintiff's argument would be along the following lines:

> 'The song has ridiculed the plaintiff and exposed her to the ridicule of others in the community by cutting and pasting recorded snippets of the plaintiff's spoken words, creating an absurd monologue that speaks about matters of sexuality which the plaintiff would not usually discuss and which the plaintiff would certainly not discuss in the way presented.'

The plaintiff would not need to argue that the song conveyed any meanings, nor would she need to argue that it in any way tended to make people think the less of her. On its face, the work would seem to be actionable because it exposes her to more than a trivial degree of ridicule.[107]

I have already argued that the ridicule test tends to protect a plaintiff's self-worth rather than their reputation. In these circumstances, one can be certain that Hanson's feelings would have been hurt by the ridicule, but it is still not clear how the form of the publication tarnishes the plaintiff's reputation. Magnusson's proposal goes some way to addressing this gap.

C. The argument for a higher threshold

Magnusson argues that if the ridicule test is applied 'too leniently' then it 'becomes a remedy for harm to the plaintiff's self-image or sense of self-worth'.[108] He argues that the threshold for the ridicule test needs to be higher than 'more than a trivial degree' of ridicule and that a more appropriate threshold is that the ridicule must be 'overwhelming' or 'enduring':[109]

> [A] plaintiff who has been ridiculed to an extreme degree, so that he or she *remains* a 'preposterously ridiculous spectacle' can genuinely claim to have lost their standing in the eyes of others. Since defamation law aims to protect 'standing in the eyes of others' as an

[105] Ibid [78]; cf *Brander v Ryan*, Supreme Court (n 95 above) [31] where intention was considered in the determination.

[106] *Brander v Ryan*, Full Court (n 95 above) [88].

[107] This raises again the possibility that the defendant might justify the publication: see above, n 69 and accompanying text.

[108] Magnusson (n 93 above) 280–1.

[109] Ibid 281.

enduring quality, it should only provide a remedy for ridicule that is sufficiently extreme that it risks having an ongoing role in the plaintiff's future, compromising the plaintiff's identity through the continuing association of the plaintiff with ridicule. Ridicule that assumes a 'parasitic' role upon the plaintiff's reputation, so that he or she can 'never live it down', might truly be said to interfere with the plaintiff's standing. Lesser forms of ridicule, however, will only have a fleeting or ephemeral impact upon the plaintiff's reputation.[110]

This argument needs careful consideration. First, Magnusson draws on the *Burton* phrase of what constitutes ridicule, adds to it the requirement that the person must 'remain' the subject of ridicule, and apparently accepts the *Burton* position that a person subject to that degree of ridicule has in fact had their reputation tarnished. On what basis is it argued that reputation has been damaged? He does not adopt the explanation Hand J gave in *Burton* and instead offers a different reason. He argues that reputation is damaged by this level of ridicule because the ridicule becomes 'parasitic' upon the plaintiff's reputation such that they can 'never live it down'. In his last sentence he seems to accept that lesser ridicule can tarnish reputation, though not to the extent that it can be actionable. But what he still does *not* show is *how* overwhelming or enduring ridicule affects the plaintiff's standing in the eyes of others. It is not clear exactly what he means by 'parasitic'.

Magnusson's position is unpersuasive because it relies on an unsupported assumption about communities' criteria for moral judgment. In order to reach a conclusion that lasting exposure to ridicule is defamatory, it would need to be accepted that one of the criteria for moral judgment in the community is the absence of an enduring exposure to ridicule. Or, in positive terms, that a person who is subjected to ridicule on an enduring basis is somebody that ordinary, decent folk think the less of *because of the fact they are ridiculed*. The reason why they are subjected to ridicule would have to be irrelevant to sustain Magnusson's argument. (If the reasons for ridicule were relevant, then one would return to the principal test and the question of whether the factual imputations and/or comment tend to make people think the less of the plaintiff.)

Is it possible to argue that the fact of being ridiculed to perhaps a significant extent is a contemporary criterion for judging a person? Certainly, in the communities of the old American South it would have been possible to make such a claim because the maintenance of appearance and the avoidance of ridicule were indeed criteria for moral judgment.[111] But in contemporary Australian or English communities it seems difficult to accept that the sole fact of being ridiculed would affect a person's reputation. It might be that the community has sympathy for a person who is ridiculed, but that is not to say that their standing is diminished. It

[110] Ibid 281, emphasis in original.

[111] See Chapter 2, II(B); KS Greenberg, *Honor and Slavery* (1996); B Wyatt-Brown, *Southern Honor: Ethics and Behavior in the Old South* (1982).

is one thing to say that a person will always be associated with the ridicule once cast upon them—for instance, they are labelled with a derogatory nickname that sticks—and that may indeed cause the plaintiff considerable grief and hurt, but it still does not mean that the community's judgment of the person is in any way diminished, *unless* one accepts that the fact of being ridiculed is one of the criteria for moral judgment.

If persuaded that the community would in fact think the less of a person because they have been ridiculed then the courts might well ask whether that is a view or value that the law should recognize. This requires a consideration of the processes of ethical recognition which characterize the principal test. As discussed in section IV, there is little evidence that 'the right-thinking person' standard has been seen as a part of the ridicule test, though this would surely prompt it.

The crux of the matter is the same under the accepted standards of the ridicule test or under Magnusson's higher threshold: if nobody holds the plaintiff in lower esteem then—no matter how extreme—ridicule remains an injury to the plaintiff's self-worth. And that should not be actionable as defamation. It is not to the point that the plaintiff's self-worth would have to be more substantially diminished than is required under the established ridicule test. Without a negative moral judgment of the plaintiff, based on criteria for moral judgment that the court will recognize, a publication should not be actionable as defamation.

D. When should satire be actionable?

It was argued in section A that 'Backdoor Man' should not have been actionable under the principal test on the basis of the pleadings as Hanson presented them because the pleaded imputations were not conveyed. It was argued in section B that it should not have been actionable on the grounds that the ridicule test does not protect the plaintiff's reputation. But this does not necessarily mean that 'Backdoor Man' should be found to be incapable of defaming Ms Hanson. It was highly capable of doing so and should be actionable as defamation, though it should also be defensible.

A publication should be actionable if it tends to damage reputation. Is there something about a satirical work that tends to harm the plaintiff's reputation where other publications that expose the plaintiff to ridicule do not? That is, does satire possess a connection between ridicule and reputation that is not present in the established line of ridicule decisions? The answer to these questions is 'yes'—not because the publication *ridicules* the plaintiff, but because it *satirizes* the plaintiff.

Satire possesses a tendency to damage reputation because it conveys factual imputations that would tend to diminish the standing in which the plaintiff is held and expresses an opinion that encourages others to view the plaintiff in a negative light. The method used to do this is mockery and hyperbole. These are usually thought of as ridicule, and they may be. But satire is not simply ridicule.

It is critique. As Margaret Rose has explained it: 'By incorporating parts of the target text into the parody, parodists... ensure the closeness to a target necessary for an accurate firing of their critical arrows.'[112] Buck and Wright have studied how satire operated as political critique in colonial New South Wales.[113] 'The Poor Man' was a serial published in the *Sydney Morning Herald* in 1864, satirizing liberal arguments for free selection of land for the working classes. In doing so, it sought to portray facts in a particular way and to convey opinions about the state of the working classes and the appropriateness of the proposed land law and policy.[114] Inspired by the satire of Hitler in 1930s Berlin cabaret, Simon Hunt's strategy in creating Pauline Pantsdown was:

> based on the 'impossibility' of subject-bound satire in relation to public figures whose attributed original statements are of an extreme (ie, unable to be exaggerated) and illogical (ie, unable to be made absurd) nature.[115]

The work was 'a political critique', calling attention to and criticizing the inconsistencies, lack of logic, and content of her political position.[116]

Transposing this to the legal framework, there are two dimensions to a satirical publication. On the one hand, mockery and hyperbole are devices used to call attention to facts about the plaintiff's behaviour and motivations. The publication is in this regard no different in its substance from a news report that makes accurate statements of fact about what the plaintiff's behaviour and motivations are. If the allegations tend to harm the plaintiff's reputation then they will be actionable. Presuming they are true, they can be justified by the defendant. The second aspect of satire is that mockery and hyperbole are also deployed to express and convey an opinion that is critical of the plaintiff. In this regard, the satirical work is no different from a newspaper op-ed piece. The message it conveys to the reader is that the person being discussed should be thought of poorly because of their behaviour and motivations. The author is attempting to persuade a community that the target of the satire is in breach of the community's agreed criteria for moral judgment. The author of satire may also be challenging the norms of the community, attempting to persuade and shape the community's criteria for moral judgment.

Applying this to *Hanson*, Simon Hunt was appealing to a listenership comprised of some people who shared his view of the criteria for moral judgment in the community, and some people who did not share his views. For example, some listeners would think the less of a person who condemns people for their

[112] MA Rose, *Parody: Ancient, Modern, and Post-Modern* (1993) 52.

[113] AR Buck and NE Wright, *The Poor Man: Law and Satire in 19th Century New South Wales* (2005).

[114] Ibid 12–24.

[115] Hunt (n 94 above) 29, drawing on P Jelavich, *Berlin Cabaret* (1993).

[116] J Stratton, 'I Don't Like It: Pauline Pantsdown and the Politics of the Inauthentic' (2000) 4(4) *Perfect Beat* 3, 8; Hunt (n 94 above) 29–33.

homosexuality. Others will believe that such views are irrelevant to the judgment a community makes about a person, some may be uncertain or ambivalent, and still others will hold the speaker in higher standing when they become aware of his or her condemnatory views. The author of the satire presumes that once the first group of listeners' attention is drawn to the facts then they will lower their opinion of the plaintiff. The author then tries to persuade the remaining groups of readers to adopt certain substantive criteria for moral judgment by suggesting the value that should be attached to the facts discussed. The author is also trying to persuade all listeners that Hanson's views fall foul of the criteria he thinks should govern judgment of a person.

While the factual dimensions of satire should be able to be justified, the critical dimensions should be defensible as fair comment on a matter of public interest.[117] The defendant will have to overcome the hurdle that:

> The facts upon which fair comment is based must either be stated by the commentator or indicated by him with sufficient clarity to enable the reader or listener to ascertain the matter on which the comment is being made.[118]

This should not be insurmountable. The court is to interpret the work 'in light of all the circumstances known to those to whom the words are published [and] in particular the context in which the words appear'.[119] The basic facts concerning any issue or person that attracts satire will almost certainly be generally well-known and the appearance of words in the context of a work that is clearly identifiable as satirical (either by its form, its content or through an express statement) should combine to yield a conclusion that the facts are identified with sufficient clarity to enable the listener to ascertain the matter being commented upon. This would require the courts to come to grips with the nature of satire more than they did in *Hanson*, but the existing legal framework both requires and is capable of accommodating this.[120]

In sum, satire is a device that both calls attention to the facts and comments upon them. Such a publication should be actionable, but not simply because it takes the form of ridicule. It should be actionable because the substance of the publication has the capacity to diminish a person's reputation. Unquestionably, the ridiculing form of the publication will affect the plaintiff's sense of self-worth as well, but the action is founded on the tendency to harm reputation. Authors of satire should be able to successfully argue defences of justification and comment.

[117] A Kenyon, 'Defamation, Artistic Criticism and Fair Comment' (1996) 18 Sydney Law Review 193, 200–15 looks at the defence of comment where artistic criticism is concerned. His analysis could also be applied to satire.

[118] *Brander v Ryan*, Supreme Court (n 95 above) [58].

[119] Ibid [60], quoting P Lewis, *Gatley on Libel and Slander* (8th edn, 1981) [699].

[120] There is also the possibility that qualified privilege may provide a defence where the satire concerns government and political matters; for procedural reasons it received only minimal attention in *Brander v Ryan*, Full Court (n 95 above) [64]–[65], [112].

Conclusion

Given the aim of defamation law is to protect reputation, three main conclusions can be drawn with respect to the appropriateness of the contemporary ridicule test as the basis for actionability.

First, where the recent cases have reached the conclusion that ridicule is actionable, they have made inappropriate use of the old authorities. Those early cases do not support the proposition that ridicule was actionable in the absence of moral fault. Further, and with parallels to the 'shun and avoid' test, they bear out the point made in Chapter 6 that the absence or presence of moral fault is an inadequate conceptual tool for understanding how the ridicule test is different from the principal test. When the 'hatred, contempt, or ridicule' formulation of what is defamatory was first articulated in the early 18th century, it derived its last limb from cases where the plaintiff's reputation had been diminished. Following the confused reasoning in *Villers v Monsley* in 1769, it was possible to argue that a publication could be actionable under the ridicule limb of the test even though it did not at all diminish the plaintiff's social worth or moral standing. That is, it seemed in *Villers* that a publication could be actionable even though it did not tarnish a person's reputation. Prior to 1936, a moral aspersion was cast in every case where the plaintiff succeeded. The imputation was not always one of moral fault; it might have been a suggestion of either moral fault or immoral association or even an ascriptive moral inferiority. However, not until *Burton v Crowell* did the courts take the next step and permit actionability where there was no moral aspersion cast at all.

Secondly, the ridicule test is unnecessary in many cases because the principal test often provides an adequate basis for determining actionability where a plaintiff is ridiculed. If factual imputations are conveyed or if the publication constitutes comment that has the capacity to damage a person's reputation then their defamatory quality can be evaluated with reference to whether they tend to make ordinary decent folk in the community think the less of her or him. There is much evidence of this in the cases prior to *Burton*. This applies equally to satirical works (with the caveat that the courts need to demonstrate a more sophisticated appreciation of satire) as to works which are nothing more than mere ridicule.

Thirdly, the test is inappropriate in all other circumstances because, since *Burton v Crowell*, it has not served to protect the plaintiff's reputation. The legal shift that occurred in *Burton* brought to life the possibilities that had been laid down in *Villers*. It formally provided that a publication could be actionable even where there was no moral aspersion of any kind. The action became one which could and did protect a plaintiff's sense of self-worth in circumstances where there was no tendency to damage the plaintiff's reputation. This shift was characteristic of the actions that saw the revival of the test in the late 20th century. The recent cases bear out the self-worth aspects of the test because, like *Burton*, they rely on the form of the publication rather than its substance and fail to show how it is that the fact of being ridiculed diminishes a person's reputation. None of this is to say that the hurt felt by the ridiculed plaintiff is insubstantial. Indeed, there may be a case for reform which makes ridicule actionable under some other cause (such as privacy or the intentional infliction of emotional distress) but it should not be actionable as defamation.

This completes the analysis of the tests for actionability and the ways that reputation is and is not protected under those tests. Chapter 6 and this chapter have argued that both supplementary tests should be discarded. Only the principal test for actionability protects reputation. The next chapter examines the appropriate scope and limits of that test in the contemporary context of moral diversity.

8

Ethical Recognition, Moral Diversity, and 'The Right-thinking Person'

For almost two centuries, the stated aim of defamation law has been to protect reputation. I have argued that to achieve that goal the principal test for actionability should be retained and a sectional standards approach used, while the supplementary tests should be discarded. However, as Chapter 5 explained, not all attacks on reputation have been protected by the law: a publication will be actionable only if it tends to lower the plaintiff in the estimation of people whose values the court recognizes as decent, respectable, or right-thinking. But what it means to speak of 'the right-thinking person' has become much less clear and more highly contested. For several decades now jurisdictions in Western societies have been characterized by competing views about what is right and wrong, many of which are at odds with the traditional values that have for so long been associated with 'the right-thinking person'. As a result, there is a need to reconsider how ethical recognition operates in the law. These ruptures to the moral taxonomies of tradition and the laws of defamation are discussed in this chapter.

The aim of this chapter is to examine how, if at all, 'the right-thinking person' should form a part of the current law of defamation. Section I looks at how ethical recognition has functioned in the context of moral diversity. Here, cases concerning imputations that a white person is African-American mark a shift from ethical recognition to the refusal of ethical recognition, reflecting a change in the content of 'the right-thinking person'. To explain that shift sections II and III explore the imputation that a person is homosexual. The cases provide exemplary material for a study of ethical recognition in the common law because sexuality has in recent years been an important area of contested morals. Further, there is a relatively large body of decisions and the courts have on occasion expressly tried to grapple with the questions of recognition that are central to the law. In section II, the history of these cases shows how ethical recognition has operated in determinations of actionability while section III critiques the reasoning behind the refusal of recognition in the landmark case of *Rivkin v Amalgamated Television Services*.[1] Reflecting on this, section IV draws on liberal

[1] *Rivkin v Amalgamated Television Services Pty Ltd* [2001] NSWSC 432.

and communitarian scholarship to propose a new path where a modest shift in the presumptions associated with the views of 'the right-thinking person' will make for a more coherent, transparent, and principled approach to the determination of actionability and the legal protection of reputation.

I. Ethical Recognition and Moral Diversity

A. Moral diversity, contested criteria, and inclusive communities

A determination of defamatory capacity requires the courts to constitute a jurisdiction as a moral community. That is, the court needs to form a sense of the values that operate as moral ties, binding people together not simply within geographic boundaries or as a polity or an economy but as a community in its true sense. Before the modern era of mass communication, transport, and migration, it was not difficult to claim that the people of a locale or even a nation were a community, united by a wide-ranging consensus on the core values that should govern life—a shared idea of how things are and how things should be. But diverse, liberal-democratic, late-modern societies are in states of moral flux. There are competing and conflicting moral taxonomies in jurisdictions. People identify with multiple communities, each of which shares some values that identify it as a community defined and bound together by shared moral rules, with different degrees of importance attached to their connection to each community. For instance, one might see oneself as being located in communities of towns, workplaces, social clubs, cultural associations (formal and informal), or churches and the like, as well as in friendship, professional, or family circles. Diverse moral taxonomies pose problems for the legal protection of reputation: the matter in dispute—reputation—is founded in the concept of community, and yet courts must resolve disputes with reference to the values of jurisdictions—and those jurisdictions are no longer self-evidently communities.

Since the end of the Second World War the moral codes of Western communities have been highly contested. Traditional criteria for moral judgment have been challenged and sometimes displaced. Most notably, ascriptive characteristics (such as race, ethnicity, or gender) have been often formally and informally rejected as appropriate criteria on which to judge a person's moral status in a community. This is discernable in identity politics, social movements, shifts in social and economic mobility, and legal instruments.[2] This change to the traditional moral frameworks has distinctly modern philosophical foundations. Often associated with the law and discourse of human rights, modern liberal claims to equal moral worth are the basis for more inclusive moral communities. Racial

[2] For example, *Universal Declaration of Human Rights*; *International Convenant on Civil and Political Rights*; the US *Civil Rights Act of 1964*; the Australian *Racial Discrimination Act 1975* (Cth); and the UK *Human Rights Act 1998*.

and gender equality, for example, have become axiomatic values in the public sphere. Prejudice, bigotry, and discrimination have not disappeared but moral equality has become a defining principle of the modern liberal state and meaningfully reflects values and social life in communities. To what extent, then, has this influenced the conceptions of community that have underpinned judicial determinations of defamatory capacity?

Chapter 6 explained how the *Youssoupoff* decision would be decided differently today on the basis that right-thinking people would not think the less of a woman who had been raped. This is so regardless of whether or not there are a substantial number of people who would in fact hold the woman in lower estimation. This reflects a change in the criteria for moral judgment. The actionability of imputations of insanity or mental illness should be similarly incapable of defaming, though determinations regarding these imputations have not been discussed in any detail in the case law.[3] Again, this is not to say that there is no prejudice in communities. It simply means that courts consider the ethical limits to the legal protection of reputation and those limits apply regardless of the quantity of people who would think the less of the plaintiff. It is in this realm of identity-based claims to equal moral worth that ethical recognition most clearly intersects with contested values. The shift from exclusive to inclusive conceptions of community—and the consequent move to refuse ethical recognition to values of racial inferiority—can be seen in the cases concerning imputations that a white person is African-American.[4]

B. The defamatory capacity of imputations regarding blackness

1. *The cases*

A statement that a white person is black was the subject of many successful defamation actions in the early part of 20th century.[5] (I use the term 'blackness' deliberately here because it was in a very real sense the distinction of significance.[6]) The circumstances included mistakes in newspaper reporting, an erroneous listing in a telephone directory, public statements about a child's lineage and right to attend a white school, and the placement of a white patient in the 'coloured' ward

[3] See Chapter 6, III(B).

[4] Actions regarding statements that non-Jews are Jews share some parallels but they are primarily instances of intentional, political libel: D Reisman, 'Democracy and Defamation: Fair Game and Fair Comment I' (1942) 42 Columbia Law Review 1085, 1118–19.

[5] Earlier cases of this kind had arisen when a white man was called a mulatto: *Eden v Legare* 1 Bay 171; 1 SCL 171 (SC, 1791); *Wood v King* 1 Nott & McC 184; 10 SCL 184 (SC, 1818); *Atkinson v Hartley* 1 McC 203; 12 SCL 203 (SC, 1821) cited in *Bowen v Independent Publishing Co* 96 SE 2d 564, 564–5 (SC, 1957); generally, JH Crabb, 'Annotation: Libel and Slander: Statements Respecting Race, Color or Nationality as Actionable' (c1954) 46 American Law Reports, Annotated 2nd 1287.

[6] M Hill (ed), *Whiteness: A Critical Reader* (1997); GE Hale, *Making Whiteness: The Culture of Segregation in the South, 1890–1940* (1998); DA Lorimer, *Colour, Class and the Victorians: English Attitudes to the Negro in the Mid-Nineteenth Century* (1978).

of a hospital.[7] All parties involved accepted that an imputation of blackness would result in a white person being held in a lower esteem amongst their white associates in the community but the legal question was whether the imputation was actionable in light of the equal protection clause of the Fourteenth Amendment.

The Supreme Court had already said that legal equality did not alter social relations: 'The colored race, as a race, was abject and ignorant, and in that condition was unfitted to command the respect of those who had superior intelligence.'[8] In 1905, the Supreme Court of South Carolina held that 'to impute the condition of the negro to a white man would tend to interfere seriously with the social relation (*sic*) of the white man with his fellow white men'.[9] In Alabama the imputation was defamatory even though it 'imputes no crime, no misconduct, no mental, moral or physical fault for which one may justly be held accountable to public opinion. . .'.[10] Just as the absence of moral fault did not mean a rape victim's moral worth was undiminished,[11] the absence of moral fault in being black did not mean that black Americans had the same moral worth as whites. Blackness was an ascriptive moral inferiority. Accordingly, the court explained that in the 'peculiar social conditions' that prevailed in Alabama, there was no doubt that the imputation was defamatory.[12] Notwithstanding legal equality, the views of those who would think the less of a person for being black would be recognized by the courts.

Into the mid-20th century courts in Mississippi and South Carolina continued to find that the imputation was libellous.[13] The South Carolina Supreme Court used the *Corpus Juris Secundum* entry on libel and slander to capture what it saw as the state of the law: words would be libellous 'if they discredit the plaintiff in the minds of any considerable and respectable class in the community, taking into consideration the emotions, prejudices, and intolerance of mankind'.[14] The question was not to be considered by the courts again until the 1980s when the law would change markedly.

[7] *Upton v Times-Democrat Publishing Co* 28 Southern Reporter 970 (La, 1900) (public meeting); *Flood v News & Courier Co*; *Flood v Evening Post Publishing Co* 50 SE 637 (SC, 1905) (pedestrian accident); *Spencer v Looney* 82 Southern Reporter 745 (Va SC Apps, 1914) (child's lineage); *Jones v RL Polk & Co* 67 Southern Reporter 577 (Ala, 1915) (telephone directory); *Collins v Oklahoma State Hospital* 184 P 946 (Okla, 1919) (hospital care and records).

[8] *Strauder v West Virginia* 100 US 303, 306 (1880).

[9] *Flood v News & Courier Co* 50 SE 637, 639 (SC, 1905).

[10] *Jones v RL Polk & Co* 67 Southern Reporter 577, 577 (Ala, 1915).

[11] See Chapter 6, II(B).

[12] *Jones v RL Polk & Co* 67 Southern Reporter 577, 577 (Ala, 1915).

[13] *Natchez Times Publishing Co v Dunigan* 72 So 2d 681 (Miss, 1954); *Bowen v Independent Publishing Co* 96 SE 2d 564 (SC, 1957).

[14] *Bowen v Independent Publishing Co* 96 SE 2d 564, 565–6 (SC, 1957). This is essentially the position that was favoured by Reisman, though without condemnation of the plaintiff: D Reisman, 'Democracy and Defamation: Fair Game and Fair Comment II' (1942) 42 Columbia Law Review 1282, 1298.

In *Thomason v Times-Journal Inc*, the Georgia Court of Appeals acknowledged the existence of prejudice in the community but—in contrast to the earlier cases—refused to recognize prejudiced views in determining actionability:

> It would ignore reality to suggest that racial and ethnic prejudices do not exist or that all manifestations of those prejudices have been eliminated... The Constitution cannot control such prejudices but neither can it tolerate them. Private biases may be outside the reach of the law, but the law cannot, directly or indirectly, give them effect.[15]

Thomason stands almost alone in the defamation case law. The only other case on point is *Polygram Records Inc v Superior Court*.[16] There was a suggestion in that case that it could be defamatory for a comedian to derogatorily associate a wine with African-American consumers on the basis that they were perceived as 'a socio-economic group of persons commonly considered to be the antithesis of wine connoisseurs... who harbour obviously unsophisticated tastes in wines'.[17] The court held this proposition to be 'utterly untenable'.[18] The plaintiff would not be permitted 'to recover damages based on a theory that his wine had been disparaged by association with a particular racial or ethnic group, or a segment thereof. Courts will not condone theories of recovery which promote or effectuate discriminatory conduct.'[19] *Thomason* and *Polygram* sit in stark contrast to the earlier decisions. On what basis did the courts change their views and ignore the earlier approach to the defamatory capacity of blackness imputations?

2. *Explaining the shift: the refusal of ethical recognition*

Times had changed. An ethos of racial equality had emerged. The cultural and political changes associated with landmark desegregation decisions such as *Brown v Board of Education of Topeka* and the Civil Rights Act of 1964 almost undoubtedly must be at the root of the shift but, nonetheless, it does not easily follow that the imputation of blackness is incapable of being defamatory.[20] Put simply, empirical change cannot support the decision in *Thomason*. This can be illustrated by looking at cases where a plaintiff has sued on an imputation that they hold an objectionable political belief.

The political belief cases rely on the 'the temper of the times' to ascertain whether an imputation is defamatory. The major line of cases considered in the 1940s and 1950s held that it would be defamatory to say a person was a communist.[21] The times, it was said, were such that respectable people would think the less of a person

[15] *Thomason v Times-Journal Inc* 379 SE 2d 551, 553 (Ga Ct App, 1989) quoting the Supreme Court in *Palmore v Sidoti* 466 US 429, 433 (1984).

[16] *Polygram Records Inc v Superior Court* 216 Cal Rptr 252 (Cal Ct App, 1985), though cf *Ledsinger v Burmeister* 318 NW 2d 558 (Mich Ct App, 1982) which concerned racist abuse.

[17] *Polygram Records Inc v Superior Court* 216 Cal Rptr 252, 261 (Cal Ct App, 1985).

[18] Ibid.

[19] Ibid.

[20] *Brown v Board of Education of Topeka, Kansas* 347 US 483 (1954).

[21] See Chapter 5, III(A).

for being a communist. That is, an imputation not previously defamatory became so because the temper of times meant that respectable segments of the community held particular views. With respect to civil rights, the temper of the times had certainly changed; a large and respectable portion of the community now believed in racial equality—but that change does not explain the result in *Thomason*.[22] In the political belief cases the courts said that imputations were actionable *because* of the temper of the times (the temper being a belief in the evils of communism). In *Thomason*, the imputation was not actionable *in spite of* the temper of the times (the temper being a significant portion of the community believing in racial inferiority, in spite of a widespread ethos of equality). To put it differently, the implication of the political belief cases is that the court follows community sentiment. In the blackness cases, the implication is that the court will not follow community sentiment.

In *Thomason*, the relevant point of reference for determining actionability should have been those in the jurisdiction who did *not* believe in racial equality. Under the law, the views of this group could be rejected on either quantitative or qualitative grounds. The judgments clearly indicated that recognition could not be refused on a quantitative basis (ie, they acknowledged that the racist segment of the community was not so small as to be insubstantial).[23] So, the rationale must have been qualitative: the views were not 'respectable' or not 'right-thinking' or (in the language of *Connelly*) were so anti-social that the court could not recognize them. However, this language was not used. Instead, the process of ethical recognition was concealed by making the justification in constitutional terms. The constitutional basis for the decision was not necessary for the decision the court reached, though the proposition that it would be discriminatory to find the imputation actionable points to a moral wrong that the court would no longer give effect to.[24]

The common law provides room for the ethical recognition (or rejection) of criteria for moral judgment. The rejection of criteria does not deny the existence of prejudice or of harm to a person labelled as black. It just says that there are ethical limits on what slurs will be actionable. What is missing from *Thomason* and, indeed, from any of the cases regarding blackness imputations, is a sense of principle. There is no explanation of why some criteria for moral judgment will be recognized by the courts and why some will not be. The concepts of discrimination that underpin the decision must themselves come down to ethical recognition,

[22] That change could mean that an allegation that a person engaged in racial discrimination might well be defamatory where in the past it would not have been defamatory: *Calore v Powell-Savory Corp* 251 NYS 2d 732 (NY SC App Div, 1964).

[23] This is apparent from the use of *Palmore v Sidoti*: *Thomason v Times-Journal Inc* 379 SE 2d 551, 553 (Ga Ct App, 1989); *Polygram Records Inc v Superior Court* 216 Cal Rptr 252, 261 (Cal Ct App, 1985).

[24] The Australian common law has embodied similar themes, perhaps most famously in the recognition of native title where Brennan J stressed the importance of ensuring that 'the common law should neither be nor be seen to be frozen in an age of racial discrimination': *Mabo v Queensland (No 2)* (1992) 175 CLR 1, 41–2.

but what is it that makes a discriminatory application of the law inappropriate? This requires seeing the refusal of ethical recognition of racist views as part of a wider shift away from traditional moral frameworks and towards the recognition of equal moral worth and inclusive moral community.

The judicial view that an imputation that a person is African-American no longer has the capacity to defame a person is suggestive of changes to the moral community envisaged and maintained by the United States' laws. This is important because it provides (albeit without reasoning and in only a few cases) an example of a reconstituted and inclusive moral community.[25] Moreover, it allows us to contemplate even more inclusive communities. In looking at such possibilities, cases concerning imputations regarding sexuality are of special interest.

II. Ethical Recognition in the Sexuality Cases

There are two reasons why determinations of the defamatory capacity of imputations of homosexuality are especially useful for understanding ethical recognition. First, the cases have almost always been decided using the principal test for what is defamatory. As the preceding chapters explained, the moral fault distinction has enabled problematic issues of ethical recognition to be avoided or ignored by applying supplementary tests. Secondly, these cases are useful because the moral status of homosexuality is presently highly contested in Western liberal democracies. As such, questions of ethical recognition have recently been difficult to avoid which means the reasons for recognition or its refusal are more visible here than in the blackness cases. The following sections will show how modern questions of ethical recognition have taken a very particular form and rely on presumptions which are inherently skewed against inclusive conceptions of community.[26]

A. Imputations of homosexuality in England

The first of the few relevant English cases is *Woods & Pirie v Gordon* which went to the House of Lords around 1820.[27] Two boarding school mistresses were

[25] It also shows plainly that Learned Hand was wrong when he said in *Grant v Reader's Digest Association Inc* 151 F 2d 733, 735 (2nd Cir, 1945) that the informing cases were the only instance where 'the right-thinking person' was used to limit actionability and were an exception to the general operation of the law. This view may have been sufficiently accurate at the time *Grant* was decided but it no longer stands up to scrutiny. The informing cases are undoubtedly an application of a general principle.

[26] It will be presumed that what it means to be 'homosexual' is not in dispute among the parties; cf HE Ware, 'Celebrity, Privacy Rights and Free Speech: Recalibrating Tort Remedies for "Outed" Celebrities' (1997) 32 Harvard Civil Rights & Civil Liberties LR 449, 472.

[27] Ten years of litigation preceded the hearing in the House of Lords but the case was never reported. W Roughhead, 'Closed Doors' (1929) 41 Juridical Review 91 draws on a set of papers retained by counsel to provide a lengthy description of this case, replete with maps of the school and sleeping quarters, though pervaded by racial prejudice against the perpetrator of the rumour.

alleged to have been in a lesbian relationship. The decision ultimately went in their favour but 'because of the delicacy of the matter, the decision was never reported and the papers associated with the case were ordered by the court to be destroyed'.[28] When *Kerr v Kennedy* was decided in 1942, an imputation of homosexuality was the central issue but there was no discussion as to whether that imputation might not be defamatory—it was clearly beyond question that it was.[29]

Nearly two decades later, the glamorous American pianist and showman Liberace was described by the *Daily Mirror* as:

> the summit of sex—the pinnacle of Masculine, Feminine and Neuter. Everything that He, She or It can ever want . . . a deadly, winking, sniggering, snuggling, chromium-plated, scent-impregnated, luminous, quivering, giggling, fruit-flavored, mincing, ice-covered heap of mother love.[30]

There was dispute over whether the words could convey an imputation that the plaintiff was homosexual but, again, there was no doubt that the imputation would be defamatory if it was conveyed. It is clear that in the late 1950s, it was accepted that 'right-thinking men generally' would think the less of a person for their homosexuality.

The issue was next raised in 1992 when pop-singer and actor Jason Donovan sued *The Face* magazine for libel.[31] Through manipulated images, the magazine's cover pictured Donovan wearing a shirt with the words 'Queer As Fuck' emblazoned on the front. He did not plead an imputation that the defendant magazine had claimed he was homosexual. Instead, Donovan framed his claim as a hypocrisy allegation, arguing that the magazine had suggested he was 'lying and deceitful about his sexuality'.[32] The plaintiff's arguments expressly stated that there was nothing defamatory about being called a homosexual and, in the absence of argument from the defendant, the court offered no opinion on the matter. While the pleadings no doubt reflect Donovan's true views on sexuality and equality, these same pleadings could have been drafted to prevent any adverse publicity from perceived bigotry. Whether the plaintiff or the jury really thought that the sting of the libel lay in hypocrisy is uncertain, but Donovan was awarded £200,000 damages.[33]

[28] Ibid 91.

[29] *Kerr v Kennedy* [1942] 1 KB 409.

[30] *Liberace v Daily Mirror Newspapers* The Times, 17 and 18 June 1959.

[31] The *Donovan* judgment is unreported; I have drawn on numerous media reports, including 'Sex, Lies and Libel Laws' *The Times*, 5 April 1992; 'Face-Saving Formula' *The Times*, 7 April 1992.

[32] 'Sex, Lies and Libel Laws' *The Times*, 5 April 1992.

[33] Donovan did not seek to enforce the judgment and went to some lengths to ensure that the magazine was not ruined: 'Sex, lies and libel laws' *The Times*, 5 April 1992; 'Face-saving formula' *The Times*, 7 April 1992. The Court of Appeal seemed to accept in *Cruise v Mirror Newspapers PLC* [1999] QB 931, CA that an imputation of homosexuality is still capable of defaming a person.

B. Imputations of homosexuality in the United States

Around 60 American defamation cases deal with imputations of homosexuality.[34] Courts in the United States have consistently found the imputation to be capable of defaming a person.[35] In libel cases, courts and parties have consistently proceeded on the basis that there is no doubt an imputation of homosexuality is defamatory.[36] In slander cases, defamatory capacity has generally turned on whether the defendant's words fell into categories of slander per se.[37] It was traditionally held that an allegation of homosexuality against a man implied he had committed sodomy and thus imputed a criminal offence.[38] Suggestions a woman was homosexual were said to impute unchastity.[39] Although the defamatory capacity of the imputation was rarely in doubt, the cases help show how the courts have dealt with the contested moral status of sexuality and how 'the temper of the times' is taken into account in making determinations.

As the sodomy statutes have slowly been repealed and public feeling has changed, the United States courts have been less willing to find that an imputation of

[34] A good coverage of the case law can be found in EM Koehler, 'The Variable Nature of Defamation: Social Mores and Accusations of Homosexuality' (1999) 76 Journalism & Mass Communication Quarterly 217.

[35] A brief explanation of the law may be helpful in understanding the US cases. The distinction between libel and slander as, respectively, written and oral defamation is the same in US states as it is in the common law of England and Australia. However, the US cases can become confusing in their use of the terms 'per se' and 'per quod'. In slander actions in England, Australia, and the US, 'slander per se' refers to slander that falls within one of the established categories of slander that is actionable without special damage. 'Slander per quod' is used in the US to refer to slander that will only be actionable upon proof of special damage. In libel actions, the 'per se' and 'per quod' distinctions are not found in English or Australian law and they are not analogous to 'slander per se' and 'slander per quod'. A publication that is 'libellous per se' will be libellous on its face. In some states, this is a determination of law and will mean that the jury has no role to play. 'Libel per quod', on the other hand refers to a publication that relies on the proof of extrinsic facts to establish the libel. Thus, the American libel distinctions are more concerned with what is understood as innuendo and the conveying of imputations in English and Australian law.

[36] *Keys v Interstate Circuit Inc* 408 SW 2d 485 (Tex Civ App, 1971); *Justice v Belo Broadcasting Corporation* 472 F Supp 145 (N Dist Tex, 1979); *Neiman-Marcus v Lait* 107 F Supp 96 (S Dist NY, 1952); *Neiman-Marcus v Lait* 13 FRD 311 (S Dist NY, 1952); *Wetherby v Retail Credit Company* 201 A 2d 344 (Md, 1964); *Boy Scouts of America v Teal* 374 F Supp 1276 (E Dist Pa, 1974); *Manale v City of New Orleans Department of Police* 673 F 2d 122 (5th Cir, 1982).

[37] A statement is slanderous per se if it imputes to any person the commission of a crime; the existence of a loathsome disease; incompetence in their trade or profession; or unchastity to a woman. If the imputation does not fit into a category then special damage must be proved, which is often difficult in slander. WL Prosser, *Handbook of The Law of Torts* (4th edn, 1971) 760 suggested that homosexuality might be directly constituted as a fifth category of slander per se. This suggestion was rejected in *Moricoli v Schwartz* 361 NE 2d 74, 76 per Stamos J (Ill App Ct, 1977) though adopted in obiter in *Privitera v Phelps* 79 A 2d 1, 3 (NY SC App Div, 1981). The suggestion was not included in the next edition: WP Keeton *et al*, *Prosser & Keeton on the Law of Torts* (5th edn, 1984).

[38] *Buck v Savage* 323 SW 2d 363 (Tex Civ App, 1959); *Head v Newton* 596 SW 2d 211 (Tex Civ App, 1980); *Mazart v State of New York* 441 NYS 2d 600 (NY Ct of Claims, 1981).

[39] *Schomer v Smidt* 170 Cal Rptr 662 (Cal Ct App, 1980); *Nazeri v Missouri Valley College* 860 SW 2d 303 (Mo, 1993).

homosexuality against either a male or female is slanderous per se. One approach has been to find that a statement that a person is homosexual does not of itself give rise to an imputation of unlawful sexual activity and is thus not actionable as slander.[40] Where unchastity is concerned, the courts have acknowledged that opinions about sex have changed but this has not resulted in a substantial change in the law.[41] For example, when the Colorado Court of Appeals considered whether the imputation was slanderous per se in 1992, Dubofsky J said that persons deserving of social reprobation included thieves, murderers, and prostitutes, and the court:

> should not classify homosexuals with those miscreants who have engaged in actions that deserve the reprobation and scorn which is implicitly a part of the slander/libel per se classification. For a characterization of a person to warrant a per se classification, it should, without equivocation, expose the plaintiff to public hatred or contempt... However, there is no empirical evidence in this record demonstrating that homosexuals are held by society in such poor esteem. Indeed, it appears that the community view towards homosexuals is mixed.[42]

The refusal to adopt a slander per se classification is still, however, a long way from finding that an imputation of homosexuality is not at all capable of defaming a person under the general libel test.

Emergent social inclusion and the challenges it raises for the law are similarly apparent in libel cases. In *Matherson v Marcello*, for instance, the Appellate Division of the New York Supreme Court first stated the legal principle: a defamatory statement is one that tends to 'induce an evil opinion of [the plaintiff] in the minds of right-thinking persons....'[43] Then, applying this, the court held:

> It cannot be said that social opprobrium of homosexuality does not remain with us today. Rightly or wrongly, many individuals still view homosexuality as immoral... [D]espite

[40] *Stein v Trager* 232 NYS 2d 362 (NY SC, 1962); *Matherson v Marchello* 473 NYS 2d 998 (NY SC App Div, 1984); *Moricoli v Schwartz* 361 NE 2d 74 (Ill Ct App, 1977). *Boehm v American Bankers Insurance Group Inc* 557 So 2d 91, 94 & n 1 (Fla Dist Ct App, 1990) held that 'the modern view ... has not found statements concerning sexual preference to constitute slander per se', but the reasoning in the case is unpersuasive. *Boehm* relies on *Morrisette v Beatte* 17 A 2d 464 (RI, 1941) and *Boy Scouts of America v Teal* 374 F Supp 1276 (E Dist Pa, 1974) as authority for the proposition that the imputation is not slanderous per se. Neither case supports that view. On the contrary, they tend to adhere to the traditional position.

[41] *Donovan & Hunter v Fiumara* 442 SE 2d 572 (NC Ct App, 1994); cf *Random House Australia Pty Ltd v Costello & Abbott* (1999) 167 ALR 224, 236–7, FCA; see Chapter 5, II(A).

[42] *Hayes v Smith* 832 P 2d 1022, 1025 (Colo Ct App, 1992). The reasoning is not without its problems. It does not consider whether the imputation might be appropriately placed in one of the original four categories but is completely predicated, it seems, on the basis that a new category would have to be established if the imputation is to be slanderous per se. A discussion of homosexual sex as no longer being a criminal offence is not directed at the inclusion of the imputation in that category; rather, homosexuality 'is not of such a character as to be slanderous per se'. There is no reference to right-thinking persons or the like but the normative premise is unquestionably present in his comparative evaluation of who the court should classify as warranting public scorn.

[43] *Matherson v Marchello* 473 NYS 2d 998, 1001–2 (Titone J delivering the opinion of the court) (NY SC App Div, 1984), references omitted.

the fact that an increasing number of homosexuals are publicly expressing satisfaction and even pride in their status, the potential and probable harm of a false charge of homosexuality in terms of a social and economic impact cannot be ignored.[44]

The reasoning neglects the crucial legal issue. Where Titone J suggests that 'rightly or wrongly' there is a lesser opinion of homosexuals in society, he continues as if this does not matter; the non sequitur is that he has stated that it does indeed matter by the very words of the test.

It is a failure of United States courts that they have not at all considered that the social acceptance of homosexuality may be legally significant with respect to the principles of ethical recognition stated in the test for what is defamatory. At most, the American case law indicates that segments of the community hold different views about whether a person's sexuality is a criterion of moral judgment. This does mean courts may find that a statement that a person is *homophobic* will be defamatory.[45] However, there is nothing to indicate that the courts are moving towards a refusal to recognize the moral taxonomies that devalue persons on the basis of their homosexuality.

The upshot of the decisions in England and the United States is that until the late 1990s neither libel nor slander cases had seriously addressed the proposition that an imputation of homosexuality should not be defamatory as a matter of law based on the threshold terms of 'right-thinking' or 'respectable' or 'anti-social'. This is so even though the blackness cases might have suggested the possibility of successfully running such an argument.

C. Imputations of homosexuality in Australia

Australian courts have occasionally dealt with imputations of homosexuality. In 1991 the Supreme Court of Western Australia relied on *Kerr v Kennedy* when it held that a statement a woman was a lesbian was actionable as slander per se because it imputed unchastity to the woman.[46] The imputation was actionable in *Harris v Perkins*, a libel case, though the jury there found it was not defamatory of the plaintiff.[47] In *Hanson v Australian Broadcasting Corporation* the opinion at first instance included a statement similar in tone to the American decision of *Matherson*:

I think the current view is that [homosexuals] constitute about 5 per cent of the community and I think it's clear that [a significant percentage of] people who are of heterosexual

[44] Ibid 1005. Similar views are expressed in *Nazeri v Missouri Valley College* 860 SW 2d 303, 312 (Mo, 1993); *Mazart v State of New York* 441 NYS 2d 600, 603–4 (NY Ct of Claims, 1981).

[45] *Lester v Powers* 596 A 2d 65 (Me, 1991); *Vail v Plain Dealer Publishing Company* 649 NE 2d 182 (Ohio, 1995).

[46] *Harrison v Galuszko* (West Aust SC, 8 November 1991).

[47] *Harris v Perkins* (NSW SC, 24 March 1999); *Harris v 718932 Pty Ltd* [2000] NSWSC 784; *Harris v Perkins* [2001] NSWSC 258; J Eisenberg, 'Sex, Satire and "Middle-Class Morality": Reflections on Some Recent Defamation Cases' (1999) 92 Media Information Australia 19, 27.

disposition... hold homosexuals in contempt and don't accept that form of lifestyle. Now whether they're right or wrong, that's the fact of the matter. I think lots of people who are not of homosexual disposition, but are of heterosexual orientation look down upon, rightly or wrongly, homosexuals...[48]

Justice Ambrose goes on to explain that this would generate ridicule and contempt, and the case proceeds on that footing rather than under the principal test.

In two matters imputations of homosexuality have received significant attention. Both cases are significant because defamatory capacity was challenged under the principal test. Both are decisions of a single judge in the Supreme Court of New South Wales. In *Horner v Goulburn City Council* Levine J found the imputation was capable of defaming a person.[49] In *Rivkin v Amalgamated Television Services* Bell J reached the opposite conclusion.[50] They proceed quite differently but each is a useful vehicle for exploring the issues, and each is significantly flawed.

The action in *Horner* arose from a workplace disagreement. The plaintiffs were senior managers and complained that an internal performance review implied they were in a homosexual relationship.[51] The defendant argued that the imputation was incapable of being defamatory.[52]

Justice Levine held that in December 1997 an imputation of homosexuality was capable of defaming a plaintiff:

The question of law is whether the statement constituting the imputation could cause ordinary members of the community to think the less of the plaintiff... Community attitudes to an assertion of a homosexual relationship may range from sympathetic tolerance and understanding to an irrational abhorrence... I do not consider that it can conclusively be said that even towards the end of this century's last decade that there can be, among ordinary members of the community, a view that to say of a person that that person is in a homosexual relationship is not disparaging or is not likely to lower that person in the estimation of such people.[53]

While the reasoning resembles that in *Matherson*, it is different because Levine J states that the test is whether the imputation 'could cause ordinary members of the community to think the less of the plaintiff'.[54] This statement of the test is incomplete; the correct test refers not just to ordinary members of the community, but to ordinary *decent* members of the community.[55] The misstatement of

[48] *Hanson v Australian Broadcasting Corporation* (Qld SC, 1 September 1997), cited in E Handsley and G Davis, 'Defamation and Satire: *Hanson v Australian Broadcasting Corporation*' (2000) 9 Torts Law Journal 1, 13–14. See further Chapter 7, IV.

[49] *Horner v Goulburn City Council* (NSW SC, 5 December 1997). For a later decision by Levine J see *Kelly v John Fairfax Publications Pty Ltd* [2003] NSWSC 586 [31]–[44].

[50] *Rivkin v Amalgamated Television Services Pty Ltd* [2001] NSWSC 432.

[51] *Horner v Goulburn City Council* (NSW SC, 5 December 1997) [3].

[52] Ibid [4].

[53] Ibid [5].

[54] Ibid.

[55] *Boyd v Mirror Newspapers Ltd* [1980] 2 NSWLR 449, 452, NSW SC.

law allows Levine J to avoid the critical question of ethical recognition with more subtlety than Titone J could do in *Matherson*. Still, three observations can be made about ethical recognition in *Horner*. The first concerns the reasoning; the second considers the case as authority for a legal principle; and the third turns to the place of defences.

First, although not addressing the place of 'the right-thinking person' in the test, the court implicitly engages in the ethical recognition process by using the values of those who would hold a person in lower esteem on the basis of their sexuality as the relevant point of reference. The criteria for moral judgment are subsumed within the 'ordinary person' test.[56] By applying the standards of 'ordinary people'—divorced from any investigation of decency—Levine J needs to consider only the prevalence of homophobia and prejudice and can ignore any questions about its moral acceptability. The reasoning relies on and authorizes the exclusion of homosexuals from the moral community envisioned by the court. Justice Levine's understanding of how ordinary people might think of homosexuality is revealing in this regard: at best he can comprehend no more than 'sympathetic tolerance and understanding' from an ordinary person.[57] There is not a possibility, it appears, that ordinary members of the community would accept, endorse, or approve of a homosexual relationship, let alone enjoy it. Most certainly, homosexuals and others whose attitudes towards homosexual relationships go beyond sympathetic tolerance are not among the ordinary people which Levine J sees from the Bench.

Secondly, when the case is considered as authority, without looking at the misstatement of law in the reasoning, the necessary implication is that in the eyes of the law one can be a decent or right-thinking or respectable person in the community and still think the less of another on the grounds of their sexuality. The implication remains that homosexuals are not respectable; quite literally, they are not worthy of legal respect. The court's failure to consider the ethical recognition elements of the test skews the tenor of the judgment. It may appear on its face that the decision is a step forward for gays and lesbians because, by acknowledging the reality of homophobia among ordinary people, it gives at least some legal recognition to the existence of prejudice. But such an interpretation would be misplaced: the decision does not just give legal *recognition* to bigotry, but legal *legitimacy*. It recognizes homophobia as a characteristic of ordinary decent, respectable, right-thinking people.

A final observation can be made regarding exclusion and the defence of justification. On the reasoning of Levine J, the ostracism or intolerance of homosexuals is only unacceptable with regard to a person who is *wrongly* said to be gay or lesbian. A person incorrectly said to be gay or lesbian can recover for the harm they suffer. If the allegation can be proved true, the plaintiff will fail. The

[56] The same logic is used in the homicide case of *Green v The Queen* (1997) 191 CLR 334 where for the defence of provocation the ordinary person is imbued with a moral standard.
[57] *Horner v Goulburn City Council* (NSW SC, 5 December 1997) [5].

implication is that the law will not permit the reputation of heterosexuals to be disparaged, but will allow the reputation of a homosexual person to be damaged. In Robert Post's framework, the unsuccessful plaintiff is 'discredited and stigmatised as a person unworthy of being treated with civility; in effect he will be subject to exclusion from belonging as a respected and responsible member of society'.[58] It is 'an authoritative confirmation of his own stigma'.[59]

Like the American courts, the New South Wales Supreme Court has acknowledged the existence of prejudice but—unlike the decisions regarding blackness imputations—the imputation of homosexuality has remained defamatory.[60] This position has recently been the subject of a significant legal change.

III. The Refusal of Ethical Recognition in the Sexuality Cases

A. *Rivkin v Amalgamated Television Services*

The plaintiff in *Rivkin v Amalgamated Television Services* was a high-profile stockbroker.[61] The defendant broadcast a programme that linked Rivkin to a man named Gordon Wood, the suspect in a murder case. A number of imputations were pleaded, including 'that the plaintiff had engaged in homosexual intercourse with Gordon Wood'.[62]

The court summarized the submissions by the defendant's counsel:

> [Mr Stitt] submitted that there had been a change in the social and moral standards of the community such that, as a matter of law, it could [no longer] be said that right thinking members of the society generally would hold that the mere fact of homosexual intercourse lowered a man in their estimate. In support of his submission Mr Stitt drew attention to a framework of legislation at the State and Federal level which he contended reflected the change in community attitudes on the topic of homosexuality.[63]

The legislation included the de-criminalization of homosexual intercourse as well as amendments to anti-discrimination, family, immigration, and employment laws which sought to protect citizens against discrimination based on sexuality.[64]

Against this, the plaintiff submitted that the enactment of discrimination laws 'did not speak to the question of whether ordinary right thinking members of the

[58] RC Post, 'The Social Foundations of Defamation Law: Reputation and the Constitution' (1986) 74 California Law Review 691, 711, references omitted.

[59] Ibid 713.

[60] For a discussion of the position in Canada, see B MacDougall, *Queer Judgments: Homosexuality, Expression and the Courts in Canada* (2000); in New Zealand, but with a wider focus, see DR Knight, '"I'm Not Gay—Not That There's Anything Wrong With That!" Are Unwanted Imputations of Gayness Defamatory?' (2006) 37 Victoria University of Wellington Law Review 249.

[61] *Rivkin v Amalgamated Television Services Pty Ltd* [2001] NSWSC 432.

[62] Ibid [3].

[63] Ibid [19]–[20].

[64] Ibid [20].

community might not entertain an adverse reaction to a man who had homosexual intercourse'.[65] Justice Bell noted also that the plaintiff 'drew attention to the fact that many reasonable persons holding religious convictions would consider engagement in homosexual relations to be a sin'.[66]

Actionability was decided under the general standards test.[67] Justice Bell 'accept[ed] that reasonable members of the community, by reason of religious belief, may think the less of a man who engages in homosexual intercourse', but concluded that wider community attitudes must prevail, and those attitudes were indicated by legislative provisions that generally sought to treat people equally regardless of their sexuality.[68] The defendant's arguments were adopted by the court, though the term 'reasonable' was used rather than 'right-thinking'.

> In [Mr Stitt's] submission it is no longer open to contend that the shared social and moral standards with which the ordinary reasonable member of the community is imbued include that of holding homosexual men (or men who engage in homosexual sex) in lesser regard on account of that fact alone. I accept that submission.[69]

It is unfortunate that the position is not expressed a little more carefully and precisely. This needs to be flagged lest the relevant judicial statement be misconstrued. The statement should be read as meaning the 'ordinary *right-thinking* member of the community', which was in fact the wording in the defendant's submission.[70] Leaving this to one side, the statement of law is clear and succinct, but narrow.[71] The principle does not have the wide sweep it might on its face appear to have. It is limited in two significant respects.

First, the legal principle stated in *Rivkin* refers to moral standards 'of holding homosexual men (or men who engage in homosexual sex) in lesser regard'.[72] While the legislative basis of the reasoning almost certainly implies that Justice Bell's decision should equally apply to both homosexual women and men, it could be argued that if read in conjunction with the defamation case law that conclusion might not necessarily follow. An imputation that a woman is a lesbian

[65] Ibid [21]. [66] Ibid [22].

[67] *Reader's Digest Services Pty Ltd v Lamb* (1982) 150 CLR 500, 506 (Brennan J), cited in *Rivkin v Amalgamated Television Services Pty Ltd* [2001] NSWSC 432 [24]. Interestingly, *Hepburn v TCN Channel Nine Pty Ltd* [1983] 2 NSWLR 682, NSW CA—in which a sectional standards approach was taken—was not mentioned in either *Horner* or *Rivkin*.

[68] *Rivkin v Amalgamated Television Services Pty Ltd* [2001] NSWSC 432 [19], [26], [30].

[69] Ibid [30].

[70] Ibid [17]. The reasonable reader, as discussed earlier, is the standard applied when determining whether an imputation has been conveyed. On the defamatory quality of the imputation, the arguments and judgment unquestionably view the significance of the expression 'right-thinking' as a matter of morality: ibid [17]–[29].

[71] The reasoning surpasses that in *Horner*, not least because the correct statement of law is applied and the issues are considered in the appropriate legal terms. Soon after *Rivkin*, Levine J indicated that he preferred the position taken by Bell J rather than his earlier decision in *Horner's* case: *Obermann v ACP Publishing Pty Ltd* [2001] NSWSC 1022 [21], though cf his decision in *Kelly v John Fairfax Publications Pty Ltd* [2003] NSW SC 586 [40] where his Honour expressed some doubts.

[72] *Rivkin v Amalgamated Television Services Pty Ltd* [2001] NSWSC 432 [30].

has historically been defamatory because it imputes unchastity to her.[73] More recently, *Costello & Abbott* makes it clear that chastity remains a live issue for Australian defamation law and shows that the courts view the sexual behaviour of women very differently to the sexual behaviour of men.[74]

Secondly, the principle in *Rivkin* is qualified by Justice Bell's statement that while a simple imputation of homosexuality alone cannot be defamatory, such a publication could easily raise defamatory imputations of hypocrisy, infidelity, or abuse of power or trust.[75] Accordingly, leave was granted to amend the pleadings and Rivkin then alleged that the broadcast conveyed the following imputations:

> That the plaintiff engaged in homosexual intercourse with Gordon Wood, a man who was an employee of his, much younger than him, who viewed him as a father figure, upon whom he lavished gifts and who was engaged to be married.
>
> The plaintiff procured a male employee to have sexual intercourse with him by lavishing presents on him; an abuse of wealth and power.[76]

This aspect of the decision confirms that even the most basic pleading of hypocrisy can go to the jury.[77] Of course, a publication may convey more damaging imputations. Moreover, it might be thought that where a heterosexual person is said to be homosexual (or, presumably, vice versa) it is serious because it suggests a breach of trust at an intimately personal level; it suggests that a person has hidden from their partner something central to their personal identity and the very nature of their relationship. So, I am not arguing that more complex imputations cannot arise from a statement that a person is homosexual, however, if the legal principle arising from the *Rivkin* judgment is to have any real significance then pleaded imputations must be genuine and meaningful, not merely pleaded as a way of restating the homosexuality imputation.

B. The basis for the shift to the refusal of recognition

In spite of its limits, *Rivkin* still represents a marked shift in the law and the reasoning warrants close attention. Having decided that a general community standard needed to be applied, what persuaded Bell J that the statement of law

[73] *Schomer v Smidt* 170 Cal Rptr 662 (Cal Ct App, 1985); *Harrison v Galuszko* (West Aust SC, 8 November 1991); *Donovan & Hunter v Fiumara* 442 SE 2d 572 (NC Ct App, 1994).

[74] *Random House Australia Pty Ltd v Costello & Abbott* (1999) 167 ALR 224, FCA; see Chapter 5, II(A).

[75] *Rivkin v Amalgamated Television Services Pty Ltd* [2001] NSWSC 432 [30]. Cf J Harkess, 'A Linguistic Inspection of the Law of Defamation' (1998) 8 Auckland University Law Review 653. Harkess brings an interesting linguistic analysis to bear on the conveying of imputations though tends to conflate the questions of whether imputations are conveyed and whether they are defamatory.

[76] Ibid [32]

[77] Ibid [35]–[36].

regarding the defamatory capacity of an imputation of homosexuality should change? There were two lines of reasoning used in finding that a shift from ethical recognition to the refusal of recognition was warranted. They revolved around precedent and legislative change.

1. *The use of precedent in* Rivkin

The decision referred to just three cases. The first was the action just a month earlier where Rivkin had sued two newspapers over relevantly identical imputations though the defendants did not contest the defamatory capacity of the sexuality imputation.[78] Second, *Horner's* case was mentioned but distinguished because the defendant's argument put to Bell J had not been put to Levine J in 1997.[79] Finally, and most interestingly, the defendants supported their argument with a 1998 Scots case, *Quilty v Windsor*, where it had been held that an imputation of homosexuality was incapable of defaming a person.[80] *Quilty* concerned a letter written by an inmate about a prison officer. It alleged, among other things, that the officer was homosexual. Justice Bell quotes Lord Kingarth's finding that 'merely to refer to a person as being homosexual would not now generally at least be regarded—if it ever was—as defamatory per se'.[81] Lord Kingarth's decision needs closer attention than Bell J gives it. The reasoning is not especially persuasive.

Lord Kingarth seriously considered that it might *never* have been defamatory to say that a person is homosexual. This distorts the history of defamation law and the 1917 case of *AB v XY* on which His Lordship draws for support. In *Quilty* it was said that in *AB v XY* 'the allegation was not of mere homosexuality but of the alleged engagement by [the plaintiff] in what was then criminal activity'.[82] A reading of *AB v XY* shows that while the imputations are mostly framed in those terms, the court at first instance and on appeal sees the slur on reputation as lying in the plaintiffs' alleged homosexual behaviour, regardless of its criminality.[83]

Secondly, the decision in *Quilty* places some reliance on *Prophit v British Broadcasting Corporation*, a 1997 case where it was argued that an imputation had arisen that the plaintiff, a nun, was a lesbian.[84] Lord Kingarth finds that *Prophit*

[78] *Rivkin v John Fairfax Publications* (NSW SC, 18 April 2001), cited in *Rivkin v Amalgamated Television Services Pty Ltd* [2001] NSWSC 432 [28]. The action against Fairfax was unsuccessful in what was held on appeal to be a perverse verdict by the jury when they found that none of the pleaded imputations were conveyed: *Rivkin v John Fairfax Publications* [2002] NSWCA 87; *John Fairfax Publications v Rivkin* [2003] HCA 50. The defamatory capacity of a homosexuality imputation was not argued in this case, though in the High Court Kirby J expressed an inconclusive view on the issue. He suggested that it could not be said that the imputation was incapable of being defamatory 'for all purposes and all people' and that it could be defamatory if it raised issues of hypocrisy or it could be defamatory 'for people who treat their sexuality as private or secret': [140].

[79] *Rivkin v Amalgamated Television Services Pty Ltd* [2001] NSWSC 432 [28].

[80] *Quilty v Windsor* [1999] SLT 346, OH.

[81] Ibid 354, cited in *Rivkin v Amalgamated Television Services Pty Ltd* [2001] NSWSC 432 [29].

[82] *Quilty v Windsor* [1999] SLT 346, 350, OH, referring to *AB v XY* [1917] SC 15.

[83] *AB v XY* [1917] SC 15, 16–17.

[84] *Prophit v British Broadcasting Corporation* [1997] SLT 745.

does not assist the plaintiff in *Quilty*.[85] This seems superficially correct as Coutts TJ stated in *Prophit* that 'it is unnecessary for me to consider at this stage as a matter of law whether a suggestion of lesbianism remains defamatory these days'.[86] However, the action in *Prophit* proceeded on the basis that the imputation would indeed have been defamatory which meant it was least consistent with the plaintiff's submission in *Quilty* that the imputation was defamatory.

The strongest basis for Lord Kingarth's decision is his reliance on the developments of the common law: 'Matters have so moved on, it was stressed, that the court has recognised the right of a single man living in a stable relationship to adopt a child.'[87] His Lordship then makes reference to a speech in the House of Lords to the effect that where partners guarantee debts, the law should provide the same protection for homosexual couples as it does for married heterosexual couples.[88] While these developments are appropriate matters for consideration, the decision proceeds more by assertion than argument because there is not really an adequate explanation of *how* they are relevant. My point is not that Lord Kingarth *could not* have supported the decision using the common law developments, but rather that he *did not* do so adequately.

Although the decision in *Rivkin* makes reference to *Quilty v Windsor*, the strength of Justice Bell's reasoning lies not in its reliance on precedent, but in its use of the legislation as the basis for determining defamatory capacity. There are, nonetheless, some concerns about the use of legislation.

2. *The use of legislation in* Rivkin

The second limb of the reasoning in *Rivkin* relies on legislative change as an indicator of change in community attitudes. Justice Bell sought to explain that the legislative provisions were relevant because they reflected 'the change in community attitudes' and 'such a framework spoke strongly of the change in recent years in social and moral values concerning homosexuality'.[89] This use of legislation is quite novel in Australian defamation law and neither supported nor precluded by the authorities. Still, it seems a useful starting point when looking for a set of external indicators that might support a conclusion as to what views are held by 'right-thinking' people. Where homosexuality imputations are concerned, this has been considered by Randy Fogle as part of a public policy approach.[90] His position is not the same as the approach taken by Bell J but is certainly not inconsistent with it.

[85] *Quilty v Windsor* [1999] SLT 346, 352, 355, OH.
[86] *Prophit v British Broadcasting Corporation* [1997] SLT 745, 748.
[87] *Quilty v Windsor* [1999] SLT 346, 350, OH.
[88] Ibid, referring to *Barclays Bank v O'Brien* [1994] 1 AC 198, HL.
[89] *Rivkin v Amalgamated Television Services Pty Ltd* [2001] NSWSC 432 [19], [30].
[90] R Fogle, 'Is Calling Someone "Gay" Defamatory?: The Meaning of Reputation, Community Mores, Gay Rights and Free Speech' (1993) 3 Law and Sexuality 165; also RM Wrightson, 'Gray Cloud Obscures the Rainbow: Why Homosexuality as Defamation Contradicts New Jersey Public Policy to Combat Homophobia and Promote Equal Protection' (2002) 10 Journal of Law and Policy

The logic behind Fogle's argument is that '"right-mindedness" appears to exclude those people whose attitudes directly conflict with public policy'.[91] Public policy, argues Fogle, is indicated by local legislative provisions such as anti-discrimination or gay-rights laws to obtain an indicator of community standards.[92] If the local laws are at odds with a particular group's views, then the court will not recognize the views of that group; because they are contrary to public policy, they are not 'right-minded'. There are some problems associated with the use of legislation as an external indicator of community attitudes.

As Fogle himself notes, the application of such criteria would be difficult for numerous reasons, including establishing whether the laws are an accurate reflection of community attitudes about homosexuality; the problem of interpreting community values in jurisdictions with no legislative provisions on homosexuality; and the difficulty of interpreting community values about homosexuality when there are conflicting laws.[93] While Fogle considers that the effects of such problems can be sufficiently minimized, I disagree. Statutes may provide a basic external indicator, but without a remarkably strong and consistent legislative regime, the reliance on statutes as a standard of public policy will at best legitimize a choice made by the courts rather than provide a clear indicator of moral standards that should be applied by the courts.

Some of these difficulties are manifest in *Rivkin*. Most importantly, the limits of anti-discrimination legislation are not identified, let alone considered in terms of how they might be relevant to the test for what is defamatory. These limits include significant exemptions and limitations when it comes to housing, education, employment, and business partnerships.[94] Criminal statutes differentiate between heterosexual and homosexual activities.[95] It is not difficult to conceive of a judgment that would point to these gaps as an indication that the legislature still maintains some discrimination against homosexuals and that such discrimination is an indicator of community standards which should be taken account of when determining the capacity to defame in the eyes of decent folk. Ultimately, legislation provides

635; cf P Arend, 'Defamation in an Age of Political Correctness: Should a False Public Statement that a Person is Gay be Defamatory' (1997) 18 Northern Illinois University Law Review 99.

[91] Fogle, ibid 173. This claim requires much more support than Fogle provides. It is certainly not true for the informers cases, and the blackness cases would need a good deal more analysis before such an assertion can be confidently made.

[92] This is distinct from using public policy to override an otherwise defamatory imputation: cf *Shaha v Dardiryan* ca 466/83, PD 39 (4) 734 (1985), Israel SC; Chapter 5, III(B)(2).

[93] Fogle (n 90 above) 187–92.

[94] *Anti-Discrimination Act 1977* (NSW), ss 49ZH(3) (employment), 49ZK (business partnerships), 49ZO(3) (education), 49ZQ(3) (accommodation).

[95] The differences include aspects of consent—the age of consent is lower for women than for men—and penalties associated with homosexual criminal offences are greater than those for the same criminal acts that constitute heterosexual offences. Compare, for instance, the following sections of the *Crimes Act 1900* (NSW): s 66A, cf. s 78H; s 66C, cf s 78K; s 61N, cf ss 78Q and 78R. Conflicting laws in the United States are discussed in EK Yatar, 'Defamation, Privacy and the Changing Social Status of Homosexuality: Re-Thinking Supreme Court Gay Rights Jurisprudence' (2003) 12 Law & Sexuality 119, 135–48.

a useful but not adequate foundation for the refusal to recognize the criteria for moral judgment.

In sum, the decision in *Rivkin* constitutes a shift from recognition of a moral taxonomy that devalues people on the basis of their sexuality, to rejection of such a taxonomy. However, the reasoning in *Rivkin* is an inappropriate, insufficient, and insecure foundation for legal change. Neither the reliance on precedent nor legislation provide an adequate foundation for the shift from recognition to rejection.

IV. The Presumptive Content of 'the Right-Thinking Person'

Rivkin is the best judicial attempt to deal with the limits to the legal protection of reputation and yet it is ultimately unsuccessful. It does not articulate any firm grounds upon which the court can refuse to recognize criteria for moral judgment which devalue a person on the basis of sexuality. I want to now suggest a way of approaching the issues that can more effectively and appropriately take account of contemporary diverse and conflicting moral taxonomies. At the core of the approach is a critical focus on the presumptions associated with the conceptual tool that is 'the right-thinking person'. The application of the law in *Rivkin* provides a pathway in to these matters.

A. Determining the ethical good

Actionability in *Rivkin* was decided under the general standards test which relies on a 'moral or social standard... common to society generally'.[96] Under this approach if the scales are quantitatively tipped in favour of one view then less favoured views will be excluded. This raises an important question about how virtue is legally determined. The question becomes apparent when one extends Justice Bell's analysis to a sectional standards approach which, as Chapter 5 explained, could recognize a range of differing views in a jurisdiction, subject to a qualitative ethical limit.

Justice Bell accepted that there was one stream of thought in the jurisdiction that saw homosexuals as morally equal and another in which 'reasonable members of the community by reason of religious belief may think the less of a man who engages in homosexual intercourse'.[97] There was no indication that recognition of either view would be refused on ethical grounds. Thus, it seems that the imputation would have been capable of defaming a person under the sectional standards test.

[96] *Rivkin v Amalgamated Television Services Pty Ltd* [2001] NSWSC 432 [24], [26], [30], referring to the test in *Reader's Digest Services Pty Ltd v Lamb* (1982) 150 CLR 501, 506 (Brennan J), references omitted.

[97] *Rivkin v Amalgamated Television Services Pty Ltd* [2001] NSWSC 432 [26], [30].

At the qualitative level, a sectional standards approach of this type would give a judicial imprimatur to bigotry that is no different from that which underpins the decisions prior to *Rivkin*. It grants ethical recognition to moral taxonomies under which a person's worth is diminished on the grounds of their homosexuality. It does so on the basis that there are people in the community whose religious beliefs lead them to see homosexuality as immoral. This exposes a deep-seated inconsistency in the processes and principles of ethical recognition. Where sexuality is concerned, the decision to grant or refuse ethical recognition is not based on whether any given view is inherently morally acceptable or unacceptable but, instead, the decision is made by looking at whether the people who hold such views are accepted as respectable people in the community. This is inconsistent with the approach to ethical recognition in other categories of cases. In the informing cases, courts considered whether a low opinion of informers had the requisite moral goodness that it should be recognized as decent or respectable or as a quality of 'the right-thinking person'. The contemporary cases on imputations regarding race similarly define the content of racist views as undeserving of recognition regardless of who holds those views.[98] Judicial statements that the courts will no longer find a *Youssoupoff*-type rape imputation to be defamatory also presume that the ethical status of a view is not dependent upon the standing of those who hold it.[99]

As Chapter 5 explained, it is clear from the cases that ethical recognition is not determined empirically. Courts will not necessarily see a view as having a positive moral status simply because it is widely held. Even if reputation is determined by the reality of opinion in a jurisdiction, its legal protection has been determined on a different basis. 'The right-thinking person' has been an idea and not a reference to specific people or groups of people. The contrast between the established categories of cases and the contested moral status of sexuality illuminates a major uncertainty at the heart of the principal test for what is defamatory: should the decision to recognize or refuse to recognize criteria for moral judgment be made with reference to the intrinsic moral quality of the criteria, or with reference to people who hold the views at issue and who might generally be seen as 'right-thinking' or 'decent' or 'respectable' on other grounds?

The case law has neither provided nor required any resolution of this question. Until relatively recently, tradition has been the source of the criteria for moral judgment in communities. The values of the politically dominant classes have been morally dominant and so perceptions of intrinsic moral rightness have been inherently commensurate with social standing.[100] It is no longer clear that this is the case. As Chapter 1 and this chapter have discussed, the criteria for moral judgment and the bases of criteria are being re-thought in Western societies. As such, the conceptual tools used for adjudicating slurs on reputation must also be re-thought if the courts are to make well-reasoned decisions about what is

[98] See this chapter, I(C).

[99] See Chapter 6, II(C).

[100] See Chapter 5, I(C).

actionable as defamation. This is a challenge that has not yet been addressed by the courts and it has only been touched on in the defamation literature. As the following sections will argue, it is the intrinsic moral quality of the criteria that should be the point of reference. How that quality is to be determined needs close attention.

B. Ethical presumptions and inclusive communities

The conceptual tool that has been used to determine the scope and limits of the legal protection of reputation is 'the right-thinking person'. In the past, that concept has had content comprised of what I have called traditional values. Derived as they were from traditions of God-ordained moral and social order, and later from a secular appropriation of those Christian ethical codes, those values were an expression and source of moral certainty and social stability. But traditional values have now come adrift from their epistemological moorings. No longer anchored to religious truth and often inconsistent with the experience of social life in modern Western societies, the old ethical codes have become highly vulnerable to challenge and critique and the moral certainty of their content has diminished. This has gradually had a subtle but quite profound effect on defamation law. As the blackness and sexuality cases indicate, the traditional values of 'the right-thinking person' are no longer a fixed and certain point of reference but now function as *presumptions*. Their dominance is contingent rather than certain. They will prevail only if they are not displaced by the judicial recognition of competing moral taxonomies. Traditional values should now be thought of as the 'presumptive content' of 'the right-thinking person'.

The presumptions of tradition include presumptions about the way the jurisdiction is constituted as a moral community in determinations of defamatory capacity. The moral community has traditionally been an exclusionary one. As the blackness and sexuality cases show, when a defendant tries to persuade the court that it should refuse to recognize criteria which devalue a person on the basis of ascriptive identity-based factors, the court is being asked to envision the jurisdiction differently. It is being asked to reconstitute the jurisdiction as a moral community in which individuals obtain equal moral worth by virtue of their humanity.

Exclusionary presumptions are unsatisfactory in a modern, pluralist, liberal state. Instead, defamation law should rest on a presumption that jurisdictions are inclusive moral communities. Upon what can the court rely as the ethical rule(s) or moral value(s) that bind the people in the jurisdiction together as a community? The various collectivities in late-modern societies can be said to constitute communities by virtue of their shared commitment to the liberal premises of equal moral worth, the freedom to choose the values by which one would like to live (to the extent that they are consistent with a commitment to equal moral worth), the protection from harm that is a consequence and condition of those premises, and the moral diversity that flows from these.[101] It may seem ironic, but the commitment to moral diversity is a substantive value that identifies the shared moral unity of the people in the jurisdiction. The fact that groups with diverse moral taxonomies co-exist by consent in a democratic jurisdiction makes it appropriate for the common law to recognize the commitment to liberal premises and principles as unifying connectors.

For defamation law, this holds two implications. First, Chapter 5 proposed that a sectional standards test should be adopted because it acknowledges the social reality of moral diversity. That argument is strengthened because it now obtains a philosophical coherence. Secondly, the presumptive content of 'the right-thinking person' should change to reflect the bases of moral unity described above. The 'revised' or 'liberal presumptive content' (as I will call it) of 'the right-thinking person' consists of the inclusive values that bind the people in a liberal jurisdiction together as a community. That is, 'the right-thinking person' is presumed to be committed to equal moral worth, freedom of moral choice, protection from harm and moral diversity.

On this analysis, the principles and processes of ethical recognition operate in the same way they have in the past, but the burden of persuasion no longer falls on those who want equal moral worth recognized. It now lies on those who would seek to invoke criteria for moral judgment that are inconsistent with an inclusive liberal conception of community. The consequence is that the court in a case like *Rivkin* would not be asking (as it did) whether exclusionary criteria for moral judgment should be *refused* recognition in the determination of defamatory capacity. Instead, the court would be asking whether exclusionary values should be *granted* recognition. That is, under the revised presumptive content of 'the right-thinking person', unless a court was persuaded that 'the right-thinking person' would think the less of someone on the grounds of their sexuality then the default position would be that an imputation of homosexuality is not defamatory.

A vast range of imputations would be actionable under a liberal framework for the presumptive content of 'the right-thinking person'. In fact, most imputations that arise in defamation actions would be actionable because the various and diverse values to which they appeal are consistent with liberal principles. As Rawls has expressed it in his thesis on political liberalism, an 'overlapping consensus' of 'reasonable comprehensive religious, philosophical and moral doctrines' is an

[101] These are consistent with several of the major elements of the keystone work of modern liberal theory, John Rawls' theory of justice as fairness: *A Theory of Justice* (1971); see Chapter 1, III(C). The commitment with respect to harm is drawn from traditional liberal theory rather than from Rawls. The harm principle in its traditional sense is not Rawls' concern but nevertheless falls within his general theory. The commitments are framed as presumptions, rather than fixed content, and are thus at once consistent with and represent a more modest argument than, for example, Dworkin's claims that a commitment to 'equal concern and respect' is required: R Dworkin, 'Liberalism' in S Hampshire (ed), *Public and Private Morality* (1978) 113, 127–8; and generally, R Dworkin, *Freedom's Law: The Moral Reading of the American Constitution* (1996).

essential feature of liberal democracy.[102] This 'reasonable pluralism' contemplates a range of 'permissible conceptions of the [moral] good'.[103] What makes a moral code 'reasonable'? A code will be reasonable provided that it does not undermine the conditions that enable fairness for all (which in Rawls' work is itself justice), including the affirmation of equal moral worth and the freedom to choose one's own conception of the moral good, protection from harm and the moral diversity or pluralism that flows from these conditions.[104] Applied to defamation, this means that the test for what is defamatory will be necessarily framed in a sectional standards way and will be able to accommodate any criteria for moral judgment which do not undermine the liberal presumptive content of 'the right-thinking person'. The criteria of most interest which have the potential to undermine that content are criteria under which a person is to be judged negatively on the basis of ascriptive factors. These questions, more than any others, mark out the clash between tradition and modernity.

It is inappropriate to recognize ascriptive criteria for moral judgment because the existence of diverse moral taxonomies—including those with exclusionary criteria for moral judgment—relies on the shared liberal commitment to moral diversity that makes the jurisdiction a community. It is the shared liberal affirmation of equal worth and consequent commitment to moral diversity that permits the existence of competing and conflicting moral taxonomies. If a court recognizes criteria for moral judgment that are inconsistent with those presumptions then it undermines the premises upon which the exclusionary moral taxonomies obtain a legitimate presence in the jurisdiction in the first place.[105]

In either its traditional or liberal forms, the presumptive content of 'the right-thinking person' is just that—a set of presumptions that can be displaced. It does not mean that moral community is not or cannot be formed around other values. Just as the traditional presumptive content has been displaced in the blackness cases, it is possible that a revised liberal presumptive content could also be displaced. That is, a court may recognize moral taxonomies that include criteria under which an individual will be negatively judged if they exhibit behaviour or characteristics that are at odds with the community's traditional sense of the moral good *even though the behaviour or characteristics would not prompt a negative judgment under liberal values.* On what basis, however, might a court grant ethical

[102] J Rawls, *Political Liberalism* (1993) 36–9, 133–72.

[103] Ibid 24–5, 180.

[104] See Rawls (n 102 above) 139, for example. Rawls actually has a broader conception of justice as fairness, including economic reciprocity. As such, the claims advanced here are a very modest application of Rawls' liberalism.

[105] This argument suggests that modern liberalism contains a conception of the good. This is in contrast to the sense of liberalism proposed by Rawls in *A Theory of Justice* (n 101 above) under which justice was purely fairness. His later work acknowledged the strength of the communitarian criticisms and he re-framed liberalism as 'political liberalism' under which justice was a moral conception with content (rather than being purely about fairness): Rawls, *Political Liberalism* (n 102 above) 147. For a position that advocates more strongly an inherent liberal conception of the good, see WA Galston, *Liberal Purposes: Good, Virtues, and Diversity in the Liberal State* (1991).

recognition to such exclusionary criteria for moral judgment when determining the scope of the legal protection for reputation? The strongest argument for displacing inclusive liberal presumptions in determinations of actionability can be derived from communitarian ethics.

C. Ethical recognition of exclusionary criteria for moral judgment

Exclusionary criteria for moral judgment might gain ethical recognition in the courts on communitarian grounds. Communitarianism directly meets the problems raised by conflicting moral taxonomies whose points of difference centre around the clash between traditional and modern values that have been the focus of this chapter.

Like any conception of moral community, communitarian claims identify and express a vision (in Bailey's words) of 'how things are and how things should be'.[106] They clarify a community's moral commitments.[107] The sexuality cases are a good example. For instance, a court may identify heterosexuality as a behaviour or characteristic traditionally regarded by the people in the jurisdiction as having such positive and unifying moral value that it can be legitimately seen as an ethical good that deserves recognition by the court. This is the basis on which the court may displace the revised presumptive content of 'the right-thinking person' and, thus, it would be defamatory to say of a person that they are homosexual. However, there are two reasons why a court should be extremely wary of recognizing exclusionary values that are inconsistent with the revised presumptive content of 'the right-thinking person'.

First, there are strong arguments to see at least some strands of communitarian theory as consistent with the same substantive moral presumptions that underpin political liberalism.[108] One of the most thoroughly worked positions has been taken by Philip Selznick who explains the import of the communitarian critique of liberalism as being that it 'cannot accept as moral a consensus marred by bigotry' and there must be a 'threshold standard' of what he calls 'critical morality'.[109] There is a requirement

[106] FG Bailey, 'Gifts and Poison' in FG Bailey (ed), *Gifts and Poison: The Politics of Reputation* (1971) 1, 8.

[107] I draw this phrase from Selznick who uses it in a slightly different context: P Selznick, *The Moral Commonwealth: Social Theory and the Promise of Community* (1992) 453.

[108] The split between liberals and their communitarian critics is not by any means a sharp one on this or other issues. Philip Selznick, ibid, on whom I will draw a deal, describes his project as one of 'communitarian liberalism'. However, he quite clearly falls at the communitarian end of the spectrum (cf. ibid ix). By contrast, Galston (n 105 above) is critical of liberal theory but in developing his idea of 'purposive liberalism' he clearly remains a liberal. It has been suggested that Rawls himself can be interpreted as having acquired a communitarian sensibility in his development of 'political liberalism' as a response to his critics: S Mulhall and A Swift, *Liberals & Communitarians* (1992) 198–205.

[109] Selznick (n 107 above) 409. Critical morality, he argues, derives from reason and sits in opposition to conventional morality that is derived from custom. He does not see this as a complete split: 392–4.

of 'baseline equality'.[110] The content of that morality and equality is derived from the premises of equal moral worth that are usually associated with liberalism:

> Moral equality is the postulate that all persons have the same intrinsic moral worth… [E]veryone who is a person is presumptively entitled to recognition of that personhood… [P]ersons are equal as moral actors and as objects of moral concern. [A]s a starting point for moral reasoning, no individual's well-being is more worthy of consideration than any other's…What is appropriate is moral equality or treatment as an equal. We cannot be genuinely other-regarding, whatever the circumstances, if we do not accept the idea that everyone has the same intrinsic worth.[111]

On this argument, the moral threshold implied by communitarianism is the same as that implied by liberalism. It is:

> wholly compatible with rich diversity so long as that diversity does not undermine equality of membership… [T]he effect of moral stigma is to rank some people as intrinsically less worthy than others.[112]

The moral threshold of communitarianism carries the same implications as liberalism does for the recognition of exclusionary criteria for moral judgment: communitarian theory suggests that ascriptive criteria should not be granted ethical recognition in determinations of actionability as they undermine equal moral worth.

The communitarian critique also leans towards a second inclusive dimension. Given the communitarian premise that justice is derived from tradition then it seems beyond question that—more than two centuries after the Enlightenment—the core claims of liberalism have themselves become 'traditions', albeit traditions that compete with what is usually understood as traditional morality. Foundational liberal principles are what William Galston has called 'central tendencies: strong and enduring aggregations of belief that substantially define a political culture'.[113] Selznick has argued that the shared historical experience of 'customary morality' may be subject to reasoned critique, but the liberal principles are not merely abstractions. Embodied in the American constitutional framework, they represent 'an operative covenant [that] underpins the institutions and guides the development of a living community'.[114] The construction of community in this way is not, as Lidsky would have it, a myth.[115] Although the Americans have stated the covenant more explicitly than have other Western

[110] Ibid 484. [111] Ibid 483, 491 [112] Ibid 489.

[113] Galston (n 105 above) 16.

[114] Selznick (n 107 above) 480–4; also 392–4.

[115] LB Lidsky, 'Defamation, Reputation and the Myth of Community' (1996) 71 Washington Law Review 1, 38, 42–3. Lidsky argues that the sense of 'national community' in the United States is limited to 'certain norms that command widespread consensus. The vast majority of Americans would condemn child molestation, cold-blooded murder, or treachery to friends, family or country.' Other, more far-reaching senses of community are, she argues, mythical. The values Lidsky identifies as possibly making a community are not inconsistent with liberal values.

liberal democracies, liberal principles also deserve recognition as tradition in those other democracies:

> The principle of moral equality is drawn from experience. In embracing it we take into account the evils that ensue when its message is rejected or ignored; the limits thereby put on what it means to be genuinely other-regarding; the vision thereby dimmed of human dignity and personhood.[116]

In Australia, for example, historical experience—in both its positive and negative aspects—has frequently provided the terms in which the nation has mapped its reflections on its social, legal, and political relationships.[117]

If liberalism is seen as a tradition then even on a communitarian argument it is difficult to justify the ethical recognition of exclusionary ascriptive criteria in determinations of actionability. There will without question be competing traditions of exclusionary moral taxonomies in a jurisdiction but that will not of itself mean the liberal presumptions can be easily displaced. In particular, the numerical strength of an exclusionary taxonomy will not be enough to justify its recognition under a communitarian argument. The communitarian rationale for recognition is not simply a majoritarian claim.[118] Nor is it what Rawls has referred to as a '*modus vivendi*' that reflects and depends upon the distribution of power between opposing views.[119] The extent to which values are held in a jurisdiction is not irrelevant. Certainly, a court could appeal to a quantitative dimension of moral codes to justify ethical recognition, *but that recognition must be explained and justified as the moral choice that it is.* If a court is to recognize the ethical value of criteria for moral judgment then it must do so in ethical terms. If a court is to recognize exclusionary ascriptive criteria then it must state expressly the foundation and implications of its determination: the jurisdiction does not constitute a community that is bound together by a valuing of and commitment to recognizing the intrinsic equal moral worth of all its members.

116 Selznick (n 107 above) 482–3.

117 Cf *Mabo v Queensland (No 2)* (1992) 175 CLR 1; The Hon P Keating, Prime Minister, 'Australian Launch of the International Year for the World's Indigenous People' (the 'Redfern Park Speech'), 10 December 1992, reproduced in Native Title and Aboriginal and Torres Strait Islander Land Fund Senate Committee, *Sixteenth Report: Consistency of the Native Title Amendment Act 1998 with Australia's International Obligations under the Convention on the Elimination of all Forms of Racial Discrimination (CERD)* (2000) 270; L McNamara, 'History, Memory and Judgment: Holocaust Denial, The History Wars and Law's Problems with the Past' (2004) 26 Sydney Law Review 353, 364–8, 387–92. R Dworkin, *Taking Rights Seriously* (1977) 254 also makes an experiential observation: '[T]he belief that prejudices, personal aversions and rationalizations do not justify restricting another's freedom...occupies a critical and fundamental position in our popular morality.' This idea of 'the fair go' is axiomatic in the moral and political rhetoric of Australian life: for example, a search of Prime Minister John Howard's speeches showed that he used the expression around 120 times in speeches during five years to 2005: <http://www.pm.gov.au/media/index.cfm> (1 September 2005).

118 See, for example, Selznick (n 107 above) 408.

119 Rawls, *Political Liberalism* (n 102 above) 146–7. My description of Rawls' use of the term draws on the pithy explanation of this point by Mulhall and Swift (n 108 above) 187.

This analysis is consistent with the case law on defamation. The cases show that numbers alone will not be enough: recognition *must* have an ethical basis. As the blackness cases show, a criterion for moral judgment was refused recognition even though (or regardless of whether) it may have been widely held. The *Youssoupoff*-type rape imputation might also be counted an example. Unless the claim to recognition is made in ethical terms then it cannot be justified. This compels the courts to articulate their reasons precisely, transparently, and in the language of ethics if the inclusive presumptive content of 'the right-thinking person' is to be displaced.[120]

D. Resolving difficult imputations

It has been argued in the preceding sections that an imputation should be actionable if it possesses a tendency to cause 'the right-thinking person' to think the less of the plaintiff. 'The right-thinking person' is presumed to be a person who values equal moral worth, freedom of moral choice, protection from harm and moral diversity. Where it is argued that 'the right-thinking person' should be taken to mean something at odds with these values then that requires the court to explain in ethical terms the values which bind the jurisdiction as a community. Before concluding, it is appropriate to be clear about how this position would apply to the determinations of actionability regarding the main imputations that have been discussed and which have raised difficult issues for the courts with respect to their capacity to defame. These are imputations relating to: (1) the ascriptive factors of homosexuality, blackness, and mental illness; (2) objectionable political beliefs; (3) informing the police about a crime; (4) statements that a doctor performs abortions.

For each, I first identify the imputation, the criteria for moral judgment to which the plaintiff would be appealing, and the defendant's position. Next, I explain how the test for what is defamatory would apply where 'the right-thinking

[120] Lidsky (n 115 above) 43, 47–8, has also called for transparency in the reasoning related to determinations of actionability. She argues that the effect of constructing community has been that 'public policy choices are made in a relatively unexamined fashion' and judges 'should face this choice directly, rather than camouflaging it beneath the cloak of identifying the community's values'. My call for transparency is a little different. It is not merely a demand for an 'elaboration and explanation' of public policy goals (that Lidsky suggests will be fruitful). Rather, it is a demand to elaborate and explain the ethical rules that dictate a sense of 'how things are and how they should be'. That is necessary because those rules—which express the moral good—dictate the sorts of policy goals a jurisdiction might have. They explain not just what particular policy goals are but also *why* those goals should be pursued. To articulate policy goals (as Lidsky advocates) presupposes rather than problematizes the moral good. By demanding an ethical articulation of the values that make the jurisdiction a community—the values that make sense of policy choices—the courts are not applying a camouflage. On the contrary, they are removing it. It might be that Lidsky seeks a similar explanation when she wants courts to identify the 'assumptions about community life' that lie beneath the 'covert' policy choices made by judges. However, the conflation of the assumptions and the policy choices is not as helpful as it might be.

person' has a liberal presumptive content. It will be stated whether the imputation is capable of being defamatory. Thirdly, I explain the position a court would have to take to displace the inclusive presumptions and thus reverse the determination regarding defamatory capacity. At the risk of being repetitive, I have tried for the purposes of comparison and clarity to use roughly the same terminology when discussing the different imputations. The section concludes by very briefly summarizing the most important aspects of the application of the law and its implications.

1. *Ascriptive criteria: sexuality, blackness, and mental illness*

Is a publication that states the plaintiff is homosexual, is black, or has a mental illness capable of being defamatory? The plaintiff will argue that some people in the jurisdiction would think the less of him or her. Those are people whose moral codes include the following criterion for moral judgment:

> A person who is homosexual, black or has a mental illness should be judged negatively.

The defendant will argue that the publication is incapable of being defamatory because even though it might tend to make some people in the jurisdiction think the less of the plaintiff, it would not tend to make the 'the right-thinking person' think less of the plaintiff.

The court would apply the test: could the statement tend to make 'the right-thinking person' in the community think the less of the plaintiff? Its decision would be to the following effect:

> The test requires the court to ask whether this criterion for moral judgment is inconsistent with the liberal presumptive content of 'the right-thinking person'? That is, is it inconsistent with commitments to equal moral worth, freedom of moral choice, the protection from harm, or moral diversity that bind the people in the jurisdiction together as a community?
>
> The conclusion must be that this criterion for moral judgment is inconsistent with the commitment to the equal moral worth of human beings. This is because it devalues people on the basis of an ascriptive feature of their personhood. 'The right-thinking person' could not think the less of someone on these grounds because that would be inconsistent with their belief in equal moral worth. The imputation would not be actionable.

Can the court nevertheless grant ethical recognition to the criterion for moral judgment and thus hold that the imputation is capable of being defamatory? Yes, it can, but it would have to displace the liberal presumptions by stating that:

> 'The right-thinking person' in the community may think the less of someone on ascriptive grounds. 'The right-thinking person' is prepared to accept that people do not have the same intrinsic equal moral worth by virtue of their humanity. This is because jurisdiction does not as a community recognize the equal moral worth of individuals on the basis of their humanity. This is how things are and how things should be.

2. *Objectionable or unpopular political beliefs*

Is a publication that states the plaintiff holds an objectionable or unpopular political belief capable of being defamatory? The plaintiff will argue that some people in the jurisdiction would think the less of him or her. Those are people whose moral codes include the following general criterion for moral judgment:

A person who holds to [*the particular political belief*] should be judged negatively.

The defendant will argue that the publication is incapable of being defamatory because even though it might tend to make some people in the jurisdiction think the less of the plaintiff, it would not tend to make the 'the right-thinking person' think less of the plaintiff.

The court would apply the test: could the statement tend to make 'the right-thinking person' in the community think the less of the plaintiff? Its decision would be to the following effect:

The test requires the court to ask whether this criterion for moral judgment is inconsistent with the liberal presumptive content of 'the right-thinking person'? That is, is it inconsistent with commitments to equal moral worth, freedom of moral choice, the protection from harm, or moral diversity that bind the people in the jurisdiction together as a community?

The conclusion must be that the defamatory capacity of an imputation regarding political belief will depend on the content of the particular political belief in issue and the particular criteria for moral judgment to which the plaintiff is appealing.

Imputations may be actionable in two circumstances. First, where the political belief is ascriptively oppressive then the imputation may be actionable. Consider, for example, a publication that says the plaintiff is pursuing a racist political agenda. Here, the plaintiff is appealing to a criterion for moral judgment that says: 'a person who has a racist political agenda should be judged negatively'. This criterion is consistent with the commitments of 'the right-thinking person'. In particular, it is consistent with the commitment to equal moral worth. So, it could be actionable to say that a person is pursuing a racist political agenda or any other ascriptively oppressive politics.

Secondly, where a political belief has a violent agenda then it will be actionable. Consider, for example, a publication that says the plaintiff is pursuing a political agenda that advocates violence as a strategy to achieve its goals. Here, the plaintiff is appealing to a criterion for moral judgment that says: 'a person who has a violent political agenda should be judged negatively'. This criterion is consistent with the commitments of 'the right-thinking person'. In particular, it is consistent with the commitment to the protection from harm which is premised on equal moral worth and which maintains the conditions for freedom of moral choice and moral diversity. So, it could be actionable to say that a person has a violent political agenda.

Where an imputation concerns any other political belief then it will not be actionable. This is because the jurisdiction as a community is committed to moral diversity that flows from the adherence to equal moral worth and freedom of moral choice.[121] Holding a particular political belief is an exercise of that moral choice and 'the right-thinking

[121] Cf *Garriga v Richfield* 20 NYS 2d 544 (NY SC, 1940).

person' could not think the less of a person on these grounds, provided that the particular political belief is not inconsistent with and does not undermine liberal commitments.

It should be noted that it would be difficult to establish that a political position is ascriptively oppressive or has a violent agenda. A person might advocate a position that has significant discriminatory effects but which falls well short of undermining equal moral worth, or might advocate substantial and activist protest but which is not inconsistent with the harm principle. Usually, then, an allegation that a person holds a particular political belief should not be actionable.

Can the court nevertheless say an imputation is actionable even though the particular political belief does not undermine liberal commitments? Yes, the court can do this, but it would have to displace the liberal presumptions by stating that:

> 'The right-thinking person' may think the less of someone on the grounds that they hold any political belief, regardless of its content. This is because the jurisdiction is not as a community committed to freedom of moral choice and moral diversity that is premised upon and maintains the conditions for a commitment to equal moral worth. This is how things are and how things should be.

Conversely, can the court say an imputation is *not* actionable even though the particular political belief *does* undermine liberal premises? Can it say, for example, that 'the right-thinking person' would not think the less of someone for holding a political belief that has a racist or violent agenda? Yes, the court can say this, but it would have to displace the liberal presumptions by stating that:

> 'The right-thinking person' could not think the less of someone on the grounds that they hold a political belief which, for example, has an agenda that denies the equal moral worth of people in the jurisdiction or advocates harm as a part of its political programme. It is morally acceptable to pursue any political agenda. This is because the jurisdiction does not as a community recognize people as beings that possess intrinsic equal moral worth, that have a freedom of moral choice, or that are entitled to a protection from harm so that they may make their moral choices (which do not negatively affect anyone else) as they wish. This is how things are and how things should be.

3. *Informing*

Is a publication that states the plaintiff has informed the police about criminal activity capable of being defamatory? The plaintiff will argue that some people in the jurisdiction would think the less of him or her. Those are people whose moral codes include the following general criterion for moral judgment:

> A person who has informed the police about criminal activity should be judged negatively.

The defendant will argue that the publication is incapable of being defamatory because even though it might tend to make some people in the jurisdiction think the less of the plaintiff, it would not tend to make the 'the right-thinking person' think less of the plaintiff.

The court would apply the test: could the statement tend to make 'the right-thinking person' in the community think the less of the plaintiff? Its decision would be to the following effect:

The test requires the court to ask whether this criterion for moral judgment is inconsistent with the liberal presumptive content of 'the right-thinking person'? That is, is it inconsistent with commitments to equal moral worth, freedom of moral choice, the protection from harm, or moral diversity that bind the people in the jurisdiction together as a community?

The conclusion must be that the defamatory capacity of an imputation that concerns informing the police will depend on the nature of the crime that is the subject of the information.

There are two circumstances where imputations of informing will not be actionable. First, where the crime in question breaches the harm principle then the imputation of informing the police about that crime will not be actionable. Consider, for example, a publication stating that the plaintiff had provided information to the police about a crime of rape. Here, the plaintiff is appealing to a criterion for moral judgment that says in a general form: 'a person who informs the police about a crime of personal violence should be judged negatively'. This criterion is inconsistent with the commitments of 'the right-thinking person'. In particular, it is inconsistent with the commitment to the protection from harm which is premised on equal moral worth and which maintains the conditions for freedom of moral choice and moral diversity. So, it will not be actionable to say that a person has informed the police about a crime of rape.

Secondly, where a crime would undermine the security of the jurisdiction to such an extent that the presumptive jurisdictional commitment to equal moral worth and moral diversity is endangered then an imputation of informing should not be actionable. Consider, for example, a publication stating that the plaintiff had informed the police of a crime that related to the pursuit of terrorism or sedition: this undermines the security of the jurisdiction. Here, the plaintiff is appealing to a criterion for moral judgment that says in a general form: 'a person who informs the police about a crime that undermines the jurisdiction's security should be judged negatively'. This criterion is inconsistent with the commitments of 'the right-thinking person'. It is inconsistent with the commitments to all of equal moral worth, freedom of moral choice, the protection from harm and moral diversity because it undermines the ability of the jurisdiction to constitute itself as a liberal moral community. So, it will not be actionable to say a person has informed the police of a crime that relates to terrorism or sedition.

Where an imputation concerns informing about any other type of crime then it will be actionable. This is because the jurisdiction as a community is committed to freedom of moral choice. That must necessarily include a choice about the taking a position as to moral rightness of criminalizing particular behaviour or engaging in behaviour that has been criminalized, except where the behaviour is inconsistent with the presumptive liberal commitments of the jurisdiction. As such, informing the police about a crime may sometimes prompt a negative moral judgment in a liberal community and thus imputations about informing may sometimes be actionable.

Can the court nevertheless say an imputation is not actionable even though the particular crime neither breaches the harm principle nor imperils the jurisdiction's ability to constitute itself as a liberal moral community? For example, might it be held that it is not actionable to say a person has informed the police about a crime where a person has consumed illicit drugs? Yes, the court can do this. One of two paths might be taken. On the one hand the court might directly find that the imputation is not actionable because it does not possess the requisite tendency. Here, it would have to displace the liberal presumptions by stating that:

> 'The right-thinking person' could not think the less of someone on the grounds that they have informed the police about a crime, no matter what the crime is. It is irrelevant that the crime does not breach the harm principle or endanger jurisdictional security. The imputation cannot be actionable because the jurisdiction is not as a community committed to a freedom of moral choice about taking a position as to the rightness of criminalizing particular behaviour or engaging in behaviour that has been criminalized, even where the behaviour in question is consistent with maintaining the conditions under which all of equal moral worth, moral choice, protection from harm and moral diversity should be respected. This is how things are in the jurisdiction and how things should be.[122]

As discussed in Chapter 5, there is an alternative path. A court may accept the liberal presumptions and find that an imputation of informing does have a tendency to make 'the right-thinking person' think less of the plaintiff but, nevertheless, reach a conclusion on policy grounds that the imputation is not actionable because there is a competing moral good that is so highly valued by the jurisdiction that it can be seen as a value which binds people together as a community and which overrides the defamatory tendency of the imputation. That competing moral good might be the maintenance of the state because it contributes to security or well-being of the population on other grounds.[123]

The converse question does not meaningfully arise. The history of the cases suggests a court will simply not be called upon to find that an imputation is *not* actionable even though the particular crime either breaches the harm principle or imperils the ability of the jurisdiction to constitute itself as a liberal moral community.

4. *Abortion*

Is a publication that states a doctor has performed abortions capable of being defamatory? The plaintiff doctor will argue that some people in the jurisdiction

[122] In the normal course of events, informing the police about crime maintains the security of the state. The analysis here presumes that the imputation of informing carries no other overwhelming opprobrium as it did in *Berry v Irish Times* where the imputation was inherently one of national treachery (see Chapter 5, III(C)(2)). In those circumstances, even if the information does concern a crime of violence then the informing imputation might still be actionable. This would arguably be consistent with liberal commitments because informing the police historically served to undermine the maintenance and respect for equal moral worth of the people in the jurisdiction who were victims of an oppressive political regime.

[123] See, for example, the analysis of *Shaha v Dardiryan* ca 466/83, PD 39 (4) 734 (1985), Israel SC, in Chapter 5, III(B)(2).

would think the less of her or him. Those are people whose moral codes include the following criterion for moral judgment:

A person who performs an abortion should be judged negatively.

The defendant will argue that the publication is incapable of being defamatory because even though it might tend to make some people in the jurisdiction think the less of the plaintiff, it would not tend to make the 'the right-thinking person' think less of the plaintiff.

The court would apply the test: could the statement tend to make 'the right-thinking person' in the community think the less of the plaintiff? Its decision would be to the following effect:

The test requires the court to ask whether this criterion for moral judgment is inconsistent with the liberal presumptive content of 'the right-thinking person'? That is, is it inconsistent with commitments to equal moral worth, freedom of moral choice, the protection from harm or moral diversity that bind the people in the jurisdiction together as a community?

The conclusion must be that the defamatory capacity of an imputation regarding abortion will depend on whether the foetus is viewed as having the status of 'a person'. This matter is itself premised on the troubling assumption that it can be said that the pregnant woman and her foetus either are or are not independent people. There is a body of literature that challenges and critiques this assumption, suggesting that the liberal sense of the individual cannot accommodate the status of the pregnant woman or her unborn child.[124] That difficulty may be put to one side for the moment.

Where a foetus *does not* have the status of personhood then the individuals of concern are the plaintiff doctor and the woman who may have had an abortion; the foetus is not 'a person'—a liberal subject—to whom the liberal commitments apply. On this view, 'the right-thinking person' could not think the less of a doctor for performing an abortion. This is because the criterion for moral judgment is inconsistent with commitment to freedom of moral choice. That freedom must necessarily include a woman's choice and a doctor's choice about the moral rightness of engaging in behaviour that is not inconsistent with the presumptive liberal commitments. Here, the choice to have or perform an abortion does not breach the harm principle because the foetus is not 'a person' to whom the protection from harm applies. The imputation will not be actionable if the foetus is not 'a person'.

To reach the opposite conclusion, the liberal presumptions would have to be displaced by stating that: 'The jurisdiction does not as a community recognize pregnant women as having a freedom of moral choice that is equal to that of all other women and men. This is, necessarily, to deny that pregnant women are people of the same intrinsic moral worth as all other women and men because their freedom of moral choice is limited in a way that other people's choices are not. This is how things are in the jurisdiction and how things should be.'

[124] J Seymour, *Childbirth and the Law* (2000) esp 189–202; I Karpin, 'Legislating the Female Body: Reproductive Technology and the Reconstructed Woman' (1992) 3 Columbia Journal of Gender and Law 325, 329–1; E Jackson, *Regulating Reproduction: Law, Technology and Autonomy* (2001); R Scott, *Rights, Duties and the Body: Law and the Ethics of the Maternal-Fetal Conflict* (2002).

Where a foetus *does* have personhood status then the position would be different: 'the right-thinking person' may think the less of a doctor for performing an abortion. This is because the individuals of concern now include the foetus which is a liberal subject to whom liberal commitments apply. With its life at stake, the foetus must take primacy as the individual of concern. In these circumstances, the criterion for moral judgment is entirely consistent with the liberal commitments that 'the right-thinking person' has towards that individual. The imputation will be actionable if the foetus is 'a person'.

To reach the opposite conclusion in these circumstances, the liberal presumptions would have to be displaced by stating that: 'The jurisdiction does not as a community recognize the foetus as being a person whose intrinsic moral worth is equal to that of all other people. This is how things are in the jurisdiction and how things should be.'

Returning now to the problematic assumption that underlies these alternatives, how should the court view the status of the foetus for the purposes of determining actionability? And, for that matter, how should it view the moral worth of the pregnant woman? The liberal presumptive content of 'the right-thinking person' is ultimately premised on equal moral worth. While there may be doubt about whether the pregnant woman and the foetus are 'individuals' in the liberal sense, it is appropriate *for the purposes of defamation law* to recognize the possibility that both of them have a moral status equivalent to that of liberal individuals. This means an imputation that a doctor has performed an abortion would be actionable because the criterion for negative moral judgment is consistent with the proposition that the foetus is a being of equal moral worth (entitled to protection from harm). However, that does not deny the equal moral worth of the pregnant woman. Rather, it means that it could also be actionable to say of a doctor that he or she *refused* to perform an abortion. An action there would appeal to the criterion for moral judgment that 'a person who refuses to perform an abortion should be judged negatively'. This criterion for moral judgment is consistent with the proposition that the woman is a being of equal moral worth (entitled to freedom of moral choice).[125]

This position regarding the equal status of the foetus and the pregnant woman is suitable for the purposes of defamation law but it may not be suitable for other aspects of regulation or adjudication where equal moral status and liberal commitments are ultimately incommensurable because only one of the existence of the foetus or the choice of the woman can prevail.[126]

5. *Displacing inclusive presumptions*

The position regarding the imputations can be summarized shortly and, for the (much needed) purpose of simplicity, in general rather than precise terms. Where

[125] By contrast, where the foetus is 'a person' under the traditional framework then an imputation that a doctor refused to perform an abortion would not be actionable: 'the right-thinking person' could not think the less of someone for preserving life. Any criterion for moral judgment which is to the contrary would be at odds with liberal commitments.

[126] Although Seymour does not consider defamation questions, this argument is consistent with his position that the interdependent status of the foetus and the pregnant woman can and should be treated differently depending on the legal action and question involved. J Seymour, 'The Legal Status of the Fetus: An International Review' (2002) 10 Journal of Law and Medicine 28, 39–40.

'the right-thinking person' is presumed to have a commitment to liberal values then, on the face of it:

> It will not be actionable to say a person is homosexual, is black, or has a mental illness.
>
> It will be actionable to say a person has informed the police about a minor crime that harms no one, but it will not be actionable to say they provided information about significant crimes.
>
> It will not be actionable to say a person holds any particular political belief unless that belief has some ascriptively oppressive agenda (which is at odds with liberal commitments to equal moral worth) or a violent agenda (which is at odds with the protection from harm).
>
> It will be actionable to say that a doctor performs abortions and equally actionable to say that a doctor refuses to perform abortions.

Every determination regarding actionability may be reversed by displacing the liberal presumptions of 'the right-thinking person'. In order to do so, however, there is a point of major significancc:

> In every instance the actionability determination can only be reversed if a court rejects the proposition that the jurisdiction affirms and values people as beings of intrinsically equal moral worth.

In some instances that reversal requires an express rejection of the commitment to equal moral worth. In other instances, the rejection of liberal presumptions is an affirmation, acceptance, or acquiescence in conditions that undermine the commitment to equal moral worth, either limiting or circumscribing that commitment. It contemplates and affirms that the jurisdiction might be constituted as a community whose legitimate moral possibilities are neither limited nor enhanced by a commitment to the proposition that all people are—by virtue of the fact of their humanity—beings of intrinsically equal moral worth.

Conclusion

As a concept, 'the right-thinking person' should remain a part of the law of defamation. It might easily enough be called by other names—'the decent person' or 'the respectable person'—but it performs a consistent function: it is a tool which the law is able to use to evaluate whether an attack on reputation should be actionable as defamation. The content of the concept has historically been comprised of traditional values. That conception of 'the right-thinking person' has been undermined by the reality of moral diversity in late-modern societies, and the ongoing philosophical clash of tradition and modernity. For defamation law, this has raised problems: the validity of the fundamental concept it uses to adjudicate has been thrown into doubt.

In some respects, the case law and the concept have survived these ruptures in remarkably good shape. There has been little judicial inquiry into just what it is that makes 'the right-thinking person' 'right-thinking'. Instead, there has been a tendency to proceed by intuition or assertion. The cases on imputations of blackness show a shift in the legal position, but with no explanation of why the old approach was to be discarded. The cases on imputations of homosexuality were of more assistance. It became clear that what was previously certain could now only be presumed. The presumptions of tradition, however, are no longer satisfactory. An era of deontological liberal ethics, equal moral worth, and human rights demands a presumption that the jurisdiction as a moral community is inclusive. As a consequence, the presumptive content of 'the right-thinking person' must also be inclusive. The recognition of exclusionary criteria for moral judgment is by no means precluded, but recognition must be articulated as the ethical choice that it is. Communitarian political theory provides a way that recognition might proceed.

This analysis holds an important implication for the way that determinations of actionability are characterized. By understanding how 'the right-thinking person' functions as a presumptive concept, by seeing how the presumptive content of the concept should become liberal rather than traditional, and by seeing how the revised liberal presumptions might nevertheless be displaced, an intuitively compelling illusion can be dispelled: the determination of defamatory capacity does not involve a choice between 'realism' and 'idealism'.[127] Traditional values and liberal values are both real and ideal: they are ideas about how things are and how things should be. Just as the values of tradition are very much present in the jurisdictions I have discussed, the values of liberalism have an equally real presence in those same jurisdictions. And just as liberalism idealizes the individual, the communitarian project idealizes a sense of community that it claims has been lost. There is still a choice to be made but it is not appropriate to describe it a choice between realism and idealism.

As a change to the central conceptual tool in determining actionability, a move to an inclusive conception of 'the right-thinking person' will have an important bearing on the test for what is defamatory that will be proposed in the concluding chapter.

[127] Cf R Magnusson, 'Freedom of Speech in Australian Defamation Law: Ridicule, Satire and Other Challenges' (2001) 9 Torts Law Journal 269, 278–80; LK Treiger-Bar-Am, 'Defamation Law in a Changing Society: The Case of *Youssoupoff v Metro-Goldwyn Mayer*' (2001) 21 LS 291, 307ff; also above, Introduction, II(B).

Conclusion

Re-thinking the Tests for What is Defamatory

The question this study set out to answer was: if reputation is the interest to be protected by defamation law then what should be the test(s) for what is defamatory? The stated aim was to fill a gap in the common law by providing a principled, theoretically coherent statement of law regarding what is defamatory.

In developing a theoretical framework, it was argued that an individual's reputation is a social judgment of the person based upon facts considered relevant by a community. Accordingly, damage to reputation is a diminution in a person's social worth and, it was argued, because reputation is founded in community, that diminution necessarily involves a negative moral judgment. The consequence is that to say a person's reputation has been damaged is to say that the person's moral status (or moral standing or moral worth) is diminished in the eyes of the community. Reputation can best be understood in different contexts by looking at the criteria for moral judgment—the moral taxonomies—which govern it in different communities. Where defamation law encounters reputation, the courts are required to form a sense of how the jurisdiction forms a community. This may not be straightforward because contemporary Western jurisdictions are not easily seen as sharing a commitment to common values. Instead, they are characterized by moral diversity. They are not self-evidently 'communities'. By looking at the development and operation of the law in these terms it was possible to see how the tests for what is defamatory have and have not functioned to protect reputation, and the scope and limits of that protection.

It has been argued that only the principal test for what is defamatory should be retained. This is because the principal test is the only one that meaningfully protects reputation. It does so by taking account of the centrality of moral judgment in reputation. The conceptual tool through which it does this is 'the right-thinking person'. The effect of this argument is that there should be one test for what is defamatory and it should be stated in the following terms:

> A publication will be defamatory if it has a tendency to cause 'the right-thinking person' in the community to think the less of the plaintiff.

The operation of this proposed test should be clarified, especially with respect to the liberal presumptive content of 'the right-thinking person':

> In the jurisdictions of Western liberal democracies 'the right-thinking person' is presumed to be committed to the equal moral worth of human beings, freedom of moral choice (that is, the freedom to choose the values by which one would like to live, to the extent that they are consistent with a commitment to equal moral worth), the protection from harm that is a consequence and condition of those premises, and the moral diversity that flows from these.
>
> Where a criterion for moral judgment is inconsistent with these commitments then it should not generally be recognized by courts as a legitimate consideration in the determination of actionability. If inconsistent criteria for moral judgment are to be recognized then the reasons for recognition must be explained and justified in terms of the values which unite the people of the jurisdiction as a community. The court must explain how and why the value in question is a moral good that binds the people in the jurisdiction together as a community with such strength that it can be said to displace the foundational liberal commitments of the jurisdiction and thus warrant recognition under the common law.

This proposal takes account of three very fundamental dimensions of the critique of the current legal framework that has been advanced. These can be addressed in order of the difficulty they pose for the courts.

The first point of note is that, by attributing a narrow range of presumptive commitments to 'the right-thinking person', the proposed test encompasses a sectional standards approach rather than a general standards approach. This is appropriate because of the fact of moral diversity in contemporary Western societies and because the commitment to moral diversity is one of the foundational elements of those societies. The rejection of a general standards approach should not necessarily pose great difficulty for the Australian courts, at least in some circumstances. As Chapter 5 explained, the decision of the High Court in *Reader's Digest v Lamb* would not have to be overturned where there is a clear division of opinion in the jurisdiction, and *Hepburn v TCN Channel Nine* provides appellate court authority for adopting a sectional standards approach. Where the opinion in question is a minority one then it might be that *Lamb* would have to be overturned.[1] The position is roughly the same in the English courts.[2] The American courts already use a sectional standards approach. All things considered, the move away from a general standards test is a fairly modest proposal.

Secondly, the proposed test should be the sole test for what is defamatory. As Chapters 6 and 7 argued, the supplementary tests of 'shun and avoid' and ridicule should not form a part of the legal framework. These tests have developed in a way that means in some instances they go beyond the protection of reputation and instead protect a plaintiff's sense of self-worth. It might well be that there are good arguments for protecting self-worth, but a defamation action should not be a vehicle for that protection. The rejection of these tests should pose little difficulty for the courts.

[1] See Chapter 5, Part II.
[2] Ibid.

The 'shun and avoid' test does not have a solid foundation in precedent. It was said in *Youssoupoff* that it derived from cases on disease and insanity. Neither strand of the case law supports that claim. The recent judicial statements that qualify the 'shun and avoid' test by saying (correctly) that 'the right-thinking person' is the yardstick in that test mean that any publication which was actionable under the 'shun and avoid' test would be actionable under the principal test. At most, the disposal of the 'shun and avoid' test would require the courts to acknowledge that the confusion in the law arose in part from the inappropriate application of slander principles to libel laws and to reject as authoritative the 1769 decision of *Villers v Monsley*. Doctrinally, there are no other obstacles to disposing of the 'shun and avoid' test.

Similarly, precedent places few hurdles in the way of rejecting the ridicule test. With the exception of the uncertainty created by *Villers v Monsley*, all the relevant case law until *Burton v Crowell* in 1936 is consistent with the protection of reputation. The decision in *Burton* and its adoption in cases such as *Ettingshausen* and *Berkoff* would need to be revisited. There is good reason to do so because it is quite plain that the tests are not framed in a way that protects reputation meaningfully or appropriately, and material that tends to damage reputation will be more appropriately actionable under the principal test.

Thirdly, the proposed legal framework proposes a shift in the presumptions that are associated with 'the right-thinking person'. It argues that the common law should dispose of the traditional, exclusive presumptions that form the content of 'the right-thinking person' and instead use inclusive presumptions that are premised upon an acceptance of equal moral worth. A shift of this kind would see a distinct change in the complexion of the common law, but it is not at all precluded by precedent or principle. It is well-established that the defamatory capacity of an imputation may change over time. The shift to inclusive presumptions is less demanding than that line of authority permits. That is, the argument does not say there must be a change. It simply says that the presumptions underlying the analytical point of departure must change. As Chapter 8 argued, there are ample grounds on which to see those presumptions as being based in 'realism' and not simply 'idealism'. More than 200 years after the Enlightenment and the emergence of the liberal democratic polity, it should be thoroughly uncontroversial for the courts to see a commitment to the equal moral worth of human beings as a commitment that binds the jurisdiction as a community.

It has been suggested that these inclusive presumptions may be displaced. Any displacement should be controversial. A departure from the commitment to equal moral worth should be made only with great care and caution. If the jurisdiction's moral possibilities are to be limited in a way that is inconsistent with the foundational commitments that enable the very existence of diverse possibilities then there needs to be a thoroughly considered rationale.

The proposed reform has implications beyond the cause of action in defamation and these need to be flagged. The proposed reform has clear implications for freedom of speech. There are various imputations which would no longer be defamatory and this would expand the scope of what is publishable without fear of defamation action. Moreover, the removal of the supplementary tests would enhance free speech, especially with respect to satire. As a consequence of these implications, some plaintiffs who have suffered harm to their reputations and to their sense of self-worth may be left without a remedy. For example, the plaintiff who is wrongly said to be homosexual would need to rely on anti-discrimination or privacy laws. Where those remedies do not exist then the legislatures should address that. These issues can be neither avoided nor addressed by maintaining an unsound law of defamation. The better path is to look at the nature of the harm suffered and identify appropriately the law's role in remedying that harm.

The test for what is defamatory that has been proposed should be one that poses little trouble for the courts. It is a test that is developed around the legal protection of reputation which (so it is said) defamation law aims to protect. It is a test that is based on and founded in the doctrine of precedent. It is a test that draws on the simplest and most basic of commitments for its foundations: that human beings obtain equal moral worth by virtue of their humanity. It is inappropriate that the modern common law should be founded upon any other proposition.

APPENDIX

Notes on Historical Sources

Chapter 1 discussed the way that the history of defamation law has been recounted in the literature, observing that there is little to distinguish the major sources. The earliest key works are by Frank Carr and Van Vechten Veeder.[1] The history of the English common law of defamation is chronicled in the defamation sections of the major legal histories.[2] A number of journal articles take a similar path.[3]

In Chapters 3 and 4, the literature on the early English courts inevitably draws significantly on the major works of legal history, including Pollock and Maitland's *History of English Law Before the Time of Edward I*, Holdsworth's *History of English Law*, and publications of the Selden Society.[4] Richard Helmholz's relatively recent archival research on defamation cases to 1600 has been invaluable, often testing what are otherwise theories and impressions about the development of the law.[5] For cases from the local courts I have relied principally, but not solely, upon the decisions translated and reproduced in

[1] F Carr, 'The English Law of Defamation, Parts I & II', (1902) 18 LQR 255, 388; VV Veeder, 'The History and Theory of Defamation Law I & II' (1903) 3 Columbia Law Review 546, (1904) 4 Columbia Law Review 33; VV Veeder, 'The History of the Law of Defamation' in *Select Essays in Anglo-American Legal History* (1909) 446. The last was a re-written version of part I of Veeder's Columbia Law Review pieces.

[2] JH Baker, *An Introduction to English Legal History* (3rd edn, 1990) 495–508; CHS Fifoot, *History and Sources of the Common Law: Tort and Contract* (1949) 126–53; W Holdsworth, *A History of English Law in Sixteen Volumes* (3rd edn, 1945), Vol 8, 333–78, also published as W Holdsworth, 'Defamation in the Sixteenth and Seventeenth Centuries, I-III' (1924) 40 LQR 302, 397, (1925) 41 LQR 13; SFC Milsom, *Historical Foundations of the Common Law* (1969) 332–44; TF Plucknett, *A Concise History of the Common Law* (3rd edn, 1940) 427–45; E Jenks, *A Short History of English Law* (2nd edn, 1920) 145–9, 316–9; AKR Kiralfy, *Potter's Historical Introduction to English Law and its Institutions* (4th edn, 1962) 429–38.

[3] NStJ Green, 'Slander and Libel' (1871) 6 American Law Review 593; CR Lovell, 'The "Reception" of Defamation by the Common Law' (1962) 15 Vanderbilt Law Review 1051; RC Donelly, 'The History of Defamation' [1949] Wisconsin Law Review 99; WR Jones, '"Actions for Slaunder"—Defamation in English Law, Language and History' (1971) 57 Quarterly Journal of Speech 274.

[4] FW Maitland, *Select Pleas in Manorial and other Seignorial Courts, Volume I: Publications of the Selden Society, Vol 2* (1888); FW Maitland and WP Baildon, *The Court Baron: Precedents of Pleading in Manorial and other Local Courts: Publications of the Selden Society, Vol 4* (1890); IS Leadem (ed), *Select Cases Before the King's Council in the Star Chamber commonly called the Court of Star Chamber, 1477–1509, Vol 16* (1902/03); M Bateson, *Borough Customs, Volume I: Publications of the Selden Society, Vol 18* (1904); C Gross, *Select Cases Concerning the Law Merchant, 1270–1638, Volume 1: Publications of the Selden Society, Vol 23* (1908); CG Bayne, *Select Cases in the Council of Henry VII: Publications of the Selden Society, Vol 75* (1958); JH Baker, *The Reports of Sir John Spelman, Volume II: Publications of the Selden Society, Vol 94* (1977).

[5] RH Helmholz (ed), *Select Cases on Defamation to 1600: Publications of the Selden Society, Vol 101* (1985).

the Selden Society publications.[6] Cases from the church courts have been more difficult to obtain. While some have been published in the works cited above, I have also drawn on research and analysis by Martin Ingram, among others.[7] The *scandalum magnatum* statutes attract some attention in the defamation sections of major works, and a number of cases can be found in the law reports, but it appears the only substantial examination of these actions was undertaken by John Lassiter in 1978.[8] Without doubt, there are more medieval defamation cases that could be located in published archival material but the coverage of cases is consistent with that addressed in the literature to date and my research does not suggest that the analysis would be different were a greater number of cases to be consulted.[9]

At times, the historical discussion necessarily moves in broad brush strokes. There is a deal of uncertainty in the literature about, for example, the periods during which the church and local courts had most influence and the points at which they fell into decline.[10] There is also much disagreement about the relationship between the church courts and the King's courts. Helmholz has argued legal historians have traditionally been too heavily influenced by what the royal courts said was the proper jurisdiction of the church courts and thus minimized or misinterpreted the significance of the church courts. He argued in the 1970s that the statutes that formally limited the operation of the church courts, he suggests, were by no means as restrictive as the literature often suggests.[11] Since then, this argument has been borne out further in the research and, more generally, a wide body of research has documented the significant role of the church courts even after the common

[6] The indexes of all Selden Society volumes have been searched through to 2004. In addition, several cases have been taken from other works that have reproduced local court cases, such as AKR Kiralfy, *A Source Book of English Law* (1957) and Fifoot (n 2 above), though there is some overlap with the Selden Society volumes. Citation of the older cases does not appear to follow a standard form. I have adopted Kiralfy's method for consistency with the usual format of case citation, though also identifying the court where possible. In a few instances the cases are also reproduced in other sources but I have provided only the citations to the Selden Society volumes.

[7] M Ingram, *Church Courts, Sex and Marriage in England, 1570–1640* (1987); CA Haigh, 'Slander and the Church Courts in the Sixteenth Century' (1975) 78 Transactions of the Lancashire and Cheshire Antiquarian Society 1; D Neal, 'Suits Make the Man: Masculinity in Two English Courts, c.1500' (2002) 37 Canadian Journal of History 1; LR Poos, 'Sex, Lies and the Church Courts of Pre-Reformation England' (1995) 25 Journal of Interdisciplinary History 585; JA Sharpe, *Defamation and Sexual Slander in Early Modern England: The Church Courts at York (Borthwick Papers No 58)* (c1980). Ingram, ibid 8, notes that until the mid-20th century the records of the church courts were highly inaccessible. It was still the case in 1971 that the records were 'unprinted and scattered in archives throughout England': RH Helmholz, 'Canonical Defamation in Medieval England' (1971) 15 American Journal of Legal History 255, 255.

[8] JC Lassiter, 'Defamation of Peers: The Rise and Decline of the Action for *Scandalum Magnatum*, 1497–1773' (1978) 22 American Journal of Legal History 216.

[9] A small number of court rolls or Year Books that have been published by academic historians or local historical societies were also consulted but yielded nothing relevant. For further local court matters, Donnelly cites material that I was unable to access: RC Donnelly, 'History of Defamation' [1949] Wisconsin Law Review 99, 101, n 5. There is no indication in his article that those sources contradicted the views in the literature as it then stood. Helmholz (n 5 above) xlviii, notes that 'no systematic study of defamation in [the local court rolls]' had been undertaken until his own research in 1985. It does not appear there has been any such study since Helmholz.

[10] See Chapter 3, II.

[11] Helmholz (n 7 above) 255 cf W Holdsworth , 'Defamation in the Sixteenth and Seventeenth Centuries I' (n 2 above) 304.

law remedy emerged.[12] As Chapter 4 notes, there is uncertainty also about exactly when and why the common law courts first allowed actions on the case for defamation.[13] While there is much that might be said about the various conflicting accounts, the scope of the disagreement does not generally affect the analysis and so I have largely put it to one side.

Knowledge about the Star Chamber's work is really derived from only a few key sources. The Selden Society works are again of assistance.[14] There is a deal of material written in the 20th century histories of defamation about the Star Chamber's treatment of libel but much of it adds little to the Holdsworth's analysis in his *History of English Law.*[15] The records of the court having largely been lost, Holdsworth, identifies his most significant resources as the contemporary works of Hawarde's *Reports*, Coke's *Institutes*, and Hudson's *Treatise on the Court of Star Chamber.* Hudson, an advocate before the Star Chamber from 1605 until his death in 1635, is viewed in conflicting lights. Leadem described him as an apologist for the Court.[16] Holdsworth is more generous, but still somewhat cautious: 'As we might expect, he was identified with the lawyers who supported the prerogative... [While impartial, he was] not a discriminating critic of development of which he does not approve [and] he entirely suppresses the fact that it used torture to extort confessions and information.'[17] Much of the Star Chamber discussion in Chapter 4 draws on Holdsworth, with comparison and support drawn from elsewhere as need be.

The analysis of the development of the common law action relies on the sources referred to above, the reported decisions and a selection of other historical works, including Kiralfy's *The Action on the Case.*[18] Several early treatises on defamation law are discussed in some detail in Chapter 4 (especially, Starkie, Townshend, and Odgers)[19] but the law is addressed in many works. Among them, one could perhaps add Hugh Fraser's text to the major defamation texts.[20] The main treatises on tort law in the United States and England all addressed defamation. The major English works that were first written in the 19th century included (in chronological order) those by Addison,[21] Underhill,[22] Pollock,[23]

[12] Ingram (n 7 above); Haigh (n 7 above); Sharpe, (n 7 above); SM Waddams, *Sexual Slander in Nineteenth-Century England: Defamation in the Ecclesiastical Courts, 1815–1855* (2000). After a weakened ecclesiastical jurisdiction was reinstated following the Restoration, defamation actions in the church courts fell away steadily during the 18th century but were still to be found until the power of those courts to hear them was formally terminated by statute in 1855.

[13] See Chapter 4, I(A).

[14] Bayne (n 4 above); Leadem (n 4 above).

[15] W Holdsworth, *A History of English Law in Sixteen Volumes* (3rd edn, 1945) Vol 5, 155–214, esp 205–12; Vol 8, 333–46.

[16] Leadem (n 4 above) x.

[17] Holdsworth (n 15 above) 164–5.

[18] AK Kiralfy, *The Action on The Case* (1951). See also the texts and treatises, below.

[19] See Chapter 4, II.

[20] H Fraser, *The Law of Libel in its Relation to the Press* (1889); *Principles and Practice of the Law of Libel and Slander* (1893), (2nd edn, 1897), (3rd edn, 1901), (4th edn, 1908), (5th edn, 1917), (6th edn, 1925).

[21] CG Addison, *Wrongs and their Remedies, being a Treatise on the Law of Torts* (1860), (2nd edn, 1864), (3rd edn, 1870), (4th edn, 1873), (5th edn, 1879), (6th edn, 1887), (7th edn, 1893), (8th edn, 1906).

[22] A Underhill, *A Summary of the Law of Torts* (1873) (2nd edn, 1878), (3rd edn, 1881), (4th edn, 1884), (6th edn, 1894), (7th edn, 1900), (8th edn, 1906), (9th edn, 1912), (10th edn, 1922).

[23] F Pollock, *The Law of Torts* (1887) (2nd edn, 1890), (3rd edn, 1892), (4th edn, 1895), (5th edn, 1897), (6th edn, 1901), (7th edn, 1904), (8th edn, 1908), (9th edn, 1912), (10th edn, 1916), (11th edn, 1920), (12th edn, 1923), (13th edn, 1929), (14th edn, 1939), (15th edn, 1951).

Ringwood,[24] and Clerk and Lindsell.[25] In the United States, the key works of the time included Hilliard,[26] Bigelow,[27] and Cooley,[28] though Burdick (writing a little later) might also fairly be included.[29] There were also some shorter defamation books, though they essentially reflected the major publications.[30] From the late-19th century books appeared that were directed at a press audience rather than a legal one.[31] Most recently, Mitchell has explored how modern defamation action law took shape, though the aspects of the law that he addresses are different from those I have been concerned with.[32]

24 R Ringwood, *Outlines of the Law of Torts* (2nd edn, 1894), (3rd edn, 1898), (4th edn, 1906), (5th edn, 1924).

25 JF Clerk and WHB Lindsell, *The Law of Torts* (1889), (2nd edn, 1896), (3rd edn, 1904), (4th edn, 1906), (5th edn, 1909), (6th edn, 1912), (7th edn, 1921), (8th edn, 1929), (9th edn, *Clerk & Lindsell on the Law of Torts*, 1937), (10th edn, 1947), (11th edn, 1954).

26 F Hilliard, *The Law of Torts or Private Wrongs* (1859), (2nd edn, 1861).

27 MM Bigelow, *Elements of The Law of Torts* (1878), (2nd edn, 1882), (3rd edn, 1886), (4th edn, 1891), (5th edn, 1894), (6th edn, 1896), (7th edn, *The Law of Torts*, 1901), (8th edn, 1907); *Elements of The Law of Torts* (1st Eng edn, 1889), (2nd Eng edn, *The Law of Torts*, 1903).

28 TM Cooley, *A Treatise on the Law of Torts or the Wrongs which arise Independently of Contract* (1878), (2nd edn, 1888), (3rd edn, 1906), (4th edn, 1932).

29 Francis M Burdick, *The Law of Torts* (1906), (2nd edn, 1908), (3rd edn, 1913), (4th edn, 1926).

30 GW Cooke, *A Treatise on the Law of Defamation* (1844); JCH Flood, *A Treatise on the Law Concerning Libel and Slander* (1880).

31 RJ Kelly, *The Law of Newspaper Libel* (1889); WV Ball, *The Law of Libel as Affecting Newspapers and Journalists* (1912); C Pilley, *Law for Journalists* (1924); T Dawson, *The Law of the Press* (1927).

32 P Mitchell, *The Making of the Modern Law of Defamation* (2005).

References

Addison, CG, *Wrongs and their Remedies, being a Treatise on the Law of Torts* (Stevens & Sons, London, 1860); (2nd edn, 1864); (3rd edn, FSP Wolferstan, London, 1870); (4th edn, FSP Wolferstan, Stevens, London, 1873 and Banks & Bros, New York, 1874); (5th edn, LW Cave, Stevens & Sons, London, 1879); (6th edn, H Smith, 1887); (7th edn, WE Gordon & APP Keep, 1893); (8th edn, WE Gordon & WH Griffith, 1906).

Allestree, R, *The Whole Duty of Man* (Printed for John Baskett London, 1726 (First published: c1657)).

Andrew, DT, 'The Code of Honour and its Critics: The Opposition to Duelling in England, 1700–1850' (1980) 5 Social History 409.

Arend, P, 'Defamation in an Age of Political Correctness: Should a False Public Statement that a Person is Gay be Defamatory' (1997) 18 Northern Illinois University Law Review 99.

Bailey FG (ed), *Gifts and Poison: The Politics of Reputation* (Schocken Books, New York, 1971).

Baker, JH, *An Introduction to English Legal History* (3rd edn, Butterworths, London, 1990).

Baker, JH, *The Reports of Sir John Spelman, Volume II: Publications of the Selden Society, Vol 94, 1977* (Selden Society, London, 1977).

Baker, R, *Deciding Defamation* (Communications Law Centre, Sydney, 2004).

Ball, WV, *The Law of Libel as Affecting Newspapers and Journalists* (Stevens & Sons, London, 1912).

Barber, CL, *The Idea of Honour in the English Drama 1591–1700* (Gothenburg Studies in English VI, Goteborg, 1957).

Barendt, E, 'What is the Point of Libel Law?' (1999) 52 Current Legal Problems 110.

Bateson, M, *Borough Customs, Volume I: Publications of the Selden Society, Vol 18, 1904* (Professional Books Ltd, London, 1972).

Bayne, CG, *Select Cases in the Council of Henry VII: Publications of the Selden Society, Vol 75, 1956* (Bernard Quaritch, London, 1958).

Bell, C, and Newby, H (eds), *The Sociology of Community* (Frank Cass & Co, London, 1974).

Bell, D, 'Communitarianism' in EN Zalta (ed), *The Stanford Encyclopedia of Philosophy (Winter 2001 Edn)* at <http://plato.stanford.edu/archives/win2001/entries/communitarianism/> (19 November 2003).

Bell, D, *Communitarianism and its Critics* (Clarendon Press, Oxford, 1993).

Bellah, R, 'The Meaning of Reputation in American Society' (1986) 74 California Law Review 743.

Bellah, R, Madsen, R, Sullivan, WM, Swidler, A, and Tipton, SM, *Habits of the Heart: Individualism and Commitment in American Life* (Updated edn, University of California Press, Berkeley, 1996 (First published: 1985)).

Bigelow, MM, *Elements of The Law of Torts* (1st Eng edn, University Press, Cambridge, 1889); (2nd Eng edn, *The Law of Torts*, 1903).

Bigelow, MM, *Elements of The Law of Torts* (Little Brown & Co, Boston, 1878); (2nd edn, 1882); (3rd edn, 1886); (4th edn, 1891); (5th edn, 1894); (6th edn, 1896); (7th edn, *The Law of Torts*, 1901); (8th edn, 1907).

Billacois, F, *The Duel: Its Rise and Fall in Early Modern France* (ed and trans by T Selous) (Yale University Press, New Haven & London, 1990 (First pub in French as: *Le Duel*, 1986)).

Blackstone, W, *Commentaries on the Laws of England* (9th edn continued by R Burn, Printed for W Strahan & T Cadell, London and D Prince, Oxford, 1783 (Reproduced in facsimile Garland Publishing, New York, 1978)).

Boorstin, D, 'Tradition and Method in Legal History' (1941) 54 Harvard Law Review 424.

Borkowksi, A, *Textbook on Roman Law* (Blackstone Press, London, 1994).

Bower, GS, *A Code of the Law of Actionable Defamation* (2nd edn, Butterworth & Co, London, 1923 (Reproduced in facsimile by Legal Books, Sydney, 1990)) (1st edn, Sweet & Maxwell, London, 1909).

Bowers, F, *Elizabethan Revenge Tragedy 1587–1642* (Princeton University Press, Princeton, 1940).

Brandes, S, 'Reflections on Honor and Shame in the Mediterranean' in DD Gilmore (ed), *Honor and Shame and the Unity of the Mediterranean* (American Anthropological Association, Washington, 1987) 121.

Buck, AR, and Wright, NE, *The Poor Man: Law and Satire in 19th Century New South Wales* (Australian Scholarly Publishing, Melbourne, 2005).

Burdick, FM, *The Law of Torts* (Banks & Co, Albany NY, 1906); (2nd edn, 1908); (3rd edn, 1913); (4th edn, CK Burdick, 1926).

Burdick, WL, *The Principles of Roman Law and Their Relation to Modern Law* (Lawyers Co-operative Publishing Co, Rochester NY, 1938 (Reprinted in facsimile, WM Gaunt & Sons, Holmes Beach FLA, 1989)).

Burrows, J, and Cheer, U, *Media Law in New Zealand* (4th edn, Oxford University Press, Auckland, 1999).

Burrows, J, 'Media Law' (2004) 4 New Zealand Law Review 787.

Butler, D, and Rodrick, S, *Australian Media Law* (2nd edn, LBC, Sydney, 2004).

Campbell, J, *Honour, Family and Patronage* (Oxford University Press, Oxford, 1964).

Cardon, RL, 'Libel and Slander—Charge of Communism as Libel' (1947) 45 Michigan Law Review 518.

Carr, F, 'The English Law of Defamation, Parts I & II' (1902) 18 LQR 255, 388.

Carter, AT, *A History of English Legal Institutions* (4th edn, Butterworth & Co, London, 1910).

Clerk, JF, and Lindsell, WHB, *The Law of Torts* (Sweet & Maxwell, London, 1889); (2nd edn, 1896); (3rd edn, Wyatt Paine, 1904); (4th edn, 1906); (5th edn, 1909); (6th edn, 1912); (7th edn, 1921); (8th edn, WA MacFarlane & GW Wrangham, 1929); (9th edn, *Clerk & Lindsell on the Law of Torts*, by H Potter *et al*, 1937); (10th edn, 1947); (11th edn, P Burke & J Allsop, 1954).

Collini, S, *Public Moralists: Political Thought and Intellectual Life in Britain* (Clarendon Press, Oxford, 1991).

Communications Law Centre, *National Defamation Research Project: Submission to the Attorney-General of Australia concerning proposals for a National Defamation Law* (Communications Law Centre, Sydney, 2004).

Cooke, GW, *A Treatise on the Law of Defamation* (Owen Richards, London, 1844).

Cooley, TM, *A Treatise on the Law of Torts or the Wrongs which arise Independently of Contract* (Callaghan & Co, Chicago, 1878); (2nd edn, 1888); (3rd edn, John Lewis, Callaghan & Co, Chicago, 1906); (4th edn, D Avery Haggard, 1932).
Cooper, FT, *The Law of Defamation and Verbal Injury* (2nd edn revised by DO Dykes, William Green & Sons, Edinburgh, 1906).
Cottrell, J, 'What Does "Defamatory" Mean? Reflections on *Berkoff v Burchill*' [1998] Tort Law Review 149
Crabb, JH, 'Annotation: Libel and Slander: Statements Respecting Race, Color or Nationality as Actionable' (c1954) 46 American Law Reports, Annotated 2nd 1287.
Darwin, C, *On the Origin of Species* (John Murray, London, 1859 (Reproduced in facsimile with an introduction by E Mayr, Harvard University Press, Cambridge MA, 1966)).
Davies, W, and Fouracre, P (eds), *The Settlement of Disputes in Early Medieval Europe* (Cambridge University Press, Cambridge, 1986).
Dawson, T, *The Law of the Press* (PS King & Son, London, 1927).
De Tocqueville, A *Democracy in America, Vols I & II* (The Henry Reeve text as revised by F Bowen; further editing by P Bradley) (Vintage Books, New York, 1945 (First published in English: 1835)).
de Villiers, Melius, 'The Roman Law of Defamation' (1918) 34 LQR 412.
De Zulueta, F (ed and trans), *The Institutes of Gaius: Part I—Text with Critical Notes and Translation* (Clarendon Press, Oxford, 1946).
De Zulueta, F (ed and trans), *The Institutes of Gaius: Part II—Commentary* (Clarendon Press, Oxford, 1953).
Donnelly, RC, 'History of Defamation' [1949] Wisconsin Law Review 99.
Dudley, E, *The Tree of Commonwealth*, edited and with an introduction by DM Brodie (Cambridge University Press, Cambridge, 1948 (First pub: c1510)).
Dworkin, R, *Taking Rights Seriously* (Duckworth, London, 1977).
Dworkin, R, 'Liberalism' in S Hampshire (ed), *Public and Private Morality* (Cambridge University Press, Cambridge, 1978) 113.
Dworkin, R, 'What Justice Isn't' *The New York Review of Books*, 14 April 1983; republished in R Dworkin, *A Matter of Principle* (Harvard University Press, Cambridge MA & London, 1985) 214.
Dworkin, R, *Law's Empire* (Fontana Press, London, 1986).
Dworkin, R, 'Liberal Community' (1989) 77 California Law Review 479.
Dworkin, R, *Freedom's Law: The Moral Reading of the American Constitution* (Harvard University Press, Cambridge MA, 1996).
Eisenberg, J, 'Sex, Satire and "Middle-Class Morality": Reflections on Some Recent Defamation Cases' (1999) 92 Media Information Australia 19.
Elias, N, 'Towards a Theory of Communities' in C Bell and H Newby (eds), *The Sociology of Community* (Frank Cass & Co, London, 1974) ix.
Elias, N, *The Civilizing Process* (revised edn (trans by E Jephcott), Blackwell, Oxford, 2000 (First pub in German, 1939)).
Etzioni, A, *The Spirit of Community: Rights, Responsibilities, and the Communitarian Agenda* (Crown Publishers, New York, c1993).
Etzioni, A (ed), *New Communitarian Thinking: Person, Virtues, Institutions and Communities* (University Press of Virginia, Charlottesville & London, 1995).
Etzioni, A (ed), *Rights and the Common Good: The Communitarian Perspective* (St Martin's Press, New York, 1995).

Etzioni, A, *The New Golden Rule: Community and Morality in a Democratic Society* (Basic Books, New York, 1996).

Evans, M, and Jack, I, *Sources of English Legal and Constitutional History* (Butterworths, Sydney, 1984).

Fifoot, CHS, *History and Sources of the Common Law: Tort and Contract* (Stevens & Sons, London, 1949).

Fisher, JR, 'A Chapter in the History of the Law of Libel' (1894) 10 LQR 158.

Fitzgerald, T, 'Telling the Truth, Laughing' (1999) 92 Media Information Australia 11.

Flood, JCH, *A Treatise on the Law Concerning Libel and Slander* (W Maxwell & Son, London, 1880).

Fogle, R, 'Is Calling Someone "Gay" Defamatory?: The Meaning of Reputation, Community Mores, Gay Rights and Free Speech' (1993) 3 Law and Sexuality 165.

Folkard, HC, *The Law of Slander & Libel, founded upon the Treatise of the late Thomas Starkie* ['*Folkard's Starkie on Slander and Libel*'] (3rd edn, Butterworths, London, 1869); (4th edn, 1876); (4th edn with American notes by H G Wood, Banks & Bros, New York, 1877); (5th edn, Butterworth & Co, London, 1876); (6th edn, William Clowes & Sons, London 1897); (7th edn, Butterworth & Co, London, 1908).

Fraser, H, *Principles and Practice of the Law of Libel and Slander* (William Clowes & Sons, London 1893); (2nd edn, 1897); (3rd edn, Butterworth & Co, London 1901); (4th edn, 1908); (5th edn, 1917); (6th edn, 1925).

Fraser, H, *The Law of Libel in its Relation to the Press* (Reeves & Turner, London, 1889).

Frazer, E, and Lacey, N, *The Politics of Community: A Feminist Critique of the Liberal-Communitarian Debate* (Harvester Wheatsheaf, Hemel Hempstead, 1993).

Frazer, E, *The Problems of Communitarian Politics* (Oxford University Press, Oxford, 1999).

Fricke, G, 'The Criterion of Defamation' (1958) 32 Australian Law Journal 7.

Friedman, LM, 'Name Robbers: Privacy, Blackmail, and Assorted Matters in Legal History' (2002) 30 Hofstra Law Review 1093.

Galston, WA, 'Community, Democracy, Philosophy: The Political Thought of Michael Walzer' (1987) 17 Political Theory 119.

Galston, WA, *Liberal Purposes: Good, Virtues, and Diversity in the Liberal State* (Cambridge University Press, Cambridge, 1991).

Gatley, C, *Law and Practice of Libel and Slander in a Civil Action* (Sweet & Maxwell, London, 1924); (2nd edn, 1929); (3rd edn, R Sullivan, *Libel and Slander in a Civil Action*, 1938); (4th edn, *Gatley on Libel and Slander in a Civil Action*, by R O'Sullivan and R Brown, 1953); (5th edn, *Gatley on Libel and Slander*, by R O'Sullivan and R McEwen, 1960); (6th edn by RL McEwen and P Lewis, 1967); (7th edn, 1974); (8th edn by P Lewis, 1981); (9th edn by P Milmo and WVH Rogers, 1998); (10th edn, 2004).

Gibbons, T, 'Defamation Reconsidered' (1996) 16 OJLS 587.

Gibbons, T, 'Personality Rights: The Limits of Personal Accountability' in E Barendt (ed), *The Yearbook of Media and Entertainment Law, 1997/98* (Clarendon Press, Oxford, 1997) 53.

Gillooly, M, *The Law of Defamation in Australia & New Zealand* (Federation Press, Sydney, 1998).

Gilmore, DD (ed), *Honor and Shame and the Unity of the Mediterranean* (American Anthropological Association, Washington, 1987).

Gilmore, DD, 'Honor, Honesty, Shame: Male Status in Contemporary Andalusia' in DD Gilmore (ed), *Honor and Shame and the Unity of the Mediterranean* (American Anthropological Association, Washington, 1987), 90.

Gilmore, DD, 'Introduction: The Shame of Dishonor' in DD Gilmore (ed), *Honor and Shame and the Unity of the Mediterranean* (American Anthropological Association, Washington, 1987) 2.

Gong, G, *The Standard of Civilisation in International Society* (Clarendon Press, Oxford, 1994).

Gordon, RW, 'J Willard Hurst and the Common Law Tradition in American Legal Historiography' (1975) 10 Law & Society Review 9.

Graves, EB, 'Circumspecte Agatis' (1928) 43 English Historical Review 1.

Greaves, RL, *Society and Religion in Elizabethan England* (University of Minnesota Press, Minneapolis, 1981).

Green, NStJ, 'Slander and Libel' (1871) 6 American Law Review 593.

Greenberg, KS, *Honor and Slavery* (Princeton University Press, Princeton, 1996).

Grisewood, H (ed), *Ideas and Beliefs of the Victorians: An Historic Revaluation of the Victorian Age* (Sylvan Press, London, 1949).

Gross, C, *Select Cases Concerning the Law Merchant, 1270–1638, Volume 1: Publications of the Selden Society, Vol 23, 1908* (Bernard Quaritch, London, 1908).

Gutmann, A, 'Communitarian Critics of Liberalism' (1985) 14 Philosophy & Public Affairs 308.

Haigh, CA, 'Slander and the Church Courts in the Sixteenth Century' (1975) 78 Transactions of the Lancashire and Cheshire Antiquarian Society 1.

Hale, GE, *Making Whiteness: The Culture of Segregation in the South, 1890–1940* (Pantheon Books, New York, 1998).

Halsbury's Laws of England (Butterworths, London: 1st edn (General editor: Lord Hailsham of St Marylebone) Vol 18, 1911; 2nd edn (General editor: Lord Hailsham) Vol 20, 1936; 3rd edn (General editor: Lord Simonds) Vol 24, 1958; 4th edn (General editor: Lord Hailsham of St Marleybone) Vol 28, 1974, reissued 1997 and updated).

Hanawalt, BA, *'Of Good and Ill Repute': Gender and Social Control in Medieval England* (Oxford University Press, New York, 1998).

Handford, PR, 'Tort Liability for Threatening or Insulting Words' (1976) 54 Canadian Bar Review 563.

Handsley, E, and Davis, G, 'Defamation and Satire: *Hanson v Australian Broadcasting Corporation*' (2000) 9 Torts Law Journal 1.

Harding, A, *England in the Thirteenth Century* (Cambridge University Press, Cambridge, 1993).

Harding, A, *Medieval Law and the Foundations of the State* (Oxford University Press, Oxford, 2002).

Harkess, J, 'A Linguistic Inspection of the Law of Defamation' (1998) 8 Auckland University Law Review 653.

Hawkins, W, *A Treatise of the Pleas of the Crown* (Printed for Eliz Nutt, London, 1716 (Reproduced in facsimile by Garland Publishing Inc, New York/London, 1978)).

Helmholz, RH (ed), *Select Cases on Defamation to 1600: Publications of the Selden Society, Vol 101, 1985* (Selden Society, London, 1985).

Helmholz, RH, 'Canonical Defamation in Medieval England' (1971) 15 American Journal of Legal History 255.

Herzfeld, M, 'Honour and Shame: Problems in the Comparative Analysis of Moral Systems' (1980) 15 Man 339.
Hill, M, (ed) *Whiteness: A Critical Reader* (New York University Press, New York & London, 1997).
Hilliard, F, *The Law of Torts or Private Wrongs* (Little Brown & Co, Boston, 1859); (2nd edn, 1861).
Himmelfarb, G, *Marriage and Morals Among the Victorians* (Faber & Faber, London, 1986).
Himmelfarb, G, *The De-Moralization of Society: from Victorian Virtues to Modern Values* (Alfred A Knopf, New York, 1995).
Himmelfarb, G, *Victorian Minds* (Weidenfeld & Nicholson, London, 1968).
Holdsworth, W, 'Defamation in the Sixteenth and Seventeenth Centuries, I-III' (1924) 40 LQR 302, 397; (1925) 41 LQR 13.
Holdsworth, W, *A History of English Law in Sixteen Volumes* (3rd edn, Methuen & Co/ Sweet & Maxwell, London, 1945).
Holt, F, *The Law of Libel* (W Reed, London, 1812 (Reproduced in facsimile by Garland Publishing Inc, New York/London, 1978)).
Hughes, S, 'Men of Steel: Dueling, Honor, and Politics in Liberal Italy' in Pieter Spierenburg (ed), *Men and Violence: Gender, Honor and Rituals in Modern Europe and America* (Ohio State University Press, Ohio, 1998) 64.
Hunt, S, '"(I'm a) Back Door Man": An Essay for the Australian Broadcasting Corporation' (2000) 4(4) Perfect Beat 29.
Ingram, M, *Church Courts, Sex and Marriage in England, 1570–1640* (Cambridge University Press, Cambridge, 1987).
Innes, LC, *The Principles of the Law of Torts* (Stevens & Sons, London, 1891).
Jackson, E, *Regulating Reproduction: Law, Technology and Autonomy* (Hart Publishing, Oxford & Portland OR, 2001).
James, M, 'English Politics and the Concept of Honour 1485–1642' [1978] Past & Present Supplement 3 1.
Jones, WR, '"Actions for Slaunder"—Defamation in English Law, Language and History' (1971) 57 Quarterly Journal of Speech 274.
Kadish, SR, 'Foreword' (1989) 77 California Law Review 475.
Karpin, I, 'Legislating the Female Body: Reproductive Technology and the Reconstructed Woman' (1992) 3 Columbia Journal of Gender and Law 325.
Keating, P, 'Australian Launch of the International Year for the World's Indigenous People' (the 'Redfern Park Speech'), 10 December 1992, reproduced in Native Title and Aboriginal and Torres Strait Islander Land Fund Senate Committee, *Sixteenth Report: Consistency of the Native Title Amendment Act 1998 with Australia's International Obligations under the Convention on the Elimination of all Forms of Racial Discrimination (CERD)* (2000) 270.
Keeton, WP, Dobbs, DB, Keeton, RE, and Owen, DG, *Prosser and Keeton on the Law of Torts* (5th edn, West Publishing, St Paul, 1984).
Kelly, RJ, *The Law of Newspaper Libel* (William Clowes & Sons, London, 1889).
Kelso, R, *The Doctrine of the English Gentleman in the Sixteenth Century* (Peter Smith, Gloucester MA, 1964 (First published: University of Illinois Press, 1929)).
Kenyon, A, 'Defamation, Artistic Criticism and Fair Comment' (1996) 18 Sydney Law Review 193.
Kenyon, A, *Defamation: Comparative Law and Practice* (UCL Press, London, 2006).

Kermode, J, and Walker, G (eds), *Women, Crime and the Courts in Early Modern England* (University of North Carolina Press, Chapel Hill, 1994).

Kiernan, VG, *The Duel in European History: Honour and the Reign of Aristocracy* (Oxford University Press, Oxford, 1988).

Kiralfy, AKR, *The Action on The Case* (Sweet & Maxwell, London, 1951).

Kiralfy, AKR, *A Source Book of English Law* (Sweet & Maxwell, London, 1957).

Kiralfy, AKR, *Potter's Historical Introduction to English Law and its Institutions* (4th edn, Sweet & Maxwell Ltd, London, 1962).

Knight, DR, 'I'm Not Gay—Not That There's Anything Wrong With That! Are Unwanted Imputations of Gayness Defamatory?" (2006) 37 Victoria University of Wellington Law Review 249

Koehler, EM, 'The Variable Nature of Defamation: Social Mores and Accusations of Homosexuality' (1999) 76 Journalism & Mass Communication Quarterly 217.

Kollman, NS, *By Honor Bound: State and Society in Early Modern Russia* (Cornell University Press, Ithaca, 1999).

Konkola, K, and McCulloch, D, 'People of the Book: The Success of the English Reformation' (2003) 53(10) History Today 23.

Kymlicka, W, *Liberalism, Community and Culture* (Clarendon Press, Oxford, 1989).

Lassiter, JC, 'Defamation of Peers: The Rise and Decline of the Action for Scandalum Magnatum, 1497–1773' (1978) 22 American Journal of Legal History 216.

Leadem, IS, *Select Cases Before the King's Council in the Star Chamber commonly called the Court of Star Chamber, 1477–1509: Publications of the Selden Society, Vol 16, 1902/1903* (Selden Society, London, 1902/1903).

Lees, S, *Ruling Passions: Sexual Violence, Reputation and the Law* (Open University Press, Buckingham, 1997).

Lever, A, 'Honour as a Red Herring' (1986) 6(3) Critique of Anthropology 83.

Lidsky, LB, 'Defamation, Reputation and the Myth of Community' (1996) 71 Washington Law Review 1.

Lorimer, DA, *Colour, Class and the Victorians: English Attitudes to the Negro in the Mid-Nineteenth Century* (Leicester University Press, Leicester/Holmes & Meier, New York, 1978).

Lovell, CR, 'The "Reception" of Defamation by the Common Law' (1962) 15 Vanderbilt Law Review 1051.

MacDougall, B, *Queer Judgments: Homosexuality, Expression and the Courts in Canada* (University of Toronto Press, Toronto, 2000).

MacIntyre, A, *After Virtue: A Study in Moral Theory* (2nd edn, University of Notre Dame Press, Notre Dame, 1984).

Magnusson, R, 'Freedom of Speech in Australian Defamation Law: Ridicule, Satire and Other Challenges' (2001) 9 Torts Law Journal 269.

Maitland, FW, *Select Pleas in Manorial and other Seignorial Courts, Volume I: Publications of the Selden Society, Vol 2, 1888* (Professional Books Ltd, London, 1974).

Maitland, FW, and Baildon, WP, *The Court Baron: Precedents of Pleading in Manorial and other Local Courts: Publications of the Selden Society, Vol 4, 1890* (Bernard Quaritch, London, 1891).

Mangan, JA, and Walvin, J (eds), *Manliness and Morality: Middle-class Masculinity in Britain and America, 1800–1940*, (St Martin's Press, New York, 1987).

March, J, *Actions for Slander and Arbitrements* (Revised edn, with revisions by 'WB', Elizabeth Walbanck, London, 1674 (First edn published in 1648)).

Mason, A, *Community, Solidarity and Belonging: Levels of Community and their Normative Significance* (Cambridge University Press, Cambridge, 2000).

Mason, G, and Tomsen, S (eds), *Homophobic Violence* (Hawkins, Sydney, 1997).

Mason, G, *The Spectacle of Violence: Homophobia, Gender and Knowledge* (Routledge, London, 2002).

McAleer, K, *Dueling: The Cult of Honour in Fin-De-Siècle Germany* (Princeton University Press, Princeton NJ, 1994).

McNamara, L, 'Bigotry, Community and the (In)visibility of Moral Exclusion: Homosexuality and the Capacity to Defame' (2001) 6 Media & Arts Law Review 271.

McNamara, L, 'History, Memory and Judgment: Holocaust Denial, The History Wars and Law's Problems with the Past' (2004) 26 Sydney Law Review 353.

Mence, R, *The Law of Libel* (Printed by W Pople and sold by various identified law booksellers, London, 1824).

Meyer, DH, *The Instructed Conscience: The Shaping of the American National Ethic* (University of Pennsylvania Press, Philadelphia, 1972).

Mill, JS, *On Liberty* in A Ryan (ed), *Mill: Text, Commentaries* (WW Norton, New York, 1997 (*On Liberty* first published: 1859)).

Milsom, SFC, *Historical Foundations of the Common Law* (Butterworths, London, 1969).

Mitchell, P, *The Making of the Modern Law of Defamation* (Hart Publishing, Oxford & Portland, 2005).

Mommsen, T (ed), with P Krueger, *The Digest of Justinian* [Trans by A Watson] (University of Pennsylvania Press, Philadelphia, 1985).

More, D, 'Informers Defamation and Public Policy' (1989) 19 Georgia Journal of International and Comparative Law 503.

Moretti, B, 'Outing: Justifiable or Unwarranted Invasion of Privacy? The Private Fact Tort as a Remedy for Disclosures of Sexual Orientation' (1993) 11 Cardozo Arts & Entertainment Law Journal 857.

Morgan, M, *Manners, Morals and Class in England, 1774–1858* (St Martin's Press, New York, 1994).

Mulhall, S, and Swift, A, *Liberals & Communitarians* (Blackwell, Oxford & Cambridge MA, 1992).

Neal, D, 'Suits Make the Man: Masculinity in Two English Courts, c.1500' (2002) 37 Canadian Journal of History 1.

Nye, RA, *Masculinity and Male Codes of Honor in Modern France* (Oxford University Press, New York & Oxford, 1993).

Nye, RA, 'Honor Codes' in PN Stearns (ed), *Encyclopedia of Social History* (Garland Publishing, London & New York, 1994) 325.

Odgers, WB, *A Digest of the Law of Libel and Slander* (Stevens & Sons, London, 1881); (2nd edn, 1887); (3rd edn, 1896); (4th edn, with JB Eames, 1905); (5th edn, 1912); (6th edn, with R Ritson, 1929).

Paton-Simpson, E, 'Private Circles and Public Squares: Invasion of Privacy by the Publication of "Private Facts"' (1998) 61 Modern Law Review 318.

Persitiany, JG, (ed), *Honour and Shame: The Values of Mediterranean Society* (University of Chicago Press, Chicago, 1966; Midway reprint, 1974).

Persitiany, JG, and Pitt-Rivers, J (eds), *Honor and Grace in Anthropology* (Cambridge University Press, Cambridge, 1992).
Pharr, C (ed and trans), *The Theodosian Code and Novels and The Sirmondian Constitutions* (Princeton University Press, Princeton, 1952).
Pilley, C, *Law for Journalists* (Sir Isaac Pitman & Sons, London, 1924).
Pink, S, *Women and Bullfighting: Gender, Sex and the Consumption of Tradition* (Berg, Oxford & New York, 1997).
Pitt-Rivers, J, 'Honour and Social Status' in JG Persitiany (ed), *Honour and Shame: The Values of Mediterranean Society* (University of Chicago Press, Chicago, 1966; Midway reprint, 1974) 21.
Pitt-Rivers, J, 'Honor' in DL Sills (ed), *International Encyclopedia of the Social Sciences, Volume 6* (MacMillan Co & The Free Press, USA, 1968) 503.
Plucknett, TF, *A Concise History of the Common Law* (3rd edn, Butterworth & Co, London, 1940).
Pollack, DA, 'Forced out of the Closet: Sexual Orientation and the Legal Dilemma of "Outing"' (1992) 46 University of Miami Law Review 711.
Pollock, F and Maitland, FW, *The History of English Law Before the Time of Edward I* (2nd edn, Cambridge University Press, Cambridge, 1968 (First pub: 1898)).
Pollock, F, *The Law of Torts* (Stevens & Sons, London, 1887); (2nd edn, 1890); (3rd edn, 1892); (4th edn, 1895); (5th edn, 1897); (6th edn, 1901); (7th edn, 1904); (8th edn, 1908); (9th edn, 1912); (10th edn, 1916); (11th edn, 1920); (12th edn, 1923); (13th edn, 1929); (14th edn, *Pollock's Law of Torts*, by PA Landon, 1939); (15th edn, 1951).
Poos, LR, 'Sex, Lies and the Church Courts of Pre-Reformation England' (1995) 25 Journal of Interdisciplinary History 585.
Post, RC, 'The Social Foundations of Defamation Law: Reputation and the Constitution' (1986) 74 California Law Review 691.
Post, RC, 'The Social Foundations of Privacy: Community and Self in the Common Law Tort' (1989) 77 California Law Review 957.
Pound, R, 'Interests of Personality' (1915) 28 Harvard Law Review 343, 445.
Prosser, WL, 'Privacy' (1960) 48 California Law Review 383.
Prosser, WL, *Handbook of The Law of Torts* (West Publishing, St Paul, 1941); (2nd edn, 1955); (3rd edn, 1964); (4th edn, 1971); (5th edn, *Prosser & Keeton on the Law of Torts*, by WP Keeton *et al*, 1984).
Putnam, RD, 'Bowling Alone: America's Declining Social Capital' (1995) 6(1) Journal of Democracy 65.
Putnam, RD, *Bowling Alone: The Collapse and Revival of American Community* (Simon & Schuster, New York, 2000).
Rawls, J, *A Theory of Justice* (Belknap Press, Cambridge MA, 1971).
Rawls, J, *Political Liberalism* (Columbia University Press, New York, 1993).
Ray, RR, 'Truth: A Defense to Libel' (1931) 16 Minnesota Law Review 43.
Reisman, D, 'Democracy and Defamation: Fair Game and Fair Comment I & II' (1942) 42 Columbia Law Review 1085, 1282.
Rigney, A, 'Fame and Defamation: Toward a Socio-Pragmatics' (1994) 99 Semiotica 53.
Ringwood, R, *Outlines of the Law of Torts* (2nd edn, Stevens & Haynes, London, 1894); (3rd edn, 1898); (4th edn, 1906); (5th edn by CH Zeigler, Sweet & Maxwell, London, 1924).
Rose, MA, *Parody: Ancient, Modern, and Post-Modern* (Cambridge University Press, Cambridge, 1993).

Rosenberg, N, *Protecting the Best Men: An Interpretive History of the Law of Libel* (University of Nth Carolina Press, Chapel Hill & London, 1986).
Rothwell, H (ed), *English Historical Documents, Vol III 1189–1327* (Eyre & Spottiswoode, London, 1975).
Roughhead, W, 'Closed Doors' (1929) 41 Juridical Review 91.
Said, E, *Orientalism: Western Conceptions of the Orient* (Penguin Books, London, 1991 (First pub: 1978)).
Sandel, M, *Liberalism and the Limits of Justice* (Cambridge University Press, Cambridge, 1982).
Schauer, F, 'Social Foundations of the Law of Defamation: A Comparative Analysis' (1980) 1 Journal of Media Law and Practice 3.
Scott, R, *Rights, Duties and the Body: Law and the Ethics of the Maternal-Fetal Conflict* (Hart Publishing, Oxford & Portland OR, 2002).
Scott, SP, *The Civil Law*, Vol 10 (Central Trust Company, Cincinnati, c1977).
Selznick, P, 'Dworkin's Unfinished Task' (1989) 77 California Law Review 505.
Selznick, P, *The Moral Commonwealth: Social Theory and the Promise of Community* (University of California Press, Berkeley & Los Angeles, 1992).
Selznick, P, *The Communitarian Persuasion* (Woodrow Wilson Center Press, Washington DC, 2002).
Seymour, J, 'The Legal Status of the Fetus: An International Review (2002) 10 Journal of Law and Medicine 28, 239–40.
Seymour, J, *Childbirth and the Law* (Oxford University Press, Oxford, 2000).
Sharpe, JA, *Defamation and Sexual Slander in Early Modern England: The Church Courts at York (Borthwick Papers No 58)* (Borthwick Institute of Historical Research, University of York, York, c1980).
Sheppard, W, *Action Upon the Case for Slander* (Printed for Ch Adams, J Starkey & T Bassett, London, 1662).
Shortt, J, *The Law Relating to Works of Literature and Art* (2nd edn, Reeves & Turner, London, 1884).
Spierenburg, P (ed), *Men and Violence: Gender, Honor and Rituals in Modern Europe and America* (Ohio State University Press, Ohio, 1998).
Stacey, M, 'The Myth of Community Studies' (1969) 20 British Journal of Sociology 134.
Stallybrass, WTS, *Salmond's Law of Torts* (9th edn, Sweet & Maxwell, London, 1936).
Starkie, T, *A Treatise on the Law of Slander, Libel, Scandalum Magnatum and False Rumours* (W Clarke & Sons, London, 1813); (2nd edn, J & WT Clarke, London, 1830).
Starkie, T, *A Treatise on the Law of Slander, Libel, Scandalum Magnatum and False Rumours* (1st American edn, G Lamson, New York, 1826); (2nd American edn with annotations by T Huntington, Collins & Hannay, New York, 1832); (3rd American edn with notes to American decisions since 1830 by JL Wendell, C Van Benthuysen, Albany, 1843); (4th American edn with notes to American decisions since 1830 by JL Wendell, J Wendell, Hartford, 1858).
Statutes of the Realm, from Original Records and Authentic Manuscripts (Dawsons of Pall Mall, London, 1810 (Reprinted 1969)).
Stephen, JF, *A History of the Criminal Law of England, Vols I-III* (MacMillan & Co, London, 1883).
Stewart, FH, *Honor* (University of Chicago Press, Chicago & London, 1994).
Stone, L, *The Crisis of the Aristocracy, 1558–1641* (Clarendon Press, Oxford, 1965).

Stratton, J 'I Don't Like It: Pauline Pantsdown and the Politics of the Inauthentic' (2000) 4(4) Perfect Beat 3.

Taylor, C, *Sources of the Self: The Making of Modern Identity* (Harvard University Press, Cambridge MA, 1989).

Thomas, JAC, *The Institutes of Justinian: Text, Translation and Commentary* (North Holland Publishing Company, Oxford, 1975).

Thompson, FML, *The Rise of Respectable Society: A Social History of Victorian Britain, 1830–1900* (Fontana Press, London, 1988).

Tönnies, F, *Community and Civil Society* [Trans & Ed: J Harris] (Cambridge University Press, Cambridge, 2001 (First published in German as *Gemeinschaft und Gesellschaft*, 1887)).

Townshend, J, *A Treatise on the Wrongs called Slander and Libel* (Baker, Voorhis & Co, New York, 1868); (2nd edn, 1872); (3rd edn, 1877); (4th edn, 1890).

Treiger-Bar-Am, LK, 'Defamation Law in a Changing Society: The Case of *Youssoupoff v Metro-Goldwyn Mayer*' (2001) 21 LS 291.

Trindade, F, 'When is Matter Considered "Defamatory" by the Courts?' [1999] Singapore Journal of Legal Studies 1.

Tucker, StG, *Blackstone's Commentaries with notes of reference to the Constitution and Law of the Federal Government of the United States and the Commonwealth of Virginia* [*'Tucker's Blackstone'*] (William Young Birch & Abraham Small, Philadelphia, 1803 (Reproduced in facsimile by Lawbook Exchange Ltd, New Jersey, 1996)).

Turner, FM, *Contesting Cultural Authority: Essays in Victorian Intellectual Life* (Cambridge University Press, Cambridge, 1993).

[unattributed] 'The Community Segment in Defamation Actions: A Dissenting Essay' (1949) 58 Yale Law Journal 1387.

[unattributed] 'With How Many People Must a Writing have a Tendency to Disgrace the Plaintiff to be Actionable' (1909) 58 University of Pennsylvania Law Review 44.

Underhill, A, *A Summary of the Law of Torts* (Butterworths, London, 1873); (2nd edn, 1878); (3rd edn, 1881); (4th edn, 1884); (6th edn, 1894); (7th edn, 1900); (8th edn with JG Pease, 1906); (9th edn, 1912); (10th edn by AC Hagon, 1922).

United Kingdom, *Report of the Committee on Defamation* (Cmnd 5909, 1975, ('The Faulks Committees Report))

Veeder, VV, 'The History and Theory of Defamation Law I & II' (1903) 3 Columbia Law Review 546; (1904) 4 Columbia Law Review 33.

Veeder, VV, 'The History of the Law of Defamation' in *Select Essays in Anglo-American Legal History* (Little, Brown & Co, Boston, 1909) 446–73.

Waddams, SM, *Sexual Slander in Nineteenth-Century England: Defamation in the Ecclesiastical Courts, 1815–1855* (University of Toronto Press, Toronto, 2000).

Wade, J, 'Tort Liability for Abusive and Insulting Words' (1950–51) 4 Vanderbilt Law Review 63.

Walker, S, 'Regulating the Media: Reputation, Truth and Privacy' (1994) 19 Melbourne University Law Review 729.

Walker, Sally, *Media Law: Commentary & Materials* (LBC, Sydney, 2000).

Wallach, JR, 'Liberals, Communitarians, and the Tasks of Political Theory' (1987) 17 Political Theory 581.

Walzer, M, *Spheres of Justice: A Defense of Pluralism and Equality* (Basic Books, New York, 1983).

Walzer, M, 'The Communitarian Critique of Liberalism' (1990) 18 Political Theory 6.

Ware, HE, 'Celebrity, Privacy Rights and Free Speech: Recalibrating Tort Remedies for "Outed" Celebrities' (1997) 32 Harvard Civil Rights & Civil Liberties Law Review 449.

Warren, SD, and Brandeis, LD, 'The Right to Privacy' (1890) 4 Harvard Law Review 193.

Watterson, R, 'What is Defamatory Today?' (1993) 67 Australian Law Journal 811.

Weaver, RL, Kenyon, A, Partlett,D, and Walker, C, *The Right to Speak Ill: Defamation, Reputation and Free Speech* (Caroline Academic Press, Durham NC, 2006).

White, E, *Tort Law in America: An Intellectual History* (Expanded edn, Oxford University Press, Oxford & New York, 2003 (First pub: 1980)).

Wikan, U, 'Shame and Honour: A Contestable Pair' (1984) 19 Man 635.

Wilson, PG, 'Reputation and Respectability: A Suggestion for Caribbean Ethnology' (1969) 4 Man 70.

Winfield, PH, *A Text-book of the Law of Tort* (Sweet & Maxwell, London, 1937).

Winfield, PH, *The Province of the Law of Tort* (Cambridge University Press, Cambridge, 1931).

Winfield, PH, *Youssoupoff v MGM* (case note) (1935) 51 LQR 281.

Wrightson, RM, 'Gray Cloud Obscures the Rainbow: Why Homosexuality as Defamation Contradicts New Jersey Public Policy to Combat Homophobia and Promote Equal Protection' (2002) 10 Journal of Law and Policy 635.

Wyatt-Brown, B, *Southern Honor: Ethics and Behavior in the Old South* (Oxford University Press, New York, 1982).

Wyatt-Brown, B, *The Shaping of Southern Culture: Honor, Grace, and War, 1760s–1890s* (University of North Carolina Press, Chapel Hill, 2001).

Yatar, EK, 'Defamation, Privacy and the Changing Social Status of Homosexuality: Re-Thinking Supreme Court Gay Rights Jurisprudence' (2003) 12 Law & Sexuality 119.

Index